SOUTH AFRICA
by road

A REGIONAL GUIDE

STRUIK
TRAVEL &
HERITAGE

CONTENTS

HOW TO USE THIS BOOK

South Africa by Road: A Regional Guide contains 29 chapters outlining the various regions of the country, supplemented by a comprehensive road guide that includes detailed regional maps and town plans of the country's major centres.

The chapters each have sections on climate, fauna and flora, and history and heritage. A special focus on noteworthy places highlights what there is to see and do in the most interesting cities, towns and villages in each region. Several text boxes contain additional background information covering a range of topics from regional cuisine, agriculture and national parks to culture, scenic drives and must-visit museums and heritage sites. A separate series of boxes lists a selection of outdoor activities, routes and trails, including hiking, horse and 4x4 trails. Did You Know? boxes draw attention to curious facts, and Driver's and Hiker's Alert boxes warn of any potential danger.

Each chapter also has a tailor-made regional map (or two) that includes national parks, nature reserves, game parks and places of interest such as grave and battle sites, heritage sites, rock art sites, hot springs and a host of others. For the driver (or his or her navigator), toll roads, passes, and national, secondary and gravel roads are shown, along with distance markers to help plan the journey.

Furthermore, each chapter has a reference box next to the map, which links the chapter to the road guide at the back of the book. Alternatively, the road-guide section can be used as a stand-alone feature, as it has its own index to help pinpoint almost any location in the country.

For an overview of the regions and maps covered in each chapter, refer to the key plan opposite. Each chapter is represented here, with its relevant page number for easy reference.

The legend below the key plan illustrates the abbreviations and symbols used in the chapter maps, while a legend preceding the road guide may be referred to for the road-guide maps.

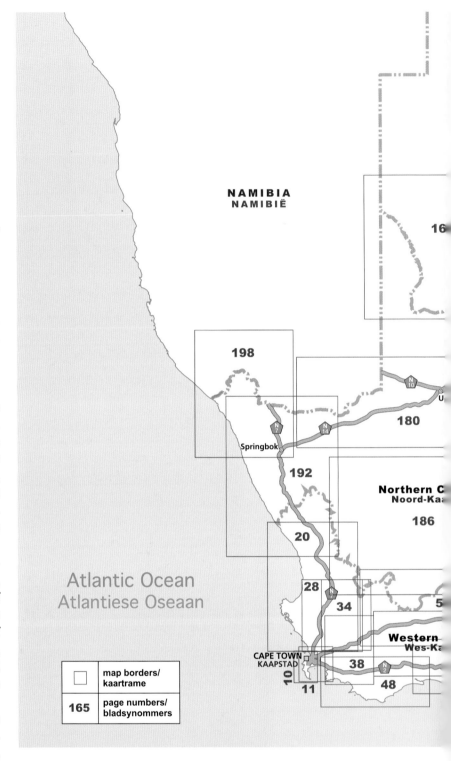

Floriskraal	lake/dam/vlei			secondary road untarred
Soetendalsvlei	marsh		*Sir Lowry's* ■■■	pass
Verneukpan	salt pan			route numbers
Lepelle	river			toll
Saldanha	bay			distance
Cape Agulhas	coastal feature			railway line
	national road			station
	main road tarred			provincial boundary
	main road untarred			country boundary
	secondary road tarred		*Sani Pass*	border post

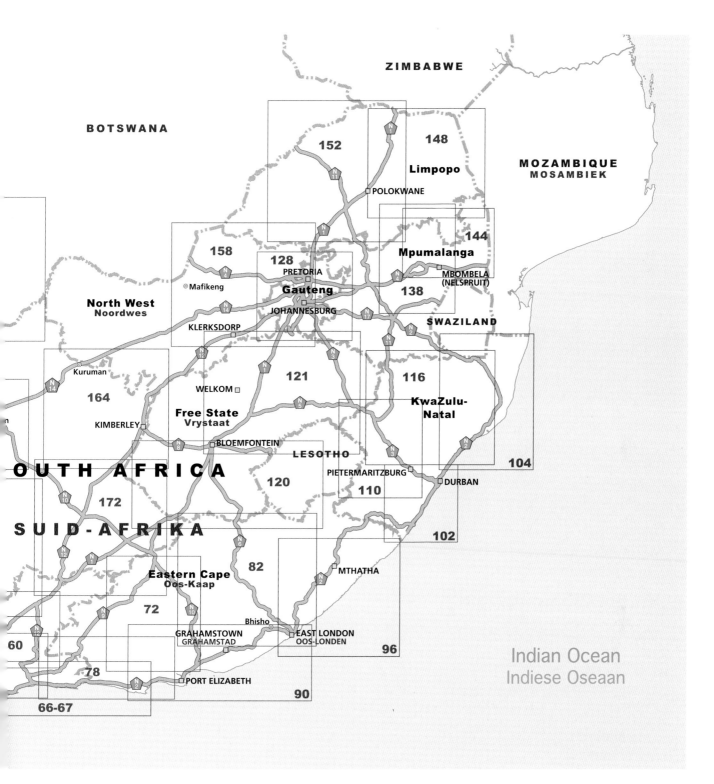

MOZAMBIQUE	country	▲ 1685m	peak
Western Cape	province	Kruger NP	park/reserve
L A N G K L O O F	area	Paul Kruger Gate/Hek	gate
JOHANNESBURG □	city/capital		accommodation
Dundee ◎	major town	Rock art/Rotskuns ★	point of interest
Brandvlei ⊙	other town	�֎	botanical garden
Tshabong ○	secondary town		battle site
Nigamoep ○	village		grave
Bulwer ↘	place out of map range	✈	airport
Langeberg	mountain	✕	airfield

ABBREVIATIONS

BR	Biosphere Reserve/ Biosfeerreservaat
GR/WR	Game Reserve/ Wildreservaat
NP	National Park/ Nasionale Park
NR	Nature Reserve/ Natuurreservaat
WHS/WE	World Heritage Site/ Wêrelderfenisgebied

CHAPTER 1

THE CAPE OF GOOD HOPE

ABOVE: Table Mountain watches over yachts in the harbour at Cape Town's V&A Waterfront.

DID YOU KNOW?

Table Mountain National Park packs more floral species into its almost 29 000 ha than New Zealand or the British Isles.

Much praise has been lavished on the beauty of Cape Town and its surrounds. In fact, the compliments have been flooding in ever since Sir Francis Drake rounded the sub-continent back in 1580 and proclaimed it 'the Fairest Cape'. Today's tourists regularly vote Cape Town one of the world's top destinations, classing it among a select number of 'places to see before you die'.

Even the briefest of visits to this historic city, sheltered in the protective embrace of Table Mountain, will reveal that there is little exaggeration in all the acclaim. The coastal drives around the peninsula offer many scenic surprises — turn a corner and find a raging sea straining against sharp cliffs, push on to the next bend and the frame becomes quietly pastoral. The vistas are matched by a history equally dramatic in which a clutch of cultures melded to form a unique community. Indigenous, Asian and European influences have added colour and variety to architecture, cuisine and entertainment.

Much of iconic Table Mountain is conserved by the Table Mountain National Park, which stretch-es across the peninsula. Besides the cable car ride up the mountain, a highlight is magnificent Cape Point at the southern tip and the rewarding views from its summit, reached by a short funicular ride. Mountains, ocean, beaches and forests offer a number of activities such as mountain biking, hiking, walking and birdwatching.

CLIMATE

The region has a Mediterranean climate. Summers are long and average 15–27°C on the coast, with an occasional heat wave. Inland temperatures are slightly higher. March and April are particularly pleasant. Winters are mild, around 7–18 °C at the coast and 5–22 °C inland, but this is the rainy season and spates of wet days are not unusual. A gusty southeasterly characterises spring and summer. Dubbed the Cape Doctor, it clears the skies of pollution and may have you chasing umbrellas on the beach, but it is great for some wind sports.

FLORA AND FAUNA

Much of the Western Cape falls into the Cape Floristic Kingdom — smallest of the six floral kingdoms of the world, but famous for its high diversity of plant species, most of them endemic. This floral wealth has earned the Cape Floristic Kingdom World Heritage Site status. Made up of eight protected areas covering 553 000 ha, this botanical heritage site includes an estimated 9 000 species of flowering plants and represents an astonishing 20% of all the floral species of Africa.

FAR LEFT: To mark his achievement of reaching the Cape, Bartolomeu Dias erected a stone cross, the *Padrão de São Filipe*, in 1488, a replica of which can be seen at Cape Point. LEFT: The Cape Peninsula has a large population of chacma baboons, many of them resident at Cape Point. BELOW: Cape Point is situated in the southern section of the Table Mountain National Park and offers splendid views of the ocean and surrounding mountains.

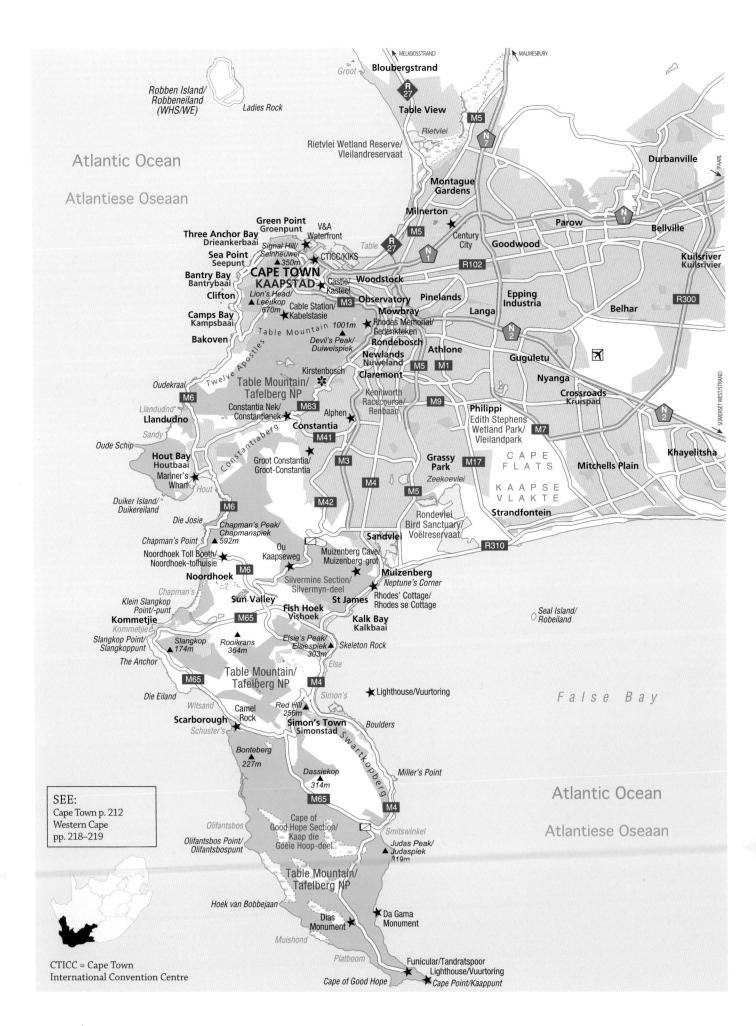

Atlantic Ocean

Atlantiese Oseaan

MELKBOSSTRAND

MALMESBURY

Groot

Bloubergstrand

R 27

Table View

M5

N 7

PAARL

Durbanville

Robben Island/
Robbeneiland
(WHS/WE)

Ladies Rock

Rietvlei Wetland Reserve/
Vleilandreservaat

Rietvlei

**Montague
Gardens**

N 1

Milnerton

M5

Century
City

Parow

Bellville

Goodwood

R 27

Green Point
Groenpunt

V&A
Waterfront

N 1

R102

Kuilsriver
Kuilsrivier

Three Anchor Bay
Drieankerbaai

Signal Hill/
Seinheuwel
▲350m

Table

CTICC/KIKS

Sea Point
Seepunt

**CAPE TOWN
KAAPSTAD**

Castle/
Kasteel

Woodstock

**Epping
Industria**

R300

Belhar

Bantry Bay
Bantrybaai

Clifton

Lion's Head/
Leeukop
▲670m

Cable Station/
Kabelstasie

M3

Observatory

Mowbray

Pinelands

Langa

Camps Bay
Kampsbaai

Table Mountain 1001m
▲

Rhodes Memorial/
Gedenkteken

N 2

Guguletu

Bakoven

Devil's Peak/
Duiwelspiek

Rondebosch

Newlands
Nuweland

Athlone

M5

M1

Nyanga

Twelve Apostles

Kirstenbosch ✿

Claremont

Crossroads
Kruispad

Oudekraal

M6

**Table Mountain/
Tafelberg NP**

Kenilworth
Racecourse/
Renbaan

M9

N 2

Llandudno

Constantia Nek/
Constantianek

M63

Alphen

Philippi

Llandudno

Sandy

Constantia

M41

Edith Stephens
Wetland Park/
Vleilandpark

M7

Oude Schip

M3

**Grassy
Park**

M17

C A P E
F L A T S

Mitchells Plain

Khayelitsha

Hout Bay
Houtbaai

Groot Constantia/
Groot-Constantia

M4

Zeekoevlei

K A A P S E
V L A K T E

Mariner's
Wharf

M42

M5

SOMERSET WEST/STRAND

Hout

Strandfontein

Duiker Island/
Duikereiland

Die Josie

Chapman's Peak/
Chapmanspiek
▲592m

Ou
Kaapseweg

Rondevlei
Bird Sanctuary/
Voëlreservaat

R310

Chapman's Point

Sandvlei

Muizenberg Cave/
Muizenberg-grot

Noordhoek Toll Booth/
Noordhoek-tolhuisie

M6

Muizenberg

Noordhoek

Silvermine Section/
Silvermyn-deel

Neptune's Corner

Chapman's

Klein Slangkop
Point/-punt

Sun Valley

Fish Hoek
Vishoek

St James

Rhodes' Cottage/
Rhodes se Cottage

Seal Island/
Robeiland

Kommetjie

M65

Kalk Bay
Kalkbaai

Kommetjie

Slangkop Point/
Slangkoppunt

Slangkop
▲174m

Rooikrans
364m

Elsie's Peak/
Elsiespiek
▲303m

Skeleton Rock

The Anchor

Else

M65

**Table Mountain/
Tafelberg NP**

M4

F a l s e   B a y

Die Eiland

Witsand

Camel
Rock

Simon's

★Lighthouse/Vuurtoring

Red Hill
256m

Scarborough

Schuster's

Simon's Town
Simonstad

Boulders

Atlantic Ocean

Bonteberg
227m

Miller's Point

Atlantiese Oseaan

Dassiekop
314m

Swartkopberg

M65

M4

Cape of
Good Hope Section/
Kaap die
Goeie Hoop-deel

Smitswinkel

Olifantsbos

Olifantsbos Point/
Olifantsbospunt

Judas Peak/
Judaspiek
▲819m

**Table Mountain/
Tafelberg NP**

Hoek van Bobbejaan

★Da Gama
Monument

Dias
Monument

Muishond

Platboom

Funicular/Tandratspoor
Lighthouse/Vuurtoring

Cape of Good Hope

Cape Point/Kaappunt

SEE:
Cape Town p. 212
Western Cape
pp. 218–219

CTICC = Cape Town
International Convention Centre

EXPERIENCE CAPE TOWN CENTRAL

Cape Town central includes the city bowl and central business district (CBD), the V&A Waterfront and the Atlantic Seaboard. It is a hive of fun and entertainment – all in one compact area – where visitors can shop, enjoy sidewalk cafés, visit heritage sites or simply soak up the beauty of this magnificent city.

City Hall and Grand Parade

Located on Darling Street, the City Hall, built in 1905, overlooks the Grand Parade that was once the parade ground of Dutch troops.

Company's Garden

Situated on Upper Adderley Street is the oldest garden in South Africa, planted by Jan van Riebeeck in 1652.

Bo-Kaap

Explore the cobbled streets, colourful houses and local restaurants of the Bo-Kaap, home to some of Cape Town's Muslim community. A visit to the Bo-Kaap Museum is a must.

Greenmarket Square

Cobblestoned Greenmarket Square hosts one of Cape Town's most popular open-air markets where local arts and crafts, clothing, sunglasses and African curios are for sale.

Green Point

This suburb is a friendly place with a number of restaurants, delis, quaint old buildings and sports facilities, not forgetting the Cape Town Stadium, renovated extensively for the 2010 FIFA World Cup™.

Sea Point

The main road of this seaboard suburb is lined with restaurants, shops and nightclubs, and has an excellent beachfront promenade for seaside walks.

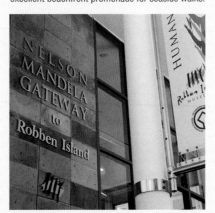

V&A Waterfront

This popular destination in Cape Town's working harbour has more than 450 stores, a wide variety of restaurants, arts and crafts markets and a world-class aquarium. It is also the gateway for tours to Robben Island.

Two Oceans Aquarium

One of the finest on the African continent, the Two Oceans Aquarium celebrates South Africa's marine treasures. It is situated at the V&A Waterfront and is a great place to visit with children.

Table Mountain Aerial Cableway

Take a 5-minute ride in the Cableway's revolving cars to the top of Table Mountain and enjoy incredible views of the city, the ocean and surrounds. There are 12 viewing sites and decks, and several marked trails.

Long Street

Although sometimes fondly referred to as a grown-up fishing village, Cape Town is a world city with a wealth of restaurants, pubs, nightclubs and entertainment venues, many of which are situated in Long Street – the hub of the city's nightlife scene.

ABOVE (CLOCKWISE FROM TOP): Colourful Bo-Kaap houses; Table Mountain cable car; Nelson Mandela Gateway, launching point of the Robben Island ferry; and Cape Town's City Hall and Grand Parade. LEFT: The candy-striped Green Point Lighthouse, built in 1824 and the oldest in the country, is situated alongside the Green Point promenade.

Fynbos ('fine bush', endemic heathland) is one of the Cape's most distinctive vegetation types and contains the three largest of more than 100 fynbos families: proteas, ericas and restios. These can be seen in abundance in the Table Mountain National Park and at Kirstenbosch National Botanical Garden.

Situated on Rhodes Drive in Newlands, the 528-ha Kirstenbosch National Botanical Garden is one of Cape Town's top attractions, renowned for its indigenous plants and themed gardens. On warm summer evenings, picnickers bring along snacks and drinks and enjoy the concerts that are held here.

Two creatures occurring along the peninsula coastline bump South Africa's famed Big Five up to a Big Seven: the great white shark and the southern right whale. When the whales arrive between June and November, whale watching becomes an exciting pastime. Cape waters attract a number of shark species, and several shark-cage diving operators offer tourists a safe, close-up experience of these predators of the deep.

HISTORY AND HERITAGE

Long before European settlers arrived, family groups of San hunter-gatherers occupied southern Africa, from the hot Kalahari Desert and the desiccated Karoo to the more temperate eastern and western coastal lowlands. About 2 000 years ago, a wave of new immigrants reached the Cape's shores when Khoekhoe herders, bringing with them cattle, sheep and the craft of pottery, moved into the region. Today the two groups are collectively referred to as the Khoe-San.

In 1488 Bartolomeu Dias became the first European to round the Cape, thereby opening a route to the East and heralding a frenzied period of empire building by the nations of the Northern Hemisphere. For nearly two centuries thereafter the Cape became a refreshment and repair stop for passing ships. English sailors had expressed an interest in annexing it in the early 17th century, but King James I was not keen. Neither were the Dutch, until the Dutch East India Company received a report by surviving sailors from the company trader *Haerlem* that had run aground in Table Bay during a storm in 1647. Based on their favourable description, the Company decided to establish a permanent refreshment station at the tip of Africa, and in 1652 Jan van Riebeeck was dispatched to the Cape to build a fort and lay out a

THE KRAMATS OF THE CAPE

Some of the Muslim holy men brought to the Cape as political prisoners were of noble birth; those who died here were buried in shrines known as kramats or mazaars. The kramats, many of which look like miniature mosques, can be found from Muizenberg to Mowbray, with four on Signal Hill. The most visited by pilgrims is that of Sheikh Yusuf, in the dunes at Macassar. He was the first to read from the Qur'an in South Africa, and is regarded as the father of local Islam. Other important kramats are those of the last Malaccan sultan, Sheikh Abdurahman Matebe Shah, at the gates to Klein Constantia, and of Sheikh Sayed Abdurahman Maturu on Robben Island.

VISIT A MUSEUM

Castle of Good Hope

Completed in 1679, the Castle of Good Hope is the oldest building still in use in South Africa. It is designed in the shape of a pentagon; its thick stone walls were once lined on the inside with residences, government offices, storerooms and stables. The entrance, planned to resemble the brick-and-stone town approaches common in the Netherlands, was topped by a belfry in 1682. A few years later, the internal courtyard was divided in two by a Kat, or defensive wall. On either side were the official quarters of the governor and senior staff, as well as a great hall with an ornamental balcony from where official proclamations were read out.

The best preserved of all the Dutch East India Company castles, it was declared a national monument in 1936. Extensively renovated during the 1980s, it is today the Western Cape headquarters of the South African army, and open to visitors. On show are a number of military exhibits, the Castle Military Museum and the William Fehr Collection of artworks depicting early life at the Cape. Around November, it hosts the annual Cape Town Military Tattoo.

Robben Island

Once a symbol of oppression, Robben Island was declared a World Heritage Site in 1999. The island lies in Table Bay and has superb views of Cape Town, 9 km away. On its highest point, Minto Hill (only 30 m above sea level), rises one of the oldest lighthouses in the Southern Hemisphere.

But it is as a place of banishment and exile that it achieved notoriety. Miscreant sailors were offloaded here, as were Muslim activists rebelling against Dutch colonisation in the East. The British banished troublesome chiefs here, and for a time it was used as a leper colony. Finally, in 1960, the government constructed a maximum-security prison on the island to incarcerate anti-apartheid activists, among them Nelson Mandela.

Robben Island is now a living museum. Tours leave from the Nelson Mandela Gateway at the V&A Waterfront and include a boat trip across Table Bay, a visit to the prison and a bus tour of the island.

Groot Constantia

Commander Simon van der Stel was appointed governor of the Dutch settlement at the Cape in 1679. Six years later he was granted the right to select a tract of land for his personal use and chose a valley he named Constantia. There he planted vines, orchards and oak trees, and built the first of the great Cape homesteads. Today, Groot Constantia is one of the leading tourist attractions of the region.

Accessed along an avenue of oaks, the manor house features gables, dungeons and a stone bath in which the slaves washed their feet before pressing grapes. A wine cellar with a pediment depicting Ganymede and Bacchus was added later.

After the death of Van der Stel in 1712, the estate was divided into three: Groot Constantia, Klein Constantia and Buitenverwachting, all of which constitute the Constantia Wine Route.

Iziko Museums of Cape Town maintains three venues at Groot Constantia: the beautifully restored Manor House is a must for those interested in early Cape history; the Orientation Centre contains artefacts from the early days of the estate; and the original Cloete Cellar houses historical drinking vessels and wine-making equipment. There are also conference facilities and the fine Jonkershuis Restaurant, which specialises in Cape Malay cuisine. Weather permitting, there is no better way to enjoy this national heritage site than with a picnic on the lawns overlooking the vineyards.

Iziko South African Museum & Planetarium

Founded in 1825, this museum focuses on natural history and the human sciences. Its nucleus is a social and maritime history collection obtained in the 19th and early 20th centuries. The oldest museum in the country, it is set in the Company's Garden in central Cape Town. A modern planetarium was added in 1987.

District Six Museum

The sixth municipal district in Cape Town once housed a racially mixed community of freed slaves, merchants, artisans, labourers and immigrants and was renowned for its vibrancy. But it was brought to an end by apartheid – its residents were forced to leave; their homes flattened by bulldozers. The District Six Museum preserves memories of the once lively area, as well as the history of forced removals, through collections, exhibitions and education programmes. It is located in the old Methodist Mission church in Buitenkant Street.

garden. From then on the bay and its settlement would be known as the Tavern of the Seas.

Colonisation by the Dutch, and their encroachment on land used by the nomadic Khoekhoen, inevitably led to conflict, and a series of wars raged between 1659 and 1677. About that time, in 1657, the first slaves were brought to the small settlement at the Cape. Later, the Company also shipped in political prisoners who had been fighting for independence from Dutch rule in Indonesia. Among these were teachers of Islam, or Auliyah ('friends of Allah').

The biggest problem facing the Dutch was protecting their sea route to the East, which they were able to do until 1795. At that time the Netherlands was under French occupation and so, to prevent the Cape from falling into the hands of Napoleon Bonaparte, British forces engaged the Dutch at the Battle of Muizenberg. Britain handed the Cape back to the Dutch in 1803 when the situation in the Netherlands had improved, but retook it three years later at the Battle of Blaauwberg when French control strengthened again, and so began 155 years of British rule.

All of these influences have left a mark on the architecture of the region, the most notable of which is the Cape Dutch style characterised by ornate gables on buildings, many of which were laid out in an 'H' shape. Outbuildings included stables, coach houses, wine cellars

BELOW: The historic walls of The Castle of Good Hope are dramatically lit at night.

ABOVE RIGHT: Rhodes Memorial, built in remembrance of Cecil John Rhodes, offers a panoramic view of Cape Town's southern suburbs and beyond.

SCENIC DRIVES

Cape Town and its surrounds are best explored by car, and there are a number of wonderful drives that showcase the extraordinary natural beauty of the peninsula.

Cape Point Route

Starting in Cape Town's CBD, follow the M6 through Sea Point and Bantry Bay all the way to Clifton and Camps Bay. Then continue past Bakoven and Llandudno to Hout Bay.

Continue to Noordhoek via scenic Chapman's Peak Drive. Continue along the M6 until Sun Valley. At the crossroads turn right onto the M65 to reach Kommetjie, then continue along the M65 to Scarborough.

Drive through Scarborough, and about 4 km after the village turn right into Plateau Drive. The entrance to the Cape Point section of the Table Mountain National Park will be on the right.

On leaving the park, take a right turn towards Smitswinkel Bay, then follow the M4 to Simon's Town and the many small villages beyond.

From Muizenberg, follow Main Road back to the city via the suburbs of Diep River, Wynberg, Kenilworth, Claremont, Newlands, Rondebosch, Observatory and Woodstock. Or, just past Lakeside, turn left onto the M42 and left again onto the M3 highway, then take a side trip to Constantia before returning to the M3 and heading back to the city.

Chapman's Peak Drive

Renowned for its incredible views as the road twists and turns some 160 m above the ocean, this is one of the world's most scenic drives. It is operated as a toll road section of

and slave quarters. Later Capetonians favoured flat-roofed, double-storey homes in the style of the Koopmans–De Wet House in Strand Street (Cape Town), now a museum. Other architectural styles to look out for are the colourful homes and mosques of the Bo-Kaap, the Herbert Baker influences of the 1890s in constructions such as Rhodes Memorial and St George's cathedral, and the art deco buildings of the 1930s and 1940s in the CBD. More recent trends include the modern, geometric mansions overlooking the beaches of Clifton and Bantry Bay, their vast windows making the most of the Atlantic Seaboard's spectacular views, and the spurt of boutique hotels featuring 'afro-chic' interiors.

NOTEWORTHY PLACES

Cape Town

Cape Town is one of the world's most picturesque cities. The cosmopolitan centre is framed by majestic Table Mountain on one side and the blue Atlantic Ocean on the other. It is an ultra-modern African metropolis where high-rise buildings housing big corporates dwarf historic monuments. This is a city comfortable with its contrasts; one that celebrates its diversity. It also boasts many gorgeous beaches, Camps Bay and Clifton being the hot favourites nearest to the city bowl.

Simon's Town

Simon's Town, beneath a ridge of mountains in False Bay, is South Africa's principal naval base. In its time, it has seen everything from pirate brigs and slavers to the ships of the world's leading navies.

There is a lot to do in and around this town, including visiting four excellent museums: Simon's Town Museum, the South African Naval Museum, the Warrior Toy Museum and the Heritage Museum. Visitors can also go on guided historical walks (starting just beyond the railway station alongside Admiralty House) to explore the town's heritage (booking is essential). A visit to Boulders Beach, where you can stroll along a boardwalk to see the African penguins, is an absolute must.

Kalk Bay

Kalk Bay is idyllically set on a slip of land between mountain and sea. This tranquil village is

the M6, but is frequently closed due to rock falls, so it is a good idea to check if the road is open beforehand on www.chapmanspeakdrive.co.za.

Clarence Drive

Take the N2 from Cape Town to Somerset West, passing Langa, Guguletu, Mitchells Plain and Khayelitsha. Continue on to Strand and Gordon's Bay. The R44 between Gordon's Bay and Kleinmond, also called Clarence Drive, winds its way over steep cliffs to the Overberg. It is known as the Helderberg's 'Chapman's Peak' because it offers excellent views over False Bay.

Cape Town northbound route

Take a day and head along the R27 via Milnerton and Table View to Bloubergstrand and Melkbosstrand.

LEFT: Simon's Town's main road has a variety of shops, galleries and restaurants to entertain the passer-by. BELOW: Chapman's Peak Drive – one of the finest routes along the Atlantic Seaboard – affords spectacular views.

perfect for a lazy day spent ambling along and viewing the many antique, curio and clothing shops that line the main road. It is a place where people go to dine, and there are a number of excellent restaurants to choose from. Feasting on prawns and beer at the legendary Brass Bell is an enticing prospect. This eatery is situated on the seaside of the railway line; incredible ocean views are served as part of the deal.

A highlight is a visit to the colourful working harbour where fresh fish can be bought as they come off the boat. For a taste of local culture, the famous Kalky's offers the best fish and chips. For energetic visitors, the mountain behind Kalk Bay is pocked with caves to explore.

Noordhoek, Kommetjie and Scarborough

Fantastic beaches can be found along this stretch of the Cape Peninsula. Horse riding on Noordhoek's Long Beach is very popular and there are a number of riding schools in the area. You can also work up an appetite by walking along the beach to the wreck of the *Kakapo* (1900). Noordhoek Farm Village has some lovely shops and eateries, or try the famed Red Herring restaurant and bar.

Near Kommetjie, you can join the Masiphumelele Township walking tour and learn about the local Xhosa community. Scarborough is a sleepy little beach town, great for picnics, surfing and sundowners. While here, see if you can spot the aptly named Camel Rock.

A visit to the nearby Cape Point section of the Table Mountain National Park is a must. The point was initially called *Cabo Tormentoso* (Cape of Storms) by Bartolomeu Dias when he made his first tumultuous rounding; King John II of Portugal later changed it to *Cabo da Boa Esperança* (Cape of Good Hope) as the turn of the land gave hope for finding a sea route to India.

RIGHT: Kalk Bay is a bona fide fishing harbour and a great place to buy fresh fish straight off the boat. FAR RIGHT: Seagulls serenade in Hout Bay harbour, another great spot to buy the catch of the day and enjoy the sights and sounds of a working harbour. BELOW: The colourful Cape Minstrel Carnival, also known as *Tweede Nuwe Jaar* (second New Year), epitomises local Cape culture.

FESTIVALS

Not to be missed is the Cape Minstrel Carnival that takes place on 2 January each year, when troops of colourfully dressed minstrels take to the streets sporting banjos, umbrellas and painted faces as they sing traditional Kaapse Klopse songs. Jazz lovers will enjoy the annual Cape Town Jazz Festival during March/April. May brings the annual two-week Cape Gourmet Festival for food and wine lovers, and for avid readers the Cape Town Book Fair is held in June. Not to be left out, fashionistas can see and be seen during Cape Town Fashion Week, which showcases local design talent in August.

Cape Town also has a vibrant gay scene: December's Mother City Queer Project is a roaring dress-up bash to start the silly season, and Cape Town Pride is held around February each year.

Apart from dramatic, pristine beaches, fynbos, baboon, buck, zebra and ostriches, highlights include the old lighthouse (238 m above the ocean), the Vasco da Gama beacon and Dias cross, the *Padrão de São Filipe*.

Hout Bay

Take a drive over Chapman's Peak to visit Hout Bay harbour and enjoy seafood at the Mariner's Wharf restaurant. There's a great fish market here, too, and trips to see the seals on Duiker Island can be booked in the harbour, where there is also a small museum.

ADVENTURE SPORTS

- Dungeons big wave surfing off Hout Bay
- Tandem skydiving at Melkbosstrand
- Paragliding from Lion's Head
- Abseiling from Table Mountain

ROUTES AND TRAILS

There are excellent hiking trails in and around Cape Town – too many to mention in detail, but maps are available at the Information Centre at the V&A Waterfront. Some popular choices are:
- The guided 'slackpacking' Hoerikwaggo Trail (3 days), starting at the V&A Waterfront and ending at Kirstenbosch National Botanical Garden
- Pipe Track (1–3 hours) from Kloof Nek
- Lion's Head walk (2 hours) from Signal Hill Road, especially popular on a full-moon night, when hikers ascend in time to watch the sun set and the moon rise
- Skeleton Gorge and Nursery Ravine hikes (2–3 hours each) from Kirstenbosch National Botanical Garden
- Platteklip Gorge (3 hours one way) from Tafelberg Road to the top of Table Mountain, with the option of either walking both ways or taking the cable car in one direction
- Constantia Corner Path (3.5 hours) from Constantia Nek

Constantia

The historical suburb of Constantia, reached from Hout Bay via Houtbay Road, is closely linked to the wine heritage of the Western Cape. The leafy, upmarket suburb is home to the Constantia Wine Route and some of the oldest vineyards in the country. This green belt lies to the south of Kirstenbosch and is known for its oak trees, farm stalls, Cape Dutch architecture and wines. The five vineyards that make up the Constantia area are Groot Constantia, Klein Constantia, Buitenverwachting, Constantia Uitsig and Steenberg. There are several award-wining restaurants here, making it a food-and-wine lover's heaven.

Observatory

This funky suburb in the southern suburbs is known for its fun restaurants, bars, coffee shops and somewhat bohemian vibe. Close to the University of Cape Town, the large student population of 'Obz' peacefully co-exists alongside other residents who have made this arty suburb their home. There are quaint houses situated along the narrow Victorian streets and excellent food stores, street cafes and unpretentious pubs on Lower Main Road. The Groote Schuur Hospital overlooks Observatory from a distance.

East of Cape Town

Framed by the Hottentots Holland and Helderberg mountain ranges, this scenic part of the Cape offers a mix of attractions. The townships of Crossroads, Langa, Nyanga, Guguletu and Khayelitsha are home to a vast number of Western Cape residents. There are various guided township tours in these sprawling communities. Visitors usually get the chance to see a local shebeen (bar), visit a sangoma (traditional healer), and browse in an arts and craft centre. The Lwandle Migrant Labour Museum outside Somerset West commemorates the township's origins. Lwandle was established in 1958 as a single-sex hostel to house migrant labourers working in the fruit and canning industry in the Western Cape.

For nature lovers there is the Edith Stephens Wetland Park in Philippi with 37 bird species and a number of reptiles, as well as the endangered *Isoetes capensis* plant (a diminutive water fern on the Red Data List of Threatened Species) that dates back some 200 million years. The Helderberg Nature Reserve on the outskirts of Somerset West is well known for its 100-year-old oak trees and excellent hikes.

LEFT: Abseiling down Table Mountain is a popular choice for adventure-seekers visiting the Mother City.

CHAPTER 2

THE WEST COAST

ABOVE: The West Coast is a place of laid-back hospitality and unassuming natural beauty.

The West Coast is known for its scenic beauty, warm hospitality and great seafood. This coastline is best explored slowly, on a loose itinerary without rigid time constraints. Drive north along the N7 or R27 from Cape Town and watch the pace of life slow down as the hustle and bustle of the city is replaced by picturesque fishing towns.

The West Coast has contrasting landscapes — there is the beautiful and sometimes desolate coastline, rolling wine and grain farms, the rugged Groot Winterhoek and Cederberg wilderness areas and the fertile Olifants River Valley.

Wind-blown shores along the West Coast are stabilised by hardy vegetation. Granite can be found in low outcrops as you approach the Langebaan area, and from the road you can see pronounced hills, often covered in fynbos, between the ocean and lagoon.

CLIMATE

The cold Benguela Current accounts for the chilly winter weather, and an icy ocean — even in summer, when the West Coast is hot and dry with frequent strong winds. Spring is a great time to visit when temperatures are mild and the plant life is prolific, most splendidly evident in the displays of wild flowers.

The climate in the Olifants River Valley varies from that of the coastal region. Winters in the valley are chilly and wet, while summers are generally hot and dry, with temperatures sometimes soaring to 40 °C. Rain falls in winter, from May to September, and the area is often covered in mist in autumn. The climate is suitable for citrus farming and the citrus blossoms are a sight to behold. Millions of cases of fruit are packed here during the picking season that stretches from May to October.

FLORA AND FAUNA

Fishing has been part of life along the West Coast for hundreds of years. The major concentration of fish in these waters is due to vast amounts of plankton and nutrients brought in by the north-flowing Benguela Current. Seventy percent of all line-fish caught on the West Coast (mainly snoek) is landed at Yzerfontein harbour. Crayfish season extends from November until the Easter weekend each year, but you need a permit to catch a daily quota. Fynbos grows in this part of the world and in spring-time the West Coast is renowned for its colourful displays of wild flowers.

Away from the coast, in the Olifants River Valley, mountain fynbos predominates. On the lower slopes of the Cederberg, visitors will find yellow daisies, wild olive trees, laurel proteas, buchu, rooibos tea and ridderspoor. Clanwilliam cedars grow on the upper cliffs, high above sea level. Wildlife is abundant, particularly in the Cederberg Wilderness Area where there are baboon, Cape clawless otter, aardvark, leopard and a variety of antelope, including klipspringer, duiker, grysbok and grey rhebok. Small predators include cacaral, bat-eared fox, African wild cat and Cape fox. More than a hundred bird species can be spotted, including a number of raptors such as rock kestrel, jackal buzzard and Verreaux's (black) eagle.

HISTORY AND HERITAGE

A number of monuments, museums and memorials commemorate the history of the West Coast. Long before European explorers braved the oceans around the Fairest Cape, the indigenous Khoekhoen populated the area. Their clans included the GrigriQua, ChariGuriQua and CochoQua.

Vasco da Gama, the Portuguese seafarer, made amicable contact with the GrigriQua when he landed at St Helena Bay in 1497. Unfortunately, expansion of the small settlement at the Cape and exploration of the northern coastal region

HISTORICAL HIGHLIGHTS

• The Hildebrand Monument, on the R27 near Darling, commands a glorious view of the countryside. It was here on 12 November 1901 that the Republican officer Field Cornet CP Hildebrand was killed in a South African War skirmish and was hastily buried.

• The area surrounding Langebaan Lagoon has various old buildings. The first person to build a shore cottage here was William Smith, a British sailor. Later, in the 1820s, Governor Lord Charles Somerset erected a hunting lodge on a farm opposite the lagoon. The ruins of another building, Oudepost, an old Dutch fort, can be seen at Kraalbaai on the western shore.

• On the farm Kliprug, just outside Saldanha Bay, is the 1863 grave of New York-born Simeon Cummings, third engineer of the Confederate raider, the *Alabama*, who accidentally shot himself.

BELOW: That Darling is a prime agricultural centre is evident in the many vineyards and wheat, dairy and sheep farms, as well as striking, yellow canola fields.

brought the later 17th-century colonists in conflict with various bands of the local Khoehoen. These indigenous people were nomadic and followed set grazing routes throughout the year that coincided with the availability of seasonal grazing lands for their cattle. This practice of transhumance, the antithesis of private property, resulted in land disputes and eventually conflict between the Khoekhoen and the colonists. Today, a mixed bunch of people make up the lively human landscape of the West Coast.

NOTEWORTHY PLACES ALONG THE COAST

Negotiating the West Coast is easy, and there are a number of small towns and villages that deserve a visit, so make sure you have time on your itinerary.

Mamre

The picturesque mission village of Mamre, with its oak trees and small whitewashed cottages, is an architectural gem. It was established as a cattle post in 1701 to protect the settlers' cattle

DRIVER'S ALERT

The bridge crossing the Olifants River at Kriedouwkrans between Citrusdal and Clanwilliam is sometimes flooded in winter. There are alternative routes, so make enquiries before you start your journey.

SEE:
Western Cape pp. 218–219
Western & Northern Cape p. 224
Northern Cape p. 225

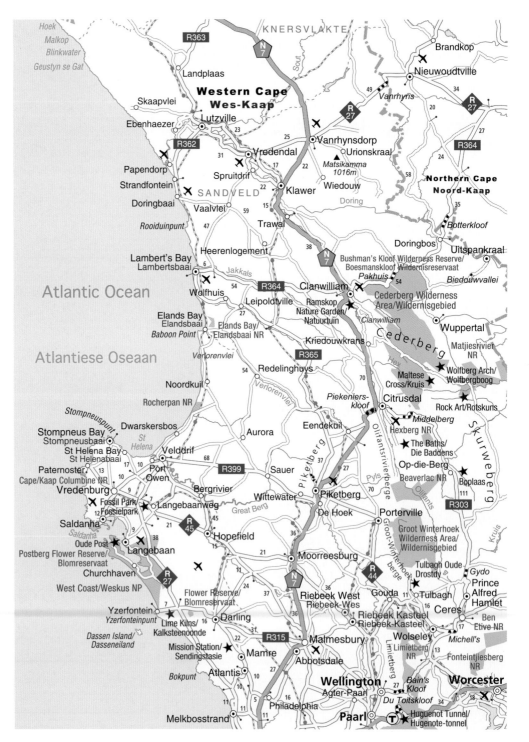

WEST COAST FOOD

A trip to the West Coast is likely to be somewhat of a seafood safari. The region is renowned for its marine delicacies, mostly prepared according to simple but tasty recipes that reflect the traditions of the various fishing communities. Prawns, calamari, crayfish and mussels are cooked, steamed or grilled to produce mouth-watering dishes.

Bokkoms, too, are synonymous with the West Coast, in particular with the town of Velddrif. This local delicacy – salted, sundried fish, usually mullet – is the marine variant of biltong, and is best enjoyed with apricot jam on bread and washed down with white wine or a cup of strong, black coffee.

from being stolen by the Khoekhoen. In 1807, the year after the Cape Colony once again came under British control, three farms in the area belonging to the former Dutch East India Company were transferred to the Moravian Missionary Society, and Mamre became a thriving mission station. There are several historical buildings in Mamre including the Old Mamre Moravian church, the Mamre School, the parsonage, the Old Mill and the Long House.

Yzerfontein

Yzerfontein is some 80 km north of Cape Town. The name, meaning 'iron fountain', is derived from a spring in an ironstone formation about 3 km inland. Yzerfontein is renowned for its long beach and beautiful holiday homes. Whale watching is also a favourite pastime in these parts, with whales mating and calving in the bay during the winter months. Cormorants and seagulls abound on the little island of Meeurots ('gull rock').

Dassen Island, just 10 km southwest of Yzerfontein, is the main breeding ground of the African penguin. There are some 68 000 penguins on this 4,5-km-long by 2-km-wide island. Travellers can go to Dassen Island by boat and either enjoy sundowners on board or kayak around the island while watching the birds return to roost.

Darling

Travel along the R315 from Yzerfontein towards Malmesbury to reach the quaint town of Darling. The area is famed for its fynbos and wild spring flowers (more than 1 000 species). There are a number of private floral reserves in the area as well as one of the largest orchid nurseries in South Africa – Duckitt Nurseries on Oudepost Farm. The town has been made famous by South African satirist Pieter-Dirk Uys, and visitors are welcome to book tickets for performances at his theatre, Evita se Perron, at Darling station. Apart from theatre, Evita se Perron showcases arts and crafts made by the local community. Woodwork, pottery, beading and jewellery can be bought at Evita's shop, and most of the proceeds go to community projects.

Langebaan

Families from all over South Africa head to Langebaan during the school holidays for seaside fun and recreation. This beach resort sits on the eastern shore of Langebaan Lagoon, which stretches some 17 km northwest to Saldanha Bay, and is well loved by water sports enthusiasts. Langebaan once supported the largest whaling station in the southern hemisphere; today it is the gateway to the West Coast National Park.

ABOVE: The Evita se Perron theatre is the brainchild of one of Darling's best-loved residents, satirist Pieter-Dirk Uys.

DID YOU KNOW?

During the 1940s lime was produced from the shells of black mussels in large kilns constructed near present-day Yzerfontein. Passers-by will notice the remnants of two round kilns situated approximately 5 km outside Yzerfontein on the R315. The kilns were declared heritage sites in 1980. The lime was mainly used to whitewash the walls of dwellings or as a type of cement.

RIGHT: The beautiful Langebaan Lagoon is popular for its excellent water sports opportunities. BELOW: Die Winkel op Paternoster offers anything from home-baked biscuits to collectables and antiques. BELOW RIGHT: Visitors to Velddrif can try *bokkoms*, a dried fish delicacy found along the West Coast.

Hopefield

This town is particularly popular in spring when flowers blossom en masse. Founded on the banks of the Zoute River in 1853, there are fossil displays at the nearby Elandsfontein farm, and the cast of 'Saldanha Man', an early hominid, can be seen at the local tourism office.

Saldanha

The country's largest natural harbour, the port of Saldanha, lies with the West Coast National Park to its south and the Berg River mouth to its north. Fishing, oyster farming and the processing and exportation of iron ore are the major industries here that provide employment for many people along the West Coast. Visit the French Huguenot memorial for a touch of history. Hiking, flower viewing, whale watching and water sports are popular activities.

Vredenburg

North of Saldanha lies the town of Vredenburg, the commercial heartland of the West Coast and a major distribution centre. It was founded as a Dutch Reformed parish close to a spring called Twisfontein in 1875. These days the main activities are wheat and sheep farming. If you are on a self-catering holiday, Vredenburg's well-stocked supermarkets are an excellent place for buying supplies before filling up on fuel and continuing your journey along the coast.

About 10 km southeast of Vredenburg is the West Coast Fossil Park. Founded in 1998, it is one the richest fossil sites in the world. Displays include fascinating information on species that have been extinct for 5 million odd years, among them sabre-toothed cats, giant bears and several kinds of animals that were previously unknown.

THE WEST COAST NATIONAL PARK

This Jewel of the West Coast is celebrated for its incredible bird life and wealth of spring flowers that bloom when sunny skies chase away the winter rains. The expansive Langebaan Lagoon, with its lovely beach, is the focal point of the park. At Kraalbaai, on the western side of the lagoon, stop to see *Die Preekstoel* ('pulpit rock'), a fascinating 4-m rocky outcrop.

Within the park is the Postberg Flower Reserve, open to the public only for the flower season in August and September. Further north is the West Coast Fossil Park, a place rich in fossils that is regularly visited by palaeontologists.

Paternoster

The West Coast really comes into its own about 20 km northwest of Vredenburg as you approach the quaint fishing village of Paternoster, whose name is said to come from the prayers uttered by Portuguese sailors crawling ashore from a shipwreck in the adjacent bay. Crayfish netting and fishing are the principal economic activities in Paternoster, yet the seaside village is also gaining a reputation for some excellent restaurants and upmarket guest houses. Just 5 km from Paternoster you will find Cape Columbine Nature Reserve, which was established to conserve the indigenous sandveld fynbos. Along the road from Paternoster to the reserve, you pass the Cape Columbine lighthouse, built in 1936.

St Helena Bay

St Helena Bay has an interesting claim to fame – it is said to be the only major centre along the West Coast where the sun rises over the sea. It was here that Vasco da Gama first set foot on South African soil during his epic voyage around the Cape in 1497, and the Vasco da Gama Nautical Museum at Shelley Point is a must-see. St Helena Bay offers great opportunities for both whale and dolphin watching and is a popular holiday destination.

Velddrif

Velddrif, where the Great Berg River meets the ocean, is a laid-back fishing town. An unassuming place, it incorporates the upmarket resort of Port Owen, the scenic harbour at Laaiplek and the seaside resort of Dwarskersbos, known for its wide, inviting beaches and whale watching. Try the *bokkoms*, a West Coast dried-fish delicacy. Port Owen Marina is popular for yachting, while the Rocherpan Nature Reserve is excellent for birdwatching and is part of the Flamingo Birding Route.

Redelinghuys

This quaint West Coast village is situated on Verlorenvlei ('lost marsh'), the largest freshwater wetland on the West Coast. It boasts abundant bird life and spring wild flowers. There are many historical attractions nearby including San rock art, the South African War battle site at Vegkop, and old buildings.

Elands Bay

At the mouth of Verlorenvlei lies the relaxed village of Elands Bay. The marsh, which stretches for almost 30 km from Redelinghuys to Elands Bay, is home to a variety of bird species including pelicans, coots, ducks, Egyptian geese and flamingos. In addition to its spectacular bird life, Elands Bay is also a popular surfing destination.

Lambert's Bay

At the mouth of the Jakkals River is Lambert's Bay. Once just a fishing village, it is now a West Coast tourist magnet. Many come to visit the impressive Bird Island, which houses a busy breeding colony of Cape gannets. There is also excellent whale watching. For those who enjoy a bit of history, the Sandveld Museum has some interesting artefacts and antiques. There are a number of decent resort-type lodgings in Lambert's Bay, as well as a few good restaurants.

ABOVE: The West Coast National Park has some wonderful hiking options, including one- and two-day walks, and a cycling trail.

DID YOU KNOW?

In 1995 fossilised human footprints dating back approximately 117 000 years were discovered along the shore of Langebaan Lagoon. The oldest known footprints of an anatomically modern human, they are believed to be those of a female, and have been dubbed 'Eve's footprints'. The prints are now housed in the Iziko South African Museum in Cape Town.

ROOIBOS TEA

The Olifants River Valley is the hub of the rooibos tea industry. The story goes that when settlers arrived in the valley, they noticed that the Khoekhoen produced a potable beverage from the leaves of a 'red bush'. Today the area is said to produce more than 3000 tonnes of tea a year. You can enjoy a tasting at Rooibos Limited in Clanwilliam and enjoy the Rooibos Heritage Route between Wuppertal and Nieuwoudtville.

ABOVE: The Kardoesie farm stall in Piekeniers-kloof, with its beautiful views of the scenic and historic pass, is a great place to stop off for a bite to eat.

PIEKENIERSKLOOF PASS

The first expedition to cross the Olifants River Mountains was led by Jan Danckaert in 1660. The track, later known as Piquinierskloof Pass, was for almost two centuries one of the main routes linking the Cape with the hinterland. The treacherous crossing was made somewhat less daunting when the newly constructed Grey's Pass, engineered by Thomas Bain, was opened to great fanfare in 1858. It carried traffic over the pass between the settlements of Piketberg and Citrusdal for about a hundred years until a new pass was constructed slightly higher up along the mountain. Renamed Piekenierskloof Pass, it is still in use today.

NOTEWORTHY PLACES IN THE OLIFANTS RIVER VALLEY

Named by Dutchman Jan Danckaert, who claimed to have seen hundreds of elephant in the area, the Olifants River Valley officially forms part of the West Coast area. However, the towns here are rather different to those along the coast. This scenic river valley – running between the mountains of the Cederberg, Matsikammaberge, Bokkeveldberge and Gifberg – starts north of Ceres in the Skurweberg and Witzenberg mountains and stretches as far as the tiny coastal town of Papendorp. Despite its rugged appearance, the area's fertile soil supports abundant citrus orchards and vineyards.

Citrusdal

Like Vredenburg, Citrusdal was founded as a Dutch Reformed parish, and, as the name suggests, it is surrounded by citrus orchards. The natural hot springs, called The Baths, are a key attraction, as is the Citrusdal Museum, which pays tribute to the Khoe-San and the early pioneers. Take the Piekenierskloof Pass for glorious views of the Cederberg, orchards, valleys and wheat fields in the distance.

Cederberg Wilderness Area

Stretching from the Middelberg Pass just east of Citrusdal to the north of Pakhuis Pass at Clanwilliam is the Cederberg Wilderness Area that covers 71 000 ha of rugged, mountainous terrain. The Cederberg forms part of the Cape Fold Belt and consists mainly of Table Mountain sandstone. Two of the most impressive rock formations in the area are the Wolfberg Arch and the Maltese Cross. The Cederberg is renowned for its ancient rock art found at more than 1 000 sites including caves and rocky overhangs. The rock art dates back to between 1 000 and 10 000 years.

Clanwilliam

In 1814, some 90 years after the first settlers arrived in the Olifants River Valley, the governor of the time, Sir John Cradock, changed the name of the town from Jan Dissels Valleij (after a botanist Jan Dissel) to the current Clanwilliam (after his father-in-law, the Earl of Clanwilliam). The town has many historical attractions including the Old Gaol and Magistrate's Court that date back to 1808, St John's Anglican Church dating to 1867 and the Dutch Reformed church of 1864. The local *velskoen* factory that makes shoes from animal hide should not be missed, and visitors should stop at some of the local wine cellars that are part of the Olifants River Wine Route.

Clanwilliam Dam is a must for water sports enthusiasts. It was built in the 1930s to irrigate the area and is now a popular angling spot. The Ramskop Nature Garden, located at the dam, has various wild flower species and a great viewpoint with panoramic views over the valley.

Some 50 km from Clanwilliam is the Bushman's Kloof Wilderness Reserve and Wellness Retreat. It offers relaxing spa experiences combined with rock art excursions and hikes in the Cederberg.

ACTIVITIES

• Tandem skydiving with Skydive Cape Town just outside Atlantis
• Surfing, including windsurfing and kitesurfing, at Yzerfontein
• Sea-kayaking at Paternoster
• Scuba diving and shipwreck diving, with 37 wrecks found between Yzerfontein and Elands Bay
• Underwater photographic safaris at Paternoster and Langebaan
• Water sports such as kitesurfing, windsurfing and kayaking on Langebaan Lagoon
• Surfing at Elands Bay
• Mountain biking at Boschkloof Farm Cottage in Citrusdal and Kromrivier Cederberg Tourist Park, bordering the Cederberg Wilderness Area
• Quad biking at the Quad Farm in Citrusdal
• Quad-biking tours into the Cederberg from Clanwilliam
• Rock climbing, fishing, horse riding and rock art excursions at Kromrivier Farm in the Cederberg
• Gyrocopter trips and microlighting in Strandfontein

ROUTES AND TRAILS

• Crayfish West Coast Hiking Trail (3–4 days) from Elands Bay to Ebenhaezer
• Strandveld Educational Hiking Trail (2 days) at the West Coast National Park
• SAS Saldanha Nature Hiking Trails, including the Red Route (14,5 km), the Yellow Route (11 km), the Green Route (9,6 km) and the Blue Route (4 km)
• Various coastal hiking trails through the Cape Columbine Nature Reserve, including two day trails
• Cederberg 4x4 trails of various distances
• The Boegoeberg 4x4 Trail (30 km) near Clanwilliam
• Cederberg/Wuppertal 4x4 Route (1.5 day)
• Numerous hiking trails in the Cederberg Wilderness Area. Hikes to the Wolfberg Cracks and Wolfberg Arch require reasonable fitness levels; permits are available from one of the local farmers. Permits for the Maltese Cross can be bought at Dwarsrivier Farm.

Wuppertal

Lying in the rather remote Tra-Tra Valley, on the fringes of the Cederberg, Wuppertal is a tranquil town that was founded in the 1830s by Johann Gottlieb Leipoldt (the grandfather of author and missionary C Louis Leipoldt) who opened a Moravian mission station on a farm called Rietmond. Today's visitors can explore a number of well-mapped-out 4x4 routes or ride in a donkey cart from Wuppertal to Heuning-vlei via the Pakhuis Pass. There is also a rooibos tea factory that is open from January to April, the official tea season.

Vredendal

Established in 1944, this town is the hub of the Olifants River Valley agricultural region and is known for its fresh vegetables and grapes. Like Clanwilliam, there are numerous wine cellars nearby, which form part of the Olifants River Wine Route. For the adventurous, there is the Bergkraal 4x4 Route. It is also a good base from which to explore the Cederberg Wilderness Area before moving on to Namaqualand.

Lutzville

Dating back to 1923, Lutzville is a typical rural enclave, but it does have the second-largest wine cellar in the Southern Hemisphere, which offers tastings and cellar tours. An interesting excursion from Lutzville goes to Seal Island with its evidence of past sealing activities.

Doringbaai

Doringbaai has great ocean views and a friendly atmosphere. The most important economic activities centre on a rock-lobster processing factory and offshore marine diamond mining.

Strandfontein

Situated north of Doringbaai, Strandfontein ('beach fountain') is named after a spring that surfaces near the beach. It is a popular holiday resort and its long white beach is a major draw card.

Papendorp and Ebenhaezer

Situated close to the mouth of the Olifants River, the fishing village of Papendorp offers good angling and birdwatching opportunities. Situated further inland on the banks of the river is Ebenhaezer, a small settlement that was established in 1831. From here book your place on the Crayfish West Coast Hiking Trail.

ABOVE: The people of the West Coast are relaxed and welcoming. ABOVE LEFT: The Wupperthal shoe factory is famous for its hand-sewn *velskoene*, red ones being particularly popular.

CHAPTER 3

THE SWARTLAND

ABOVE: Rolling wheat fields and a mosaic of patterns and colours add to the allure of the Swartland.

Situated along the inland margin of the low-lying coastal plains of the Sandveld in the west, the Swartland is separated from the interior plateau by the Groot Winterhoekberge in the east. Verlorenvlei River demarcates its northern boundary, which extends southwards to Malmesbury. The gently undulating plains are punctuated by low hills, as well as Kasteelberg and Piketberg, two island mountains.

The Swartland is a mosaic of rolling grain fields, vineyards, orchards, olive groves and islands of renosterveld, vegetation characterised by renosterbos and many species of the daisy, pea and thyme families. The colours of the countryside change from emerald green in winter to golden yellow in summer, and the textures also vary, such as symmetrical rows of newly ploughed soil in autumn and neat bundles of straw bales after the harvest.

CLIMATE

The Swartland enjoys a Mediterranean climate with hot summer days that can be scorching midway through the season. Winters are cold and wet, but rainy spells are interspersed with clear blue skies and pleasant, sunny days. The high peaks of the Groot Winterhoekberge are occasionally covered by a blanket of snow in midwinter, causing temperatures to plummet below freezing.

FLORA AND FAUNA

The Swartland ('black country') is not named after the colour of the soil, but rather for the dull dark colour of the landscape in summer when the leaves of the renosterbos ('rhinoceros bush'), so called because its colour resembles the hide of the black rhinoceros, turn black. This hardy shrub dominates the indigenous vegetation.

Because renosterveld grows in more fertile soils than other vegetation types, it is generally the first land to be cultivated. Sadly, isolated patches of renosterveld are all that are left after centuries of intensive cultivation, and the herds of large game species have disappeared as wheat fields have replaced renosterveld.

Sheep farming goes hand in hand with wheat farming, and peacefully grazing flocks are a familiar sight after the harvest has been brought in – usually by the end of October. Sheep are reared for meat and wool and although wheat is still the mainstay of the Swartland's agriculture, other crops such as oats, barley, lupine and canola are also grown. In recent years, farming has diversified to include wine, table grapes, deciduous fruit and olives.

Protea, erica, reeds and rushes dominate the mountain fynbos vegetation of the Piketberg, and the Olifants River and the Groot Winterhoekberge to the east, where clusters of red disa cling to stream banks in summer.

SWARTLAND WINE ROUTE

The first vineyards in the Swartland were established in the early 1800s, but wine making has grown in importance since the 1940s. Pinotage and Chenin Blanc are the main cultivars, but the Swartland is also known for its outstanding Shiraz. Established in 1986, the Swartland Wine Route links 18 cellars, estates and cooperatives in Malmesbury, Piketberg, Porterville and the Riebeek Valley. Allesverloren (renowned for its excellent port and red wines), Meerhof Wine Cellar (named after Pieter van Meerhof, one of the early explorers) and the Swartland Wine Cellar are among the well-known producers.

LEFT AND BELOW: Allesverloren Wine Estate, on the slopes of Kasteelberg in the Riebeek Valley, has been producing wine since 1806.

Blue crane, capped wheatear, several lark species (including the Cape clapper lark and the Cape long-billed lark), black harrier and Cape longclaw are among the endemic fynbos birds to keep an eye out for.

HISTORY AND HERITAGE

San hunter-gatherers roamed the mountains before the Dutch established a refreshment station at the Cape in 1652. Rock paintings in the mountains are a testimony to these people, most of whom were dispossessed, killed or enslaved soon after the arrival of the white settlers.

The region was also home to the pastoral CochoQua, a group of indigenous Khoekhoen who grazed their herds on the plains between Saldanha Bay and present-day Malmesbury. Several expeditions were dispatched into the interior by the first commander at the Cape, Jan van Riebeeck, to obtain cattle from these herders for the fledgling settlement at the Cape and for the supply of meat to passing ships.

Corporal Jan Wintervogel reconnoitred the Swartland in March 1655 and turned back after reaching the area where Malmesbury was later established. He was followed five years later by Jan Danckaert, whose expedition encountered a herd of elephants to which the Olifants River owes its name.

In 1661, an expedition led by Corporal Pieter Cruythoff set off from the Cape in search of the Namaqua, as the local Khoekhoen had told the Dutch of a wealthy tribe further north and they hoped to establish trade with them. Their interest was further stimulated by the copper bangles of the local herdsmen that originated

SEE:
Western Cape
pp. 218–219

from the Namaqua people and the hope that these people would lead them to the fabled Empire of Monomotapa. The Cruythoff Memorial at the foot of Kasteelberg ('castle mountain'), northeast of Malmesbury, is a reminder of the expedition that honoured their commander at the Cape by naming the 946-m-high mountain Riebeeck's Kasteel ('Riebeeck's castle').

Cruythoff set off again the following year – this time in search of the Vigiti Magna, the river believed to be the frontier of Monomotapa. Early maps (based on reports of trade in gold along the east coast by Portuguese mariners) showed that Monomotapa, a kingdom believed to be extremely wealthy in gold, ivory and other goods, lay to the northeast of the settlement at the Cape. But the rugged mountain chain to the east of the Cape settlement presented a formidable barrier and explorers took the relatively easy route north – hoping that they could find a way around the mountains further inland. The expedition returned empty-handed to the Cape in 1663, but is at least remembered as the first to have used an ox-wagon.

Inevitably, Dutch expansion into the hinterland, combined with competition for grazing and water, sparked open battles between the Dutch and the indigenous herders, including a war between the settlers and the CochoQua that lasted from 1673 to 1677. Weakened by ongoing conflict, dispossession and the loss of cattle, subjugation to Dutch law and a devastating smallpox epidemic in the early 18th century, Khoekhoe society had all but disintegrated by the mid-1700s. Small groups of impoverished Khoekhoen roamed the countryside, worked as farm labourers or drifted to the mission stations established in the Cape from 1738 onwards.

The fertile, fine-grained clay soil and the climate of the Swartland were ideally suited to grain production, which gradually replaced cattle farming. By the middle of the 18th century, the Swartland was well known for its wheat and in 1795 the region was described as *de graan magazyn der colonie* (the grain store of the colony).

NOTEWORTHY PLACES
Malmesbury
Malmesbury, the largest town in the Swartland, was established on the banks of the Diep River in 1743. When it was officially proclaimed a town in 1829, it was named after the first Earl of Malmesbury in England – the father-in-law of the British governor of the Cape at the time,

MALMESBURY'S *NAGMAALPUTTE*

Malmesbury's *nagmaalputte* ('communion wells') were built in 1751 on the square adjoining the original Dutch Reformed church to provide water for members of the congregation who travelled to the town for Holy Communion. One of these wells can be seen on the premises of a well-known retail store in Piet Retief Street, while another is in Voortrekker Road.

ABOVE: Malmesbury's synagogue was built in 1911 when the town had a sizeable Jewish community. The heritage site now serves as a museum.

Sir Lowry Cole. The imposing neo-Gothic Dutch Reformed church, dating back to 1860, dominates Malmesbury's skyline, and some fine Victorian houses have survived in the historic heart of the town. The Jewish synagogue dates back to 1911 when the Jewish community was large enough to warrant its own house of prayer, but over the years their numbers have dwindled. The building today houses the Malmesbury Museum, which has an interesting photographic collection of the town's history and its Jewish community, and also depicts the story of bread.

Moorreesburg
Enormous grain silos etched against the skyline of Moorreesburg are reminders of the importance wheat has for this town. A collection of utensils, equipment and machinery is displayed in the Wheat Industry Museum. One of only three such museums in the world,

ABOVE: Piketberg, a relic of Table Mountain sandstone, rises like an island above the cultivated fields.

HEUWELTJIES

Heuweltjies (hillocks), a characteristic feature of the wheatlands, are especially abundant in the Piketberg area. These raised mounds, the remains of ancient termite mounds, have a higher clay content than the surrounding soil. As a result, the *heuweltjies* retain moisture for longer and plants growing on them are greener than those in the depressions.

DID YOU KNOW?

The town of Piketberg owes its name to a lookout post established on the slopes of the Piketberg mountain to warn pioneer stock farmers against attacks by San and Khoekhoe raiding parties. In French, a lookout manned by a small group of soldiers was called a *piquet,* and the town's name was initially spelt Piquetberg.

MEN WITH A MISSION

The Moravian Missionary Society in Herrnhut, Saxony, was the first to respond to appeals in Europe for missionaries to work among the Khoekhoen. Genadendal ('valley of grace'), the society's first mission station in the Cape, was established in the Overberg in 1738. In 1808 the society established a mission station at Mamre for Khoekhoe soldiers of the Cape Corps and their families. It later opened two mission stations near Piketberg: Wittewater ('white water') was established in 1859, while the nearby Goedverwacht ('high expectations') was founded in a fertile valley in 1888. Goedverwacht is characterised by simple whitewashed and thatched homes and features a school building, store and watermill. The church, built from local stone, dates back to 1896. The Wittewater and Goedverwacht mission stations can be reached off the R399 between Piketberg and Velddrif.

the early 1880s. Woburn Lodge in Waterkant Street, the only surviving thatch pioneer-type house in the town, was the residence of Piketberg's first magistrate. The town's history is depicted in the Piketberg Museum which is furnished in Edwardian style.

Expansive views of the wheatlands unfold in the ascent of Versfeld Pass, which was originally built by hand in 1899. The cooler climate and higher rainfall on the plateau of the mountain, commonly known as Op-die-Berg ('on the mountain'), is ideal for the cultivation of deciduous fruit and there are also several commercial wildflower farms here.

Porterville

The rugged Olifants River Mountains and the Voorberg form a dramatic backdrop to the tranquil town of Porterville. Photographs and implements depicting the history of the town and the area are displayed in the Jan Danckaert Museum housed in the old magistrate's office.

The Groot Winterhoek Wilderness Area, 33 km east of Porterville, is one of the eight separately protected areas of the Cape Floral Region, proclaimed a UNESCO World Heritage Site in 2004. The wilderness area, with its sandstone rock formations, rich diversity of proteas and several disa species, is a popular destination for outdoor enthusiasts.

Riebeek Valley

Set slightly off the main tourist track, the picturesque Riebeek Valley is a mosaic of vineyards and olive groves.

it is housed in the old Dutch Reformed mission church building.

Built in 1913, the Carnegie Library – now home to the Moorreesburg Tourism Office – features Doric columns, a barge-board gable and white plaster decorations around the windows.

The works of renowned South African artists such as Jacob Hendrik Pierneef, Maggie Laubser (who was born in the Malmesbury district) and Gregoire Boonzaier can be viewed in the Dirkie Uys Art Gallery. The collection was started years ago when matric classes donated paintings to the school on completing their secondary education.

Piketberg

Laid out in the foothills of the Piket Mountain, the pleasant country town of Piketberg lies amid undulating wheat fields. The dressed sandstone Dutch Reformed church with its unusually 'spiky' decorative turrets and plastered panels was built in Cape Gothic style in

DID YOU KNOW?

Porterville has hosted several South African and African championships and the hang-gliding ramp on the summit of Dasklip Pass is regarded as one of the best foot-launch sites in the world.

ACTIVITIES

- Cross-country paragliding and hang-gliding all across the Swartland
- Viewing sandstone rock formations, proteas and disas in the Groot Winterhoek Wilderness Area near Porterville
- Going to markets in Riebeek Valley, such as the Short Street Fine Food and Wine Market (last Saturday of every month), the Royal Hotel's Farmers' Market (last Sunday of every month) and the Riebeek West Fresh Funky Market (first Saturday of the month)

ROUTES AND TRAILS

- Various trails (2 days or longer) in the Groot Winterhoek Wilderness area

The decision to build a Dutch Reformed church at Riebeek Kasteel in 1854 caused such dissent among the congregation that a breakaway group built a church at Riebeek West in 1858, a mere 4 km away. Implements used in the cultivation of wheat and wine are displayed in the museum in the historic Oude Kerk ('old church') in Riebeek Kasteel.

Graceful Victorian houses line the streets of Riebeek Kasteel, a quaint country town with a square surrounded by art galleries, restaurants and coffee shops. The landmark Royal Hotel with its arched veranda dates back to 1862 and is the oldest hotel in South Africa.

Attracted by the Riebeek Valley's patchwork of colours and its tranquil atmosphere, a growing number of artists and crafters have settled here in recent years. Arts and crafts range from paintings, ceramics and pottery to furniture and jewellery.

The Short Street Fine Food and Wine Market is held on the last Saturday of every month in Riebeek Kasteel, while the Royal Hotel's Farmers' Market takes place on the last Sunday of every month. The Riebeek West Fresh Funky Market is held on the first Saturday of the month.

The Riebeek Valley plays host to two annual festivals: the Olive Festival in May and the Shiraz and Arts Festival in September.

Allesverloren, on the southeastern slopes of Kasteelberg, was the birthplace of Dr DF Malan, who in 1948 led the National Party to victory. Ongegund, 3 km northwest of Riebeek West, is the birthplace of one of South Africa's most famous statesmen, Jan Smuts. The thatched-roof house in which he was born and the schoolroom, coach house, dairy and stables have been restored beautifully. An interesting collection of old photographs can be viewed in one of the outbuildings, which has been turned into a museum.

LEFT: The Olive Festival of the Riebeek Valley has established itself as one of the top culinary celebrations in the Western Cape. BELOW LEFT: The rich colours, textures and tranquillity of the Riebeek Valley are an inspiration to the many artists who reside there. BELOW: The spire of the historic Oude Kerk ('old church') towers high above the Riebeek Valley and the nearby Royal Hotel.

CHAPTER 4

THE WARM BOKKEVELD

ABOVE: The Ceres Valley, distinguished for the delicious fruits grown there, has chilly winters and is often called the Switzerland of South Africa.

The Warm Bokkeveld is defined by the Gydo and Waboom mountains in the north, the Witzenberg and Skurweberg in the west and the Hex River Mountains to the south. To the east it borders on the Central Karoo.

Matroosberg, the highest point in the Hex River Mountains, rises 2 249 m above the valley. Numerous streams and tributaries of the Breede River, which has its headwaters in the Warm Bokkeveld basin, provide an abundance of water to the intensively cultivated valley, which is a tapestry of orchards, clumps and rows of pine trees, wheat fields and dams.

When the first Dutch stock farmers arrived in this corner of the inland plateau, they named it the Bokkeveld after the vast herds of springbok, wildebeest and zebra that migrated to the area in early spring. The warmer climate of the Warm Bokkeveld distinguishes it from the higher-lying Koue Bokkeveld, which has a much harsher climate.

Despite its small size, the Warm Bokkeveld is an important agricultural region and a popular destination for outdoor enthusiasts.

MICHELL'S PASS

Local farmer Jan Mostert built the first pass through the Witzenberg range in 1765, but half a century later it was still regarded as 'one of the worst and most dangerous roads in the colony'.

Work on a new pass started under the watchful eye of Andrew Geddes Bain in 1846 and the road was opened on 1 December 1848. The Toll House in the pass became operational in the same year: the fees were fixed at three pennies per wheel, two pennies per draught animal and half a penny per sheep, goat or pig.

CLIMATE

The Warm Bokkeveld enjoys a Mediterranean climate with hot summers, but the heat is tempered by the altitude as high mountains shelter the valley from strong southeasterly winds. Winters are wet and cold and heavy snowfalls are not uncommon on the mountains in midwinter. The main town, Ceres, is dubbed the 'Switzerland of South Africa' and many Capetonians flock here when good snowfalls have been reported.

HISTORY AND HERITAGE

The San, the first known people of the area, left a legacy of rock paintings in caves and overhangs in the surrounding mountains.

For more than half a century after the Dutch arrived at the Cape, the towering mountains of the Warm Bokkeveld presented a formidable barrier to the expansion of the small settlement. It was only in 1727 that the first European stock farmers crossed the Witzenberg range from the adjacent Tulbagh Valley.

The completion of Michell's Pass in 1848, which links the Warm Bokkeveld to the Breede River Valley, reduced the travelling time of a transport wagon from Cape Town to Beaufort West from 20 to 12 days. Ceres became a major staging post on the main route to the north and in the late 1860s and early 1870s the town boomed after the discovery of diamonds in the Northern Cape. Its fortunes waned, however, when the railway line between Cape Town and Kimberley was completed in 1885.

In the early 1900s, deciduous fruit farming began replacing stock and wheat farming.

FLORA AND FAUNA

A profusion of proteas, ericas, reeds, lilies, orchids and other fynbos plants grow in the mountains surrounding Ceres. The slopes are particularly attractive in spring when they are covered in masses of flowering ericas. The Ceres sugarbush is among the large variety of protea occurring in the area.

Cape grysbok, klipspringer, grey rhebok, baboon and a host of smaller mammals inhabit the mountains.

Birding enthusiasts can expect to spot typical fynbos birds such as the Cape sugarbird, protea seed-eater, Cape rock-jumper and orange-breasted sunbird.

NOTEWORTHY PLACES
Ceres

Ceres, the principal town of the Warm Bokkeveld, was named after the Roman goddess of growing plants in recognition of the valley's rich soil, and lies at the eastern end of Michell's Pass. A settlement was established on the western bank of the Dwars River in

BELOW: In winter the mountains surrounding the Warm Bokkeveld are often capped with snow.

THE QUAKE THAT SHOOK CERES
The sandstones and quartzites of the Table Mountain Group surrounding the Warm Bokkeveld basin were subjected to intense folding and warping by forces deep inside the earth's crust when the Cape Fold Belt was formed about 250 million years ago. Movements along the faults that developed during these upheavals caused a devastating earthquake that struck Ceres and Tulbagh on 29 September 1969.

1849 and further expansion came when plots were sold on the eastern bank six years later.

The surrounding orchards produce pears, apples, peaches, plums, cherries and apricots. Fruit that is not exported or sold on the local market is canned, dried, or made into juice. Visits to fruit farms can be arranged in picking season (December to April).

Ceres is an attractive town with streets lined by oak trees and well-kept gardens. It is especially attractive in autumn when the leaves change colour. Lovers' Bridge, a pedestrian

ABOVE: The brightly coloured Cape sugarbird is one of several fynbos endemics. OPPOSITE TOP: The magnificent king protea, South Africa's national flower, can be found in the region, preferring sandstone slopes or Bokkeveld shale. OPPOSITE BELOW: Canna flowers provide a blaze of red amid the verdant vineyards of the Boland.

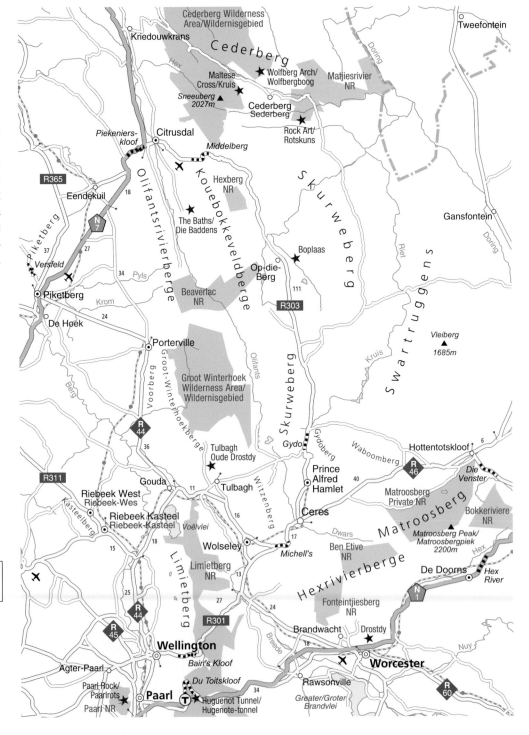

SEE:
Western Cape p. 219

walkway supported by dressed sandstone columns over the tree-lined Dwars River, is a landmark in the town.

An interesting collection of antique wagons and equipment used by farriers and wagon makers can be seen in the Togryersmuseum ('transport riders' museum').

The school chapel, built in 1864, was later enlarged to serve as St Andrew's church, while the Dutch Reformed church was consecrated in 1881.

Matroosberg Private Nature Reserve

The Matroosberg Private Nature Reserve is situated on a working deciduous fruit, onion and protea farm, 34 km east of Ceres. Covering over 1 000 ha of unspoilt mountain land, including Matroosberg Peak, the reserve offers excellent birding opportunities, a host of outdoor recreation activities, and tours of the farm. Accommodation options range from self-catering chalets and campsites to a ski hut high in the mountains.

Prince Alfred Hamlet

The village of Prince Alfred Hamlet at the foot of the Gydo Pass was laid out on the farm of Johannes Goosen in 1861, and named after the second son of Queen Victoria, who had visited South Africa a year earlier.

The Dutch Reformed church, built in 1906, was converted into a hall after a new church was consecrated in 1964. Prince Alfred Hamlet is the terminus of the branch railway that linked Wolseley and Ceres in 1912 and is a centre for the surrounding deciduous fruit farms. The area is also a major producer of table potatoes, seed potatoes and onions.

GYDO PASS

The Warm Bokkeveld was linked to the Koue Bokkeveld in 1848 when Andrew Geddes Bain built the Gydo Pass 5 km north of Prince Alfred Hamlet. The 6,5 km–long road sweeps up the slopes of the Skurweberg in a series of 27 turns and hairpin bends. Fossils have been discovered in the Bokkeveld shales along the pass, which also offers good birding prospects.

South Africa's premier hill-climbing motor rally, the King of the Mountain, is held here in November each year. The record speed is an almost unbelievable 194 km/h. The views of the Ceres Valley from the 1 018 m–high summit are magnificent, and from here the R303 continues past pear and apple orchards to the village of Op-die-Berg, 45 km beyond Ceres. Continuing towards Citrusdal, the road passes the farm Boplaas where the well-known Afrikaans writer Boerneef (Professor IW van der Merwe) was born in 1897.

CHAPTER 5

THE BOLAND

ABOVE: Neat rows of trellised vineyards nestle against the backdrop of Simonsberg near Helshoogte.

With its rich history, stately Cape Dutch houses, panoramic views, world-class wines, good food and diverse cultures, the Boland is one of the most popular tourist regions in South Africa. Spectacular valleys surrounded by towering mountain peaks, sheer cliffs and fynbos-covered slopes create breathtaking scenery. Blessed with fertile soil, crystal-clear mountain streams and an ideal climate, the Boland is the centre of South Africa's wine industry and is also the country's largest producer of deciduous fruit.

To the south the region borders on the Overberg, while the Hex River Mountains form a natural boundary with the Warm Bokkeveld to the north. The rugged Franschhoek Mountains demarcate the eastern boundary and in the west the sandy plains of the Cape Flats separate the Boland from the Cape Peninsula.

CLIMATE

The Boland has a typical Mediterranean climate with hot, dry summers. Moisture-laden air from the ocean provides some relief from the heat, but inland temperatures can reach into the mid-30s. The infamous southeasterly wind, commonly referred to as the Cape Doctor, reaches gale-force strength in summer. Winters are wet and cold, especially in midwinter when the high mountain peaks are often snow-capped. The rainy season starts in May and can last until early October. The winters are mild though with rainy spells followed by sunshine, clear blue skies and moderate to warm temperatures.

FLORA AND FAUNA

The Boland Mountain Complex is one of eight separate conservation areas of the Cape Floral

Region, which was declared a UNESCO World Heritage Site in 2004. Covering a mere 0,04% of the earth's land surface, this floristic kingdom is richer in plants than any similar-sized area in the world.

One-fifth of the total number of species that make up the Cape Floral Region has been recorded in the Boland Mountains; among them are the spectacular king protea, South Africa's national flower, and the highest concentration of *mimetes* (pagoda bush) in the Western Cape. The vegetation is especially pretty in winter and spring when the mountain slopes are covered in masses of flowering ericas and proteas. The Hottentots Holland, Jonkershoek and Limietberg nature reserves and the Kogelberg Biosphere Reserve form part of the Boland Mountain Complex.

Large mammals are poorly represented in the region but baboon, dassie (rock hyrax), klipspringer, common duiker and Cape grysbok are among species likely to be seen.

The Cape rock-jumper, orange-breasted sunbird, protea seedeater, Cape sugarbird and Victorin's warbler are among the more common endemic fynbos birds.

HISTORY AND HERITAGE

Originally, San hunter-gatherers and groups of pastoral Khoekhoen inhabited the region. The Khoekhoen grazed their livestock near Table Bay from December to March, when they would set off with their herds on a circular route that would eventually bring them back to Table Bay in the early summer.

When Jan van Riebeeck stepped ashore in April 1652 to establish a refreshment station for the Dutch East India Company, he was surprised to find hardly any Khoekhoe pastoralists in the area. They finally arrived with their herds in at the end of the year, but by mid-January they had moved on again. Van Riebeeck therefore sent several expeditions into the interior to barter for cattle in an effort to obtain fresh meat for the vessels of the Dutch East India Company. He also established gardens to supply grain and vegetables to passing ships.

The first vines were planted in 1655 and on 2 February 1659 the commander at the Cape noted in his dairy, 'Today, thanks to God, wine has been pressed for the first time from the grapes of the Cape ...'

During an inspection tour of the interior in 1679, Governor Simon van der Stel and his party camped at a spot known as Wilde Bosch ('wild bush'). Van der Stel was so enchanted by the place that he named it *De Colonie van Stellenbosch* and established an agricultural settlement there.

A cool climate and rich soils provided ideal conditions for the cultivation of grapes. Van der Stel planted 100 000 vines in the Constantia Valley in 1680 and also encouraged the establishment of vineyards further afield in Stellenbosch, Paarl and Franschhoek.

But it was the arrival of the French Huguenots in 1688 that brought about vast improvements in the Boland's early viticulture. Many of the Huguenots hailed from the wine regions of France and they brought with them an

BELOW: Members of the Royal Africa Corps built the Franschhoek Pass under the supervision of Major William Holloway. It was completed in 1825.

THE FOUR PASSES

This popular day drive incorporates four Boland passes that opened up the interior as the Cape Colony expanded. Sir Lowry's Pass, which crosses the Hottentots Holland Mountains, was completed in 1828 and named after the Governor of the Cape at the time – Sir Lowry Cole. Viljoen's Pass was built in the early 1900s to replace an earlier route which wound along the mountain slopes east of the Palmiet River. Construction of the Franschhoek Pass began in 1823 and the pass was completed two years later. Splendid views of the Franschhoek Valley unfold from the 750-m-high summit. The fourth and final pass, Helshoogte, links the Drakenstein Valley and Stellenbosch. It was built in 1854 and the name, which means 'Hell's heights', alludes to the precipitous course of the pass. The drive is a 320 km round trip from Cape Town.

SEE:
Western Cape p. 219

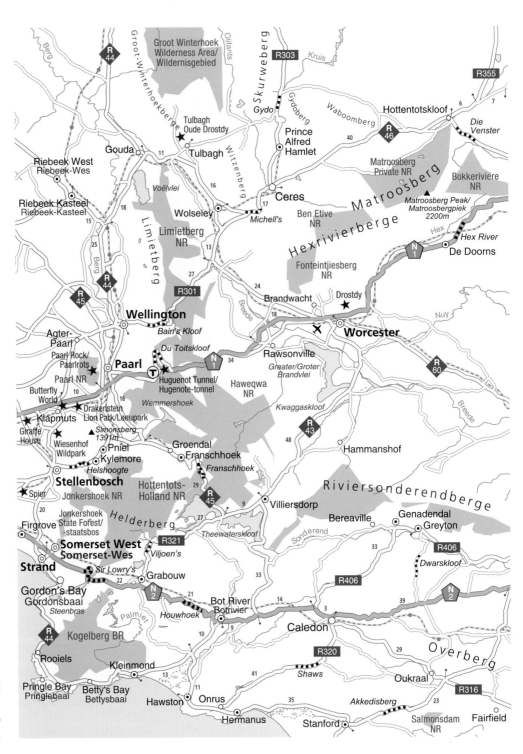

BELOW: The oldest oak trees in Stellenbosch date back to about 1760.

intimate knowledge of the art of wine making. Disaster struck in the 1880s when overproduction and an outbreak of phylloxera almost destroyed the burgeoning industry. Many wine farms in the Drakenstein Valley were bought and amalgamated under the name Rhodes Fruit Farms – a company formed by financier, magnate and politician, Cecil John Rhodes. Farming switched to deciduous fruit and the valley played an important role in the establishment of the Cape's fruit export industry. Some wine farmers persisted and replanted their vineyards, but it was the formation of the *Ko-operatieve Wijnbouwers Vereniging* (KWV) in Paarl in 1918 that laid the foundations of South Africa's modern wine industry.

NOTEWORTHY PLACES
Stellenbosch

Founded in 1679, Stellenbosch is the oldest town in South Africa after Cape Town. The ancient oak trees lining the streets are a distinctive feature of the town, which is also known as Eikestad ('oak town'). There is no better

CAPE DUTCH HOMESTEADS

The stately Cape Dutch manor houses that form the centrepiece of many historic Boland wine farms are part of the region's unique architectural heritage. A U-plan and T-plan developed from the most basic design, the L-shaped house, but the ultimate symbol of wealth and status was the elegant H-shaped layout.

An integral feature of these magnificent thatched homesteads (built up to the first half of the 1800s) is the gable that ranged from plain leg-of-mutton and holbol specimens (common during the 18th century and featuring concave–convex curves) to the baroque and neo-classical examples that became popular in the early 19th century.

ARTS AND CRAFTS

• Set amid vineyards, the Rupert Museum in Stellentia Avenue (off Dorp Street) houses a unique collection of over 350 paintings, sculptures and tapestries. The gallery has three exhibition spaces: one for international art and two for 20th-century South African art.

• The Stellenbosch University Museum consists of the US Art Gallery and the Sasol Art Museum. Regular exhibitions by contemporary artists and students of the university's Fine Arts Department are held in the US Art Gallery in the old Lutheran Church (built in 1814) in Dorp Street.

• The Sasol Art Museum has a perma-nent collection of 19th- and 20th-century art, artefacts from the Klasies River Caves (the site where the oldest known human remains in South Africa have been unearthed) and an extensive anthropo-logical collection.

• The Rembrandt van Rijn Art Gallery in Stellenbosch is at Libertas Parva, a striking Cape Dutch homestead built in 1783. The permanent collection includes sculptures by Anton van Wouw, the famous nude by the Italian sculptor Giacomo Manzù and a 3,8-m-long panorama of Cape Town in 1808, painted by Joseph Jones.

• Cultural events ranging from orches-tral music, opera and jazz to drama, dancing and ballet are staged at the Oude Libertas Amphitheatre in Stellenbosch from late November to end March. Concert-goers can enjoy spectacular views of the vineyards and mountains from the 430-seat open-air theatre on the slopes of Papegaaiberg. It has become a tradition to bring picnic baskets to the popular Sunday-night twilight concerts.

• Organic fruit and vegetables and hand-made crafts are on sale at the Organic Farmers Market held on the lawn in front of the historic Mon Repos homestead at Oude Libertas every Saturday morning.

TOP: Lanzerac's magnificent Cape Dutch manor house, in the Jonkershoek Valley, was built in 1830. ABOVE: Oom Samie se Winkel, an authentic general dealer's store in Dorp Street, is one of the town's landmarks and a major attraction in Stellenbosch.

way to experience its old-world charm than to set off on foot with a copy of the pamphlet *Historical Stellenbosch on Foot*, obtainable from the local tourism office.

Dorp Street, with its gabled Cape Dutch houses and row of early 19th-century Cape Georgian houses, is one of the most attractive streets in the country. The Braak ('village square') initially served as a military training ground. Kruithuis, a whitewashed building with a barrel-vaulted roof and surrounding wall, was built as a powder magazine in 1777, while St Mary's Anglican church on the northern side of the Braak dates back to 1852. The Rhenish complex, a mixture of Cape Dutch, typical English and Cape building styles on the western side of the Braak, is regarded as one of the best restoration projects in the country. A complex of four buildings from different periods of the town's history comprises the Stellenbosch Village Museum: the 1709 Schreuder House, the 1782 elegant, double-storied Grosvenor House, the Bletterman House (a typical 18th-century Cape Dutch building) and the home of OM Bergh.

Stellenbosch is a well-known education centre and the integration of the University of Stellenbosch campus within the townscape lends a special atmosphere to this historic town.

Paarl

Nestling in a beautiful valley of the Berg River, Paarl is also known as 'the town below the rocks'. The glistening appearance of one of the three granite domes so much resembled a pearl that Abraham Gabbema, the first Dutch official who reached the valley in October 1657, named it *Peerlberg* ('pearl mountain'). The first 23 farms along the Berg River were awarded by Governor Simon van der Stel in October 1687 and several of the Huguenots who arrived at the Cape the following year settled here.

A 2-km stroll through the town's historic heart begins at the landmark Strooidakkerk ('thatched roof church') with its scrolled gables. Consecrated in 1805, it is the oldest church building still in use in South Africa. Zeederburg Square opposite the church is overlooked by a cluster of buildings with Cape Dutch, Victorian and Georgian features. The walk ends at the Dutch Reformed parsonage (the neo-classical gable bears the date 1787) that houses the Paarl Museum. It portrays the area's history and has a fine collection of early Cape furniture, silverware and porcelain.

KWV, one of the largest wine cooperatives in the world, has its headquarters in Paarl. The world-famous Cathedral Cellar with its barrel-vaulted roof, lightly tinted windows and huge vats decorated with carvings depicting the history of wine making is the highlight of a tour of the famous cellar complex. Paarl's vineyards are renowned for their red wines, especially Shiraz.

The 11-km-long Jan Phillips Mountain Drive winds to the summit of Paarl Mountain where a scramble up Paarl Rock and Bretagne Rock is rewarded with spectacular views of vineyards, the lush Berg River Valley, Du Toit's Kloof Mountains and Table Mountain.

BIRTHPLACE OF A NEW LANGUAGE

The campaign to get Afrikaans recognised as an official language was launched in the house of Gideon Malherbe in Paarl in 1875. Today, the Afrikaans Language Museum in Gideon Malherbe House has interactive multimedia exhibitions on the diverse roots, history, development and future of Afrikaans. Dominating the southern slopes of Paarl Mountain, the imposing Afrikaans Language Monument also commemorates the origins and development of the language.

Groot Drakenstein

Groot Drakenstein lies midway between Franschhoek and Paarl. Elegant Cape Dutch manor houses grace the estates of Lekkerwijn, Meerlust, Bellingham and Rhone. Bien Donné, an experimental fruit farm, is renowned for its herb garden, lavender fields and Cape Dutch homestead with its elaborately decorated neo-classical front gable.

Built in 1812, the Boschendal manor house is widely regarded as one of the most impressive examples of Cape Dutch architecture. A ring-wall encloses the H-shaped manor house on three sides, and a historic water furrow runs along the eastern side. The wine cellar, coach house, slave quarters, poultry house with built-in nesting boxes, and a threshing floor form part of the historic farm. Boschendal manor is furnished with antiques from the 17th and 18th centuries and has a priceless collection of Ming porcelain and glassware of the VOC (Dutch East Indian Company). It is open for public viewing.

Pniel

The picturesque settlement of Pniel at the foot of Simonsberg in the Dwars River Valley was established as a refuge for freed slaves who had no abode after completing a four-year apprenticeship following the abolition of slavery in 1834. They built modest houses and established orchards, vineyards and vegetable gardens on the smallholdings allocated to them. A mission church, parsonage and school were built in 1843. The Fountain of Freedom, unveiled in 1993, is a reminder of the settlement's origin.

LEFT: The Afrikaans Language Monument, with its 57-m-high main column, is a landmark in the Paarl area. BELOW: Magnificent hand carvings on the vats in KWV's Cathedral Cellar in Paarl depict the history of wine making in South Africa.

SOLMS-DELTA WINE FARM

The history of wine making on the Solms-Delta wine farm in Groot Drakenstein dates back to the late 17th century when the first vines were planted. Housed in a wine cellar built in 1740, the Solms Museum van de Caab on the estate reflects on the history of the people who occupied the land prior to and after its establishment as a farm – from the San and the Khoekhoen to the farm workers who currently live here.

The museum and wine farm are open throughout the week. Tastings of the wine produced here are offered and pre-booked picnic lunches can be enjoyed on the banks of the river.

TOP: The striking Huguenot Memorial in Franschhoek was inaugurated in 1948 in commemoration of South Africa's French heritage. ABOVE: Fine restaurants and quaint arts and crafts outlets line the streets of Franschhoek, a tranquil Boland country town

Franschhoek

Franschhoek lies in a spectacular setting of verdant vineyards, orchards and imposing mountain peaks at the head of the Drakenstein Valley. Historic farms with names such as Chamonix, Plaisir de Merle, Cabrière and Mont Rochelle are reminders of the Huguenots who settled here after fleeing religious persecution in France in 1688. The Huguenot Memorial commemorates these immigrants and their contribution to South Africa's culture, while the adjacent Huguenot Museum is an information and research centre.

Franschhoek was proclaimed a town in 1845 and its architecture ranges from graceful Cape Dutch houses on wine estates to Victorian, Edwardian and Cape Dutch revival-style buildings. Several fine Victorian homes with cast-iron decorations line the upper end of Cabrière Street. The Dutch Reformed church with its neo-gothic and Cape Dutch features dates back to 1847, while the Old Parsonage was most likely built before 1850.

Fine cuisine complements outstanding wines – several of South Africa's most acclaimed restaurants are in Franschhoek, earning it the reputation of the 'gourmet capital of South Africa'.

One of the most unique collections of vehicles in the world can be viewed at the Franschhoek Motor Museum on the L'Ormarins wine farm.

Wellington

Overlooked by the rugged Limietberge, the settlement established on the banks of the Kromme River was originally named Limiet-

WINE AND BRANDY ROUTES

Stellenbosch Wine Route

Established in 1971, the Stellenbosch Wine Route was the first of its kind in South Africa and now consists of five sub-routes with over 146 winery members. The district is renowned for its gracious estates with their stately Cape Dutch manor houses and award-winning wines. Delheim, Alto, Spier, Blaauwklippen and Neethlingshof are among the very well-known estates.

Stellenbosch is also the starting point for the Western Cape Brandy Route, which includes 13 producers in Stellenbosch, Paarl, Wellington and Franschhoek.

Paarl Wine Route

The granitic soils of the Paarl area are ideally suited to the production of red wines and so the Paarl Wine Route is also affectionately referred to as the Red Route. Estates like Backsberg, Landskroon and Laborie have become household names, while Fairview with its characteristic 'goat tower' produces an extensive range of goat's, sheep's and cow's milk cheeses in addition to a wide range of excellent wines. The historic Nederburg is host to the prestigious Nederburg Wine Auction each year.

Franschhoek Wine Route

Established in 1984, the *Vignerons de Franschhoek* (an association of wine growers) strives to uphold the French tradition of wine making in the Franschhoek Valley. The area produces award-winning white wines, dry white blends and *Méthode Cap Classique* sparkling wines made according to the traditional French *Méthode Champenoise*.

Cabernet Sauvignon, Merlot, Shiraz and Pinotage are among the red varietals grown in the valley. The Franschhoek Wine Route comprises 19 producers, ranging from well-known estates such as Bellingham, Boschendal and L'Ormarins to boutique wineries.

Wellington Wine & Brandy Route

Blessed with an excellent climate and fertile soil, the Wellington area is a major grower of cuttings for the wine industry. Excellent white and red wines, as well as brandy, are produced by the 25 estates, cooperatives and wineries on the Wellington Wine & Brandy Route.

Tulbagh Wine Route

The sandstone and shale soils of the Tulbagh Valley are particularly well-suited to delicate white wines, but good-quality reds are also produced in the area. Theuniskraal, Twee Jonge Gezellen and Montpellier are well-known wine estates on this wine route.

Breedekloof Wine Route

The Breedekloof Wine Route meanders along the course carved by the Breede River and includes Rawsonville, Goudini and the spectacular Slanghoek Valley. This route has 23 members, among them well-known producers such as Badsberg and Slanghoek.

Worcester Wine Route

The Worcester district accounts for close to 25% of the total volume of grapes produced in South Africa for wine making. White cultivars predominate in this area, which produces excellent dry and semi-sweet white wines, dessert wines and brandies.

vallei ('border or frontier valley'). The area became famous for its wagon-making industry and, following the settlement of French Huguenots at the end of the 1600s, became known as Val du Charron ('valley of the wagon maker'). Today it is the centre of South Africa's dried fruit industry.

When the town was proclaimed in 1840, it was named in honour of the hero of the Battle of Waterloo, the Duke of Wellington, who had defeated Napoleon 25 years earlier.

The Market building, dating back to 1847, is among the fine structures fortunate to have survived a disastrous fire that destroyed most of the town's old buildings at the beginning of the 1900s. The nearby Dutch Reformed church was built in 1840, but its tower was only added 51 years later.

Ouma Granny's House, a beautiful Victorian cottage, houses a valuable collection of antiques, while an interesting collection of ancient Egyptian artefacts, traditional musical instruments and jewellery, and Stone Age artefacts can be viewed in the Wellington Museum.

The founding of the Huguenot Seminary in 1874 and the establishment of the country's first teachers' training college in 1896 in Wellington are reminders of the important role the town has played in education.

Wolseley

Wolseley was established in 1875 where the Breede River winds its way between the Waaihoekberge, Witzenberg and Watervalberg. Deciduous fruit cultivation is the main activity here, but dairy, cattle and sheep farming

ABOVE LEFT: La Concorde, the headquarters of KWV on Paarl's Main Street, features an imposing facade.
ABOVE: The chapel on Montpellier Estate in Tulbagh is a popular venue for weddings.

is also practised. Two stone blockhouses built by the British in the early 1900s to protect the railway line south of the town are reminders of the second Anglo–Boer War of 1899–1902 (also known as the South African War).

Tulbagh

Tucked away between the Ubiqua Mountains, Grootwinterhoekberge and Witzenberg, Tulbagh was founded in 1795 and named after then Governor Ryk Tulbagh.

Church Street has the largest concentration of historical buildings in the country – all of them carefully restored to their early- and mid-19th-century splendour after a devastating earthquake in 1969. Mon Bijou, a magnificent double-storied Georgian-style building, Ballotina with its unusual gable, and Paddagang, which dates back to 1821, are among the eye-catching architectural treasures in Church Street. Oude Kerk ('old church') with its elegant Baroque gable and attractive gateway is the centrepiece

of the Volksmuseum complex that also has three annexes, at 4, 14 and 22 Church Street.

The Oude Drostdy, 4 km north of the town, was built in 1806 as a seat of local government and justice. It is the headquarters of a well-known winery and is furnished with an exquisite collection of early Cape furniture.

Worcester

Also known as the 'Capital of the Breede River Valley', Worcester is the hub of the largest wine and fruit-growing district in the country.

Church Square is the historical heart of the town, which was founded in 1819 and named after the Marquis of Worcester, the brother of the British governor at the time, Lord Charles Somerset. Several gabled houses are among the fine Cape Dutch buildings in Church Street.

The Worcester Museum complex consists of four houses dating from the mid-19th century to the early 1900s. Beck House, a Cape Dutch homestead, has been furnished as a typical late 19th-century country house. Stofberg House next door dates back to 1920, while the Afrikaner Museum depicts an early 1900s doctor's consulting room, dentist room and attorney's office. A collection of paintings by two famous South African artists, Hugo Naudé and Jean Welz, is on permanent display in Hugo Naudé House.

Kleinplasie ('little farm') on the outskirts of Worcester consists of replicas of buildings representing different agricultural activities. The lifestyle of the pioneer farmers and the development of agriculture until around 1940 are portrayed in this interesting open-air museum.

BELOW LEFT: Tulbagh is renowned for its magnificent historical homes, which were meticulously rebuilt after an earthquake virtually destroyed the town in 1969.
BELOW RIGHT: A rich diversity of succulents bursts into bloom in the Karoo Desert National Botanical Garden in late winter and spring.

BAIN'S KLOOF PASS

Bain's Kloof Pass is regarded as the greatest work of famous road-builder Andrew Geddes Bain. Construction of the road up the western slopes of the Limietberge proved no challenge for him, but the upper sections of the eastern slope proved more difficult. Several kilometres along the eastern slope of the mountain above the Witte River had to be blasted out of solid rock and long sections of the road had to be supported by dry-stone retaining walls up to 20 m high in places. Construction started in 1849 and the pass was completed in 1853.

ACTIVITIES

• Rafting trips (1 day and overnight) on the Breede River near Worcester

• Exotic-butterfly viewing at Butterfly World near Klapmuts, with other attractions including an aviary, spider room, iguana cage and a meerkat enclosure

• Nineteen lions, including a rare white lion, can be seen at Drakenstein Lion Park, also near Klapmuts

• Animal viewing in environmentally friendly enclosures at Giraffe House, between Stellenbosch and Paarl, with other attractions including jungle gyms, a giraffe jumping castle and free-flying bird and reptile shows

• Guided crocodile tours, and watching crocodiles being fed in summer, at Le Bonheur Crocodile Farm, between Paarl and Franschhoek

• Picnicking, swimming, braaing and antelope viewing at Wiesenhof Wildpark, 3,5 km from Klapmuts

• Falconry and flying demonstrations at the Eagle Encounters Raptor Rehabilitation Centre and close-up views of hand-raised cheetahs at the Cheetah Outreach at Spier between Cape Town and Stellenbosch

ROUTES AND TRAILS

• Four Passes (320 km), Breede River (440 km), Paarl (155 km) and Ceres (280 km) fruit routes (round-trip distances from Cape Town)

• Limietberg Hiking Trail (2 days) in the Limietberg Nature Reserve near Paarl

• Seven different day walks (3–6 hours) in the Limietberg Nature Reserve

• Various trails (1–5 hours) in the Paarl Nature Reserve

• Nine walks (30 minutes–8 hours) in Mont Rochelle Nature Reserve near Franschhoek

• Five walks (2–7 hours) in the Jonkershoek Nature Reserve near Stellenbosch

BRANDY – THE NOBLE LIQUOR

The first brandy from Cape wine was distilled by the assistant cook of the ship De Pijl in 1672. The country's brandy industry has come a long way since Colonel Bird recorded, in 1822, that Cape brandy was 'even worse than its wine', and South African brandies have won numerous international awards in recent years.

The Western Cape Brandy Route – the first of its kind in South Africa – was established in 1997 and includes cellars in Stellenbosch, Paarl, Wellington and Grabouw. Worcester is a major producer of wine for brandy and the KWV cellar complex in town, with its 120 Woudberg copper pot stills and enormous maturation cellar, is the largest of its kind in the world. Worcester is also the starting point of the R62 Brandy Route that continues to Robertson, Montagu, Barrydale, Calitzdorp, Oudtshoorn and De Rust.

Visitors can watch demonstrations of home industries such as bread baking and soap making, as well as seasonal activities such as grape pressing and sheep shearing.

The Karoo Desert National Botanical Garden is situated in the foothills of the Brandwacht Mountains on the northern outskirts of town. It was established to conserve the rich and diverse flora of the Succulent Karoo biome. Plants from different Karoo regions can be seen in the garden's cultivated section, while the remaining 144 ha have been left untouched. The aloes and geophytes (bulbous plants) flower during autumn and winter, but it is the spectacular displays of spring flowers that draw the crowds.

Worcester is known for its educational institutions, including special schools for the hearing impaired, the deaf and the blind.

Hex River Valley

A dense patchwork of vineyards makes the Hex River Valley one of the most spectacularly scenic areas in South Africa. In summer the vineyards are deep green; in autumn the leaves are transformed into a breathtaking kaleidoscope of colours – rich reds, orange, russet and shades of brown. Bounded by the Hex River Mountains and the Kwadousberg, the valley is one of the largest producers of table grapes in the country.

The Hex River Valley is a paradise for outdoor enthusiasts with activities ranging from rock climbing, hiking and 4x4 trails to mountain biking and guided excursions to rock art sites.

ABOVE: A tour of the KWV brandy distilling cellar in Worcester provides a fascinating insight into the art of brandy making. LEFT: Jagged mountain peaks and sheer cliffs enclose the Jonkershoek Valley, just outside Stellenbosch.

CHAPTER 6

THE OVERBERG

ABOVE: Scenic Hermanus, a popular weekend getaway from Cape Town, draws visitors with its excellent beaches and whale watching.

A drive about 60 minutes east from Cape Town will take travellers over the mountain into the far southern region of the African continent. This is the scenic Overberg, quite literally 'over the mountain'. The Overberg stretches from Hangklip to the Breede River, bordered by the ocean to the south and the Langeberg mountain range to the north.

This fertile region produces fruit, flowers and wine, and there are great beaches, beautiful mountain passes, quaint towns and lots of local bonhomie. Sometimes known as the Whale Coast — so named because of the hundreds of gentle giants that visit these waters every winter — the Overberg coastline's claim to fame is that it is here, at L'Agulhas, the southernmost tip of Africa, that the Indian and Atlantic oceans meet.

CLIMATE

The Overberg has a predominantly Mediterranean climate. The days are long and warm in summer; February and March are when wine grapes are harvested and the southeaster makes its presence felt. April and May offer mild days, and sometimes there are heady north winds along the coast as well as misty conditions. June and July mark the rainy season.

FLORA AND FAUNA

The Overberg sports some of the finest expanses of indigenous fynbos vegetation and the coastline supports a variety of marine birds and wildlife. The UNESCO-recognised Kogelberg Biosphere Reserve boasts more than 1 600 species of indigenous flora and fauna.

HISTORY AND HERITAGE

The mountains of the Overberg presented a challenge even for the indigenous Khoekhoen who migrated with the seasons in search of grazing for their livestock. Later, for Jan van Riebeeck and the early settlers, the Hottentots Holland Mountains were a major obstacle that prevented expansion and exploration of the eastern interior. The first recorded crossing happened in 1662, by the fiscal Hendrik Lacus who traversed the mountain on a cattle-bartering expedition. Steep and dangerous, the pass continued to be the only link between the Cape of Good Hope and the eastern interior, and by the time of the arrival of the 1820 British settlers, an average 4 500 ox-wagons were using it annually.

In 1828, engineer Charles Michell was commissioned to build a new pass to the south of the old one. It was named after the then governor of the Cape Colony, Sir Galbraith Lowry Cole. These days, Sir Lowry's Pass offers one of the most scenic drives in the Western Cape.

NOTEWORTHY COASTAL PLACES
Hangklip to Kleinmond

Several quaint towns lie along this section of coastline. It includes Rooiels, Pringle Bay and Betty's Bay – all with excellent beaches, holiday accommodation and relaxed eateries, as well as fun outdoor activities. The area is part of the Kogelberg Biosphere Reserve, the country's first-ever proclaimed reserve of this kind. Highlights include the penguin colony at Stony Point in Betty's Bay and the wild horses in the Rooisand Nature Reserve near Kleinmond.

Hermanus

A thriving resort town, Hermanus is said to offer the best land-based whale watching in the world. Listen out for the Whale Crier who sounds a kelp horn when he sights whales, particularly from June to November when the southern right whales arrive to mate and calve in Walker Bay. The annual Hermanus Whale Festival takes place at the end of September each year and is a major event on the tourism calendar. Fine beaches, great fishing, top-notch restaurants, and numerous art galleries and curio shops all add to the attraction of this popular holiday destination.

Stanford

This small Victorian village, located on the banks of the Klein River, is situated just 33 km from Hermanus. It is a leafy, relaxed town that has retained its original village market square as well as its historical architecture. Stanford boasts a microbrewery, where five types of beer can be tasted. The Stanford area, including the nearby Salmonsdam Nature Reserve, is known for its prolific bird life.

MOUNTAIN PASSES

There are many scenic passes in the Overberg region: the Houwhoek Pass between Bot River and Grabouw is festooned with proteas; Viljoen's Pass on the R321 between Elgin and Villiersdorp offers beautiful forest vistas; and Sir Lowry's Pass on the N2 between Elgin and Somerset West is notable for its sweeping views over False Bay.

ABOVE: The striking southern double-collared sunbird is a common resident in the Overberg region. LEFT: Stanford, situated on the Klein River, is a relaxed coastal town with a distinctly Victorian feel. FAR LEFT: Hermanus boasts the world's only Whale Crier, who blows his kelp horn to alert the town that the whales are making an appearance in Walker Bay.

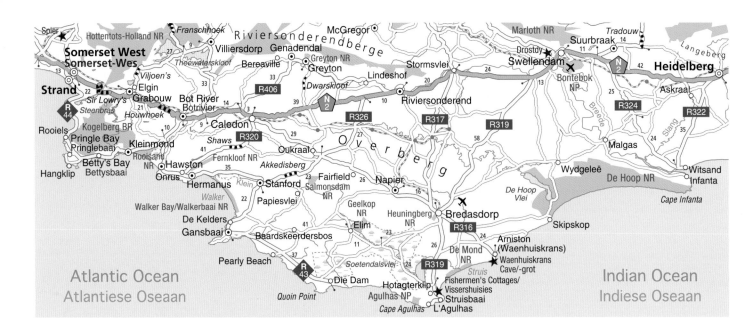

SEE:
Western Cape p. 219
Western Cape p. 220

BELOW LEFT: The quaint village of Elim, a heritage site, retains much of its 1820 charm. BELOW RIGHT: The farm stalls and country shops in Napier are a good place to stop off and buy local produce.

Gansbaai

The fishing village of Gansbaai has become synonymous with great white shark-cage diving. Visit Danger Point Lighthouse, built in 1895, with its 360-degree views of the ocean. De Kelders and Klipgat caves are notable – the former is the only freshwater cave on this coastline, and the latter contains Middle and Later Stone Age deposits that provide an insight into the lifestyles of those who lived along this coastline as much as 65 000 years ago. Further exploration of the coastline will reveal the wrecks of the *Johanna* (1682), *Nicobar* (1783) and *Birkenhead* (1852).

Elim

A national heritage site, the village of Elim is the world's southernmost Moravian mission station, founded by German missionaries in 1824. The Moravian church tower, at the centre of the village, houses the oldest working clock in South Africa. The nearby Geelkop Nature Reserve is known for its rare dwarf Elim fynbos.

Napier

A popular stopover between Cape Town and L'Agulhas, Napier is a quiet rural enclave with decent accommodation and a few eateries and farm stalls. The town developed around the Dutch Reformed church, built in 1838. See the Ox-wagon Monument, the Rose Boats & Toy Museum and the All Sorts Militaria Museum collection.

Bredasdorp

Bredasdorp, the economic heart of a dairy- and wool-farming district, is known for its shops, galleries, restaurants and historical buildings. Visit the interesting Shipwreck Museum, the

SHARK-CAGE DIVING

For adrenalin junkies, one of the major attractions along the Overberg coastline is shark-cage diving. In terms of thrills, nothing can compare to an underwater experience with a great white shark, and the seaside town of Gansbaai has become known as the shark-cage diving capital of South Africa. There are a number of tour operators in the area.

Merino Ram Statue and the Dutch Reformed church. There are three nature reserves in the vicinity – De Mond, Heuningberg and De Hoop.

L'Agulhas

Officially the southernmost town on the African continent, L'Agulhas is the meeting point of the Indian and Atlantic oceans. Early Portuguese explorers named the area *Cabo das Agulhas* ('cape of needles') when they discovered that compass needles show no real deviation between magnetic and true north here. Local attractions include excellent hiking trails at Agulhas National Park and the Cape Agulhas Lighthouse, built in 1849.

Struisbaai

Struisbaai is a relaxed, resort-type destination known for its unbroken 14-km stretch of beach. Good swimming, surfing and other water sports are offered. The harbour was built in 1959 and is worth a visit. The restored fishermen's cottages at Hotagterklip and the thatched Anglican church are heritage sites.

Arniston

Arniston was named after the nearby wreck of the British East Indiaman *Arniston* (1815). The coastal town is also known as Waenhuiskrans ('wagon house cliff'), after the Waenhuiskrans Cave, an enormous sea cave that is said to be big enough to house several ox-wagons. Arniston is a picturesque town, with quaint whitewashed cottages clustered together. It is lovely for swimming, and offers wonderful beach walks.

ABOVE: Sleepy Struisbaai is a fishing and angling paradise.
LEFT: The famous lighthouse at L'Agulhas guides vessels in both the Indian and Atlantic oceans.
BELOW LEFT: The quiet fishing village of Arniston, with its picturesque whitewashed homes and silky beaches, is an ideal seaside retreat.
BELOW: The skilful craftsmen and -women at Kapula Candles in Bredasdorp create beautiful handmade candles.

Malgas

During the 19th century, Malgas, on the western bank of the Breede River, was a busy inland port, with ships entering the river from the sea at Port Beaufort to deliver and collect goods at the small harbour. Today it is a popular weekend destination, with birding, fishing and water sports as some of its attractions. Nearby, at Cape Infanta – where the Breede River enters the sea – is the biggest whale nursery on this coast.

NOTEWORTHY INLAND PLACES
Elgin Valley

Head off the N2 near Steenbras River to the rural farming towns of Grabouw and Elgin. Fruit grows abundantly in this part of the world; the Elgin area in particular is known for its apples. Attractions include the Elgin Apple Museum on the banks of the Palmiet River, Elgin Valley tours showcasing the agriculture of the area, and eco-activities in the Hottentots Holland Nature Reserve and Kogelberg Biosphere Reserve.

There are a number of wine estates in the valley specialising in cool-climate wines such as Pinot Noir, Chardonnay and Sauvignon Blanc. Visit Paul Cluver Wines, South Hill, Elgin Vintners and the Thandi Wine Project, an initiative wholly run and managed by the local community.

Villiersdorp

Sometimes called the 'Sleeping Beauty' of the Overberg, Villiersdorp was founded in 1843. This tranquil rural village is surrounded by mountains and farmlands. The Villiersdorp Wild Flower Garden is known for its birds, fynbos and herbs. There are also numerous wine cellars in the area, and it is the only place in the country with its own Tractor Museum. Nearby Theewaterskloof Dam is popular with water-sport enthusiasts and anglers.

Caledon

Caledon is renowned for its wild flowers, natural mineral waters and hot springs, and for hosting the largest population of the endangered blue crane. There are more than 50 wine estates in the area to visit and the Caledon Hotel, Spa and Casino offers fun and entertainment.

Genadendal

Head off some 27 km from the N2, along the R406, and you will find Genadendal ('vale of grace'). Founded in 1738, it is the oldest Protestant mission station in South Africa, and the buildings around Church Square are all heritage sites. Visit the Mission Museum, Moravian church and Wagon House, and pay your respects at the famous pear tree, planted by Genadendal's first missionary in the 18th century.

BELOW LEFT: Local shops, like this one in Villiersdorp, offer the best food and wine from the area and are worth a visit. BELOW RIGHT: Historical Genadendal is home to numerous heritage sites. BOTTOM: Caledon, at the foot of the Klein Swartberge, is renowned for its rolling landscapes, wild flowers and hot springs.

Greyton

Located 6 km from Genadendal, Greyton lies in the foothills of the Riviersonderend Mountains and is a popular getaway for Capetonians. Attractions include many restored buildings such as St Andrews church, Greyton Lodge, the Post House, the Moravian church and the Smouswinkel. There are several trails through indigenous fynbos in the Greyton Nature Reserve. The Von Geusau chocolate factory should not be missed.

Riviersonderend

Situated 65 km north of Caledon on the N2, Riviersonderend lies at the centre of a wheat-farming community. It offers pristine mountain and river scenery and is renowned for its blue crane colonies.

Swellendam

Historical Swellendam, at the foot of the Langeberg Mountains, is the third-oldest town in the country. Here the Drostdy Museum is worth a visit, as is the Dutch Reformed church on Voortrek Street with its four architectural styles.

Just a short drive south of Swellendam is the Bontebok National Park that supports a population of more than 200 of the antelope for which it is named, as well as Cape mountain zebra, grysbok, red hartebeest and grey rhebok. It also offers excellent birdwatching, hiking and mountain biking opportunities. To the north of the town is the Marloth Nature Reserve, an area of mountain fynbos and afro-montane forest.

Suurbraak

Wedged in between Heidelberg and Swellendam, Suurbraak is a quiet rural town also known as *Xairu* ('paradise'). Surrounded by the majestic Langeberg Mountains, some 7 km from the Tradouw Pass, this former mission station dates back to 1812, and many of the original houses are still standing.

ABOVE: The Drostdy Museum in Swellendam was built in 1747 and was originally the seat of the landdrost, or magistrate. LEFT: A drive from Gordon's Bay to Pringle Bay along the R44 allows for dramatic views of this rugged stretch of coastline.

CHAPTER 7

THE KOUP

ABOVE: The Swartberg Pass, north of Prince Albert, is a monument to the ingenuity of master road engineer Sir Thomas Bain.

To travellers speeding along the N1 across the vast expanse of the Karoo, the landscape appears bleak and uninteresting. However, those who are prepared to set aside preconceived ideas and spend some time in the Koup will soon learn to appreciate its wide open spaces, crisp air filled with the scent of aromatic Karoo bushes, fascinating plant life and fossils galore.

One of several sub-regions of the Great Karoo, the Koup's northern boundary is formed by the rugged mountains of the Nuweveldberge, while the Swartberge form a natural border to the south. Lengthways, it extends from the town of Touws River in the southwest to Beaufort West in the northeast.

CLIMATE

The climate of the Koup is one of extremes. Summer temperatures of above 40 °C are not uncommon, while temperatures can plummet to -5 °C in winter. Rain occurs throughout the year, but peaks between January and March.

HISTORY AND HERITAGE

The arrival of the *trekboers* (migratory stock farmers) in the Koup around the 1750s resulted in the San's loss of their hunting grounds and waterholes. They retaliated by raiding farms, stealing cattle and murdering farming families. The *trekboers* responded by organising commandos to exterminate the San, whom they regarded as vermin.

Xhosa-speaking people fleeing conflicts between rival chiefs in the Eastern Cape also settled in the Karoo. Their herds of cattle needed water and grazing and this also brought them into conflict with the *trekboers*.

These clashes resulted in the proclamation of a new district under the Graaff-Reinet magistracy in November 1818. The British governor at the time, Lord Charles Somerset, named the district and the new town after his father – the fifth Duke of Beaufort. On 3 February 1837, Beaufort became the first town in South Africa to receive municipal status. It was later renamed Beaufort West to avoid confusion with Port Beaufort and Fort Beaufort.

Following the completion of the Hex River Pass in the 1860s, outspans (areas on farms where travellers and their animals could rest) were established along the wagon road to the interior. But it was the building of the railway line from the Cape to the Witwatersrand which boosted the establishment of settlements, such as Laingsburg and Leeu-Gamka, around the railway stations.

Wool sheep were introduced in the region by a farmer named Arthur Kinnear in 1836 and the Koup is now one of the country's major producers of wool and mutton.

FLORA AND FAUNA

The Koup region lies in the Nama Karoo biome, which covers nearly a third of the country's surface. A great many of the 7 000-odd plant species of the Nama Karoo occur in the Koup. Typical low Karoo *bossies* (bushes) and shrubs with descriptive names such as perdekaroo ('horses' Karoo'), gombossie ('gum bush'), springbokbos ('springbuck bush'), inkbos ('ink bush') and kapokbos ('snow bush') dominate the vegetation of the plains. Mesembs, commonly known as *vygies*, and perennial grasses are other important constituents of the Karoo vegetation.

Adapted to the harsh environment, the seeds of Karoo plants can lie dormant for up to 70 years. Germination takes place after good rains at almost any time of the year, but soaking rains in autumn and early winter, followed by 10 to 14 days of mild, overcast weather, provide the best conditions.

Uncontrolled hunting, overgrazing and the erection of fences soon wiped out the large herds of game that once freely roamed the plains, and the Koup gradually turned into a desolate landscape. The first soil conservation plan was implemented in 1954 and a new one

was introduced six years later. Despite efforts to combat overgrazing and soil erosion, just over two decades ago the Karoo region was still overstocked by almost 30%.

Proteas, ericas, reeds and rushes dominate the fynbos vegetation of the Swartberge. The dry, lower northern slopes are characterised by typical Karoo plants.

The Swartberg Complex, which lies at the centre of the Swartberge, is one of eight separate conservation areas of the Cape Floral Region, which was declared a UNESCO World Heritage Site in 2004.

NOTEWORTHY PLACES
Touws River

From the Hex River Valley, the Great North Road (N1) gains nearly 500 m in altitude as it climbs to Touws River, lying at the southwestern corner of South Africa's interior plateau.

In its heyday, during the era of steam trains,

BELOW: Near-vertical cliffs, festooned with lichens, guard the narrow northern entrance of the Swartberg Pass, which was officially opened in 1888.

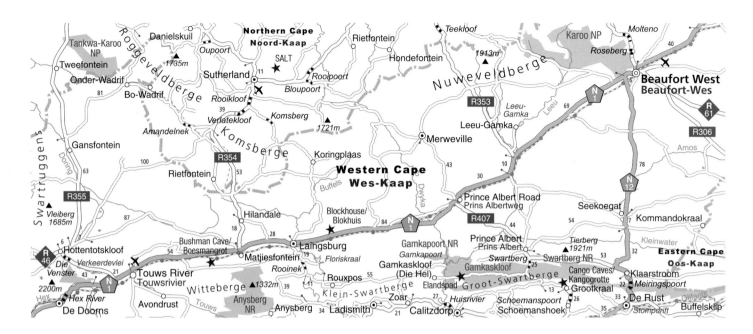

SEE:
Western Cape p. 219
Western Cape p. 220
Eastern Cape p. 221

Touws River was a busy locomotive depot and marshalling yard, but its fortunes waned when diesel locomotives were introduced.

Touws River was one of several observation stations set up in South Africa to observe the transit of Venus in December 1882. The objective of the British expedition stationed here was to measure the distance between the earth and the sun. Two concrete pillars in the grounds of the old Douglas Hotel are reminders of South African astronomy in the 19th century.

Matjiesfontein

What was once just a railway halt was transformed into a charming Victorian village by an enterprising Scotsman, James (Jimmy) Douglas Logan, in the mid-1880s.

In those days trains did not have dining wagons, and it did not take Logan long to realise that there was money to be made from the lucrative refreshment-room concessions. He began by obtaining the lease for the railway-owned hotel at Touws River Station, and eventually secured all the concessions from Cape Town to Bulawayo.

Logan began developing Matjiesfontein, then a lonely railway siding, in 1884. Here, he developed a late Victorian-style health and holiday resort that attracted famous people like Cecil John Rhodes, Lord Randolph Churchill (father of Sir Winston Churchill), the Duke of Hamilton and the Sultan of Zanzibar. Olive Schreiner, the author of Story of an African Farm, lived at Matjiesfontein for a few years.

Matjiesfontein sank into obscurity after Logan's death in 1920, but was saved from certain demise when well-known hotelier David Rawdon bought the entire village in 1968 and restored it to its former splendour.

The towered Lord Milner Hotel, the Laird's Arms Victorian country pub, the wood-and-iron Masonic Losieshuis (boarding house), the post office and the double-storied general store (now the Coffee House) are among the many outstanding buildings in the village that is a virtual open-air museum. An extensive collection of Victoriana is on display in the Marie Rawdon Museum, named after the owner's mother.

Laingsburg

A little more than a century after Laingsburg was established, the town made headlines in January 1981 when the Buffels River burst its banks after 425 mm of rain fell in its catchment area in just two days. The devastating flood

RIGHT: The Union Jack flying over Matjiesfontein further adds to the town's Victorian atmosphere.

destroyed 184 houses and killed 104 people, many of whom were swept away by the raging floodwaters. The flood-level marker opposite the Dutch Reformed church in Main Street is a reminder of one of South Africa's worst natural disasters in living memory.

Prince Albert

Laid out in the foothills of the Swartberge in 1842, Prince Albert has retained much of its old-world charm. The picturesque farming village with its *leivore* (water furrows) and tree-lined streets is an architectural gem, with building styles ranging from simple Karoo houses to Victorian homes with decorative cast-iron columns and lacework, wooden fretwork and verandas.

The town is also renowned for its Cape Dutch houses with their distinctive Prince Albert gables. These holbol gables have alternating concave and convex curves with a small round or triangular pediment on the top. The gable window is typically flanked by two pilasters, while matching horizontal moldings connect the convex moldings.

The best way to explore the town's rich architecture is to buy a copy of the *Prince Albert Historical Route* pamphlet at the tourism bureau and to explore the town on foot. The bureau is housed in the Fransie Pienaar Museum, which depicts the town's history and its surroundings.

The normally tranquil village becomes a hive of activity in May when the annual Olive Festival takes place.

Gamkaskloof (Die Hel)

In the 1830s, a group of hardy farming families settled in a remote valley in the folds of the Swartberge. Blessed with an abundance

ABOVE LEFT: Laingsburg, a centre for the surrounding farms, was an important stop on the railroad between Cape Town and Johannesburg during the days of steam trains. ABOVE RIGHT: Prince Albert is an architectural gem, its streets lined with many fine Victorian and Karoo houses. BELOW: A long and winding road leads to Gamkaskloof, a remote valley in the Swartberge.

THE ROAD TO DIE HEL

The road descending into Gamkaskloof (Die Hel) starts innocently enough, winding through fynbos (razed by fire in places) and through exuberant acid-yellow leucadendrons, then spiky Karoo veld, bright pink mesembs and the candelabra valleys of bitter aloe. Here and there is a little rocky outcrop with a perfect, natural bonsai meditation garden at its feet.

Eventually drivers will arrive at the crux of the road – a steep 4-km stretch that doubles back on itself through hairpin bends and perilous drops. This is the time to focus. The perilous journey is worth it, however, as once in the valley, another, very secluded, world is revealed.

of water and fertile soil, the *Kloovers* ('ravine people'), as they called themselves, reared livestock and cultivated wheat, fruit and vegetables. In time, the valley became renowned for its dried raisins, dried fruit and its witblits ('white lightning') – a potent home-distilled spirit.

By the early 1900s, the valley was already known as Die Hel ('the hell') – a name that was resented by the *Kloovers*. For more than 130 years, the only access into Gamkaskloof was on foot or by donkey. Prolonged droughts, followed by devastating floods, tested the mettle of the *Kloovers*.

The completion of the road from the Swartberg Pass to Gamkaskloof in 1963 finally brought about drastic changes. Young people left to attend school in the towns, the elderly and the sick moved away and an increasing number of visitors attracted by the name 'Die Hel' disturbed the tranquillity of the valley.

Gamkaskloof came under the control of CapeNature in the early 1990s – after the last inhabitants left the valley in 1992. Visitor facilities include accommodation in restored cottages; campsites with cold-water ablutions and braai facilities; and a bush camp with hot showers and braai facilities.

A four-wheel drive vehicle is essential for the 37 km journey to Gamkaskloof. The final 4 km

zigzags along the Elandspad to the valley, losing several hundred metres in altitude.

Klaarstroom

The farming village of Klaarstroom was established on the farm De Klaare Stroom ('the clear stream') after completion of the road through Meiringspoort in 1858. The first plots were laid out in 1860 along a single street and the village, with its Karoo-style and Victorian houses, general-dealer store, Victorian police station and post office has changed little since the days when it was an important stop on the wool route between the Karoo and the coast.

Leeu-Gamka

Once an outspan on the wagon route to the north, Leeu-Gamka became an important stop after diamonds were discovered at Hopetown in 1866 and at Kimberley in 1871. It received another boost when the railway reached the settlement in 1879, and many famous personalities of the time stretched their legs on the platform of the small railway station.

Disaster struck when the N1 was moved to its present position in 1943 as most motorists simply sped past. Leeu-Gamka gradually sank into obscurity. Buildings of architectural interest include the railway station, the 1898 Leeu-Gamka Hotel and the Dutch Reformed church.

BELOW: Herds of springbok roam the plains of the Karoo National Park at Beaufort West. BOTTOM: Visitors to the Karoo National Park are accommodated in Cape Dutch-style cottages.

KAROO NATIONAL PARK

Situated on the outskirts of Beaufort West, the Karoo National Park was proclaimed in 1979 to protect an area representative of the region. The municipality of Beaufort West donated 7 209 ha of commonage, the central government made money available and funds were raised by the Southern African Nature Foundation by selling stamps – each representing 1 acre of Karoo.

The park is a sanctuary for herds of springbok, gemsbok, Cape mountain zebra, buffalo, red hartebeest, black rhino and several raptor species. Eland, kudu, klipspringer, bat-eared fox, black-backed jackal are among the other animals to be seen.

The park can be explored along two self-drive routes: a tarred circular drive across the low-lying plains of Lammertjiesleegte, or a 50-km circuit through the western part of the park. Guided game drives and night drives are conducted in open vehicles.

Accommodation in the rest camp is available in self-catering Cape Dutch-style cottages, while those preferring the outdoors can opt for shady campsites. A restaurant, shop and swimming pool are other facilities in the rest camp. The Bulkraal day-visitor area has picnic sites, a swimming pool and ablution facilities.

ACTIVITIES

- Buying farm produce at the Gamkaskloof Kiosk in Gamkaskloof
- Camping in Gamkaskloof
- Tasting olives in Prince Albert, especially during the May Olive Festival
- Viewing local architecture at various locations
- Identifying Karoo bossies and other flora

ROUTES AND TRAILS

- Two 4x4 Eco Adventure Trails (2–6 hours and 5–6 hours) in the Karoo National Park
- Out-and-return 4x4 trail (54,4 km; day or overnight route) in the Swartberg Nature Reserve
- Pointer Hiking Trails (1.5–3 hours) in the Karoo National Park
- Bossie Trail (800 m) and Fossil Trail (400 m) in the Karoo National Park
- Country Walk (1.5 hours) in Prince Albert, starts and ends in Church Street
- Koppie Trail (1 hour) in Prince Albert, starts in Berg Street and ends in Crosby Street
- Karoo Walk (1 hour) in Prince Albert, starts and ends in Christina de Wit Street
- Ghost Walk (1.5 hours) in Prince Albert, starts and ends in front of the Fransie Pienaar Museum in Church Street
- Swartberg Hiking Trail (day walks to 5 days) in the Swartberg Nature Reserve
- The Donkey Trail (4 days), a guided hiking trail over the Swartberg, following the original donkey trail between Calitzdorp and Gamkaskloof, where donkeys carry the equipment

Beaufort West

Beaufort West, the largest town in the region, lies in the heart of the Great Karoo. Pear trees, cypresses and *leivore* line the main street. The Beaufort West Town Hall, which was inaugurated in 1866, is the focal point of the Beaufort West Museum complex. The historic building has been dedicated to the town's most famous son, Dr Christiaan Barnard, who performed the world's first successful human heart transplant at Groote Schuur Hospital in Cape Town in 1967. Several hundred awards and gifts presented to Dr Barnard after this medical feat are on display and there is also a reconstruction of the operating theatre.

The Dutch Reformed mission church is situated next to the town hall. It was here that the pioneer heart surgeon's father, Reverend Adam Barnard, preached to his flock from 1911 to 1948. Adjoining the mission church, which dates back to 1872, is the parsonage where young Christiaan grew up.

LEFT: Klaarstroom, a farming village near the northern entrance of Meiringspoort, has changed little in the last 150 years.
BELOW: A diorama depicting the world's first heart transplant can be seen in the Beaufort West Museum.

TREASURE HOUSE OF FOSSILS

Dinosaurs roamed the marshy floodplains and swamps that covered the Karoo basin some 240 million years ago. The skeletons of dinosaurs that died in these marshes became entombed in mud, and silica from the surrounding sediments gradually replaced the calcium in their bones to preserve them perfectly. Erosion exposed some of these fossilised creatures millions of years later and the Karoo is regarded as one of the richest areas in the world for reptile fossils.

The Fossil Trail in the Karoo National Park offers a fascinating insight into these extinct reptiles.

CHAPTER 8

THE LITTLE KAROO

ABOVE: The town of Oudtshoorn is bordered by the Swartberge to the north and the Outeniqua mountains to the south.

The Little Karoo, or *Klein Karoo* in Afrikaans, stretches from the southern slopes of the Swartberg range to the N2 highway in the Western Cape. It begins at Meiringspoort in the eastern folds of the Groot Swartberge and ends at the quaint town of Montagu. Along this, one of South Africa's most colourful and dramatic routes, travellers are always in sight of craggy mountains and never too far from a farm stall.

Highlights of this fascinating area include the astounding silence, the awesome Swartberge and Langeberg mountain ranges, the floral bio-diversity, the slightly challenging dirt road mountain passes, the tiny villages tucked into the mountain folds off Route 62 and the Cango Caves. The friendliness of local residents and the possibility of relaxing on a guest farm for a few days, doing next to nothing, are attractive antidotes to big-city living.

CLIMATE

Like the Great Karoo on the northern side of the Cape Fold Belt mountains, the Little Karoo is arid. Its hot summers are punctuated by short, spectacular thundershowers crashing against the mountain peaks. But it also has some winter rainfall, usually a soft life-giving drizzle. During cold winter spells, snow can be seen on the mountains. Spring (September to November) and autumn (March to May) are the mildest and most beautiful seasons.

FLORA AND FAUNA

The vegetation of the Little Karoo is unmistakable – drought-resistant, knee-high, aromatic shrub that can seem less than spectacular from a speeding car. But pull over, walk among the plants, crush and smell their leaves. The scents of wild rosemary, sage, camphor and lavender can immediately be recognised. These are the plants that 'season the sheep on the hoof', as the locals put it.

Punctuating the land like exclamation marks are the aloes that flower flame red in winter. Travellers who take the mountain passes, and who have sharp eyes, will notice proteas and ericas in the heights. These fynbos plants belong to the wondrously diverse Cape Floral Kingdom, one of the most extraordinary ecosystems in the world. Thriving on poor soil, unpredictable rainfall, heat and cold, they burst into magnificent flower from September to November, showing true grace in adversity.

HISTORY AND HERITAGE

The ostrich has spawned an entire industry in the Little Karoo – and a slew of colourful rural legends to go with it.

Ostrich feathers were worn during the Art Nouveau period in Europe and the United States, and by the 1880s the ostrich industry was flourishing in South Africa, with Oudtshoorn as its capital. 'Feather millionaires' were building 'feather palaces' all over town, ornate mansions that still stand; evidence of the very good business these big-eyed birds had become.

UNDERGROUND ART GALLERIES

Below the southern foothills of the Groot Swartberge is an awe-inspiring natural wonder: the Cango Group of limestone deposits where, over the millennia, rainwater has fashioned an immense complex of caves. Only a small number of these magnificent chambers are open to the public via the Cango Caves near Oudtshoorn, but their dreamlike arrangements of stalagmites, stalactites and flowstones, artfully lit, have attracted millions of tourists over the decades.

LEFT: Ostrich feathers are used to make flamboyant feather dusters. BELOW: The otherworldly Cango Caves are a fascinating attraction in the Little Karoo.

CANGO WILDLIFE RANCH

There are a number of ostrich farms open to the public. Tourists can also visit the Cango Wildlife Ranch, which is both an animal breeding centre and, arguably, the most exotic petting zoo in Africa. Here, visitors can be lowered in a cage to spend some quality underwater time with a trio of huge Nile crocodiles, or cuddle up to a cheetah cub. Among other fascinating creatures are resident white tigers and a Cape clawless otter.

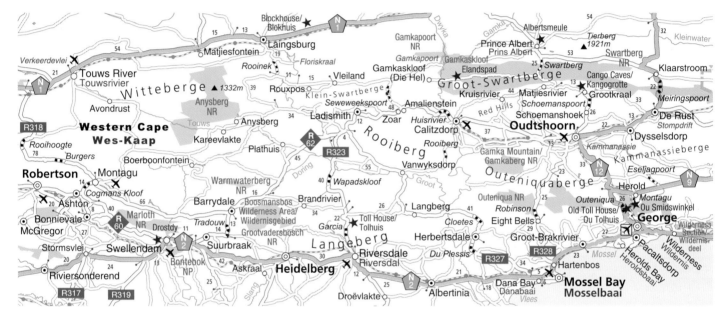

SEE:
Western Cape p. 219
Western Cape p. 220

TOP LEFT: Picturesque De Rust is situated at the southern entrance of Meiringspoort, and is worth a look-see. TOP RIGHT: Although only about 1,5 mm thick, ostrich eggshells are super strong.

Then, as the clouds of World War I gathered on the European horizon, all notions of fancy frippery were dispensed with. For nearly 30 years the South African ostrich business stood dormant, until, in the middle of World War II, ostrich farming was revived. This time it was a far more sustainable industry that was not exclusively reliant on fine feathers for its survival. Today, in a world that prefers healthy, leaner cuts of protein, ostriches are mainly farmed for their meat.

NOTEWORTHY PLACES
Meiringspoort and De Rust

Meiringspoort is the winding, stately gorge linking the Great Karoo to the Little Karoo and the town of De Rust. Meiringspoort itself is worth a slow meander, and perhaps a picnic at one of the well-appointed stopping sites. A very interesting day drive from a base in De Rust would be to head due west towards Oudtshoorn and the Cango Caves and then over the

mountains along the spectacular Swartberg Pass. Stop over at the Victorian Karoo town of Prince Albert, where ghosts are said to move in the paintings over at the local hotel, before wending homewards through Meiringspoort.

Oudtshoorn

If the Little Karoo has a capital city, then Oudtshoorn is it. Once the feather capital of the world, Oudtshoorn has reinvented itself as a bustling tourist destination and one of the cultural centres of South Africa. A highlight is the *Klein Karoo Nasionale Kunstefees* (Little Karoo National Arts Festival), held in April or May each year. The rather diverse collection of writers, singers, actors and their thousands of fans who descend gleefully on Oudtshoorn every year represents the lighter, more creative side of what used to be seen as apartheid culture.

The success of the festival has changed perceptions of Oudtshoorn, and its year-long tourism appeal has provided employment for many of

the 'non-professional' locals who make a living from the by-products of the ostrich industry – the eggs and feathers.

If time permits, try to spend a few days exploring the area. This would include the town architecture and museums, and visits to a series of interesting surrounding farms. The Gamkaberg Nature Reserve outside Oudtshoorn offers fynbos, succulent Karoo, Cape mountain zebra and several hiking trails.

Calitzdorp

This is port wine country and a more picturesque wineland setting would be hard to find. The Gamka Valley with its trellised vineyards embraces the little town of Calitzdorp, where those with a sweet tooth can feast on superior carrot cake in a place called Rose of the Karoo.

One of the better day-trip drives is to head through the Red Hills to the Kruisrivier community of fruit farmers, painters and potters.

Ladismith

Driving in the Ladismith district, traveller's eyes are magically drawn to a jagged peak called Towerkop ('bewitched peak') up on the Klein Swartberge. It stands out like a beacon and carries a quaint tale concerning a witch, a wand and fit of pique. Legend has it that she blasted the peak in two so she could get through the mountain on her way to the sea.

Ladismith itself is a charming town known for its wines, fruits and cheeses. A little more than 30 km south of Ladismith, on a good dirt road, is the mountain village of Vanwyksdorp. The drive alone makes this detour worthwhile, because the return trip through the mountains takes the magnificent Rooiberg Pass back to the R62.

Barrydale

This small town is something of a contradiction – it has the arid Little Karoo on the one side and the lushness of the Grootvadersbosch Nature Reserve on the other. Barrydale lies at the

TOP: Red Stone Hill, 14 km outside of Calitzdorp, gets its unusual colour from the iron oxide present in the rock. ABOVE LEFT: Keurbosch Farm Stall in Ladismith sells pickles, nuts, preserves and olive products from the region. ABOVE RIGHT: Ladismith, famous for its dairy offerings, makes for a great cheese-tasting sojourn.

DRIVE A PASS

The jagged Cape Fold Belt mountains divide the Great Karoo from the Little Karoo, and what a magnificent backdrop they make. Over millennia, these outcrops have been thrust upwards, warped downwards, stretched, buckled and weathered to an astonishing degree, creating the folded appearance for which they are named. In some places, the innermost creases of the folded formations have collapsed and fallen away, leaving rocky overhangs that have been used as shelters by people and animals throughout the ages.

A drive along one of the famous passes in the Little Karoo will allow the craggy beauty of these extraordinary mountains to be fully appreciated.

Swartberg Pass

Road builder Sir Thomas Bain was a genius, and his crowning achievement was the Swartberg Pass, which connects the Great Karoo village of Prince Albert with the Little Karoo town of Oudtshoorn. The hairpin bends, the wild flower displays, the spectacular views and the faultless dry-stone walling make the pass an ingenious combination of natural beauty and engineering craftsmanship. Bain performed magic with stone here, and since the opening of the pass, in 1888, no one has yet deemed it necessary to tar the road. It is great just as it is.

Montagu Pass

The Montagu Pass, opened between George and Oudtshoorn in 1847, replaced a number of notorious routes over the treacherous Outeniqua Mountains. It is still possible to visit the old toll house on the George side of the mountain crossing. According to local folklore, the ghost of a convict murdered by a fellow labourer during the construction of the pass appears at midnight to unsuspecting travellers making their way across the mountain.

Seweweekspoort

Adventurous travellers along Route 62, with the urge to put some dirt under their wheels, should take the turn-off to the Seweweekspoort at Amalienstein, between Calitzdorp and Ladismith. This track, which leads to Laingsburg, is quite simply one of the most stunning mountain passes in the country.

As the gravel road winds through what looks like a giant open-air cathedral with vertical craggy walls, the keen-eyed might spot a pair of Verreaux's eagles hunting rock rabbits near the high ledges. To truly feel the magic of the area, stop at a stream, take a walk in the water and then unpack the sandwiches.

foot of the Langeberg and has a number of good restaurants and guest houses to choose from. In recent years, it has become a hub of creativity as artists and media folk have settled here.

If time permits a detour, try the Tradouw Pass between Barrydale and Swellendam. Like the Swartberg Pass, it was built by that 'man with the theodolite eyes', Sir Thomas Bain, and it, too, has stood the test of time. There are hot springs, museums, hiking trails and gardens galore here. There are also a number of wineries in the area.

The road through Barrydale is lined with antique shops, eateries and coffee shops. Just outside the town is a nondescript little building bearing the legend 'Ronnie's Sex Shop'. Not really a sex shop, it is famous in these parts as a great little roadside bar.

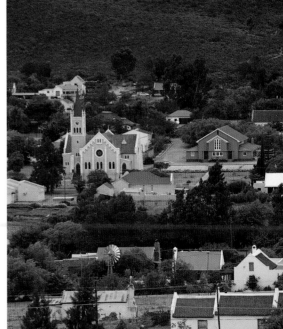

ACTIVITIES

- Crocodile-cage diving at Cango Wildlife Ranch near Oudtshoorn
- Riding ostriches in Oudtshoorn
- Touring the Cango Caves outside Oudtshoorn
- Tasting and buying port from the cellars at Calitzdorp
- Sampling local produce at the farm stalls along Route 62
- Farm stays in the Oudtshoorn, Kruisrivier and Calitzdorp districts
- Stopping at Ronnie's Sex Shop on the outskirts of Barrydale
- Hot-air ballooning from Oudtshoorn
- Birdwatching around Ladismith
- Sampling witblits (moonshine) at Barrydale and De Rust
- Cheese tasting in Ladismith
- Mountain biking throughout the Little Karoo
- Geological tours around Calitzdorp
- Meerkat Magic tour outside Oudtshoorn, where a suricate expert takes visitors to see a tame colony of meerkats
- Rock climbing and enjoying the hot springs at Montagu
- Rock climbing, abseiling, hiking and swimming in Barrydale

ROUTES AND TRAILS

- Hiking outside Montagu
- Route 62 Brandy Route (272 km) from Montagu to De Rust
- Klein Karoo Wine Route (272 km), which stretches along Route 62 from Montagu to the Langekloofberge, passing through Barrydale, Ladismith, Calitzdorp and De Rust

SEX SELLS

Ronnie Price came to live and farm in Barrydale years ago, and built a small roadside stall so he could sell fresh produce to passers-by. He called it 'Ronnie's Shop'. One night, some friends painted the word 'sex' between 'Ronnie's' and 'Shop', and people started arriving, wanting more than a pocket of potatoes. Today Ronnie's is a famous South African landmark – and a wonderful bar to boot. Overlanders and motorcycle clubs, in particular, make up much of Ronnie's trade.

Grootvadersbosch Nature Reserve

Situated near the country town of Heidelberg, the Grootvadersbosch Nature Reserve has excellent hiking and cycling routes as well as well-priced accommodation. There are more than 196 bird species in this reserve.

Montagu

One of the most sought-after villages in the Western Cape, in terms of property and retirement investment, is the exquisitely positioned Montagu in the Langeberg Valley. Drivers approaching from the direction of Cape Town on the R60 will have come through Cogmans Kloof, one of the best local examples of the Cape Fold Belt mountains and a very good area for hiking, walking and rock climbing .

More than 20 of Montagu's Cape Dutch and Victorian buildings have been declared heritage sites, and a sense of old-time elegance and history permeates its streets.

OPPOSITE TOP: Enjoy spectacular views of the Klein Karoo as you traverse the historic Montagu Pass.
OPPOSITE BOTTOM: The tranquil town of Barrydale is a typical Klein Karoo *dorp*.
ABOVE: Ronnie's Sex Shop is a popular spot to wet one's whistle.
LEFT: Apricots dry under big African skies in Montagu.

CHAPTER 9

THE GARDEN ROUTE

ABOVE: The picturesque Knysna Lagoon is a popular boating and fishing spot and forms part of the Garden Route National Park.

Stretching eastwards from Witsand to Humansdorp, the Garden Route is one of South Africa's most scenic stretches of road, an area of exquisite natural beauty and one of the country's top tourist attractions. The combination of mountains, ocean, beaches, lakes and forests makes it an ideal destination. The Garden Route National Park is well loved by those who enjoy the great outdoors and there are various other adventure attractions.

CLIMATE

Similar to other parts of the Western Cape, the Garden Route has a Mediterranean climate – winters are generally mild and wet, and summers are warm and attract beach holidaymakers in their droves. While the Garden Route falls into the winter rainfall region, there is rain almost all year round (850–1 000 mm) and as a result the countryside is green and

lush. The forests in the area thrive in this subtropical environment.

FLORA AND FAUNA

The region's diverse habitats support a rich plant and animal life; temperate forests and fynbos shelter a range of birds and small mammals. The string of coastal lakes that lie along the Wilderness coast forms a unique wetland system that includes sedges, reeds and rushes and various types of grass.

Dolphins, porpoises and whales are regularly seen. June to November is the best time for whale spotting at places such as Knysna and Plettenberg Bay.

There are a few unique birds to look out for including the Knysna turaco, the Narina trogon and the African black oystercatcher (on the Red Data List of Threatened Species). Blue duiker occur in the forests and the Cape clawless otter hunts along the rugged coastline. The rare Knysna seahorse, found only in Knysna Lagoon, is another fascinating (and highly endangered) creature.

During the 1800s, herds of elephant lived in the forests surrounding Knysna, but by 1908 their numbers had dwindled considerably as a result of ivory hunting. A century later, only three were recorded. While there continue to be rumours of sightings in the forests, your best bet of seeing one is at the Knysna Elephant Park.

HISTORY AND HERITAGE

Four hundred million years ago, the region was covered by an inland sea. When the plates of the supercontinent Gondwanaland first collided, layers of sediment were pushed upwards to form the Cape Fold Belt mountains, including the Outeniqua Mountains. Later, the land was torn apart to form the continents of Africa, South America, Australia and Antarctica.

As climate changes froze and warmed the globe intermittently, the Garden Route was alternately covered by ocean or lay deep inland. When the waters receded, rivers broadened and deepened their spectacular valleys, and dunes accumulated. During warmer times, the dunes were covered by ocean and when the sea receded yet again, lakes remained in the interdune depressions.

The resulting coastal-lake system of Wilderness is the defining feature of this region. Not only are the lakes and vleis spectacularly beautiful, they are also the spawning ground for a number of fish species such as the Knysna halfbeak, the Cape stumpnose and the spotted grunter.

The rainforests of the Garden Route are also unique. As the land iced over and thawed, rainforests spread into southern Africa but then shrank as the climate became drier. That is, except in this damp enclave where relic forests and wetlands continue to thrive.

For the San and the Outeniqua Khoekhoen, the region was paradise. The Outeniqua ('people carrying bags') got their name from the pouches they filled with the honey of wild bees that drew nectar from an abundance of wild flowers growing in the area. The Khoekhoen lived off the land, taking from it only what they needed for their survival.

However, this harmonious co-existence was disrupted within a hundred years after the arrival of the first European settlers at the Cape of Good Hope. By 1668, reports of the Garden Route's timber wealth had reached the colonists, but the region – remote and geographically

THE GARDEN ROUTE NATIONAL PARK

In 2009, three existing national parks, at Wilderness, Knysna and the Tsitsikamma, were combined with an additional 97 000 ha of forest and farmland to create a single protected area – the Garden Route National Park. The 120 500-ha megapark boasts an incredible diversity of habitats, from mountain and coastal fynbos and indigenous forest to ocean, lakes, wetlands, rivers and estuaries.

The Tsitsikamma section at the eastern end is an enclave of lush rain forest and coastal reserve. Because of the high rainfall in the area (up to 1 200 mm a year), the forest vegetation thrives and there are numerous streams and rivers in the area. (Tsitsikamma means 'place of running waters' in the language of the Khoekhoen.) The flora includes a great variety of shrubs and fynbos, as well as exquisite trees such as yellowwood, stinkwood, white alder and ironwood.

Accommodation is available in the Wilderness and Tsitsikamma sections of the park. A multitude of activities ranging from hiking, swimming, snorkelling, boating and canoeing to whale- and birdwatching are on offer.

BELOW LEFT: The lush Knysna Forest is home to majestic stinkwood, yellowwood, ironwood and Cape chestnut.
BELOW RIGHT: One of the many beautiful birds to look out for along the Garden Route is the colourful Knysna turaco.

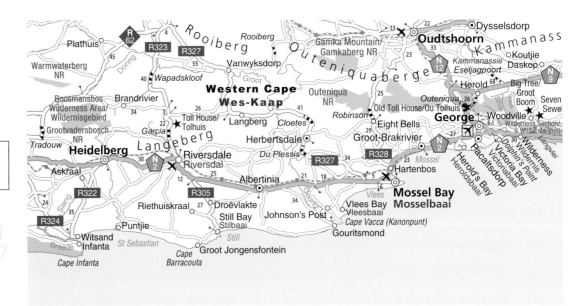

SEE:
Western Cape p. 220
Eastern Cape p. 221

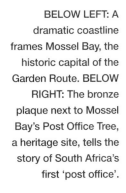

inaccessible – remained unexplored until the mid-1700s.

The settlers did not give up. A woodcutters' post was established in 1776, where the town of George now stands, and an early timber port was constructed at Plettenberg Bay in 1778. The woodcutters were the precursors of an extraordinarily hardy breed of men, referred to as the *houtkappers* (woodcutters), who were to live deep in the forest until 1939. They were a colourful lot, but for them there was precious little romance in the trade and even less money. Most of the huge profits went to the agents, the merchants at the timber ports and the ship owners.

Inexorably, and within a very short time, the forests became overexploited and the wild animals were decimated. Misguided 19th-century conservationists made matters worse by planting exotic species such as blue gum, wattle and pine to rejuvenate the forests. These aliens quickly overran the indigenous vegetation and

they remain a serious threat to this day. To preserve what is left and turn the tide, a series of national parks was declared after the 1960s. In 2009 these parks, along with parcels of former state forests and plantations, were consolidated to form the Garden Route National Park.

NOTEWORTHY PLACES

At the very start of the Garden Route, the coastal town of Witsand with its exquisite beaches and views of the Indian Ocean and the

BELOW LEFT: A dramatic coastline frames Mossel Bay, the historic capital of the Garden Route. **BELOW RIGHT:** The bronze plaque next to Mossel Bay's Post Office Tree, a heritage site, tells the story of South Africa's first 'post office'.

MOSSEL BAY'S POST OFFICE TREE

The story goes that in 1500 Commander Pedro de Ataide left a letter of great importance in a shoe under a large milkwood tree. It was found about a year later by Commander João da Nova on his way to India – and thus, the first 'post office' in the country was established. The tree still stands today.

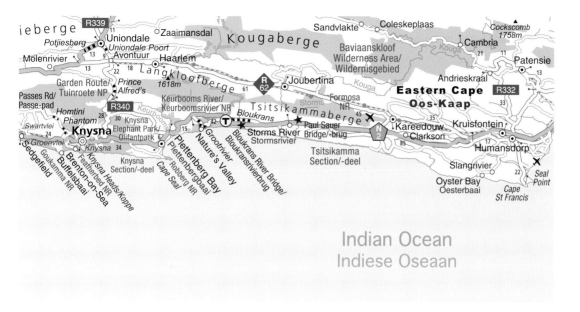

Breede River is worth a stop. Its claim to fame is that its whale nursery at St Sebastian Bay has the highest concentration of whales in the country. Witsand is also known for its variety of bird species, and blue cranes are found in these parts.

Mossel Bay

The first recorded landing of Europeans at Mossel Bay is that of Bartolomeu Dias more than 500 years ago, who after rounding the Cape of Good Hope stopped here to replenish his ship's water supply.

Situated almost halfway between Cape Town and Port Elizabeth, Mossel Bay is a friendly town with excellent beaches, interesting architecture and a few good museums, among them the Dias Museum Complex that contains a replica of Dias's vessel.

Outdoor and adventure activities include shark-cage diving, shipwreck diving, scuba diving, abseiling and yachting. St Blaize cave is a great lookout point.

George

At the foot of the Outeniqua mountain range lies the large town of George. Some of its more interesting attractions include the church of St Peter and St Paul, the oldest remaining Catholic church in the country today, the Dutch Reformed church with its stinkwood pillars, George Museum, the Outeniqua Railway Museum, and the town's great landmark, the Old Oak Tree.

The Wonki Ware ceramics studio, where beautiful one-off pieces are made by local community members, is a great stop for art enthusiasts.

Herold's Bay

This delightful holiday spot, 18 km west of George, has great beaches. The many vantage points along its coastline also make it a favourite angling and whale watching destination.

BELOW: Wilderness has long white beaches and lush surroundings. The area is known for its outdoor adventure activities and ecotourism offerings.

SEVEN PASSES ROAD

The old 82-km road between George and Knysna, known as the Seven Passes Road, is recommended for those who have some time on their hands. It winds through dense forests, down steep gorges and over several rivers, including the Kaaimans and Silver whose original stone bridges are now heritage sites. Stop at Woodville and visit the Big Tree – an ancient yellowwood reported to be around 800 years old.

ABOVE LEFT: Knysna is a gourmet destination that offers a wide variety of restaurants and eateries. ABOVE RIGHT: As Knysna is a popular boating and fishing destination, yachts are a permanent feature at both the Knysna Waterfront and Thesen Island.

Wilderness

The combination of lush foliage, white, sweeping beaches and the warm Indian Ocean makes this seaside village an ideal base for lovers of the great outdoors. Dolphin's Point is a good place to view whales and dolphins. A visit to the Wilderness section of the new Garden Route National Park, with its beaches, lakes, rivers, estuaries and excellent nature trails, is advisable. The park's Island Lake has abundant birdlife as well as excellent picnic and braai facilities. Canoeing and pedal boating along the Touws River is popular.

Sedgefield

A popular family destination, Sedgefield has wonderful beaches and nature trails. There are numerous lakes in the area including Swartvlei, Langvlei and Rondevlei, with its excellent bird sanctuary. The Goukamma Nature Reserve encompasses coastal forests and fynbos, some of the highest vegetated dunes in the country, as well as the freshwater lake, Groenvlei, and a marine protected area that stretches along 18 km of the coastline. The entire area is known for birdwatching and a variety of outdoor activities.

Knysna

Knysna is a major pit stop for travellers along the Garden Route. This popular seaside town is epitomised by the iconic Knysna Heads — facing sandstone formations that guard a narrow lagoon inlet from the sea. Situated on the Western Head is the privately owned Featherbed Nature Reserve. Visitors are ferried across the lagoon to the nature reserve where they are taken to the major lookout points by 4x4 and can enjoy a guided walk. Knysna has more than eight swimming beaches, and daily

FESTIVALS

The Pink Loerie Mardi Gras, a highlight on the gay calendar, is held in Knysna every year in April/May. This major five-day festival includes a street parade, drag competitions, beauty pageants, concerts, plays, lagoon cruises and adventure activities.

The 10-day Knysna Oyster Festival takes place every year during July and is all about feasting, sport, fun, art and entertainment. Along with much oyster eating and live music, there are sporting events, beauty pageants, oyster-shucking competitions, kids' events and charity races.

cruises on the Knysna Lagoon provide fun in warm weather. The historic Belvidere church is worth a visit, as is the King Edward VII Tree and George Rex's Grave.

The story of George Rex, the founder of Knysna, still fascinates travellers today. According to local folklore, he was the illegitimate son of King George III and a certain Hannah Lightfoot, but was packed off to the colonies when he was in his thirties to avoid embarrassment to the Crown. George Rex bought the farm Melkhoutkraal in 1804, which subsequently grew to incorporate what is known as Knysna today. Although recent genetic testing disproves his royal parentage, the legend of George Rex continues to fascinate.

Plettenberg Bay

Bordered by the Outeniqua and Tsitsikamma mountains, this resort town gets extremely busy during the summer when holidaymakers countrywide head to 'Plett' for sun, sand and sea. It is also popular with teens who descend on the town for the traditional Plett Rage each year for a period of two weeks after they have written their final matric exams.

DID YOU KNOW?

Knysna is synonymous with fresh seafood. The Knysna Quays Waterfront has a number of excellent restaurants that offer overflowing seafood platters and views of the harbour. The Knysna Oyster Company and its cosy tavern is another popular spot.

ACTIVITIES

• Abseiling on Mont Blanc Adventure Farm near Riversdale

• Water-skiing, parasailing, fishing, hiking, windsurfing and kayaking at Korentepoort Dam near Riversdale

• Shark-cage diving in Mossel Bay

• Helicopter flips over the coastline (including great white shark spotting excursions) in Mossel Bay

• Bungee jumping and bridge swinging from Gouritz River bridge near Mossel Bay and the Bloukrans River bridge near Nature's Valley

• Surfing at various locations, including Buffelsbaai and Victoria Bay

• Horse riding through the Wilderness area

• Paragliding at 24 choice paragliding sites, including Mossel Bay, Wilderness and Plettenberg Bay

ROUTES AND TRAILS

• Sleeping Beauty (4 hours) and Kristalkloof (8 hours) hiking trails in Riversdale

• 4x4 Route (60 km) in Riversdale on Mont Blanc Nature and Adventure Farm

• Noordkapper Hiking Trail (4 hours) in Still Bay

• Outeniqua Hiking Trail (7 days) between George and Plettenberg Bay

• Garden Route Trail (5 days) from Wilderness to Brenton-on-Sea

• Eden to Addo Hike for Biodiversity (18 days) from Knysna to the Addo Elephant National Park in the Eastern Cape

• Keurbooms Canoe Trail (2 days) in the Keurbooms River Nature Reserve near Plettenberg Bay

There is a wide choice of accommodation as well as a number of restaurants and relaxed eateries. It is a great place for children, who can be entertained with visits to the Crags Elephant Sanctuary, Monkeyland Primate Sanctuary, the Birds of Eden aviary (the world's largest free-flight bird sanctuary) and various beaches. There are some historical sites too, such as the Old Whaling Station, the Old Timber Shed and St Andrew's chapel. Keurbooms River Nature Reserve is an excellent place for boating, picnicking, water-skiing and windsurfing.

Storms River

The town of Storms River is situated near the river by the same name. It is a beautiful area and one of its best-known sites is the Bloukrans River bridge, the highest single-span arch bridge in the world, famous for the Bloukrans Bungee, which at 216 m is the highest commercial bungee jump in the world. Other options offered here are a bridge walking tour to the top of the arch along a metal catwalk and the Flying Fox, a 200-m cable slide out onto the archway of the bridge.

South Africa's most famous hiking trail, the Otter Trail, starts nearby, at the Storms River mouth, and ends at Nature's Valley. This popular five-day trail affords spectacular views of the ocean, forests, valleys, streams, lakes and waterfalls. Its luxury version is the shorter, two-day 'slackpacking' Dolphin Trail, where your goods are transported for you.

KEURBOOMS RIVER NATURE RESERVE

The Keurbooms River Nature Reserve is about 8 km north of Plettenberg Bay. Take a boat journey up the unspoilt river gorge or relax at one of the picnic sites on the river bank. You can also organise an overnight stay up Whiskey Gorge with local nature authorities.

LEFT: Wilderness is a popular paragliding destination that attracts adventure travellers from around the globe. BELOW: Storms River Mouth offers rugged scenery and is the starting point for the famed Otter Trail.

CHAPTER 10

THE CAMDEBOO

ABOVE: The horseshoe bend of the Sundays River embraces the historic town of Graaff-Reinet.

South of the Sneeuberg the rugged mountains give way to an extensive plain which extends southwards to Jansenville. Bounded by the Camdeboo Mountains in the west and Bruintjieshoogte in the east, the Khoekhoe name for the region, Camdeboo, is translated as 'Green Heights' or 'Green Hollow'.

In her classic book, *The Plains of Camdeboo*, author and botanist Eve Palmer, who grew up on Cranmere farm near Pearson, gave a poignant description of the Camdeboo region: 'It is a country flooded by sun; lonely, sparse, windswept, treeless on the flats for many miles' (1974, p. 12).

CLIMATE

In summer, daytime temperatures rise to the mid-30s, but the heat of the day is amply compensated for by the cool evenings and early mornings. Sub-zero temperatures are not uncommon in mid-winter when the surrounding mountains are often covered in snow. Most of the region's rainfall, which averages between 250 and 300 mm a year, falls in summer and autumn.

FLORA AND FAUNA

Dwarf Karoo *bossies* (bushes), succulents, and grasses dominate the vegetation of the Camdeboo plains, while thickets of spekboom and other shrubs occur on the mountain slopes.

The Camdeboo plains were once home to vast herds of springbok and other plains game, but a combination of hunting, fencing and agriculture led to the extermination of the game soon after the arrival of the *trekboers* (migratory stock farmers).

HISTORY AND HERITAGE

Nomadic groups of San, Khoekhoe tribes and Xhosa-speaking people already inhabited the region when the *trekboers* reached the area in the early 1770s. Conflict between the frontier farmers, the hunter-gatherer San, the pastoral

Khoekhoen and the Xhosa was inevitable. Disputes over grazing and stock theft caused the First Xhosa War (1779–81), which spilled from the Zuurveld over into Graaff-Reinet.

Enraged farmers petitioned the authorities for a magistrate and the Graaff-Reinet magistracy was proclaimed in 1786. The seat of the drostdy (magistracy) was named after the Dutch Governor of the Cape at the time, Cornelius Jacob van de Graaff and his wife, Reynet.

A commando system was introduced to defend the farmers against raiding parties of San, Khoekhoen and Xhosa. Renegade farmers, however, often took the law into their own hands and the frontier was ruled by rebellion, violence and bloody confrontations for over a century.

In early February 1795, a group of rebels arrived in Graaff-Reinet, expelled the landdrost (magistrate) and renounced the rule of the Dutch East India Company. When a commission of enquiry sent from the Cape failed to defuse the situation, the rebels set up their own administration with a president of military affairs and a president of the *heemraden* (an elected board assisting the magistrate in the administration of the district). They also appointed a provisional landdrost.

Troops were dispatched to the frontier when another rebellion broke out in Graaff-Reinet in January 1799. A general surrender took place in early April after 20 of the ring leaders were arrested, while some of the

LEFT: The stately drostdy, centrepiece of Graaff-Reinet's main street, was designed by the famous Cape architect Louis Michel Thibault. BELOW: Completed in 1812 as a Dutch Reformed parsonage, the Cape Dutch-style Reinet House is one of the finest buildings in Graaff-Reinet.

A PROUD ARCHITECTURAL HERITAGE

Graaff-Reinet has a proud history of preserving its architectural heritage, and with some 230 official heritage sites it has more proclaimed buildings than any other South African town. This preservation effort was spearheaded by the late Dr Anton Rupert, who was born in Graaff-Reinet. He was responsible for the renovation of the Drostdy and the old Dutch Reformed mission church, now the Hester Rupert Art Museum, named after his mother. One of the most representative collections of contemporary art in the country can be viewed in the museum.

The church of the London Missionary Society, Little London House, which became the John Rupert Little Theatre (named in honour of Rupert's father), and the Pierneef Museum in the Jan Rupert Centre (named after his brother) are among the many other testimonies to his passion for preserving the town's rich architecture.

instigators sought refuge across the border with Chief Gaika.

The Third Xhosa War broke out in 1799 and the *trekboers* were forced to evacuate the entire southern part of Graaff-Reinet. Farms were laid waste and tens of thousands of sheep and cattle were captured by the Xhosa.

In June 1801 storm clouds gathered again. Graaff-Reinet was besieged anew by rebel farmers, but they withdrew after British reinforcements arrived from Algoa Bay. The following year, however, the region was once more thrown into disarray when Khoekhoe and Xhosa raiders struck.

A new administration came to power at the southern point of Africa when Britain handed the Cape back to the Netherlands in 1803. Following the visits of two high-ranking officials

ROBERT SOBUKWE

In 1924, a man who would have a profound influence on South Africa was born in Graaff-Reinet. Robert Sobukwe first became active in politics during his years as a student at the University of Fort Hare, about 60 km from King William's Town. He later became secretary general of the African National Congress (ANC), but broke away in 1958 to form the Pan Africanist Congress the following year. Arrested on 21 March 1960 during the Sharpeville Massacre, he was sentenced to three years' imprisonment. Following his release, he was incarcerated on Robben Island for six years in solitary confinement and was subsequently served two five-year banning orders. Robert Sobukwe was finally released in 1974, but restricted to the town of Kimberley, where he died four years later. He was buried in Graaff-Reinet, the town of his birth.

SEE:
Eastern Cape p. 221
Eastern Cape p. 222
Northern Cape p. 227
Eastern Cape & Free
State p. 228

DID YOU KNOW?

Planted by Reverend Charles Murray in 1870, the black acorn grapevine in the garden of Reinet House was once the largest in the world. Sadly, its 1983 stem circumference of 3,1 m became victim to fungal rot.

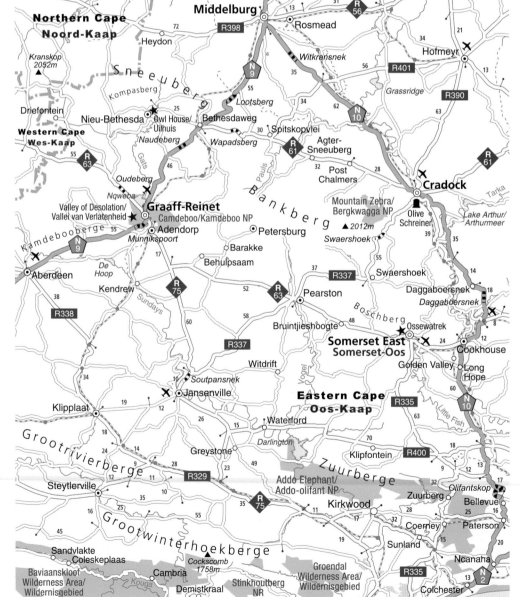

LEFT: The ornate dressed-sandstone post office and adjacent Magistrate's Court in Aberdeen was built in 1898 in the Art Nouveau style and features turrets and arches.

to the district, law and order was restored and Graaff-Reinet began to flourish.

Merino sheep were introduced into the district in 1820 with the support of Lord Charles Somerset, and Graaff-Reinet is today the centre of the country's merino industry. South Africa's mohair industry got off the ground when the first public auction of imported Angora stud goats was held in Graaff-Reinet in 1857.

NOTEWORTHY PLACES
Aberdeen
Aberdeen is easily bypassed by motorists travelling on the N9 linking Graaff-Reinet and the Garden Route. But it is hard to miss the 54,5-m-high steeple of the town's Dutch Reformed church, which is visible from 20 km away. It is said to be the second-tallest church steeple in South Africa and leans 45 cm to one side.

Aberdeen has many splendid buildings, including some fine examples of Victorian homes with turrets and porches, as well as dressed sandstone mansions built during the ostrich-feather boom of the late 19th century.

The town lies at the centre of South Africa's largest mohair-producing district.

Graaff-Reinet
Laid out in 1786 on a wide horseshoe bend of the Sundays River in the foothills of the Sneeuberg, Graaff-Reinet is South Africa's fourth-oldest town.

Cape Dutch mansions, Victorian cottages and flat-roofed Karoo houses line the streets of Graaff-Reinet, which, like many country towns, is dominated by its Dutch Reformed church, at the top end of Church Street. Built from local sandstone, the church features a slender steeple and a Gothic entrance facade and arches. It was consecrated in 1887.

The stately drostdy dominates the historic heart of Graaff-Reinet. The building with its unusual half-moon gable was completed in 1806, but served as seat of the magistracy for just 15 years. It was restored in the mid-1970s and turned into the reception and public areas of the Drostdy Hotel. Guests are accommodated in Stretch's Court, immediately behind the main building. The small, flat-roofed houses were built for emancipated slaves and labourers by an Irishman, Captain Charles Lennox Stretch, who bought the land in 1855.

The Graaff-Reinet Museum comprises a complex of five buildings: Reinet House, the Old Residency, the Old Library, Urquhart House and the Military History Museum.

Reinet House, a Cape Dutch home with a magnificent gable, is one of the town's finest buildings. It was completed in 1812 as a parsonage for the Dutch Reformed church, and was occupied from 1822 to 1904 by the Murray family. It houses a fine collection of period furniture, Cape silverware and Victorian glassware, as well as collections of dolls and clothing.

One of the finest assortments of sporting rifles in the country and the William Roe Collection featuring early photographs of Graaff-Reinet can be viewed in the Old Residency, which stands at a right angle to Reinet House.

Eclectic displays related to the life of Robert Sobukwe and the history of slavery can be viewed in the Old Library Museum. Other exhibits include Karoo fossils, Stone Age artefacts and rock art.

Urquhart House, which has a kitchen floor made from peach stones, has been turned into a period museum. A collection of Victorian furniture and farming implements, as well as displays on merino sheep breeding, are housed in this former mayoral residence.

The Military History Museum provides an overview of the military history of Graaff-Reinet, from the 1800s to more recent times.

Camdeboo National Park
Graaff-Reinet is the only town in South Africa that is virtually surrounded by a national park. The South African Nature Founda-

tion, now WWF–South Africa, played a major role in buying territory for a reserve, while the Graaff-Reinet Municipality donated town commonage. The land was transferred to the provincial conservation authorities in 1978 to establish the Karoo Nature Reserve, which was proclaimed the Camdeboo National Park in 2005.

The Valley of Desolation, a ridge of dolerite columns set against a backdrop of Karoo plains, is one of the park's main attractions. The spectacular rock columns were formed as a result of the unequal weathering of a dolerite sill, which intruded into the Beaufort Series rocks some 180 to 160 million years ago. Millions of years of weathering have eroded the softer sedimentary rock, leaving behind only the spectacular, freestanding dolerite columns.

Impressive views of Graaff-Reinet, the Camdeboo plains and the landmark Spandaukop can be enjoyed from the viewpoint close to the Valley of Desolation.

Buffalo, plains zebra, black wildebeest, springbok, blesbok and red hartebeest are among the species that can be spotted in the park's game-viewing area, which surrounds the Nqweba Dam just north of town. The eastern section of the park is only accessibly by 4x4 vehicles, or on foot.

Nieu-Bethesda

Tucked away in a secluded valley below Compassberg, Nieu-Bethesda was established in 1875 by the Reverend Charles Murray of the Dutch Reformed church at Graaff-Reinet.

The tranquil village would probably have remained just a name on the map – were it not for Helen Martins. This artist's extraordinary legacy draws crowds of tourists to the Owl House; it also provided the inspiration for acclaimed South African playwright Athol Fugard's play *The Road to Mecca*.

Life-size models of dinosaurs in the Kitching Fossil Exploration Centre, right next to the Owl House, provide an absorbing insight into what the Karoo looked like when prehistoric creatures reigned supreme. Some fossil remains, still embedded in the rock, can be seen on a short, guided walk to the nearby Gats River.

Other, more recent, attractions include the Bethesda Art Centre, a project to uplift the township community, and the stone-built Dutch Reformed church, consecrated in 1905.

The water mill on part of the farm, Uitkyk, where Nieu-Bethesda was established, can be seen on the western bank of the Gats River. The mill house dates back to 1860; the original wooden structure was later replaced by a metal one.

At the Sneeuberg Brewery, the parched can slake their thirst with Karoo ale and sample some smoked kudu salami, or cheese from the 2 Goats Deli.

Somerset East

Set against the Boschberg, the charming town of Somerset East is an important centre for surrounding sheep and angora farms. Permission was granted to farmers, who had crossed the official boundary of the Cape Colony in 1770, to settle at the foot of the Boschberg in 1775. Following a favourable report on the agricultural potential of the area, the British administration bought one of the farms in 1815 and named it Somerset Farm – after the British Governor, Lord Charles Somerset.

BELOW: An owl guards the work of Helen Martins in Nieu-Bethesda's Owl House. OPPOSITE: Spectacular dolerite columns rise from the floor of the Valley of Desolation, near Graaff-Reinet.

THE WORLD OF HELEN MARTINS

Born in Nieu-Bethesda in December 1897, Helen Martins qualified as a teacher in Graaff-Reinet and spent several years teaching in the former Transvaal. Her first marriage broke up after six years and she returned to Nieu-Bethesda in the 1930s to tend her sick parents. Following the deaths of her mother in 1941 and her father in 1945, Miss Helen, as she was known, became increasingly reclusive.

In the mid-1940s, she began turning the interior of the modest house in which she had been born into a fantasy world – in her perpetual search of light and enlightenment. Walls and ceilings were 'painted' in finely ground glass of different sizes and colours, and she used mirrors to reflect the light of candles and lamps. Her fascination with owls is evident from the intriguing cement statues that greet visitors as they step onto the veranda of what came to be known as the Owl House.

After completing the interior, Miss Helen directed her energy to the Camel Yard which is guarded by an owl perched on top of the Grand Arch. An extraordinary array of cement sculptures, including pyramids, sphinxes and a Nativity scene, created by Koos Malgas and other workmen under Miss Helen's supervision, cram the yard. Other features include the Corner of Debauchery, Moon Gate and the Pool of Healing.

Suffering from arthritis and failing eyesight, Miss Helen took her life in 1976 by drinking caustic soda, some say because she could no longer see her life's work.

ACTIVITIES

- Visiting historical buildings all over the region, especially in Graaff-Reinet
- Game viewing in the Camdeboo National Park, Graaff-Reinet
- Water-skiing, windsurfing, canoeing and angling on Nqweba Dam in the Camdeboo National Park, Graaff-Reinet
- Hiking, mountain biking, horse riding and birdwatching on farms in the region

ROUTES AND TRAILS

- Crag Lizard Trail (45 minutes) at the Valley of Desolation in the Camdeboo National Park outside Graaff-Reinet
- Eerstefontein Day Walks (2–6 hours) and Driekoppe Trail (2 days) in the Camdeboo National Park outside Graaff-Reinet
- Boschberg Hiking Trail (1 or 2 days) in Somerset East

FOOK ISLAND – THE ISLAND OF IMAGINATION

Walter Battiss, one of South Africa's foremost abstract artists, was born in Somerset East in 1906. When he was ten, the family moved to Koffiefontein in the Free State where the young Battiss became interested in rock art. These ancient paintings inspired him to discover the 'soul' of his own paintings, and in 1939 he published *The Amazing Bushmen* – the first of nine books.

Battiss undertook several visits to Europe and forged a lasting relationship with Pablo Picasso, whom he met in 1949. By the mid-1950s his paintings had become increasingly abstract and in the mid-1970s he created the imaginary Fook Island.

To Battiss, Fook was the embodiment of the 'island that is inside all of us'. He drew a map of this magic realm that was inhabited by imaginary people and where he ruled as King Ferd the Third. Fook Island had its own animals, passport, currency, stamps, drivers' licences and even its own language.

Battiss donated his personal collection of work to 'the people of Somerset East and South Africa' in 1981. It is appropriately housed in the old English Officers' Mess where his parents once ran a hotel.

ABOVE: Consecrated in 1833, the Dutch Reformed church in Somerset East is a blend of Cape Dutch and Gothic architecture.

Somerset Farm grew fresh produce for soldiers guarding the eastern border of the Colony and ensured a supply of fodder for their horses. Faced with mounting criticism from farmers unable to sell their produce at prices that could compete with those of a government-subsidised farm, the land was eventually subdivided into plots and sold by public auction.

The district of Somerset was proclaimed in 1825, and the town was renamed in 1857 to distinguish it from Somerset West, also named after Lord Charles Somerset.

Soon after the town's proclamation, land on the slopes of Boschberg was made available to the Wesleyan Missionary Society for a chapel and a graveyard. The property was transferred to the Dutch Reformed Church a few years later, and the chapel built in 1828 was converted into a double-storey parsonage in late-Georgian style in 1835. The historic residence has been converted into the Old Parsonage Museum, with displays on the history of the region and a permanent exhibition on the Slachter's Nek Rebellion.

Several well-preserved buildings can be seen in Paulet Street in the oldest part of the town.

CHAPTER 11

THE EASTERN CAPE INTERIOR

ABOVE: Mixed grasslands dominate the Upper Karoo plains of the Eastern Cape Midlands near Cradock.

The contrasting scenery of the Eastern Cape interior ranges from wild valleys and plains punctuated by hills to towering mountain peaks and spectacular sandstone formations. With five biomes meeting here, the region's natural beauty is complemented by an extremely rich variety of plants.

San hunter-gatherers, Khoekhoe and Xhosa pastoralists and Dutch *trekboers* (migratory stock farmers) converged in the region, which has a legacy of conflict. Nine bloody Xhosa Wars, also called the Wars of Land Dispossession, were fought here in the course of a hundred years.

The Eastern Cape interior covers a large area, with its extreme boundaries being the Orange River to the north, the Albany region to the south, the Transkei to the east and the Camde-

boo and Central Karoo to the west. Within the area, however, are three distinct regions, namely the Langkloof and Gamtoos Valley, the Eastern Cape Midlands and the Northern Interior, each with their own routes and attractions.

CLIMATE

The Eastern Cape interior lies in a transitional zone between the winter and summer rainfall areas (in the west and east, respectively). Most of the precipitation in the non-seasonal area occurs in autumn and spring. The mountainous regions enjoy the highest rainfall and the peaks are often covered in snow in midwinter.

Temperatures rise to the mid-30s in summer, but in winter minimum temperatures can plummet to below freezing point, especially after snow has fallen on the high mountain peaks.

FLORA AND FAUNA

Situated in an area where the Fynbos, Forest, Thicket, Nama Karoo and Grassland biomes meet, the Eastern Cape interior has an extremely rich diversity of flora.

The Fynbos biome reaches the eastern limit of its distribution in the Eastern Cape where the Cape Fold Belt finally runs out. Ericas, proteas, restios (reeds and rushes) and members of the daisy family are characteristic of the mountain fynbos vegetation.

Patches of indigenous forest occur in the Langkloof, as well as in the foothills and valleys of the Amathole Mountains (a Xhosa name meaning 'the calves of the Drakensberg') and the Katberge. Other valley flora in the region include dense thickets of evergreen and succulent trees and shrubs, grasses and herbs. Common plants are the spekboom ('pork bush', a favourite food of elephants), noorsdoring (euphorbias), aloes and thorny shrubs.

The Lower Karoo plains, north of the mountains of the Cape Fold Belt, are dominated by dwarf shrubs and succulent plants. After good summer rains the plains are transformed into waving grasslands. Mixed grasslands are characteristic of the Upper Karoo plains, while sour grasslands occur in the foothills of the Eastern Cape Drakensberg.

The region's bird life is as diverse as its flora, and birding is extremely rewarding. Cape parrot, lammergeier and high-altitude grassland endemics such as the Drakensberg rock-jumper and Drakensberg siskin are among the noteworthy species.

Huge herds of game roamed the plains of the Eastern Cape interior until the arrival of the *trekboers* with their guns. Antelope were hunted for their meat and hides as well as for sport, while large mammals like elephants were shot for their ivory and to protect crops. Predators, frequently considered vermin, were extinguished mercilessly to protect livestock. It did not take long before the great herds were wiped out – by 1937 the Cape mountain zebra was on the brink of extinction, while the number of Addo elephants – the only population of free-ranging elephants in the Eastern Cape – had been reduced to a mere 11.

HISTORY AND HERITAGE

Rock paintings in overhangs in the Southern Drakensberg and elsewhere in the region are reminders of the San hunter-gatherers who inhabited the region for thousands of years before the arrival of new groups of people – Khoekhoe and Xhosa pastoralists, as well as Dutch pioneers.

In 1689, just 37 years after the establishment of a Dutch settlement at the Cape, Ensign Isaq Schrijver explored the Langkloof Valley between the Tsitsikamma and Kouga mountains. Other explorers, hunters and Dutch *trekboers* followed in his footsteps and the second half of the 1700s saw the rapid eastward expansion of the Cape Colony's borders. The Gamtoos River was declared the eastern boundary in 1770, but

BELOW LEFT: The peaks of the Tsitsikamma and Kouga mountains rise above the tranquil Langkloof Valley, which stretches from Herold to Joubertina. BELOW RIGHT: The fertile Gamtoos Valley is a major producer of citrus fruit; vegetables, tobacco and avocados are also grown here.

RIGHT: Baviaanskloof is an unspoilt wilderness bounded by the rugged Baviaanskloof and Kouga mountains.

BAVIAANSKLOOF MEGARESERVE

The approximately 200 000-ha Baviaanskloof Nature Reserve is the focal point of the greater Baviaanskloof area, which has been identified for the development of a megareserve. This area lies in a transition zone between several of the country's biomes, and the endemic Willowmore cedar is among the over 1 150 plant species growing here.

The reserve is one of eight protected areas of the Cape Floral Region, which was declared a UNESCO World Heritage Site in 2004. Leopard, kudu, bushbuck, klipspringer and a host of small mammals occur in the reserve, while black rhino, buffalo, Cape mountain zebra, eland and red hartebeest have been reintroduced. With over 300 bird species recorded to date, birding is a major attraction.

as the colony expanded the boundary was moved east to the Great Fish River 25 years later.

As the conflict over land and grazing intensified, the eastern frontier increasingly became a violent and volatile place. Between 1779 and 1879 nine frontier wars were fought, during which colonial boundaries were redrawn, alliances were formed between the Xhosa and the Khoekhoen, and some Xhosa groups collaborated with the British authorities while others continued to resist encroachment by the colonialists. Although there were various causes of the nine wars, the struggle for land, grazing rights and stock thefts featured prominently. Other causes included leadership feuds between rival Xhosa chiefs, attacks on rival clans and the expulsion of Xhosa groups from areas they had

SEE:
Eastern Cape p. 221
Eastern Cape p. 222

APPLE EXPRESS

The *Apple Express* operates over a small section of the 283-km-long Port Elizabeth–Avontuur narrow-gauge railway line, built between 1902 and 1906 to transport fruit from the Langkloof to Port Elizabeth harbour. A steam locomotive hauls the *Apple Express* on its scenic 72-km-long journey from Port Elizabeth to Loerie. The Van Stadens Gorge crossing is one of the highlights of the excursion. The 156-m-long and 77-m-high steel and concrete bridge is the highest narrow-gauge bridge in the world. It was built in 1905. Trips are operated twice a month, usually on weekends, except in December and January when more are laid on.

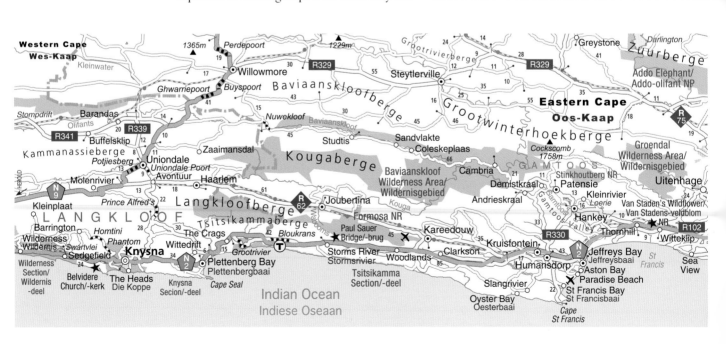

occupied. It was a restless frontier where war dragged on for up to four years at a time, with the longest period of relative peace lasting for 24 years between the Eighth (1850–53) and the Ninth (1877–79) wars.

NOTEWORTHY PLACES IN THE LANGKLOOF AND GAMTOOS VALLEY

The Langkloof ('long ravine') stretches from Herold in the Western Cape for 160 km to just east of Joubertina in the Eastern Cape. It is one of the country's major producers of apples, peaches and pears; dairy farming and timber are other important activities.

The Gamtoos Valley is situated just east of the Langkloof and includes the towns of Loerie, Hankey and Patensie. Blessed with an abundance of water and fertile soil, its agriculture centres on the production of citrus fruit, potatoes, vegetables, tobacco and lucerne.

Uniondale

Uniondale, just outside the Langkloof, was founded in 1865 when two rival villages, Hopedale and Lyon, were amalgamated. Beautiful Victorian and Edwardian buildings line the streets of this tranquil rural town, which is a centre for the surrounding sheep, goat and deciduous fruit farms. Stewart's water mill (built in 1852 and now housing a restaurant), the neo-Gothic Dutch Reformed church, the old Congregational church complex and the All Saints church are among the town's architectural treasures. There is also a factory manufacturing aloe prod-

ucts, and a hitchhiking ghost that is said to haunt the road.

Avontuur

Avontuur is the northern gateway to Prince Alfred's Pass, which links the Langkloof to the coast. The settlement grew around the farm D'Avontuur ('the adventure'), granted to Matthys Zondagh in 1765. It is the western terminus of the Port Elizabeth–Avontuur narrow-gauge railway line.

Haarlem

The tiny village of Haarlem with its whitewashed houses and orchards was laid out as a township for the rural community of the Langkloof in 1856, but developed around the mission station established by the Berlin Missionary Society in 1860. The historic church, dating back to 1870, is one of only a few in South Africa built in the shape of a Greek crucifix.

Joubertina

Joubertina, the largest town in the Langkloof, was established on the banks of the Wabooms River as a centre for the Dutch Reformed community in 1907. It is a hub for the honeybush (heuningbos) tea industry – a drink made from the leaves of a small shrub that grows wild on the mountain slopes in the area.

Kareedouw

Kareedouw, at the eastern entrance to the Langkloof, lies just 8 km off the N2. Indigenous forests of stinkwood and yellowwood grew in the valley when the first farmers settled in the area and the Forester's Statue is a reminder of Kareedouw's origins. Exquisite stinkwood, yellowwood and blackwood furniture has been manufactured in the town since 1945, and can be bought on site or made to order. The dressed sandstone Dutch Reformed church dates back to 1905.

Humansdorp

Humansdorp is a centre for the surrounding oat, sheep, wool, dairy and citrus farms. The Humansdorp Museum with its displays of farming implements, household articles and historic photographs is well worth a visit, and the Kouga Cultural Centre provides a fascinating insight into the symbolism and meaning of African architecture. Four main themes are depicted: 'Birth of the African Renaissance', 'Mother, Ancestral Mother, Mother Earth', 'Peace and Togetherness' and 'Hope for the Future'. The centre with

LEFT: A neat, colourful little garden outside a whitewashed cottage is set against the backdrop of the bare cliffs of the Baviaanskloof.

its dome-shaped roof was largely constructed from clay, timber poles and thatch from the region. Other attractions include the Humansdorp Park, which was laid out in the form of the Union Jack, and a watermill built in 1847.

Loerie

The tranquil village of Loerie most likely owes its name to the abundance of Knysna loerie (the Afrikaans name for the lourie, now called Knysna turaco) that occurred in the area when the first farmers settled here. Loerie Dam, one of Port Elizabeth's water-storage reservoirs, is a popular angling and boating spot. The limestone terminus is a reminder of the days when limestone was transported to the station along an 8-km-long overhead cableway. Two men could turn a 60-tonne locomotive on the turntable at the station through 180 degrees.

Hankey

Hankey, the oldest town in the Gamtoos Valley, developed around a mission station established by the London Missionary Society in 1822. The church, built in 1850, and the graves of the first missionaries are reminders of the town's origins. The 270-m-long William Philips Irrigation Tunnel, built between 1842 and 1844 to irrigate land in a wide horseshoe bend of the Gamtoos River, was the first irrigation tunnel in South Africa. Another interesting feature is the sundial at the foot of Vergaderingskop. With a diameter of 36,4 m it is the largest in the Southern Hemisphere.

Patensie

Colourful bougainvilleas, poinsettias and neatly tended gardens fringe the road between Hankey and Patensie. Citrus fruit, vegetables, tobacco, avocados, as well as Patensie's renowned potatoes are cultivated in the valley. Patensie is the terminus of a branch line coming off the Port Elizabeth–Avontuur narrow-gauge railway. A profile resembling the former British monarch, Queen Victoria, can be seen on a cliff face about 16 km west of the town.

NOTEWORTHY PLACES IN THE EASTERN CAPE MIDLANDS

Uitenhage

The Uitenhage district was declared in 1804, but the town was only established two years later when the first landdrost (magistrate) was appointed. The stately Cape Dutch-style drostdy (magistrate's residence), built as the administrative and judicial seat of the Uitenhage district,

SARAH BARTMANN

Vergaderingskop ('place of gathering') on Hankey's eastern outskirts is the final resting place of Sarah Bartmann, a Khoekhoe woman who was born in the area in 1787. Tempted by promises of a better life, Sarah was lured abroad in 1809, where she was displayed at London's Piccadilly Circus as a freak of nature. Four years later, and with her health deteriorating, she was sold to an animal trainer in France where her abuse continued. After her death in 1815, at the age of 28, her remains were exhibited in the Musée de l'Homme in Paris as an ethnological and sexual curiosity. Sarah's remains were returned to South Africa in 2002 and she was finally laid to rest in August that year.

was completed in 1810. It now forms part of the Uitenhage Historical Museum Complex together with the Old Railway Museum and the 1814 Cuyler Manor.

Uitenhage is an important centre for the automotive industry and is home to Volkswagen South Africa, as well as tyre and car-component manufacturers. The Volkswagen factory tour includes a guided walk through the production line and the AutoPavilion. This fascinating exhibition, with its graphic displays, interactive exhibitions and its unique collection of cars, is the first of its kind in Africa and one of only five such centres in the world.

OPPOSITE: Fort Beaufort's Martello Tower is one of only two inland fortifications of its kind in the world. LEFT: Big and small game are attracted to the waterholes in the Addo Elephant National Park – from elephant to warthog.

Addo Elephant National Park

Proclaimed in 1931 to protect the dwindling elephant population of the Eastern Cape, the Addo Elephant National Park now stretches from Darlington Dam and the Zuurberg Mountains to the Indian Ocean.

The Big Five (elephant, rhino, buffalo, lion and leopard) are the major draw card of the Main Camp game-viewing area where spotted hyaena, kudu, plains zebra, Cape grysbok, warthog, vervet monkey and a host of smaller mammals can also be seen. It is the first 'Big Seven' park in the world, as the marine section of the reserve is a sanctuary for the southern right whale (a seasonal visitor) and the great white shark.

With habitats ranging from mountains and succulent thickets to indigenous forest and ocean, Addo offers excellent birding opportunities. To date over 400 bird species have been recorded.

Activities include self-drive game viewing, guided game drives, morning or afternoon horse trails, overnight hikes and day walks. Accommodation options range from campsites, safari tents, forest cabins, rondavels and chalets (all self-catering) to privately owned luxury lodges in concession areas in the park.

Amenities in the Addo Main Camp include a restaurant, shop, filling station, swimming pool, bird hide and an underground hide overlooking a waterhole that is floodlit at night.

Fort Beaufort

Fort Beaufort, the oldest town east of the Great Fish River, was established as a military post along the Kat River in 1822 by the British government at the Cape, and played an important role in the defence of the eastern frontier.

Following the Sixth Xhosa War (1834–35) the settlement was heavily fortified. The fort included infantry barracks, a guardhouse and a military hospital. Work on the landmark Martello Tower, a massive dressed-stone circular tower, began in 1837 and was completed about six years later.

The Seventh Xhosa War (1846–47) was sparked when an axe was stolen from the general-dealer store (now the Emgwenyeni Flats). The suspect was sent to Grahamstown under escort, but managed to escape when Xhosa warriors ambushed the group and cut off the hand of the Khoekhoe prisoner to which the suspect had been handcuffed.

The best way to discover the town's turbulent history is to follow the Golden Walkway, a trail that starts at the museum. The museum is housed in the former British officers' mess, built in the 1830s.

Alice

Laid out on the banks on the Tyhume River, the town of Alice was named after the second daughter of Queen Victoria. It is dominated by the University of Fort Hare, which was built in the grounds of an 1846 fort of the same name.

The United Free Church of Scotland established the South African Native College here in 1916. Its status was raised to that of a university college in 1923. Nelson Mandela (South Africa's first democratically elected president), Oliver Tambo (founding member of the African National Congress Youth League and ANC leader in exile) and Govan Mbeki (ANC leader who was imprisoned along with Mandela, and father of Thabo Mbeki) are among Fort Hare's numerous distinguished alumni.

An important collection of documents and records of the liberation struggle are preserved in the university's archive, while the De Beers Centenary Gallery houses an extensive collection of African art. More than 7 000 items from different cultural groups in South Africa are displayed in the FS Malan Ethnological Museum.

Hogsback

Situated in the heart of the Amathole Mountains amid indigenous forests and pine plantations, Hogsback is reminiscent of an English village. It is renowned for its carefully tended gardens, which are especially attractive in spring when the rhododendrons, azaleas, silver birches and fruit trees begin to bloom. Many artists live in the area, and their arts and crafts range from paintings, pottery and glassware to wrought-iron work, candles and carpentry.

Trails and walks lead to waterfalls with alluring names such as Madonna and Child, Swallowtail, The 39 Steps and the Kettlespout. Energetic visitors can tackle the more demanding trail to the Hogsback Peaks or set off on overnight hikes.

One of the largest trees in the Eastern Cape, the eastern monarch grows in the Auckland Nature Reserve. The centuries-old Outeniqua yellowwood has a height of 38 m and a diameter of 2,71 m.

St Patrick's on the Hill, one of the smallest houses of worship in the country, the Voice of the Earth Eco-shrine and the 11-circuit Labyrinth at the Edge Mountain Retreat are among the other attractions to be explored.

SEE:
Eastern Cape
pp. 222–223
Eastern Cape & Free
State p. 228
Eastern Cape & Lesotho
p. 229

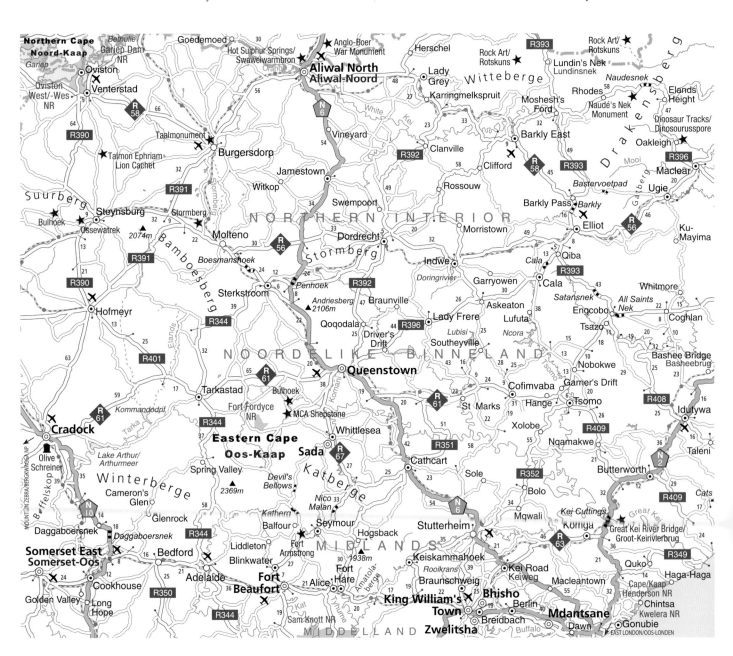

King William's Town

King William's Town was established on the banks of the Buffalo River as the administrative seat of the Province of Queen Adelaide in 1835. But due to mismanagement, just seven months later the proclamation was repealed and the territory was returned to the Xhosa.

British forces re-occupied the area after the outbreak of the Seventh Xhosa War and British Kaffraria was proclaimed on 17 December 1847, with King William's Town as its capital.

Founded in 1884, the Amathole Museum is the third-oldest museum in South Africa and its collection of mounted African mammals is the second largest in the country. One of its most famous exhibits is Huberta, the wandering hippo who undertook an epic journey along the coast from Zululand to the Keiskamma River from 1928–31.

Also of interest are the unique displays on the 1856–57 Cattle-Killing Movement (the only one of its kind in the country) and the Xhosa Gallery. A memorial on an open piece of ground in the Edward Street Cemetery marks the site of the mass grave for victims of the Great Cattle Killings.

The South African Missionary Museum, a satellite of the Amathole Museum, is housed in the old Wesleyan church built in 1855. Displays portray various aspects of missionary life in the Eastern Cape.

The Steve Biko Garden of Remembrance in Ginsberg, a township on the outskirts of King William's Town, is named in honour of the man whose fierce opposition to apartheid helped to shape South Africa's politics. Born in Ginsberg in 1946, Biko was a founder of the South African Students' Organisation that later grew into the Black Consciousness Movement. He was outlawed by the apartheid government in 1973 and banned from all political and social organisations. Arrested in August of 1977, he died in September of the same year as a result of massive head injuries sustained while in the custody of security force agents.

Bhisho

Bhisho, 3 km northeast of King William's Town, was established in the 1980s as the 'capital' of the Ciskei, a bantustan (homeland for mainly Xhosa-speaking people) created by the apartheid government in 1981. The territory was 'reintegrated' into South Africa in 1992 and Bhisho is currently the capital of the Eastern Cape province.

The Bhisho Massacre Memorial commemorates the deaths of protesters shot and killed

ABOVE LEFT: Fairytale scenes await walkers in the Hogsback forests. ABOVE RIGHT: A memorial in King William's Town honours those who died in World War I (1914–18).

on 7 September 1992 during a mass demonstration of tens of thousands of people demanding free political activity and the resignation of the Ciskei military leader, Oupa Gqozo. Soldiers of the Ciskei Defence Force opened fire when a breakaway group smashed through a barricade, killing 28 people and injuring more than 200. The memorial is opposite the Bhisho Stadium.

Queenstown

Named after Queen Victoria, Queenstown developed around the military stronghold established on the banks of the Komani River in 1853. The Hexagonal, an open space in the centre of town from where six streets radiate, was designed to give quick access to the perimeter of the settlement.

The Queenstown and Frontier Museum is housed in the old public school dating from 1897. Cultural history exhibits depict the history of the town and the region during the Xhosa Wars. Other attractions include the dressed-sandstone town hall dating back to 1842 and the St Michael and All Angels Anglican church, inaugurated in 1883.

Cradock

Cradock grew around the military garrison established on the eastern banks of the Great Fish River in 1813, and was named after Sir John Cradock, the British governor at the time.

Taking a stroll down Market Street is like stepping back 150 years. The Tuishuise ('townhouses'), a row of typical Karoo-style cottages built in the 1840s, have been restored beautifully and now serve as guest houses. Victoria Manor has presided over Market Square for over 150 years, and the landmark dressed-stone Dutch Reformed church on Central Square is a replica of St Martin's-in-the-Fields in London. Olive Schreiner, author of *The Story of an African*

Farm and many other literary works, moved to Cradock at the age of 12 and lived with her siblings in a typical Karoo cottage in Cross Street from 1868–70. Her personal library, a collection of the books she wrote and exhibitions on her life can be viewed in Schreiner House. Olive was buried on the summit of Buffelskop, 26 km south of Cradock, on 13 August 1921.

The Great Fish River Museum is housed in the Dutch Reformed parsonage, which was completed in 1825. The museum has the history of Cradock as its theme and is arranged in period rooms. A photographic display in the Cradock Four Gallery tells the story of the anti-apartheid activists – Matthew Goniwe, Fort Calata, Sicelo Mhlauli and Sparrow Mkhonto – who were tortured and brutally murdered by apartheid security force agents in June 1985. The Cradock Four, as they became know, had been travelling back from Port Elizabeth at the

RIGHT: The Garden of Remembrance in Aliwal North is a reminder of the British soldiers killed in the Anglo–Boer War. BELOW LEFT: Well-preserved Karoo-style cottages dating back to the 1840s line the streets of Cradock. BELOW RIGHT: The spire of the Anglican church in Queenstown rises to a height of 49 m. OPPOSITE: The Mountain Zebra National Park was established to save the Cape mountain zebra from becoming extinct.

The area can be explored in a sedan car, but some of the tracks are accessible for four-wheel-drive vehicles only. There are also short walks that can be undertaken.

Accommodation is in self-catering chalets and the Doornhoek Guest House. There is a campsite with hot-water ablutions. Facilities include a restaurant, shop, filling station and a swimming pool. Picnic and braai facilities are provided for day visitors.

NOTEWORTHY PLACES IN THE NORTHERN INTERIOR

Burgersdorp

The tranquil country town of Burgersdorp developed around the Dutch Reformed church built on a farm bought in 1846. Burgersdorp became the centre of the campaign to get Dutch recognised as an official language in the late 1870s. The Taalmonument ('language monument') commemorates the victory achieved when the use of Dutch in the Cape Parliament was finally allowed in 1882.

The old Reformed church parsonage and the outbuilding of the first theological seminary of the Gereformeerde Kerk (Reformed Church), which broke way from the Nederduitse Gereformeerde Kerk (Dutch Reformed Church) in 1859, are reminders of the role Burgersdorp played in religious matters. The theological school was moved to Potchefstroom in 1905 and later became the University of Potchefstroom, now North-West University.

The history of the town and its environs is portrayed in the Burgersdorp Cultural Historical Museum. There are displays on the Xhosa and the wars fought in the area, as well as collections of clothing, firearms and traditional weapons, wagons and other vehicles.

Aliwal North

Aliwal North was established at a drift (ford) on the southern bank of the Orange River in 1849.

The Kerkplein Museum is housed in the Dutch Reformed church, which was consecrated in 1864. It has fascinating reconstructions of the shops and businesses that flourished during the town's heydays. The old library built in 1876 serves as an extension of the museum.

Other attractions include three blockhouses built around the town by the British in 1901 (during the second Anglo–Boer War) to protect the rail and road bridges across the Orange River and the stone-built tollhouse on the banks of the Orange River. The Concentration Camp

time of their abduction. The memorial in the Inxuba Yethemba Municipal Park is a tribute to these freedom fighters.

Cradock Spa, a thermal spring on the banks of the Great Fish River, sports an indoor and outdoor pool. Accommodation is available in self-catering chalets and there is a campsite and picnic facilities for day visitors.

Mountain Zebra National Park

When this park was established in 1937, the Cape mountain zebra was on the brink of extinction. Since then, the species has rallied and the park has been expanded considerably. It is now also home to black rhino and herds of buffalo, gemsbok, black wildebeest, red hartebeest, eland and springbok. Cheetah, grey rhebok and mountain reedbuck also occur in the park, which has a bird checklist of over 200 species.

Garden is dedicated to the women and children who died in the camps during the second Anglo–Boer War.

The Aliwal Spa, just to the south of the town, has an indoor thermal pool, an outdoor pool, a water slide and a restaurant. Accommodation is available in self-catering chalets and there are campsites.

Lady Grey

Nestled in the foothills of the Witteberge ('white mountains'), Lady Grey was founded in 1866 and named after the wife of the British governor at the Cape, Sir George Grey.

The dressed-sandstone Dutch Reformed church was built on a hillock in the centre of the village in 1913. When the congregation was still struggling to pay off the debts 12 years later, the Koffiehuis ('coffee house') was opened to help generate funds. It now serves as a museum on the history of the town and its surroundings.

Barkly East

Barkly East was laid out in 1874 and named after the British governor at the time, Sir Henry Barkly. At an altitude of 1 813 m below the Witteberge, Barkly East is one of the highest and coldest towns in the country. It is a centre for the surrounding merino sheep, stud cattle and dairy farms; wheat, maize and potatoes are also grown in the area.

Prominent among the town's beautiful dressed-sandstone buildings is the Dutch Reformed church. The old library and municipal building dates back to 1891 and now houses the Barkly East Museum, which has a fascinating collection of traditional Xhosa beadwork, modern Xhosa art, and implements used in sheep and cattle farming.

The railway line, with its system of eight 're-verses' which were incorporated to overcome the steep gradients and sharp curves, can be seen just outside the town.

Rhodes

The tiny village of Rhodes, near the southern tip of the Drakensberg, has retained much of its old-world charm. Originally named Rossville, it was renamed in 1900 after Cecil John Rhodes. Why the remote village was named after the famous politician and financier is the subject of many tales. One explanation is that Rhodes sent a wagonload of stone pine trees to the village, while another has it that the first 100 plots were sold on condition that the village be named after Rhodes.

Rhodes comes to life in winter when the surrounding mountains are covered in snow. It is also a popular destination with fly-fishing enthusiasts and birders.

> **DID YOU KNOW?**
> Some of the toughest mountain biking, trail running and triathlons in the country are held in the Eastern Cape interior, among them the Wartrail Tri-Challenge, Sky Run Eco-Challenge, Rhodes Ultra-Marathon and Rhodes MTB Challenge.

ACTIVITIES

• Mountain biking, hiking, fishing and birdwatching in Baviaanskloof
• Game viewing, birdwatching and flower spotting in the Baviaanskloof Megareserve
• Skiing on the slopes of Ben McDhui at Tiffindell in winter
• Fly fishing in the rivers of the northeast
• Angling and boating at Loerie Dam in Loerie
• Touring the Volkswagen factory in Uitenhage
• Fly fishing, hiking and horse riding at Maclear
• Game viewing, birdwatching, camping, swimming, picnicking and braaing at Addo Elephant and Mountain Zebra national parks
• Camping, picnicking and bathing at the Cradock Spa thermal waters near Cradock
• Camping, braaing and bathing at the Aliwal Spa hot springs in Aliwal North
• Fly fishing and birdwatching at Rhodes

ROUTES AND TRAILS

• Heritage and other self-drive routes in Kouga (distance and duration depends on individual itineraries)
• 4x4 Baviaanskloof Route (205 km) from Willowmore to Patensie
• Boskloof Trail (1 hour) in Humansdorp
• Four trails (7 hours–2 days) in the Groendal Wilderness Area near Uitenhage
• Alexandria Hiking Trail (2 days) in Addo Elephant National Park
• Tree Dassie Walk (2–3 hours) in the Addo Elephant National Park
• Two walks (1 and 5 hours) in the Zuurberg in the Addo Elephant National Park
• Two walks (1 and 4 hours) in the Mountain Zebra National Park
• Walks (30 minutes–2 days) in Hogsback
• Two walks (3 hours each) in Pirie Forest near King William's Town
• Amathole Hiking Trail (2–6 days) from nearby King Williams Town to Hogsback
• Horse trails in Addo Elephant National Park

East of Rhodes, the road climbs steeply to the 2 623-m-high summit of Naudesnek Pass – the highest pass negotiable by a sedan car in South Africa.

Dordrecht

The small farming village of Dordrecht was laid out on the northern slopes of Stormberg as a parish of the Dutch Reformed church in 1856. The old part of the town is dominated by the dressed-sandstone Dutch Reformed church with its four clock-faces and imposing spire, and many Victorian houses line the main street.

A room full of photographs of rock-art sites in the area makes a visit to the Anderson Museum worthwhile for rock-art enthusiasts. Furniture and clothing of the late 19th and early 20th centuries and agricultural exhibits are also displayed.

Elliot

Spectacular sandstone formations in the Drakensberg foothills form a dramatic backdrop to the town of Elliot. North of Elliot, the Barkly Pass winds steeply upwards, and from the 2 012-m-high summit there are magnificent views of the sandstone outcrops, wild valleys and mountain streams far below. Eland, delicately painted grey rhebok and human figures are among the well-preserved rock paintings in the Dinorbin Shelter, a short way beyond the summit of the pass.

Other attractions in the area include Gatberg, a mountain with a hole through its summit, and the Bastervoetpad. This winding gravel road between Barkly Pass and Ugie should only be negotiated in a 4x4 vehicle.

Maclear

Set amid rolling hills, crystal clear streams and towering mountain peaks, Maclear was established on the banks of the Mooi River following the annexation of the area by the British Administration in 1879. The town was named in honour of the British astronomer, Sir Thomas Maclear, Her Majesty's Astronomer at the Cape at the time.

The dinosaur tracks on the farm Oakleigh, 17 km from Maclear, are among the earliest evidence of dinosaurs in Southern Africa. The tracks were made by a large, four-legged, plant-eating reptile and a smaller theropod dinosaur that ran on its hind legs. Of special interest is the tail drag of one of the prehistoric creatures.

The area is a paradise for fly fishing, hiking, horse riding.

OPPOSITE: Sandstone outcrops and grasslands dominate the landscape near Rhodes. ABOVE LEFT: Elephants and warthogs quench their thirst at a waterhole in the Addo Elephant National Park.

CHAPTER 12

THE ALBANY REGION

ABOVE: Lovely Victorian buildings line Donkin Road in Port Elizabeth.

The Albany region has from time to time been called Settler or Frontier Country. It stretches from Cape St Francis in the west to East London in the east along a scenic part of the Eastern Cape coastline, and includes the university town of Grahamstown to the north.

CLIMATE

This section of the Eastern Cape coastline is noteworthy for its lack of protection from southeasterly summer gales, which is why Port Elizabeth is often referred to as the Windy City. Then the rivers and gentle ocean are transformed into raging monsters. Many ships have met their end in Algoa Bay and along this stretch of coast.

FLORA AND FAUNA

Interesting flora of the region are yellowwood, milkwood and keurboom trees in riverine forests; dense bush interspersed with orange-scarlet French aloe; water lilies in river pools; grassed hillsides; and spring flowers. There used to be an enormous array of wildlife, but most was annihilated by the settlers. There are, however, still springbok, blue wildebeest and waterfowl to be found and private reserves are re-establishing the diversity of the area. The marine reserve of the Addo Elephant National Park is found here, with the main attractions being southern right whale and great white shark.

HISTORY AND HERITAGE

The original inhabitants of southern Africa, the San, were prolific here, as their rock art attests. But they were pushed towards the drier parts of the region by the arrival of other peoples: firstly by the Khoekhoen some 2 000 years ago, then by black tribes migrating south, and finally by white settlers pushing eastwards from the Cape.

The meeting of black and white left its indelible mark on the country. The first Dutch settlements were established here as early as 1690, but were soon abandoned. Later though, the Boers moved slowly eastwards in search of better grazing and this led to the first of nine wars with the Xhosa, fought between 1779 and 1879. The push by whites into the area increased yet further when the British occupied the Cape Colony twice in quick succession in the late 18th and early 19th centuries.

This made the need for a port in the Eastern Cape more pressing. In August 1799, during the first British occupation of the Cape, the authorities constructed a stone fort overlooking the best landing beach in Algoa Bay. Named Fort Frederick after the Duke of York, commander-in-chief of the British army at the time, it is distinguished for never having had a shot fired in anger from its parapets. The fort attracted a small community who developed a hamlet by the same name in close proximity to the garrison.

At that time, the Great Fish River formed the turbulent eastern frontier of the Cape Colony. In 1812, to stop incursions across the river, Lieutenant Colonel John Graham was instructed by Sir John Cradock, the governor, to establish a camp from which the border could be secured. The tented military camp that sprang up soon attracted the normal array of frontier people keen for protection.

Troubles intensified, culminating in the attack on Grahamstown by the mystic Makana and 10 000 followers on 22 April 1819. Lord Charles Somerset, Cradock's successor, had called for Britain to send emigrants to bolster the defences of the colony and these appeals now became more urgent. Britain, in the grip of depression since the end of the Napoleonic wars in 1815, seized the opportunity to rid itself of some of its population. Farms and transport were offered for nearly 4 000 men, women and children through advertisements that focused on Somerset's extravagant claims about the area.

The hapless pioneers were selected on the basis of good health – not their ability to farm or bear arms. It was a recipe for disaster and the unfamiliar, unfriendly countryside plagued by droughts, floods and rust drove many to Grahamstown in desperation. The town not only offered relief, but it presented the settlers with plenty of opportunities.

Shortly after the arrival of the 1820 Settlers and their dispersal into the interior, Fort Frederick was visited by the lieutenant governor of the Cape, Sir Rufane Donkin, who renamed it Port Elizabeth after his late wife. While here he had a sandstone pyramid erected in her memory, next to the site of a future lighthouse.

One side of the pyramid is inscribed to: 'One of the most perfect of human beings who has given her name to the town below'. A plaque on the opposite side reads: 'Elizabeth Frances … died at Mirat in Upper Hindoostan of a fever after seven days' illness on the 21st of August 1818, aged not quite 28 years. She left an infant in his seventh month too young to know the irreparable loss he had sustained, and a husband whose heart is still wrung by undiminished grief'.

LEFT: Sir Rufane Donkin had a sandstone pyramid erected in honour of his late wife, Lady Elizabeth Frances Donkin.

THE TRIUMPH OF DIAS

It is known that Bartolomeu Dias landed twice on the Cape south coast before sailing on until the coastline began to run perceptibly northward, where he dropped anchor at present-day Algoa Bay. The crew, realising their objective of rounding the tip of Africa had been achieved, began to mutiny when Dias suggested they continue. So Dias was forced to turn back, but not before marking the point he had reached.

On a high, bleak promontory at present-day Kwaaihoek, the crew erected the *Padrão de São Gregório*, the first of three stone crosses. Although the team had successfully rounded the Cape of Storms, Dias considered the expedition a failure, not having gone all the way to India. Today a visitor looking upon the replica of this memorial will be standing more or less in the centre of a short, narrow strip of Indian Ocean coastline. The shore is intersected by deep river gorges running from Port Elizabeth to the Great Kei River.

While this small part of South Africa is mainly remembered as the place where English culture was introduced to the country, it was also at the heart of another momentous event – the Great Trek. This search for land was undertaken by a group of fractious, independently minded and predominantly Eastern Cape boers (farmers) who were fed up with creeping British authority. Notwithstanding, the migration of a significant number of well-armed people, with specific ideas about racial superiority, into an interior already in turmoil was to have a massive impact on South African history.

NOTEWORTHY PLACES
Cape St Francis

Situated on the Eastern Cape's southernmost headland, Cape St Francis is a quaint coastal hamlet with an excellent stretch of beach (5 km) and scenic natural setting. It is a fun place with a resort feel that is known for excellent bird-watching and nature trails, and is popular with sunbathers, surfers and anglers. Seal Point, a rocky headland, marks the western limit of St Francis Bay, named in honour of the patron saint of sailors in 1575. The lighthouse here has warned ships about the dangers of the coastline since 1878. Measuring 28 m from ground level to the balcony, it is the tallest masonry lighthouse in South Africa, and is a heritage site. Penguins and other marine birds in distress are rescued by a rehabilitation centre situated in the grounds of the lighthouse.

St Francis Bay and Port St Francis

The picturesque coastal resorts of St Francis Bay and Port St Francis lie to the north of the promontory formed by Cape St Francis. St Francis Bay developed from a rustic fishing camp built in 1954 into one of the most popular coastal recreation areas in South Africa, and is arguably one of the prettiest towns along the Eastern Cape coastline. Rows and rows of whitewashed, thatched homes, built along marinas and canals leading to the Kromme River, give it a uniform visual language.

The town is surrounded by nature reserves and there are excellent walks and trails through the fynbos. St Francis Bay is known for surfing – the local break, Bruce's Beauties, being named after Bruce Brown from cult surf movie *Endless Summer*. There are also a number of restaurants and pubs in the area. The adjoining Port St Francis, at the mouth of the Kromme River, has grown from a small fishing village into a popular resort with a marina and luxury homes. The harbour is the centre of a thriving chokka (calamari) industry.

Jeffreys Bay

Jeffreys Bay, affectionately called J-Bay, is the site of South Africa's *pièce de résistance* of surf breaks. The popular seaside resort is one of the top 10 surfing destinations in the world and plays host to the Billabong Pro Competition in July each year. The locals boast that Supertubes is the best right-hand break in the world – and it is certainly a great place for surfers in search of that perfect wave. For beginners who haven't yet got the hang of it, there are a number of surf schools.

While sun worshippers are attracted to the beaches, and the energetic have a choice of water sports, there are several other attractions in

SEE:
Port Elizabeth p. 215
East London p. 215
Grahamstown p. 217
Eastern Cape
pp. 222–223

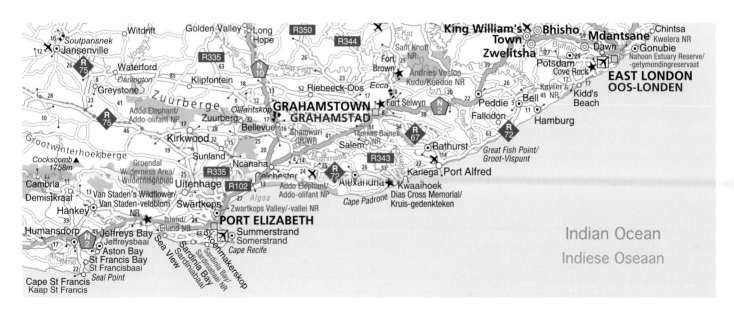

THE RED LOCATION MUSEUM

Situated in the New Brighton township of Port Elizabeth, this spectacular L-shaped facility is one of the finest Struggle for Freedom sites in South Africa. Surrounded by original housing from the establishment of the township in the early 1900s, it represents the past through interlinked installations.

Port Elizabeth

The long promenade along the coastal city of Port Elizabeth is a favourite of holidaymakers. The stretch of beaches along Summerstrand include Hobie, Humewood and King's beaches, the latter named after the royal family took a dip here during their 1947 visit. It is along this stretch where visitors will find the oceanarium.

Fort Frederick is well preserved and is the site of occasional open-air theatre productions. There is another open-air theatre in St George's Park in the heart of the city. There are fine schools here; both Grey High School and St George's Preparatory School in the beautifully restored Knockfierna are worth a visit. Especially impressive is the well-preserved inner-city architecture.

The Public Library on Market Square is one of the most beautiful buildings in South Africa. Built in 1902, it is a fine example of Art Nouveau Artistic Baronial with dramatic Elizabethan touches. The ornate, terracotta facade of the library, prefabricated and brought from England in numbered segments, features archways, oriel windows, gables, corner turrets and gargoyles behind the statue of Queen Victoria riding out towards the square. Inside it is even more stunning with original furnishings, glazed tiles, pressed steel, spiral staircases, columns, elaborate teak woodwork, stained glass windows and a splendid glass dome.

A visit to the Red Location Museum is well worth it. Other historic sites of interest are the Campanile (commemorating the arrival of the 1820 Settlers), the Horse Memorial (that remembers the horses that suffered during the second Anglo–Boer War of 1899–1902) and the statue to Black Consciousness leader Steve Biko in the city centre. In and around the city are a number of nature reserves, including the Island Nature

ABOVE LEFT: The coastal hamlet of St Francis is a great holiday destination with a laid-back resort feel.
ABOVE RIGHT: Grahamstown's Observatory Museum houses a rare Victorian camera obscura, which projects an enchanting live panorama of the town in a darkened room, in full colour.
LEFT: Shamwari Game Reserve, home to the Big Five, is situated between Port Elizabeth and Grahamstown and offers luxury accommodation for the discerning traveller.

this little town. The Jeffreys Bay Museum focuses on the history and development of surfing, and the pioneers and legends behind the sport. Also, the coast of St Francis Bay is world-renowned for its incredible variety of marine shells and a fascinating collection of over 600 of them are displayed in the Shell Museum. Ragged-tooth and leopard sharks, as well as stingrays, are among the marine creatures that can be seen at the Shark Aquarium.

The town is bordered by the Noorsekloof, Kabeljous and Seekoei nature reserves, all with excellent bird life and several hiking trails on offer. There are surf shops, pubs and restaurants in town and the Jeffreys Bay Golf Club is nearby.

Reserve, Seaview Game Park, Sardinia Bay Sea Reserve, Sylvic Nature Reserve and Cape Recife Nature Reserve.

Grahamstown

Grahamstown is filled with the romanticism of a bygone era, evident in the architecture, history, legend and mystique that veil it like the mists that roll in from the nearby ocean.

Within a short time after its establishment, Grahamstown had grown to the second largest centre in the Cape Colony. It was also one of the most elegant, where footpaths and huts gave way to fine buildings and tree-lined streets wide enough for a wagon and span of 14 oxen to turn. Most of these buildings — a watercolour of pinks, blues, greens, yellows and purples decorated with clocks, carvings, garlands, gables and swirls — are now heritage sites.

Once the turbulence of its past receded, so the town began to lose its strategic importance. With this, Grahamstown began a process of transformation into a leading centre for learning. St Andrew's College was opened in the mid-19th century and many fine institutions followed, culminating in the opening of Rhodes University in 1904. Today the town is renowned for hosting one of the country's great arts festivals, each July. There are a number of private game lodges close to the town. Most noteworthy is Shamwari Game Reserve, which has won a number of international awards.

Bathurst

Originally intended as the main centre for the 1820 Settlers, this living museum now prides itself as the 'pineapple capital of South Africa'. Both the Methodist church and the Anglican church of St John date back to this period. The Pig 'n Whistle in Kowie Street is the oldest licensed pub in the country.

FESTIVAL TIME

For the duration of the National Arts Festival, over 11 days each July, the streets of Grahamstown are transformed by colourful posters, buskers and a range of stalls selling everything from food to beads, baubles and bangles. Festival-goers can choose between hundreds of plays, dance shows, films, art exhibitions, music recitals, circus acts and blues, jazz and rock concerts.

CITY OF GHOSTS

The most fun way to get a feel for the history of the area is to take a ghost tour through Grahamstown. Here the spirits of the many that met an untimely end are among the most restless in the land.

Makana's Kop

The Xhosa, in the early part of the 19th century, were not only threatened by the British, but also by deep internal divisions. It was a time ripe for the emergence of a prophet. Makana, a commoner influenced by a mix of traditional practices and Christian beliefs, was convinced he could deliver his people by throwing off the yoke of white authority. Claiming his divine powers would resurrect the ancestors to assist in the battle, he raised an army of 10 000 to attack Grahamstown. As Makana had convinced them that bullets from British guns would turn to water when fired, they had reduced much of the effectiveness of their assegais by shortening the shafts for close-range fighting. The Xhosa were massacred. Today wispy figures, it is said, can still be seen running in formation down the hill.

The Old Gaol and Drostdy Gateway

Grahamstown is known as the City of Saints, but it was not always so blessed. Under martial law for much of its early existence, its main social occasion appears to have been public beatings and hangings.

The Old Gaol was commissioned in 1823. Designed to hold 200 in small, dank, dark cells, it often overflowed with anything up to 3 000 inmates. Those sentenced to be flogged or condemned to death were shackled and led along a path through the nearby Drostdy Gateway (now the entrance to Rhodes University) to the military parade ground where the punishment was administered.

Henry Nicholls was the subject of the last public execution in the Eastern Cape, in 1862. Nicholls had pleaded guilty to rape and there were many who felt the sentence of hanging was harsh. Apparently, his spirit can still be seen on the dead man's walk between the Old Gaol and the place where the gallows once stood.

The Provost

The Provost was once military detention barracks. Its ingenious panopticon, based on an 18th-century plan by Jeremy Bentham, gives strategically placed guards in a circular tower an unimpeded view of their section of the cells fanning out below.

The Provost was hastily completed in 1838 for the detention of mutinous Khoekhoen in the service of the Cape Mounted Rifles. Seventeen years earlier Khoekhoe deserters of the corps had been rounded up by Ensign Crowe and held at Fraser's Camp. The detainees, fearing the harsh military justice of the time, overpowered their jailers, killing Crowe. Five were rearrested and incarcerated at the Provost. Of these, Corporal Myers and Stephanus Windvogel were sentenced to death. Kingswood schoolboys have claimed to have seen a pair of ghosts near the scene of the executions.

ACTIVITIES

- Surfing, jet-skiing, canoeing, windsurfing and rubber-ducking in Port Elizabeth
- Surfing in St Francis Bay and Jeffreys Bay
- Scuba diving in and around Cape Recife and Jeffreys Bay
- Fresh-water, deep-sea and surf angling at various locations
- Rock-fishing at Jeffreys Bay
- Quad biking with Green Adventures at numerous locations, including a farm 60 km outside of Port Elizabeth
- Paragliding from various launch sites including the Maitlands River mouth, 15 km outside of Port Elizabeth, several inland thermal sites and a well-known launch site just outside Grahamstown
- Birdwatching at Cape St Francis, Jeffreys Bay, Zwartkops Valley Nature Reserve in Port Elizabeth and Nahoon Estuary Reserve in East London
- Golf at Jeffreys Bay Golf Club in Jeffreys Bay

ROUTES AND TRAILS

- The Oldenburgia Hiking Trail (2 days) is a circular trail that traverses the Thomas Baines Nature Reserve, starting at the Grahamstown Municipal Caravan Park
- The Mosslands Two River Trail (2 days) meanders along the Assegaai and Kariega rivers on Mosslands farm, 18 km from Grahamstown and hikers stay overnight in reed cabins
- The River Walk (1.5 hours) and Forest Walk (2.5 hours) at Van Staden's Wildflower Nature Reserve, 40 km west of Port Elizabeth
- The Bushbuck Walk (1.5 hours) at the Island Nature Reserve, 25 km from Port Elizabeth
- The Sacramento Trail (4 hours) in Sardinia Bay Nature Reserve between Skoenmakerskop and Sardinia Bay
- Hikes in the Gonubie Nature Reserve on a number of marked trails outside Gonubie near East London

Port Alfred

Port Alfred is the premier coastal resort in the region, although it has lost some of its charm from over-development. The sandbar at the river mouth is navigable by the small craft that dock at the marina, which dates back to the 1840s. The 1826 Methodist church is a heritage site.

East London

By 1836, the colonial frontier had been pushed further east after the Sixth Xhosa War. Sir Benjamin D'Urban, the then Cape governor, ordered the mouth of the Buffalo River to be surveyed as a possible port to supply frontier garrisons. The British overruled D'Urban and nothing came of it until after the Seventh Xhosa War, in 1847, when the new governor, Sir Harry Smith, decided to reinvestigate its feasibility. There he established Fort Glamorgan and named the settlement East London. Today it is the only river port in South Africa.

This was the port of entry for a number of German immigrants, who are commemorated by a statue on the esplanade. Other than a port, the city is best known as a beach-holiday destination. Most popular are nearby Kidd's Beach and Gonubie.

SACRED SITES

The enormous Cove Rock, also known as Gompo, and caves along the coast near East London are among the most sacred sites in Xhosa tradition. For the Xhosa, Gompo is the ancestral grounds of the rulers of the 'people of the river and sea'. When waves thunder here during storms the Xhosa believe the water spirits are communicating with them.

LEFT: Birdwatching is a pleasant way to pass the time in the Albany region. BELOW: The Steve Biko memorial in East London pays tribute to one of the Struggle's most prominent political heroes. BOTTOM: Along with other fascinating exhibits, this unique artwork may be seen at the East London Museum.

CHAPTER 13

THE TRANSKEI AND WILD COAST

ABOVE: The rugged Wild Coast has one of the most pristine coastlines in southern Africa.

DID YOU KNOW?

Many mariners and passengers shipwrecked along the Wild Coast were assimilated into Xhosa culture.

The greater Transkei region is bordered by Port Edward in the northeast and the East London in the southwest, while the Indian Ocean and the highlands that stretch towards the Drakensberg make up the southeastern and northwestern frontiers respectively. The coastal section of this area of the Eastern Cape, known as the Wild Coast, is probably the most rugged, unspoilt stretch of coastline in South Africa. Here you will find waterfalls, densely forested areas, deep river gorges, long beaches that seem to go on forever and incredible rock formations shaped over the ages by mighty waves. Most visitors come here for the scenic beauty and hiking trails.

This place of gentle green hills is home to the Xhosa people. It was here that the struggle for freedom was born from oppression, and was nurtured by some of the greatest political icons of the modern age.

CLIMATE

The Transkei region is a temperate summer rainfall area with spells of truly wild weather ranging from tornadoes to blizzards and howling gales along the coast. The geology and weather combine to make the Wild Coast among the most treacherous waters in the world, as the many shipwrecks along this stretch attest. On 26 February 1852, the troopship the

Birkenhead, an iron paddle steamer, sank along the Cape south coast. This incident entered seafaring lore as soldiers helped women and children onto lifeboats before lining up on deck to go down with the ship to the beat of a drummer. It is, however, a myth that the *Birkenhead* established the practice of 'women and children first'. This honour, in fact, goes to the *Abercrombie Robinson*, which sank in Table Bay a decade earlier.

In fact, the Wild Coast is more notorious for dishonour in shipping. When the *Jacaranda* cargo ship ran aground here in 1971, it is alleged that the captain was in his cabin with a prostitute while his drunken crew were all incapacitated, save for the 16-year-old at the helm. Two decades later the captain and most of the crew of the *Oceanos* abandoned ship and passengers when the Greek liner foundered in the same waters, leaving it to the South African entertainment staff to avert tragedy.

FLORA AND FAUNA

The Wild Coast is twitcher heaven with approximately 320 bird species, but the greatest attraction is the ocean – where dolphins and whales are regularly spotted and where the fishing is excellent. A new marine national park is planned for the Pondoland area.

Dwesa and Cwebe are two small nature reserves situated in the central region of the Wild Coast. Bordered by the Indian Ocean and grasslands, both nature reserves are covered by lowland forest but acacia scrub and grasslands can also be found in these parts. The reserves are known for a wealth of bird species and small mammals. At Dwesa, rare bird species such as the mangrove kingfisher and the Narina trogon can be seen, as well as a number of typical forest mammals including blue duiker, bushbuck, tree hyrax and samango monkey. Crocociles have also been introduced to the rivers. At Cwebe the bird life is excellent particularly at the Mbhanyana River where one can also spot Cape clawless otter.

HISTORY AND HERITAGE

Pre-1994, South African history is a litany of conflicts and rivalries between the many groups that lived or had interests in the region. These began shortly after the Dutch settlers arrived in 1652, but the most serious took place from 1779 onwards when white farmers moving eastwards came up against black groups for the first time.

There were nine Xhosa or Cape Frontier Wars between 1779 and 1879. In these, the Xhosa were pushed back, first beyond the Great Fish River and then the Great Kei River. In April 1856, between the Eighth and Ninth wars, disaster struck when the tribe acted upon a redemptive vision by a teenage girl from the Centane district, Nongqawuse. They slaughtered their cattle and destroyed their crops in the belief that this would drive the whites into the sea. It was an act that devastated them, leading to mass starvation and impoverishment, and so weakened the nation that it eased white

ABOVE: With more than 320 bird species on offer, including kingfisher, the Wild Coast is a twitcher's paradise. LEFT: Traditional Xhosa homesteads, with their expertly thatched roofs, dot the hills of the Transkei.

incursions into their area, which was incorporated into the Cape after the last war.

But the National Party did not want the Transkei when they came to power in 1948, preferring to confer nominal independence upon it. In the mid-1950s the Tomlinson Commission – an initiative of the Ministry of Native Affairs under the architect of apartheid, Hendrik Verwoerd – issued a report that would form the basis for the Promotion of Bantu Self Government Act, which created eight ethnic Bantustans, later called homelands, and became the foundation for grand apartheid.

The central premise of the homelands policy was that there was no black majority, but rather groups of ethnic minorities, of which whites were one. Only the whites were South Africans, as all the black splinter groups belonged in clearly defined areas to be excised from South Africa and eventually given 'independence'. As part of this scheme the Xhosa homeland of Transkei was given self-governing status in 1963, which was extended to full 'independence' in 1976. It was reincorporated back into South Africa prior to the first democratic elections in 1994.

NOTEWORTHY PLACES
Chintsa

Once known as Cintsa, this sleepy coastal village is situated some 45 km to the northeast of East London. While technically falling just outside the Transkei, it is often considered the gateway the region. Picturesque in the extreme, with unspoilt stretches of thick indigenous forests, this seaside village is popular with families who are privy to this coastline's best-kept secret. The lagoon provides hours of fun for children and the area is also known for rock-fishing. A few choice accommodation options are available and there are one or two renowned seafood restaurants in the area.

Haga-Haga

Another quaint village on the Wild Coast, Haga-Haga, is the haunt of travellers who have the inside track on its spectacular beaches and fantastic fauna, including blue duiker and Cape clawless otter. Situated where the Nyara and Quko rivers meet, Haga-Haga is a conservancy area with a strong Xhosa heritage. Hiking, deep-sea fishing and nature trails are popular and it is a great place to buy Xhosa arts and crafts.

SEE:
Eastern Cape p. 223
Eastern Cape & Lesotho p. 229
Eastern Cape & KwaZulu-Natal p. 230

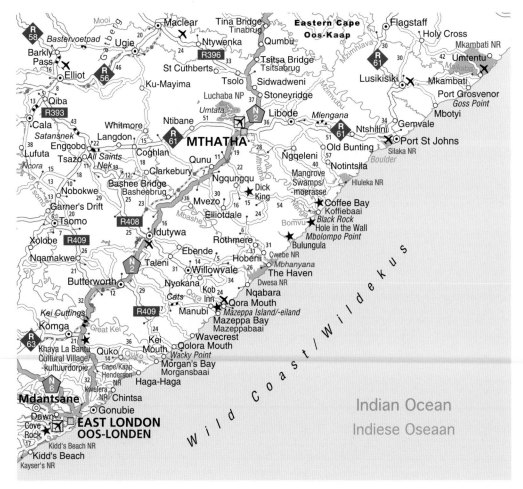

NELSON MANDELA HERITAGE

The Nelson Mandela National Museum in Mthatha is a living memorial to this struggle legend.

South African liberation and international peace icon Nelson Rolihlahla Mandela was born of Tembu royal lineage at Mvezo in the Eastern Cape on 18 July 1918. Arriving in Johannesburg in the early 1940s, he enrolled at the University of South Africa (UNISA) to complete his law degree started at the University College of Fort Hare in the eastern Cape.

He joined the African National Congress (ANC) and in August 1943 took part in his first march in support of the Alexandra bus boycott. Soon the youthful Mandela was pushing to the front of resistance marches. He was also at the forefront of changing the direction of the ANC.

He was instrumental in establishing the movement's Youth League in 1944 and its armed wing, Umkhonto weSizwe (MK), after it was forced underground. In 1963, while serving a three-year sentence for leaving the country illegally and inciting workers to strike, he was charged with treason and sentenced to life in prison.

Mandela was released on 11 February 1990 and played a pivotal role in South Africa's peaceful transition, becoming the country's first democratically elected president in 1994. For his efforts he was awarded the Nobel Peace Prize. As a tribute to the man and his work, the Nelson Mandela Museum was opened on 11 February 2000.

The museum focuses on three sites in the Transkei region of the Eastern Cape. At the impressive Bhunga building in Mthatha, the story of his life is celebrated in his own words alongside gifts he received during his presidency.

At Mvezo visitors can see where he was born. And at the Qunu Museum in Qunu, the village where he was raised, a youth and heritage centre has been built.

Morgan's Bay

Situated some 85 km northeast of East London, Morgan's Bay used to be rather difficult to get to because of shoddy roads, but the now-tarred road from Kei Mouth makes the journey easier than in the old days. Known for its great beaches and laid-back holiday feel, Morgan's Bay is also celebrated for its contrasting natural beauty consisting of savannah, valley thickets, forest and fynbos. There are over 271 bird species in the area.

Kei Mouth

Kei Mouth is situated where the Wild Coast and Sunshine Coast tourism regions meet at the Great Kei River. Once a sleepy little coastal village, Kei Mouth has seen some major development in the past 10 years, and although it continues to be a laid-back seaside resort, there are a number of accommodation options to choose from. This village is a great place for family holidays. The beaches offer excellent surfing and swimming opportunities (Wacky Point in particular is a well-known surf spot), and there are excellent fishing opportunities in the area.

Mthatha

This was the capital of the nominally independent Transkei, and is the biggest centre in the region. Of interest here is the Nelson Mandela National Museum and old colonial buildings.

ABOVE: The Nelson Mandela National Museum in Mthatha celebrates the life and times of this great man, who was born in nearby Mvezo in 1918.

The St James and All Saints churches are notable and the Umtata Museum covers the natural and cultural history of the Transkei and is worth a look. The Umtata Dam is popular for outdoor activities and the Madiba hiking trail is a favourite for visitors to the area.

Mazeppa Bay

With wide stretches of beach and a magnificent lagoon, Mazeppa Bay is something of a fishing haven along the Wild Coast. First Beach is extremely popular and travellers can walk over a 100-m-long suspension bridge to reach Mazeppa Island (which is sometimes only accessible by the bridge at high tide). The lagoon is popular for water sports and there are a number of hiking trails in the area.

The Haven

The Haven Hotel is an institution. Located between the Cwebe and Dwesa nature reserves, the establishment has been going for over 50 years and is still going strong. Family-type activities on offer include horse riding (on the beach), golf, hiking, canoeing, snorkelling and lots of activities for kids. The fishing is excellent in this part of the world.

Coffee Bay

Situated at the mouth of the Nenga River, Coffee Bay is relaxed in the extreme. Rolling hills, long beaches and friendly locals make it a great holiday spot. A highlight is the spectacular rock formation known as Hole in the Wall, a rugged natural attraction sculpted by the ocean and the elements, situated some 8 km south of Coffee Bay.

There are a few notable eateries and pubs in the area, as well as several hiking trails, but otherwise life revolves around the beach. The Coffee Shack, a backpackers lodge situated at the Bomvu River mouth, is renowned for its bonhomie (and great New Year's parties).

Port St Johns

Something of a hippie hideaway, Port St Johns, at the mouth of the Mzimvubu River, retains a casual but slightly decadent demeanour. Besides the beautifully painted museum, there are none of the typical attractions of most towns. Rather, it offers a raucous marketplace and beautiful beaches accessed through thick forest. There are intriguing trails leading from the town into verdant hills, but it is advisable to take a guide before venturing out.

ACTIVITIES

- Horse riding along the beach at various locations
- Fishing all along the Transkei coastline, including Bulungula, Chintsa, Coffee Bay, Haga-Haga and Kei Mouth
- Big-game fishing in spring and autumn and most of the resorts offer deep-sea charters
- Birdwatching at Cwebe and Dwesa nature reserves
- Lazing in a hammock at the Coffee Shack in Coffee Bay

XHOSA CULTURE

The Xhosa number approximately 7,1 million, the majority living in the Eastern Cape.

They are descended from the Nguni, who migrated from central and northern Africa to settle in Southern Africa. They comprise a number of clans such as the Gcaleka, Ngqika, Ndlambe, Dushane, Qayi and the Gqunkhwebe of Khoe-San origin. Their language is often called the 'click' language because of the three dominant clicks inherited from the languages of their Khoe-San ancestors.

Xhosa women wear heavy dresses and matching turbans, and coloured dots decorate their faces. Beadwork similar to the Ndebele's is an integral aspect of their culture. It forms part of the ornamentation that reflects the different stages of a woman's life.

The man is head of the home and it is the responsibility of a woman to be respectful to him and the elders at all times. As is tradition in many African groups, the man is accorded a higher status and can have more than one wife. Each family has a head, and each clan a chief (Inkosi). Chieftainship is conferred by the mother's lineage, even if she's not accorded political authority. In each clan the land is communally held and everything is shared, with great emphasis on helping one another, whether with hut building or harvesting.

The Xhosa recognise the presence of ancestral spirits and a supreme authority. The ceremonial slaughtering of animals is one of the many ways in which ancestors are called.

The Xhosa way of life can be experienced at the Khaya La Bantu cultural village near East London.

ROUTES AND TRAILS

- Wild Coast Meander (6 days) from Kob Inn on the Qora River to Morgan's Bay
- The Wild Coast Amble Meander (5 days) from Kei Mouth to Chintsa
- Strandloper Meander (5 days) from Kei Mouth to Gonubie
- Wild Coast Pondo Walk – three multi-directional day walks from Mbotyi
- A hike (3 hours) from the Coffee Shack at Coffee Bay, which takes in waterfalls, Baby Hole and Hole in the Wall
- Various horse riding trails (1 hour–6 days), including Mkulu Kei Horse Trails (2 hours–12 days), from Morgan's Bay
- Ranching holidays along the Wild Coast and horse-riding offered by Wild Coast Horse Trails in Kei Mouth

CHAPTER 14

DURBAN AND THE KWAZULU-NATAL COAST

DID YOU KNOW?

Durban harbour is the busiest in South Africa and one of the 10 largest in the world.

The KwaZulu-Natal coast stretches from Port Edward in the southwestern corner of the province all the way northeast to Maputaland on the Mozambique border. It is lapped by the warm waters of the Indian Ocean and incorporates many charming bucket-and-spade destinations along the way. The KwaZulu-Natal province is bordered by Mpumalanga in the north.

Durban, sometimes called eThekwini, hugs a wide lagoon of the Umgeni River. It is KwaZulu-Natal's commercial hub and Johannesburg's seaside playground. Luxury high-rise hotels define its Golden Mile beachfront where the vibe is always laid-back and friendly. The city has much to offer in the way of fantastic restaurants, fun

hangouts and leisure venues. And for those who love the great outdoors, it is a beach and surfer's paradise. Durban is also home to one of the largest Indian communities outside of India, and no visit to the city would be complete without an exploration into this fascinating culture.

CLIMATE

The area is hot and humid in summer and warm in winter, which is why it is a year-round destination. One of the biggest selling points of the KwaZulu-Natal coastline is that 320 days of sunshine per year are guaranteed. During the summer months temperatures are frequently in the early 30s, but can reach over 40 °C in places like Maputaland.

FLORA AND FAUNA

Durban's mangrove-girt and lush vegetation give it a tropical feel. Birds are plentiful as are small mammals, especially vervet monkeys. But it is the ocean that provides most interest. uShaka Marine World, the fifth largest aquarium complex in the world, is the ultimate marine fantasy park, housing 0,5 km of viewing tanks, 7 massive aquariums and 25 additional marine exhibits. The complex encompasses restaurants, shops and water fun rides.

A highlight on the calendar is the 'sardine run' around mid-June to July. In an annual migration, millions of sardines, hungrily pursued by a host of predators – from sea birds to sharks and dolphins – are swept north up the coast from their breeding grounds near the Agulhas Bank off the Cape coast. If the gigantic shoals come close enough inshore, locals and holiday-makers rush to gather up the little fish in buckets, nets or whatever they have to hand. Ragged-tooth sharks, nicknamed 'raggies', are found along the Aliwal Shoal off Durban's South Coast. The South Coast is also a great place for dolphin watching, and it contains tropical sea life and corals as well as cold-water fish and sponges.

HISTORY AND HERITAGE

When Vasco da Gama sailed past on Christmas Day 1497, he named the area Terro do Natalia ('territory of the nativity'). Natalia was later shortened to Natal. In 1824 Henry Francis Fynn obtained land from King Shaka, the famous chief and military genius who reigned over the Zulus until he was murdered by his half-brothers in 1828. Fynn established a trading and ivory-hunting post at the port.

The town grew and in June 1835 the residents changed its name to D'Urban in honour of Cape governor of the time, Sir Benjamin D'Urban.

The arrival of the Voortrekkers from the Cape startled King Dingane, Shaka's successor, leading to the Battle of Blood River on 16 December 1838, in which the Zulus were defeated.

In 1842 the British came, but they were soon held under siege at Old Fort by the Boers. A long month later reinforcements arrived from Port Elizabeth and the Boers were defeated. When the British annexed Durban as a dependency of the Cape Colony in 1845, most of the Boers trekked again.

Durban took on a very British air until 1860, when the first Indian immigrants arrived on board the *Truro* as indentured labourers to work on sugar-cane farms. From the outset these new arrivals faced intense discrimination, which led to them taking a leading role in the Struggle for Freedom that started with the arrival of Mohandas Gandhi, later known as Mahatma ('great soul') Gandhi, in 1893.

Gandhi was born in India and arrived in the British colony of Natal to take up a position as advisor to a Durban law firm. He had intended to spend only a year in South Africa, but the racial slights he experienced convinced him that his help was needed to change things; he stayed for 20 years. In 1894 he founded the Natal Indian Congress, which later would be at the forefront of the struggle. Its philosophy was one of passive resistance, but when this proved inadequate he reformulated it into Satyagraha, Sanskrit for 'truth and firmness'.

Spearheading a seven-year campaign of strikes and burning of registration cards, Gandhi was jailed on a number of occasions. While the government was able to violently quell this resistance, their methods caused an outcry, forcing

DID YOU KNOW?

Although Shaka's successor Dingane clashed with Henry Fynn on numerous occasions, Dingane recognised him as a 'great chief' and, in 1831, gave him nine wives. Today, the Fynn clan is part of the fascinating cultural mix found in KwaZulu-Natal.

BELOW: The monument to Dick King and his horse, Somerset, was erected on Durban's Victoria Embankment in 1915.

THE 'SAVIOUR' OF NATAL

Dick King, an English trader and colonist who was on board the trading vessel *Mazeppa* when the Boers held the British under siege at Old Fort in 1842, was recruited to take a plea requesting assistance to Fort Pedi near Grahamstown. To avoid Boer lookouts, he was ferried to Salisbury Island with his 16-year-old servant Ndongeni and two horses, from where they followed a secret path back to the mainland. Riding 1000 km over rough, dangerous countryside and crossing 122 rivers, King reached Grahamstown 10 days later.

Old Fort later became the headquarters of the Durban Light Infantry until they relocated to new premises in 1897. The fort was preserved by Brigadier-General G Molyneux and, together with the small chapel of St Peter's in Chains and the Warrior's Gate building, it now forms the nucleus of a historic complex set in beautiful gardens in KE Masinga (Old Fort) Road. The building is rumoured to be haunted by Ensign Prior who died during the siege, and apparently Molyneux, too, refuses to leave the gardens that were named in his honour.

SEE:
Durban p. 216
Eastern Cape &
KwaZulu-Natal p. 230
KwaZulu-Natal p. 231

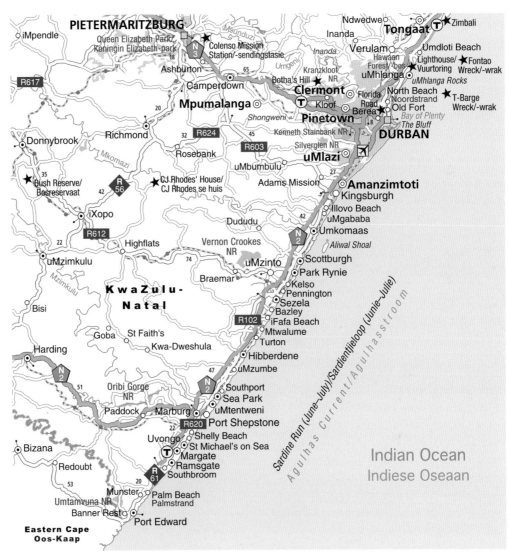

them to negotiate concessions with him. Conditional on this, though, was that he leave the country, and in 1914 he returned to India.

But Gandhi's stay here is not forgotten and there are a number of memorials to him in the Durban area.

NOTEWORTHY PLACES ON THE SOUTH COAST

The South Coast, also known as the Hibiscus Coast, offers such an array of beach holiday destinations that visitors are spoilt for choice. It starts at Port Edward, ending at, but not including, Durban. The area is known for family beach holidays and resort apartments, and during the summer season hordes of holiday-makers from Gauteng make their way to the South Coast to enjoy fun in the sun. Umbrellas dot the beaches and small coastal businesses, shops and restaurants thrive in the holiday season.

Port Shepstone is the major town along this strip of coast; the famed Oribi Gorge Nature

Reserve is about 40 km from here. Umkomaas lies at a river mouth, where visitors can hire boats and explore upriver. Other pleasant towns with typical beach attractions include: Southbroom, Ramsgate, Margate, Uvongo, St Michael's on Sea, Shelly Beach, Pennington, Scottburgh, Illovo Beach and Amanzimtoti.

NOTEWORTHY PLACES IN DURBAN

Durban's Golden Mile between uShaka Marine World and the Suncoast Casino is the most frequented beach area in South Africa. Here, modern hotels rub shoulders with Art Deco establishments, restaurants, clubs, entertainment venues, and arts and crafts outlets. Running between the built-up area and the golden beach is a promenade that is a firm favourite of joggers, strollers, rollerbladers and buskers. Here too is the renowned Fitzsimmons Snake Park, and ornate rickshaws pulled by elaborately dressed Zulu men can be hired for a unique sightseeing spin.

DID YOU KNOW?

Jummah Mosque in central Durban is the largest in the Southern Hemisphere.

DID YOU KNOW?

Mahatma Gandhi was the first lawyer of colour to be admitted to the Supreme Court in South Africa.

Berea

Berea, an exclusive suburb of Durban, is perched on a ridge overlooking the city. Known for its varied architectural styles including Edwardian, Art Deco, Victorian and super modern, it is a lovely quarter whose streets are lined with trees.

Durban's Botanic Gardens were founded in 1848 and today include an array of orchids, palms and sub-tropical trees as well as a mixed arboretum of Asian, American and African trees. The lovely Mitchell Park is a popular picnic area.

Greyville Racecourse is located in Berea and is one of the country's famed courses, known especially for the Vodacom Durban July horse race that is a well-visited annual event.

Florida Road

Durban's Florida Road is the place to be for visitors in search of great restaurants and clubs away from the frenzy of the beach area.

Over 30 eateries cater for nearly every taste, and, apart from these fashionable establishments, there is also a variety of eclectic shops, two boutique hotels and a number of comfortable B & Bs.

NOTEWORTHY PLACES ON THE NORTH COAST

The shore from Durban to the Tugela River further north is known as the Dolphin Coast and offers some of the best beaches in South Africa with regular sightings of its namesake. The North Coast, however, stretches all the way until the Mozambican border, and its last section is called Maputaland. There are a variety of coastal towns to choose from and travellers can quite comfortably meander along the coast on a succession of wide toll roads and stop where the mood strikes them. While the more popular destinations are described below, other, quieter possibilities include Umdloti Beach, Umhlali, Sheffield Beach, Blythedale Beach and Zinkwazi Beach.

uMhlanga Rocks

Durban's suburb of uMhlanga Rocks has grown from a seaside village into an entertainment and business hub. uMhlanga is a family destination offering resort-type accommodation and child-friendly facilities. The boardwalk that stretches along the beachfront from the Breakers Resort to the postcard-pretty uMhlanga lighthouse is a favourite with joggers and power-walkers. In past years it has taken a beating from Mother Nature, when massive waves and flooding did some serious damage, but is slowly being rebuilt.

Home to local mogul Sol Kerzner's first hotel, The Beverley Hills (also known as the 'Heavenly Bills'), and the historic Oyster Box Hotel, the area now features glitzy high-rise establishments and apartments to rival Miami's in stature and style.

There is much to do in the area. An informative visit to the Natal Shark's Board (the shark research centre responsible for protecting South Africa's beaches and renowned for its painstaking marine research and conservation work along this coastline) is recommended. A number of cruise operators offer opportunities to enjoy sun-

ABOVE LEFT: Uvongo, on the South Coast, is a popular destination during the summer school holidays when families take time off to romp in the lagoon.
ABOVE RIGHT: Yachts are a familiar sight in Durban. The city has two yacht clubs, namely Royal Natal and Point.

DID YOU KNOW?
Nelson Mandela voted at Ohlange High School in Inanda in South Africa's first democratic elections on 27 April 1994.

downers at sea and dolphin watching. For nature-lovers, the Hawaan Forest is recommended.

Fashionistas and shoppers will not want to miss the Gateway Theatre of Shopping, a gargantuan mall with cinemas (including an Imax theatre), shops, restaurants, fun activities for children and its very own wave park called Wave House.

Zimbali

Zimbali Coastal Resort, situated along the Dolphin Coast some 45 km north of Durban, is a residential, resort and golfing development sprawling over 700 ha that offers exquisite ocean views from various vantage points. Zimbali has two private championship golf courses and numerous activities are available.

Ballito Bay

Willard Beach, the main swimming beach at Ballito Bay, is safe for bathers as it is watched by lifeguards seven days a week and protected by shark nets. Ballito is a firm favourite along this coastline.

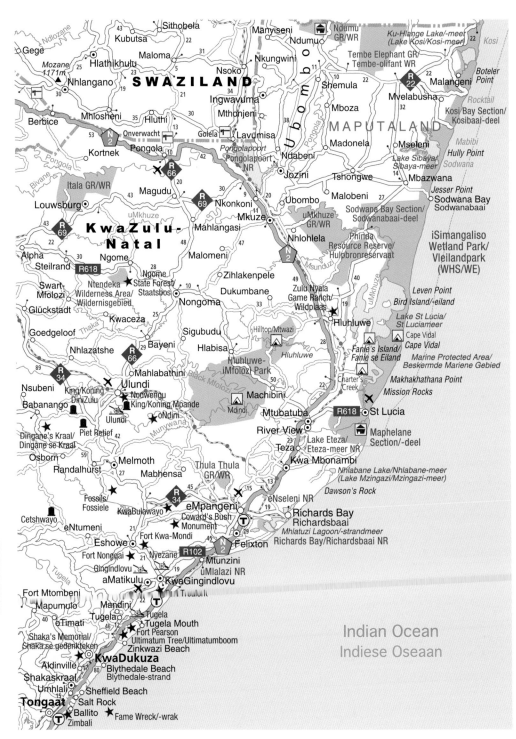

SEE:
Durban p. 216
KwaZulu-Natal p. 231
KwaZulu-Natal &
Swaziland p. 239

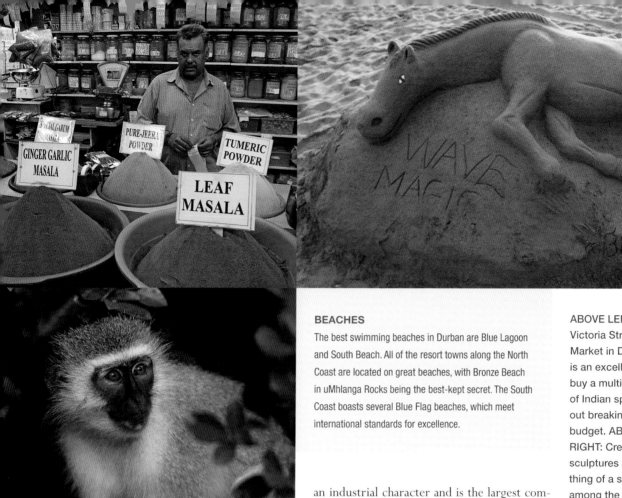

BEACHES

The best swimming beaches in Durban are Blue Lagoon and South Beach. All of the resort towns along the North Coast are located on great beaches, with Bronze Beach in uMhlanga Rocks being the best-kept secret. The South Coast boasts several Blue Flag beaches, which meet international standards for excellence.

Salt Rock

Salt Rock is yet another fabulous destination for family holidays. There are beautiful beaches complete with tidal pools, and there are lifeguards on duty. On the way to Umhlali passersby will find the Flag Animal Farm with its playgrounds, tea garden and various activities for the children, including milking demonstrations and a petting farmyard.

Tugela Mouth

This small village at the mouth of the Tugela River has an old fort dating back to before the Anglo–Zulu War. The Ultimatum Tree, a massive wild fig under which Cetshwayo was presented with the challenge that led to that war, is a national heritage site. The prevalent bird life and excellent fishing, both from the shore and deep sea, are its biggest attractions. The nearby Harold Johnson Nature Reserve has picnic and braai facilities, and there are several campsites for overnight visitors.

Richards Bay

Richards Bay is South Africa's largest harbour for bulk cargo of coal and steel. The town has an industrial character and is the largest commercial centre in the region. It boasts an airport that provides convenient access to Maputaland from the rest of the country.

St Lucia

A sleepy fishing village-cum-holiday resort, St Lucia is a good base for visitors heading off to the iSimangaliso Wetland Park and its major attractions, including Cape Vidal, Mission Rocks and Charter's Creek. The Lake St Lucia Estuary is a well-known fishing spot and the coast off St Lucia is known for game fishing. Visitors can take a sundowner cruise across Lake St Lucia and spot crocs and hippos. Modest, but air-conditioned resort-type accommodation is available in town and there are a number of B & Bs.

Hluhluwe-iMfolozi Park

The world-famous Hluhluwe-iMfolozi Park is the largest of the province's game reserves and considered by many to be its finest. Proclaimed as far back as 1895 as two separate parks – Hluhluwe and Umfolozi – the combined park currently preserves 96 000 ha.

Umfolozi gained international acclaim in the 1950s for its conservation project 'Operation Rhino' aimed at saving the white rhino from extinction. One of southern Africa's densest populations of this once-threatened species, along with their black cousins, enjoys protection in today's Hluhluwe-iMfolozi Park.

DID YOU KNOW?
KwaDukuza (Stanger) is the burial place of King Shaka.

Apart from the rhino, the remaining members of the Big Five are residents here, as is the rare endangered wild dog and a wide variety of other animals. Bird life is also prolific, and more than 300 species can be found here, including African finfoot, Rudd's apalis, eastern bronze-naped pigeon and eastern nicator.

Visitors to the park can self-drive or take an open 4x4 game drive. Alternatives to exploring the parks include boat cruises on Hluhluwe Dam or self-guided walks. There are a number of beautiful picnic sites of offer, which provide ablution and barbecue facilities.

iSimangaliso Wetland Park

The jewel in the crown of Zululand is undoubtedly the iSimangaliso Wetland Park. Its Zulu name tells you that 'you are in the land of miracles'. It is said that when Shaka died his aide Ujeqe fled, as it was customary for them to be buried along with their monarch.

Ujeqe wandered into Thongaland (present-day Maputaland) and on his return exclaimed, 'I saw wonders and miracles in the flat land and lakes of Thonga'. iSimangaliso was declared a World Heritage Site in 1999. It covers approximately 332 000 ha, including 220 km of pristine Indian Ocean coastline, and extends from the northerly Kosi Bay, where ancient fishing communities thrived, to past Maphelane in the south. The park is a robust interaction of eight interlinking ecosystems that are home to a profusion of fish, fauna and flora. Then there are the 25 000-year-old coastal dunes, which are among the highest in the world.

Sodwana Bay

The South African version of the Great Barrier Reef, Sodwana Bay with its coral reefs is a favoured holiday spot of divers and snorkellers. The bay boasts a continental reef close to the shoreline, which makes for deep waters that

BELOW: White rhino, although herbivores, are massive beasts, typically weighing between 1 400 and 3 600 kg. BOTTOM LEFT: Lake St Lucia forms part of the iSimangaliso Wetland Park, and is hippo and crocodile country. BOTTOM RIGHT: Game viewing on the St Lucia Estuary is best done from the safety of a sundowner cruise.

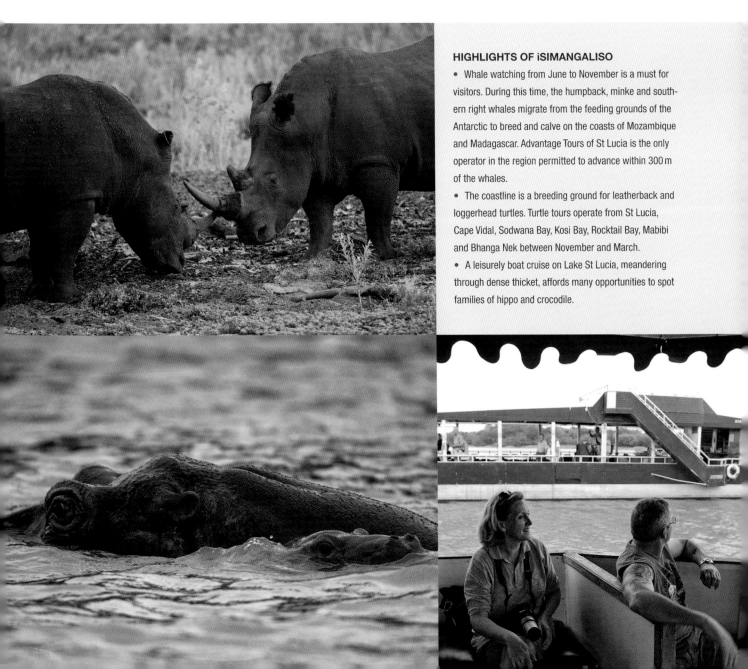

HIGHLIGHTS OF iSIMANGALISO

• Whale watching from June to November is a must for visitors. During this time, the humpback, minke and southern right whales migrate from the feeding grounds of the Antarctic to breed and calve on the coasts of Mozambique and Madagascar. Advantage Tours of St Lucia is the only operator in the region permitted to advance within 300 m of the whales.

• The coastline is a breeding ground for leatherback and loggerhead turtles. Turtle tours operate from St Lucia, Cape Vidal, Sodwana Bay, Kosi Bay, Rocktail Bay, Mabibi and Bhanga Nek between November and March.

• A leisurely boat cruise on Lake St Lucia, meandering through dense thicket, affords many opportunities to spot families of hippo and crocodile.

ACTIVITIES

- Surfing and swimming at a number of excellent beaches in Durban, including Blue Lagoon, North Beach and South Beach.
- Airplane hops over the city and coastline from Virginia Airport, Durban North
- Charter and yacht cruises from uMhlanga Rocks main beach
- Go out to sea with the Natal Sharks Board
- Wreck diving off the coastline; popular sites include the *Fame* off Ballito, the *Fontao* off the coast of uMhlanga and the *T-Barge* between Durban and uMhlanga
- Kayak safaris out to sea from uMhlanga or Ballito
- Kitesurfing down the North Coast, especially at Ballito
- Snorkelling at Cape Vidal and at Aliwal Shoal, which is one of the top five sites in the world, off Durban's South Coast
- Diving in Sodwana Bay, rated one of the world's top 10 dive sites
- Picnicking, braaing and camping at the Harold Johnson Nature Reserve near Tugela Mouth

ROUTES AND TRAILS

- Three interlinked trails (10 minutes–1 hour) at the Burman Bush Nature Reserve, just 8 km from Durban city centre: the Pithi Trail (180 m); the Hadeda Trail (500 m); and the Umgeni Trail (1 km)
- Six trails (45 minutes–6 hours) in Krantzkloof Nature Reserve in Kloof
- Walk (2 hours) in Silverglen Nature Reserve in Durban
- Four interlinked trails (15 minutes–1 hour) along the Palmiet River Valley in Palmiet Nature Reserve in the greater Durban area
- Red Trail (2 hours) at the Kenneth Stainbank Nature Reserve in the greater Durban area
- Oriental Walkabout (2–3 hours) that takes in the Indian culture of the city, starting and ending at the Durban Tourist Junction, and visiting Jummah Mosque, the historical Grey Street business precinct and the famous Victoria Street Market
- Inanda Heritage Route (1/2 day) that begins in the Phoenix section of Inanda Township and ends at the Muti Market, taking in the site where Gandhi's first ashram (Hindu religious retreat) stood; Ohlange High School in Inanda, founded by the first president of the ANC, John Dube; and Inanda Seminary
- Shembe Pilgrimage (3 days) by members of the Shembe religious sect (and anyone else), which covers 80 km each New Year's Day from the church's headquarters at Ebhohleni, Durban, to the Holy Mountain, Nhlangagazi, near Ndwedwe

are popular with fisherman. Places like Mabibi and Rocktail Bay can only be reached by 4x4.

Kosi Bay

This exquisite bay consists of four lakes that feed into the ocean and form part of the iSimangaliso Wetland Park. Kosi is known for its traditional fishing kraals, or fish traps, used by the Tsonga people for centuries. It is also a breeding ground for leatherback turtles, and eco-friendly turtle tours take place from November to February. Accommodation is available with local communities, but this needs to be organised in advance by contacting the provincial parks authority, Ezemvelo KZN Wildlife.

TOP: Durban, with its warm sea, great swell and practically year-round summer climate, is a surfer's paradise.
ABOVE: Reminiscent of prehistoric creatures, leatherback turtles may be seen at Kosi Bay.

CHAPTER 15

THE MIDLANDS AND DRAKENSBERG

ABOVE: The rugged peaks and clear streams of the Drakensberg are best explored by hiking one of the many trails that lead up into the mountains. Depicted here is the formation known as the Amphitheatre.

This area is bordered by the Free State to the north, Zululand to the east, Lesotho to the west and the Eastern Cape to the south. It is one of the most beautiful parts of South Africa, featuring the Midlands and the dramatic uKhahlamba Drakensberg Park, a World Heritage Site.

CLIMATE

This is a summer rainfall region, and is quite temperate. Here, away from the ocean, winters are much colder, and there are regular snowfalls in both the Midlands and the high mountains.

FLORA AND FAUNA

The Midlands and Drakensberg fall within the Grasslands biome. Although the term 'grasslands' implies only grass species, only one in six species in the biome is, in fact, a grass. The remainder consist of bulbous plants such as arum lily, orchid, red-hot poker, aloe, watsonia, gladiolius and ground orchid.

The region is renowned for especially eland, which can be seen in the uKhahlamba Drakensberg Park as well as the Umgeni Valley Nature Reserve, and the endangered bearded vulture (lammergeier) in the Drakensberg.

HISTORY AND HERITAGE

This region was largely spared the racial turmoil that gripped the rest of the country, but it had its moments during the first and second Anglo–Boer wars (1880–1881 and 1899–1902).

On 15 July 1842, Pietermaritzburg in the Umzunduze Valley surrendered to the British. It had been the capital of the short-lived Boer republic of Natalia, and would continue as the seat of government in the province.

In 1850 the British government obtained a single-storey Cape Dutch–style house in Pietermaritzburg as residence for the first English governor of Natal, Benjamin Pine. It was from here that the campaigns of the Anglo–Zulu War and first Anglo–Boer War were strategised. After subjugating the Zulu during the Anglo–Zulu War, the British turned their attention on the Boer republic of Transvaal. In 1877 they annexed it, which led to the start of the first Anglo–Boer War (known by the Boers as the War of Independence) on 16 December 1880. After a number of battles the combatants met at Majuba Hill, just inside the Natal border with the Transvaal, on 27 February 1881.

The British commander, Major General Sir George Colley, had occupied the summit of the hill on the previous day, presumably to outflank the Boer positions at Laing's Nek. Colley, who until then was highly regarded, took no artillery with him and did not ask his troops to dig in.

While he assumed the Boers would disperse when they became aware of his position, which was made abundantly clear by Highlanders shouting and waving their fists, they instead organised a storming party led by Nicolaas Smit. Just after midnight the Boers reached the summit and engaged the enemy with tremendous fire while avoiding hand-to-hand combat. This battle led to the British signing a truce on 6 March and a peace treaty two weeks later. But it would soon be the scene of military action with the outbreak of the second Anglo–Boer War in 1899.

Transvaal President Paul Kruger snatched the initiative in October 1899 when British troops were still being rushed to southern Africa and those in the field were outnumbered two to one. To make the most of this advantage the Boers immediately took the offensive on four fronts: north into Rhodesia; west into the northern Cape; south into the northeastern Cape; and east into Natal, where they fought the first battle of the second Anglo–Boer War at Talana Hill near Dundee on 20 October.

The following day the Boers suffered their first defeat at Elandslaagte. In the first five months of the war, however, that setback was a rarity. The Boers swept south and 'Mournful Monday' (30 October) was a bad day for the British, as losses in the vicinity of Ladysmith soared to 1 272 men. Two days later, the Boers pushed Sir George White and his 13 500 men into Ladysmith and laid siege to the town. Ladysmith is best remembered for the slaughter of British troops at Spioenkop on the morning of 24 January 1900.

NOTEWORTHY PLACES
Pietermaritzburg

The old part of the city is the most beautiful. Along streets lined with oak and jacaranda are Gothic Revival and Edwardian and Victorian homes set in lush gardens. It is a favourite of watercolour artists.

BELOW: The graves of those who fell in the famous Battle of Talana can be found in Dundee.

THE TALE OF TWO BISHOPS

Pietermaritzburg was at the centre of a schism that threatened to tear the local Anglican Church apart in the mid-19th century. John Colenso in 1853 was offered the newly created See of Natal by the Bishop of Cape Town, Robert Gray. But he soon came into conflict with the colonial administration, which replaced him with Bishop Macrorie. The problem was that Colenso successfully appealed to the Anglican powers in England, which led to the farcical situation of the small city having two Anglican bishops, each with his own cathedral and a divided congregation that refused to acknowledge or speak to the other.

RIGHT: Gracious Edwardian and Victorian architecture forms a historical backdrop in the busy student town of Pietermaritzburg.

DID YOU KNOW?

The annual Comrades Marathon was started in 1921 by thirty-four runners to commemorate comrades who had fallen in World War I.

It is known by residents as Sleepy Hollow, a most appropriate moniker but for the occasional rousing. Initially established in 1839 by the *trekboers*, Pietermaritzburg slipped into a deep slumber after its conquest by the British – a condition only briefly unsettled by the Anglo–Boer wars. Not that the city was threatened, only that there was an influx of noisy troops to disturb the peace.

Highlights of Pietermaritzburg are a historical walking tour that takes in the city's well-preserved architecture; the Natal Museum, which is the largest national museum in the province; the Railway Museum at Mason's Mill, which features restored locomotives dating back to 1888; the Tatham Art Gallery, considered one of the best galleries in the country; the National Botanical Gardens, which attract a huge variety of bird life; the Butterfly House

SEE:
Pietermaritzburg p. 217
Eastern Cape &
KwaZulu-Natal p. 230
Free State, Mpumalanga
& KwaZulu-Natal p. 238

LEFT: The Howick Falls, located in the KwaZulu-Natal Midlands, is just one of the many spectacular waterfalls found in the area. BELOW LEFT: Quaint guest houses and relaxed B&Bs along the Midlands Meander add to this route's abundant charms. BELOW RIGHT: Although best known for its annual swimming-endurance race, the Midmar Mile, Midmar Dam invites water sports throughout the year.

at Queen Elizabeth Park; and the exquisite Victorian Pavilion in Alexandra Park.

The city is on the edge of the Midlands and is close to all the major natural attractions in the region.

Midlands Meander

The Midlands Meander is one of the most popular tourism routes in the country, stretching from Hilton to Mooi River along the R103, taking in Howick, Lidgetton, Balgowan and Nottingham Road along the way. The route offers arts and crafts, outdoor activities, accommodation and cuisine in a scenic country setting.

Hilton

There are a number of arts and crafts outlets here and a shop and gallery specialising in stained-glass items. In the way of food,

there are several quaint bistros and eateries in the area.

Howick

One of the highlights of Howick is a visit to the Howick Falls, with its dramatic 95-m drop. Nearby, Umgeni Valley Nature Reserve is a great spot for picnics and walks, where there are zebra, antelope, giraffe and more than 270 bird species. Howick is close to Midmar Dam, site of the Midmar Mile endurance swim that takes place in February every year. If you are the adventurous type, then take a drive off to Karkloof Nature Reserve and take part in a canopy tour.

Lidgetton

While meandering towards Balgowan you will pass through the Lidgetton Valley. The

ABOVE: Breathtaking Sani Pass offers an enticing challenge for 4x4 enthusiasts and adventure travellers. RIGHT: Nottingham Road Hotel is a firm favourite among the locals, who spend many a merry night in Notties Pub. Not surprisingly, the town has its own microbrewery – the Nottingham Road Brewing Company.

breweries, can be found at Rawdons Hotel. A few kilometres outside of town is The Stables Wine Estate, which attracts visitors from far and wide during its Vine Budding, Blues, Grape Crushing and Winter Solstice festivals.

acclaimed Ardmore Ceramic Arts studio is situated here, and is worth a visit.

Balgowan
About 30 km from Howick, towards Nottingham Road, lies Michaelhouse, the Anglican Diocesan College of Natal. Founded in 1896, it is one of South Africa's most well-known and prestigious boarding schools. Nearby is the Bosch Hoek Golf & Country Estate, for those who are looking for a bit of golfing rest and recreation.

Nottingham Road
Despite its myriad art galleries, shops and studios, Nottingham Road is famous for one thing: beer! Nottingham Road Brewing Company, one of the country's most successful micro-

Mooi River
The pretty town of Mooi River is a textile and farming hub, and there are many excellent racehorse studs in the vicinity. In the town itself, history buffs should visit the Rhode House Museum, which has exhibits on local farming history. Passing through Mooi River towards Giant's Castle you will find Hartford House, which serves fantastic cuisine in a picturesque setting.

Southern Drakensberg
This area is a mix between the gently undulating landscape of the Midlands and the mountains of the Drakensberg. Major towns are Kokstad, Harding, Ixopo, Underberg, Sani Pass and Himeville. Do not miss the annual Splashy Fen Music Festival at Underberg, usually held around Easter.

The Central Drakensberg

The uKhahlamba Drakensberg Park predominantly occupies the Central Drakensberg. The 243 000-ha area was declared a UNESCO World Heritage Site in 2000 because of its incredibly scenic natural beauty and the rock art paintings that commemorate the San heritage of the area.

The dominant feature of this region is the Drakensberg, which stretches from the Eastern Cape to Mpumalanga. The range was created millions of years ago when an ancient seabed reared up to form a great escarpment that was then sculpted by erosion. It is a scenic wonder, most awesome in the Champagne Valley of the Central Drakensberg.

This is a region that has moved artists through the ages. The San decorated its caves and rock faces with fine rock art, and it galvanised the Tungay family to found the internationally renowned Drakensberg Boys' Choir School in 1967. It is not difficult to see why. At the heart of its attraction is an Eden of gentle, rolling hills and vertical mountain faces, of domes and cowls and spear-like pinnacles, of endless valleys and plunging waterfalls, of giant yellowwoods and dazzling winter snows.

There are numerous hotels and resorts here, including Champagne Castle Hotel, The Nest Drakensberg Resort Hotel, Drakensberg Sun Lifestyle Resort, Champagne Sports Resort, Alpine Heath, Cathedral Peak Hotel and Monk's Cowl, a pretty country lodge known for its golf course and spectacular views of the Champagne Valley.

Northern Drakensberg

The Royal Natal National Park is situated in the uKhahlamba Drakensberg Park, and although it is known as a 'national park' it is actually a provincial park, managed by Ezemvelo KZN Wildlife. The main feature of the park is the spectacular Amphitheatre situated between the Sentinel and the Eastern Buttress of the Drakensberg, with a number of domes, including the largest, Mont-Aux-Sources, rising from a relatively flat plateau.

One of the most spectacular sites found in the Royal Natal National Park are the Thukela Falls (previously known as the Tugela Falls); the spectacular 947-m cascade can be reached by a number of hiking trails. Popular hotels include the Montusi Mountain Lodge and Orion Mont-Aux-Sources Resort. The Northern Drakensberg is the most popular area of the 'Berg.

LEFT: The splendid Valley of a Thousand Hills provides a breathtakingly green landscape as far as the eye can see.
ABOVE: The beautiful statue of Mahatma Gandhi is among several attractions best seen on foot on a walking tour of Pietermaritzburg.

CHAPTER 16

ZULULAND

ABOVE: This poignant memorial commemorates the Battle of Isandlwana, which took place here in 1879.

Bounded by Swaziland and Mpumalanga in the north and the Midlands in the west, the savannah-clad hills and valleys of northeast KwaZulu-Natal are known as the land of the Zulu – the 'People of the Heavens'. Many visitors come here to experience Zulu culture, but there are plenty of other highlights in this region, including some of the best-known battlefield routes in the country.

CLIMATE

Summer brings not only rain but also intense heat to Zululand. By contrast, spring and autumn are more moderate while the winters can get extremely cold.

HISTORY AND HERITAGE

Zululand is where some of South Africa's most

KING SHAKA

Shaka, a great military strategist, was born in 1785. His father was a minor chief and his mother unranked, yet he went on to head up the Zulu nation by conquering the Nguni clans of present-day KwaZulu-Natal. Among his most famous victories were those against the Ndwandwe at Gqoki Hill, and Mhlatuze River. In 1828 Shaka was assassinated by a group that was led by his half-brother Dingane.

famous and bloody battles were fought, and there are numerous battle sites, Zulu cultural villages, British forts and Boer monuments that bear testimony to this turbulent time in the country's history.

THE BATTLE OF ISANDLWANA AND THE DEFENCE OF RORKE'S DRIFT

After the British annexed Natal they let Zululand be for some time, but a desire for a federation of states in southern Africa soon changed their focus. One of the obstacles to this was the existence of the Boer republics and the Zulu kingdom. The Transvaal was annexed in 1877, after which British attention turned to the Zulu under Cetshwayo. The spark for war was provided by border incidents, especially along a disputed strip of land on the Zululand border with Natal, running from Rorke's Drift to the Pongola River. An ultimatum was delivered to Cetshwayo on 11 December 1878.

When Cetshwayo did not respond, Lord Chelmsford invaded Zululand in January the following year. A column advancing from Rorke's Drift encamped at Isandlwana on 20 January under Lieutenant Colonel Henry Pulleine, while Chelmsford moved on to join a reconnaisance party.

Underestimating the Zulu might, and not knowing that 20 000 warriors were advancing, Chelmsford did not order Pulleine to entrench. The Zulu army under Dabulamanzi kaMpande had outmanoeuvred Chelmsford with the intention of attacking the rear of the British forces on 23 January. When their position in the Ngwebeni Valley was detected by a scouting party led by Lieutenant Raw the following day, they decided to go on the offensive. With the Zulu in pursuit, Raw sent a messenger to warn Pulleine that an attack was imminent.

When the Zulu reached Isandlwana, kaMpande arranged his warriors into the traditional attack formation to encircle the British. This involved a strong central force (the chest) and flanking 'horns' that would close around the enemy. Able to see only those impi comprising the chest and right horn, Pulleine miscalculated the mortal threat and decided to meet the Zulu head on, instructing six companies to fan out. Until noon the British appeared to be holding their own against the centre, but then matters changed dramatically.

As soon as Pulleine realised that his soldiers were about to be encircled, he ordered a retreat back to the camp, where the battle continued for three hours before the British were finally overrun. It was the Zulu nation's most glorious moment as assegais and ox-hide shields triumphed over the most modern weaponry of the day. And, while some historians have blamed the British defeat on a shortage of ammunition, it is more likely that Pulleine blundered by spreading his men along too wide a perimeter.

From Isandlwana, a reserve group of 4 000 Zulu soldiers advanced on the nearby trading post and mission at Rorke's Drift, situated at a natural ford over the Buffalo River. Chelmsford had left a member of his staff, Major Spalding, in charge of this small garrison of 139 soldiers when he entered Zululand.

Unaware of the happenings at Isandlwana, Spalding rode out to ascertain the position of one of his companies, placing Lieutenant Chard in temporary command. Chard, a military engineer, was at the drift repairing pontoons when two survivors of Isandlwana, Lieutenants Vaine and Adendorff, rode in to warn of impending attack. A defensive perimeter was hastily constructed and the buildings fortified.

Late that afternoon, news arrived that the Zulu were crossing the river at Fugitive's Drift. This resulted in a number of desertions, effectively halving the British garrison. Soon under furious attack, the tiny British force was able to hold out until four o'clock the next morning, when the Zulu retreated at last.

The defence of Rorke's Drift, considered one of the most noteworthy in history, resulted in the award of 11 Victoria Crosses, as well as several medals for Distinguished Conduct.

ABOVE: The graves at Rorke's Drift are a popular stop along the Battlefields Route.

In 1838 the Battle of Blood River/Ncome took place to avenge the murder of Voortrekker leader, Piet Retief. It was here that the Boers defeated the Zulus and their chief, Dingane, and declared the Republic of Natalia, which included much of present-day KwaZulu-Natal. Some four decades later, this part of the world saw more bloodshed during the Anglo–Zulu War in which the Zulu impis routed the British forces at Isandlwana. In the same year, the British army retaliated and defeated the Zulus at Ulundi.

The second Anglo–Boer War, also known as the South African War, took place from 1899 to 1902. Two of the war's decisive events took place in Zululand: the 118-day siege of Ladysmith, which ended on 28 February 1900, and the Battle of Spioenkop that took place on 23 and 24 January that same year.

FLORA AND FAUNA

Rolling grasslands, thornveld valleys and riverine forests are a feature of the Zululand landscape. This part of the world is known for its exceptional bird life; zebra, giraffe and wildebeest can also be found in various ecoreserves such as the Isibindi Game Reserve near Rorke's Drift. Trout fishing is a popular pastime.

NOTEWORTHY PLACES

Several of the towns in the Zululand region contain notable battlefield sites, the most famous ones being Isandlwana, Rorke's Drift and Fugitive's Drift.

KwaGingindlovu

The small town of KwaGingindlovu was once the place of the military kraal of Cetshwayo,

DID YOU KNOW?

The number of Victoria Crosses awarded for the defence of Rorke's Drift is the most ever for a single action by a single regiment.

and the site of one of the battles of the Anglo–Zulu War. It was named KwaGingindlovu ('the swallower of the elephant') when Cetshwayo defeated his brothers for chieftainship.

Eshowe
Shaka's capital KwaBulawayo was in the vicinity of Eshowe, and Cetshwayo also had a kraal in the area. The fascinating Vukani Collection Museum exhibits an excellent display of Zulu art and culture. The Battle of Nyezane, the opening battle of the Anglo–Zulu War, took place near the town from 22 January to 2 April 1879.

Ulundi
Ulundi was the place where, in 1879, the final phase of the Anglo–Zulu War took place. It was during the Battle of Ulundi that the Brit-

ish army finally defeated the Zulus. In the area was Ondini ('high place'), the site of Cetshwayo's royal residence, which was destroyed during the battle. The remains of Ondini have since been restored, and now form part of the Ondini Historical Complex, which includes the KwaZulu Cultural Museum. You can also visit the graves of King Mpande (Cetshwayo's father), King Dinuzulu (Cetshwayo's son) and Voortrekker leader Piet Retief. For nature lovers, the Ophathe Game Reserve, known for its bird life, is well worth a visit.

Dundee
Named by a coal miner from Dundee in Scotland, this town has the highest concentration of battlefield sites in South Africa. It was here that the Battle of Blood River/Ncome took place

SEE:
Free State, Mpumalanga
& KwaZulu-Natal p. 238
KwaZulu-Natal &
Swaziland p. 239

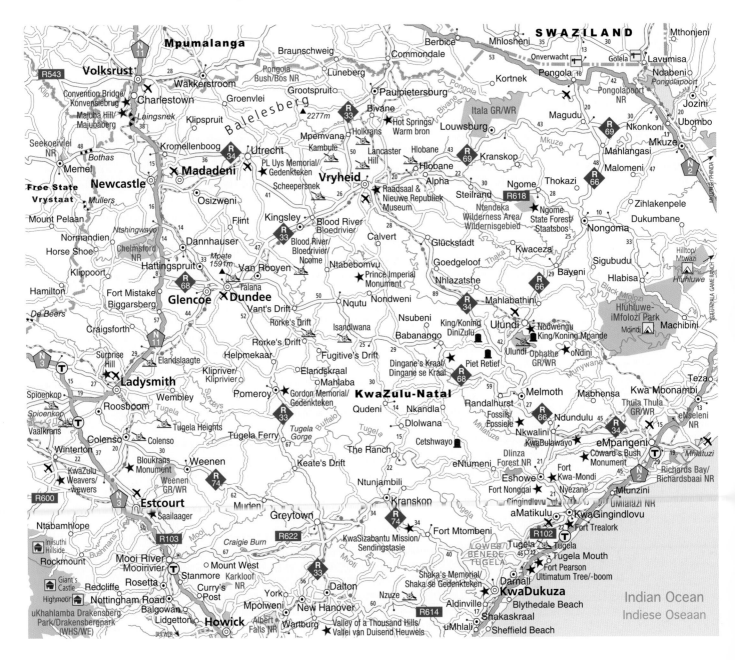

on 16 December 1838. Today one can visit the Blood River Monument where 64 bronze ox-wagons in laager formation commemorate the turbulent events of 1838, and the Ncome Museum, which offers a reinterpretation of the famous clash. In 1998 a memorial was inaugurated for the over 3 000 Zulu soldiers who died in the battle. Other historic battle sites in the area include Talana, Isandlwana and Rorke's Drift.

Vryheid

Vryheid has a multicultural heritage and its battlefield attractions include the Anglo–Zulu War sites of Hlobane and Khambule. The battle of Hlobane, during which Colonel Henry Evelyn Wood and his men suffered a bitter defeat by the Zulus, took place on 28 March 1879.

ACTIVITIES

- Birdwatching in Ophathe Game Reserve in Ulundi
- Champagne cruises on the Pongolapoort Dam near Mkuze
- Game drives in Thula Thula Game Reserve near Richards Bay
- Battlefield tours at Fugitive's Drift, southwest of Dundee
- Fishing at various sites along the Buffalo River

ROUTES AND TRAILS

- Day walks for guests at the Battlefields Country Lodge and Penny Farthing Country House in Dundee
- Izemfene Hiking Trail (2 days) in the Biggarsberg near Glencoe
- Several trails (3 hours–full day) in the Ntendeka Wilderness Area near Vryheid
- Guided tours of Isandlwana (5 hours) and Rorke's Drift (3 hours), from Fugitive's Drift Lodge near Dundee
- Hiking at the Entumeni Nature Reserve outside Eshowe
- Conducted walks at Zulu Nyala Game Ranch near Hluhluwe

There are also Anglo–Boer War sites at Lancaster Hill, Scheepersnek and Holkrans, where an entire Boer commando was defeated just a few days before the peace treaty of 1902 was signed.

In the town itself, a number of historical attractions are worth visiting, including the 1908 Carnegie Public Library, Lucas Meyer House and the Old Raadsaal.

Ladysmith

Ladysmith was besieged by the British from 2 November 1899 to 28 February 1900 during the most crucial stage of the second Anglo–Boer War.

One of the best-loved anecdotes of this town is that on 25 December 1899 the Boers fired a shell containing a Christmas pudding and a note into town, instead of explosives. There are a number of historical buildings and attractions worth visiting, including the All Saints Anglican church, the Castor & Pollux cannons outside the Town Hall, the Court House (1889) and the Lord Vishnu Temple with its statue of Mahatma Gandhi.

Numerous battlefield sites in the vicinity include those at Spioenkop, Vaalkrans, Colenso, Tugela Heights, Elandslaagte and Surprise Hill.

ZULU CULTURE

A once disparate group of clans and chieftainships, the Zulu people were melded into a mighty kingdom in the early 19th century by Shaka, whose spirit lives on to this day.

The Zulu hold their culture in high esteem, observing many old traditions, rituals and ceremonies. They believe that the ancestral spirits (*amadlozi* or *abaphansi*) are essential in their day-to-day lives, while the Supreme Creator, known as uMveliqangi ('the one who came first'), or uNkulunkulu ('the very big one'), is not that intricately involved.

The typical nuclear family (*umndeni*), which still exists in rural Zululand, includes all those people who are related to each other by blood, marriage or adoption. They dwell in a homestead often made up of circular, fenced huts with thatched roofs. A man is always the head of the household and his wife, or wives, and their children will always defer to his authority.

KwaZulu-Natal has a choice of cultural villages where traditional Zulu culture can be experienced. The best known of these is Shakaland, which is on the R66 from Eshowe to Melmoth.

BELOW LEFT: On the site of the infamous Battle of Blood River/Ncome, a laager of 64 bronze ox wagons has been erected, vividly depicting the Boer defence system against the Zulu impis.
BELOW: Following his assassination, King Shaka's corpse was unceremoniously dumped. A memorial in Stanger marks the possible burial site of this great Zulu leader.

CHAPTER 17

THE FREE STATE

ABOVE: Rolling farmlands, big skies, abundant cosmos and rocky outcrops comprise a typically eastern Free State scene.

The Free State is located on the interior plateau in the heart of the country. This province is bounded by the Drakensberg and the Kingdom of Lesotho to the east, the Vaal River to the far north and the Orange River to the south. To the west are the Northern Cape and the North West Province.

It is known as 'the bread basket' of the country, with more than 70% of the country's grain produced here, but despite its thriving agricultural industry it is a laid-back kind of place. Apart from Bloemfontein, there is not much urban life – and it seems the locals like it that way.

Known for cattle, sheep, dairy and wheat farming, the plains of the Free State offer tranquil driving spaces and home-grown hospit-ality. This is the heart of *boerekos* (farm food) country, and big skies and rugby really do rule the day here. On the other end of the cultural spectrum, a township like Botshabelo is definitely worth the detour, as is an informative visit to a cultural village.

CLIMATE

The climate is typical of the interior plateau – winters are cold, rain generally falls in summer and there is lots of sunshine. Bloemfontein's maximum summer temperature is a warm 26 °C and its maximum winter average is 16 °C.

Towns on the Eastern Highlands (Clarens, Harrismith and Bethlehem) and the Golden

Gate Highlands National Park lie at a much higher altitude than the rest of the country, which means that snow falls on mountain peaks during winter and the roads can be icy.

FLORA AND FAUNA

There is a joke that goes if you are lying flat on the ground in the Free State you can see 14 days into the future. The flat interior landscape does, however, boast a wealth of grasslands and magnificent trees such as the sweet thorn. Many tree species are restricted to river banks and valleys, but there are some exceptions. The rare *Psilotum nudum* is an ancient fossil fern, dating back millions of years, that is found in the seepages of sandstone caves in places like the Korannaberg. Typical Karoo-type vegetation is also found in the southwestern Free State, where visitors will see wild pomegranate, red cancer bush and a number of succulents.

When it comes to fauna, the Free State is certainly not Big Five country, but it does have prolific wildlife in sanctuaries such as the Gold-en Gate Highlands National Park and other nature reserves throughout the province.

GOLDEN GATE HIGHLANDS NATIONAL PARK

This 32 608-ha mountainous park, renowned for its imposing cliff faces and breathtaking vistas, is ideal for hiking, abseiling, horse riding and game watching. There are a number of grassland antelope, including black wildebeest, eland, red hartebeest, blesbok, grey rhebok and mountain reedbuck as well as oribi (on the endangered list) and zebra. Cape vulture, the endangered bearded vulture and southern bald ibis are sighted regularly.

HISTORY AND HERITAGE

The wars that swept across southeast Africa and the interior from the 1750s until the late 1830s, known as the Mfecane ('the crushing'), or Difaqane, permanently altered the political structure of African society in much of the region. The series of upheavals triggered by expansionism and battles for power and territory fractured communities and led to the demise of once powerful chiefdoms and the formation of new ones. The southern Highveld, part of present-day Free State, was not immune to the conflict. Here, the Sotho leader Moshoeshoe managed to resist attacks by Difaqane marauders while expanding his influence and consolidating the Sotho nation under his paramountcy. Remnants of various defeated clans who moved into the area joined Moshoeshoe, who gave them refuge in return for protection of his kingdom. The Sotho had lived and farmed in the lowlands between the Caledon River and the Maluti Mountains, before eventually occupying the mountain fastness of Thaba Bosiu in present-day Lesotho.

Also in search of agricultural land were the *trekboers* (migrant stock farmers) who arrived in the central interior in 1824 from the Cape Colony. In 1836, they were followed by the first parties of the Great Trek, escaping British rule in the Cape. The Boers soon clashed with the Ndebele, led by Mzilikazi, who was routed by a combined Afrikaner, Griqua and Barolong force at Mosega. The Ndebele were finally driven out by the Voortrekkers in 1837, and settled in the Matopo Hills in present-day Zimbabwe.

Other newcomers to the region were the British, who sought to impose Her Majesty's rule on the territories across the Orange River. When in 1848 the Governor of the Cape,

BASOTHO CULTURAL VILLAGE

The Basotho Cultural Village in the QwaQwa section of the Golden Gate Highlands National Park provides an authentic perspective on the life and times of the Southern Sotho. There is a living museum that documents traditional homesteads from the early 1700s to the present. Storytelling and traditional games form part of the experience and you can also get to meet the local chief.

LEFT: The iconic sandstone Sentinel, also known as The Brandwag, watches over the Golden Gate Highlands National Park and is a dramatic sight at sunset, when it becomes a canvas of pink, orange and golden hues.

ABOVE: The Gariep Dam is South Africa's largest storage reservoir. RIGHT: Built in 1870 and used to store ammunition, the Kruithuis ('gunpowder house') is located just outside Philippolis.

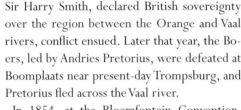

SOTHO CULTURE

Traditionally, the Sotho lived in villages that were organised according to *kgoro* – groups of households clustered along paternal family lines. Houses were built around a central area that also served as a meeting place, cattle kraal and graveyard. These villages, ruled by a chief, could grow to accommodate hundreds of people.

SEE:
Bloemfontein p. 216
Eastern Cape & Free State p. 228
Eastern Cape & Lesotho p. 229
Free State & North West p. 236
Free State & Gauteng p. 237

Sir Harry Smith, declared British sovereignty over the region between the Orange and Vaal rivers, conflict ensued. Later that year, the Boers, led by Andries Pretorius, were defeated at Boomplaats near present-day Trompsburg, and Pretorius fled across the Vaal river.

In 1854, at the Bloemfontein Convention, Britain granted the Boers independence in the Orange River Sovereignty, paving the way for the establishment of the Orange Free State republic. The convention precipitated a series of wars, with disagreements over the boundaries of the new republic and competing land claims being the main sources of strife. Increasingly desperate, Moshoeshoe appealed to the British for protection, and in 1868 the British annexed what was left of the land belonging to the Sotho as the Basutoland protectorate.

By the time the second Anglo–Boer War (also known as the South African War) broke out in 1899, Basutoland was under direct rule from Britain, protecting the mountain kingdom from being drawn into the escalating conflict between the British and the Boers.

In an effort to contain the Anglo–Boer War, British commander-in-chief, Lord Kitchener,

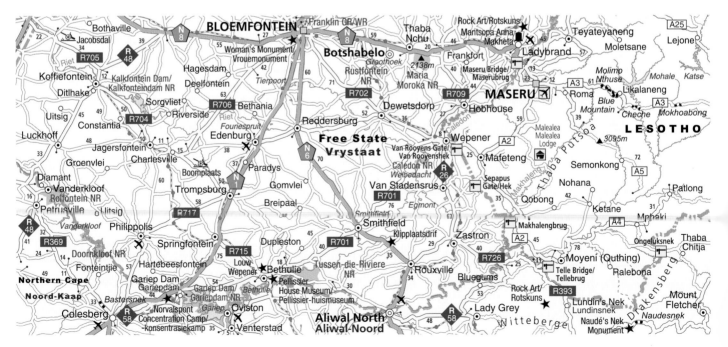

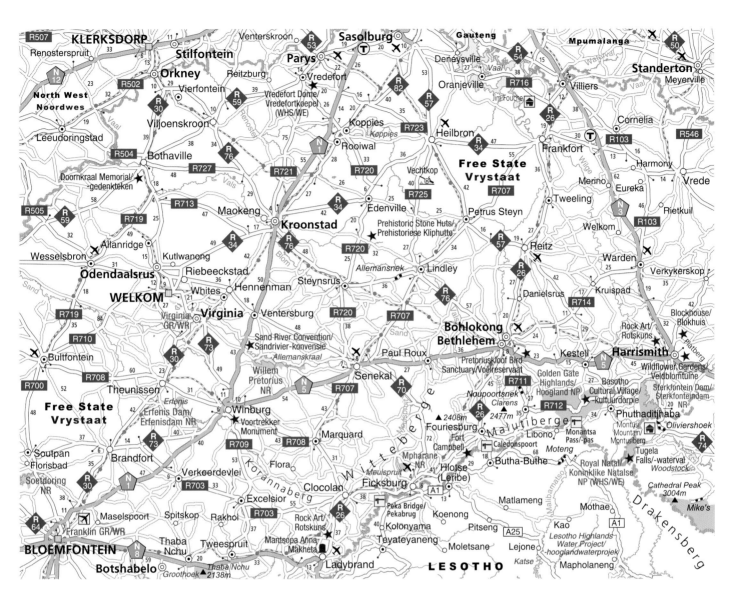

introduced the notorious scorched-earth policy in March 1901. The intention was to sweep the country bare of anything that could sustain the Boers, including burning their farmsteads and destroying their crops. The English forces deported women, children and black farm assistants to concentration camps, where thousands of them succumbed to illness in poor living conditions. Many of these camps were in the Free State. At the end of the Anglo–Boer War, Bloemfontein was made the capital of the Orange River Colony. When the Union of South Africa was proclaimed in 1910, Bloemfontein became the judicial capital of the country.

NOTEWORTHY PLACES
Gariep Dam

The Gariep Dam, formerly known as Hendrik Verwoerd Dam, is the largest reservoir in the country. Now a popular place for water sports and outdoor activities, the town of Gariep Dam is one of the newest in South Africa. Attractions include the Gariep Dam Nature Reserve and a fish hatchery. A short distance from the town is the Norvalspont Concentration Camp, which was laid out in February 1901 and closed down in October 1902.

Philippolis

Once a missionary outpost, Philippolis is the oldest settlement in the Free State. In 1822 a small Griqua community, under Adam Kok III, joined other groups already living here and the town began to thrive. However, in 1862 the government of the Republic of the Orange Free State bought all the land owned by the Griqua for £4000. The Griqua people left and eventually settled near present-day Kokstad. Attractions include the Adam Kok House, Gariep Museum, historic cannons, and the Van Der Post Memorial Garden. Visitors can also spend the night in the Philippolis Old Gaol.

SEE:
Bloemfontein p. 216
Free State & North West p. 236
Free State & Gauteng p. 237
Free State, Mpumalanga & KwaZulu-Natal p. 238

DID YOU KNOW?

Every year the Philippolis Witblits Festival is held in March or April, and the entire town celebrates the local moonshine that kicks like a mule. Lots of fun activities are on offer for the whole family at this time.

ABOVE LEFT: The city of Bloemfontein is home to the Supreme Court of Appeal, and is also South Africa's judicial capital. ABOVE RIGHT: Sunflower fields are found across the Thaba Nchu region.

SANDSTONE ARCHITECTURE

There are a number of interesting sandstone buildings worth visiting, such as the Nagmaal Cottage in Fouriesburg and the Dutch Reformed churches in Ficksburg and Ladybrand.

Bethulie

This small town was founded in 1929 as a French mission station, and is now best known as the birthplace of local actor Patrick Mynhardt (1932–2007), famous for his one-man show *Boy from Bethulie* and for portraying the Herman Charles Bosman character Oom Schalk Lourens on stage. The DH Steyn sandstone bridge is impressive and there are a number of historical landmarks including the Dutch Reformed church (1887), South African War Concentration Camp (1899–1902), Louw Wepener Monument, Ox-Wagon Monument and Pellissier House Museum. There is also the Tussen-die-Riviere Nature Reserve for game viewing.

Smithfield

Smithfield is something of an artists' haven. It is an eclectic place and even has a UFO sighting centre. Activities and attractions include San rock art, the Basotho War Memorial located in front of the City Hall, the Caledon River Museum, General De Wet House and Market Square.

Jagersfontein

Jagersfontein was once the property of Jacobus Jagers, a Griqua farmer. In the 1870s the farm was declared open for public diggings after a 50-carat diamond was found here. In 1873, Jagersfontein yielded the 972-carat Excelsior diamond and in 1895 the 637-carat Reitz dia-

mond was also found here. Although there is no mining today, Jagersfontein still has the feel of a pioneer town. Visit the Open Mine Museum and the Old Mine. There is also the three-day Diggers Groot Gat Hiking Trail.

Bloemfontein

Bloemfontein, the epicentre of the Motheo region, is the Free State's capital city and South Africa's judicial capital. There are a number of examples of historical architecture, such as the imposing City Hall, the 1849 First *Raadsaal* (parliament), the 1892 Fourth *Raadsaal*, the fascinating National Museum and the celebrated Oliewenhuis Art Museum.

The history of the Anglo-Boer conflict is explored at the famous Anglo–Boer War Museum in Bloemfontein. A series of art collections, dioramas and exhibits highlights the causes of the war and its development, and provides a glimpse into life in the concentration and prisoner-of-war camps. Adjacent to the museum is the Women's Memorial. Erected in 1913, it is dedicated 'to the glorious memory of the mothers, women and children, who, during the recent war, passed away, or had otherwise suffered bitterly, either in the concentration camps or outside'.

For great views of the town (and a good spot for sundowners) go to Naval Hill, the site of an old observatory built in 1927 and the Franklin Game Reserve established in 1928. For restaurants, shops and entertainment under one roof, the Loch Logan Waterfront is a good choice.

To the northeast of the city is the scenic Soetdoring Nature Reserve, a 7 500-ha reserve that is home to an array of plants and birds. African wild dog and lion can be found at the predator park.

DID YOU KNOW?

At King's Park there are over 4000 rose bushes, which is why Bloemfontein is also known as the 'City of Roses'.

Botshabelo

Head along the N8 for some 45 km to reach Botshabelo, the second largest township in South Africa. Visit the Botshabelo library to see Sotho arts and crafts exhibitions, as well as Onverwacht farm, which was the very first settlement in Botshabelo. For rest and relaxation there is the Rustfontein Nature Reserve where visitors can enjoy boating, angling and game drives.

Thaba Nchu

To the east of Bloemfontein is Thaba Nchu, meaning 'black mountain'. At the heart of this settlement is the 2 138-m-high Thaba Nchu Mountain, once the stronghold of the Barolong people. There are a few notable attractions here including the Wesleyan mission station, which houses Chief Moroka's grave, Moroka House, the Mabana Cultural Centre and a number of arts and crafts outlets. There are also plaques marking the trails made by Voortrekkers during the Great Trek. For nature lovers, there is the Maria Moroka Nature Reserve. Known for its bird- and wildlife species, it also incorporates the Groothoek Dam.

Ladybrand

Situated 18km from Maseru and founded in 1867 after the Basotho wars, Ladybrand has a fascinating history, which is recounted in various exhibits at the local Heritage Museum. The Ladybrand area is famous for its many rock-art sites, including the paintings that can be seen on the walls of the Modderpoort and Tandjiesberg caves.

Modderpoort, just outside Ladybrand, is famous for the Cave Church, also known as the Rose Chapel, a shelter once occupied by the San and now used as a pilgrimage site. The grave of the Sotho prophetess Mantsopa Makheta is also worth a visit.

Clocolan

Clocolan was once home to the Basotho, who were driven out of the area in the early 1800s. This quaint town, laid out in 1906, is an important farming centre; wheat, maize, sunflowers and asparagus are all farmed in the vicinity. Visitors can take a tour of the Deemsters Asparagus Factory.

Great examples of San rock art can be seen at the De Hoek and Nebo farms, while in town more contemporary creations are produced by numerous arts and crafts projects.

Ficksburg

The annual Cherry Festival takes place every year during November in the small town of Ficksburg, where fun and festivities are the order of the day. Ficksburg has a number of interesting attractions; the Ficksburg Jail and the Fick Memorial, as well as numerous rock-art sites on surrounding farms, are all worth a visit. There is also the Meulspruit Dam and the Mpharane Nature Reserve, and a number of outdoor activities including hiking, game viewing, trout fishing and mountain biking are available.

Clarens

Sitting in the foothills of the Maluti Mountains, Clarens is framed by sandstone peaks. Fittingly called 'Jewel of the Free State', this charming little town has become a haven for artists, whose work can be viewed at the numerous galleries that make up the Artists' Amble. A gallery of a different kind, the cave at Schaap-

ABOVE LEFT: All sorts of fascinating shops can be found in Ficksburg, including the Blik Plek where everything has been made out of recycled goods. ABOVE RIGHT: Ladybrand is renowned for its sandstone architecture and elegant historic buildings that date back to the early 1900s.

DID YOU KNOW?

The suburb of Dikgareteng ('place of curtains') in Mangaung township near Bloemfontein got its name from the then government's attempt to build a buffer line of smart houses along the route of the Royal Visit in 1947. Township residents dismissed this window-dressing as the 'curtains' hiding poverty and squalid conditions of the area.

plaats Farm is adorned with San rock paintings. Surrender Hill, a historic second Anglo–Boer War site, is nearby (en route to Fouriesburg). The Fertility Cave near Surrender Hill is used by sangomas who believe that it has special healing powers. The traditional healers live in the cave and drink the 'holy water' that drips from cracks in the rocks. During February and October, people come here to seek their curative powers.

Harrismith

Founded in 1849 by Sir Harry Smith, the town of Harrismith is surrounded by hills and is something of an economic crossroads in the Free State. The Platberg ('flat mountain') sits at 2377 m and is the town's visual landmark. For outdoor enthusiasts, the Sterkfontein Dam (the third-largest dam in the country) is an excellent spot for fishing and water sports and is surrounded by the Sterkfontein Dam Nature Reserve. Other attractions include Anglo–Boer War memorials, the Debora Retief Garden with its 250-million-year-old fossilised tree and the Harrismith Wildflower Gardens that contain 20% of the region's plant species and an Anglo–Boer war blockhouse.

Bethlehem

Situated at the foot of the Maluti Mountains, Bethlehem ('house of bread') falls into the Thabo Mofutsanyana District, and it is the commercial centre of the area. This is wheat country and the region produces 65% of the country's crop, which is how the town got its name. The Ash River flows alongside the town and it is a favourite spot for canoeists and water-sport enthusiasts. For history buffs, there are numerous sites worth visiting including the Battle of Bethlehem Monument, the Nazareth Mission church (housing Bethlehem Museum), the Sol Plaatje Memorial and Baartman House, which among other things has exhibits of wagons and horse carriages. There is a delightful walk that goes past numerous sandstone buildings, many of which are heritage sites.

Frankfort

Located on the banks of the Wilge River, Frankfort offers Edwardian architecture and a decidedly homely atmosphere with something of a resort feel. The Wilge River is the place for dinghy adventures, and there are also 4x4 options.

Parys

The story goes that Parys was named by a German land surveyor who said that the Vaal River reminded him of the River Seine in Paris – but this is where the resemblance between this town and its famous namesake ends. You can, however, visit the mini Eiffel Tower outside the Parys Information and Tourism office on Water

RIGHT: The little town of Parys is a great weekend getaway for visitors from Johannesburg and Pretoria in search of some R&R. FAR RIGHT: Clarens has a wonderful bohemian atmosphere, with its fun arts and crafts shops, galleries and eateries.

VAAL DAM

The Vaal Dam is popular for sailing, angling, yachting and all manner of water sports. Deneysville, in particular, is known for its yachting enthusiasts.

ACTIVITIES

- Horse riding safaris (2 hours–10 days) with Bokpoort Horse Safaris in Bokpoort, just outside of Clarens
- River rafting on the Ash River near Clarens
- Hot-air ballooning over Clarens
- Pony trekking in the Maluti Mountains
- Boating, angling and game drives at Rustfontein Nature Reserve near Botshabelo
- Game viewing and birdwatching at the Maria Moroka Nature Reserve near Thaba Nchu
- Fishing at the Meulspruit Dam in Ficksburg

ROUTES AND TRAILS

- The Sandstone Route stretches from Clarens to Ladybrand
- Waterkloof Hiking Trail (2 days) near Ficksburg
- The Rhebok Trail (2 days) in the Golden Gate Highlands National Park
- Dome trails (1–2 days), a canoe trail and a mountain-bike route at Vredefort Dome
- Diggers Groot Gat Hiking Trail (3 days) at Jagersfontein

Street and inspect a second miniature replica of the tower as well as a mini version of the Arc de Triomphe on Karl Preller Avenue.

Parys may not be a cosmopolitan city, but it is a great getaway destination and is growing as an arty hideaway for stressed-out city dwellers. Water sports are popular here too, and there are numerous accommodation options including B & Bs and guest houses. There are also good restaurants.

Parys lies near the centre of the Vredefort Dome, an enormous impact crater that dates back some two billion years, making it the oldest meteoric impact site in the world. With a radius of 190 km, it is also one of the largest on earth. The Vredefort Dome was declared a World Heritage Site in 2005.

Vredefort

Like Parys, Vredefort is situated in the Vredefort Dome World Heritage Site. It is a small mining town that is known for its adventure activities as well as San rock art.

Kroonstad

Just two hours from Gauteng, Kroonstad is a growing town and a wealthy agricultural area. It is at the heart of the region's agricultural industry and is also known for its fishing opportunities on the Vals River.

Virginia

A quaint town on the banks of the Sand River, Virginia got its name by courtesy of a few railway surveyors who etched the name of their birth town on a boulder here. There are a few fun activities in town including a trip to the Virginia Game Reserve, a tour of a nearby gold mine and a visit to a biltong factory. There are also several hiking trails, such as the Hamerkop and Paradise Flycatcher trails.

Welkom

Welkom is the principal town in this area and the second largest in the Free State. It flourished after gold was discovered on the farm Welkom in 1946. Attractions include the Clock Tower, the Gold Museum, the Welkom Museum, the Flamingo Pan and the Ernest Oppenheimer Theatre.

A number of parks add greenery to the city. Situated just outside the town is the Oppenheimer Park Golf Course. The Phakisa Freeway with its Grand Prix racing circuit is also situated in Welkom.

TOP: The Vaal Dam, fed by the Vaal and the Wilge rivers, was constructed in 1938.
ABOVE LEFT: The Vaal River near Parys offers grade one, two and three level rapids, so there is something for everyone.

CHAPTER 18

GAUTENG

ABOVE: Paul Kruger, affectionately called 'Oom Paul', presides over Church Square in Pretoria.

DID YOU KNOW?

The Witwatersrand gold-fields are estimated to be 30 times richer than any others, anywhere on earth.

Surrounded by Limpopo, Free State, Mpumalanga and North West Province, Gauteng may be South Africa's smallest province, but it is the country's economic powerhouse. It is broken by the ridges of the Witwatersrand, which form the watershed between the Indian Ocean in the east and the Atlantic in the west. Below its surface lie magnificent treasures, from the largest diamonds ever found to reefs of ore containing the world's greatest gold deposits.

But Gauteng is not just about mineral wealth, as it is here, more than three million years ago, that pre-human Australopithecines or southern ape-men roamed southern Africa. Now the search for the roots of human existence is focused on the cave system beneath the Sterkfontein Valley, which is part of the Cradle of Humankind World Heritage Site near Johannesburg.

It is also in Gauteng that apartheid took form and the struggle against it was rooted. That is now in the past; today, Gauteng is characterised by a fantastic urban vibe, cultural routes and ecotourism opportunities.

CLIMATE

Gauteng has a temperate climate, making it a year-round destination. It enjoys summer rainfall with frequent spectacular thunderstorms. It rarely receives snow, but winter frost is common.

FLORA AND FAUNA

Gauteng has very little open space with most of the land being covered by urban sprawl. Bankenveld vegetation, which is typical of Highveld grasslands, is well conserved in the Cradle of Humankind. Most of the province's endemic plant species are conserved in the botanical gardens in Pretoria, Johannesburg and Kloofendal. There are 27 animal species in the province, many of them threatened.

HISTORY AND HERITAGE –
JOHANNESBURG

'I come from the newly discovered goldfields at Kliprivier, especially from a farm owned by a certain Gert Oosthuizen,' declared George Harrison on 24 July 1886 in an affidavit to the Pretoria Mines Department. 'I have long experience as an Australian gold digger, and I think it is a payable goldfield.'

SPEND TIME IN A MUSEUM

Johannesburg and Pretoria are home to three national museums: the Transvaal Museum of Natural History and the African Window in Pretoria, and the South African National Museum of Military History in Johannesburg. With 5 million objects, the African Window has the largest collection of artefacts and records in South Africa.

There are numerous other, smaller institutions focusing on everything from fashion to photography.

Within months of this discovery the landscape was strewn with wagons and tents organised in camps along streams and interconnected by a trail that would later become Commissioner Street. In its first few years, the place was more of an Eldorado – a temporary mining camp where you got rich quickly before the gold petered out, as it had done everywhere else. In 1889 it was found that the character of the ore at a depth of about 100 m changed and traditional forms of gold recovery were no longer effective. Thanks mainly to the effectiveness of the MacArthur Forrest process of cyanide extraction and advances in technology to permit deep-level mining, Johannesburg was able to bounce back. This required even more financing, and the pioneers of yore were quickly replaced by engineers and other professionals, giving the fledgling city a more settled character.

No city on earth grew faster, but not everyone benefited. With the fortune seekers came black people in search of work. Matters for them were complicated; the discovery of diamonds and gold in the last three decades of the 19th century wrought overwhelming changes. Prior to 1870 most black South Africans lived in independent chiefdoms, but as tribal lands were absorbed by British colonisers and Boer settlers, so black people lost their freedom and the ability to support themselves independently. The only way to prevent starvation was to provide cheap labour to white farmers and industrialists.

DID YOU KNOW?
The Old Fort is the only prison in the world where two international peace icons were once incarcerated – Nelson Mandela and Mahatma Gandhi.

BELOW LEFT: Gold Reef City, a theme park based on Johannesburg's gold rush days, is one of the city's most popular attractions. BELOW RIGHT: Founded upon the discovery of gold, Johannesburg soon developed from a makeshift shantytown into a bustling metropolis.

OPPOSITE (CLOCK-WISE FROM TOP): Johannesburg is rich in Struggle history and there are a number of attractions that should not be missed, including the Hector Peterson Museum in Soweto; Constitution Hill, home of the Constitutional Court of South Africa; Walter Sisulu Square in the heart of Kliptown where the Freedom Charter was signed in 1955; and the world-class Apartheid Museum, just across the way from Gold Reef City.

Not all employers were able to house their workers on the premises; some moved into servants' quarters in the backyards of their white employers while others found accommodation in the teeming, rat-infested inner-city slums. The most notorious of these was the multiracial Brickfields, adjacent to the busy brick manufacturing works along the Fordsburg Spruit, in the western quadrant of the city. An outbreak of bubonic plague in 1904 presented the Johannesburg City Council with the opportunity to clear this 'den' and move the 1 358 black residents 13 km from Johannesburg to Klipspruit, which would later become Pimville and eventually Soweto.

Brickfields was burnt to the ground and the district renamed Newtown. A produce and livestock market, a mill, an abattoir and a power station were erected in what soon became the trading hub of the city.

HISTORY AND HERITAGE – SOWETO

Soweto became a symbol of oppression during apartheid because of its history, size and struggles. By law, no black people were permitted to live in Johannesburg after the founding of So-

weto, situated in the bowl of the municipal sewage works (cynically chosen because it was the one piece of land that would be of no interest to whites). Life for black people became more complex and more ferocious when the National Party came to power in 1948, driven by a political vision that marginalised black people as the providers of cheap manual labour.

This provided fertile ground for the African National Congress Youth League (ANCYL), which appealed to the hundreds of thousands of educated urban black youths. To counter white repression, it advocated a plan of action that included boycotts, passive resistance, strikes, civil disobedience and work stayaways. As the campaign escalated, so repressive measures intensified.

It was through this campaign of resistance that the leaders of the ANC Youth League changed the direction of the ANC to a mass-based movement intent on liberation. On 25 and 26 June 1955 thousands of delegates from the ANC, South African Indian Congress, Coloured People's Organisation and the mainly white Congress of Democrats met on a dusty field in Kliptown, a multiracial, freehold area originally intended as

SEE:
Johannesburg p. 213
Pretoria p. 214
Free State & Gauteng p. 237
Limpopo, North West & Gauteng p. 245

DID YOU KNOW?
Hastings Ndlovu, a Soweto student leader, was the first person killed during the Soweto Uprising, not Hector Peterson as is commonly believed.

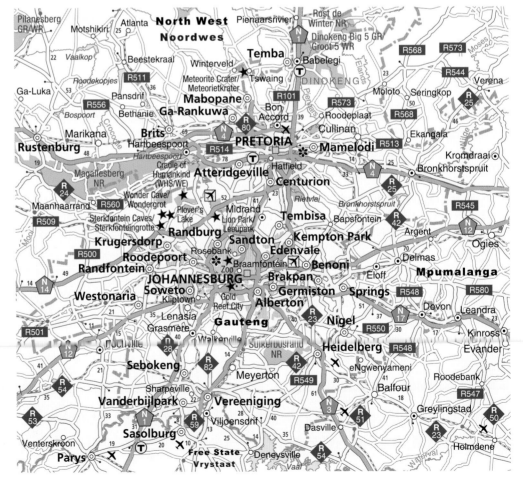

STRUGGLE FOR FREEDOM SITES

The Apartheid Museum

The policy of apartheid led to growing resistance, which brought greater oppression and a reign of terror by the security establishment. The struggle for freedom is the focus of the Apartheid Museum at Gold Reef City, between Johannesburg and Soweto. Set in 7 ha of superbly landscaped grounds, it has 22 exhibition areas designed by a team of curators, filmmakers and historians. Film footage, text panels and artefacts are arranged in such a way as to recreate the experience of what it was like to live under apartheid. There are conference facilities, a shop and coffee shop while next door is a fun theme park and Gold Reef City, a recreation of early Johannesburg.

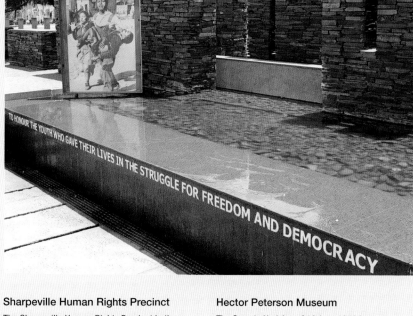

Sharpeville Human Rights Precinct

The Sharpeville Human Rights Precinct in the Vereeniging township of Sharpeville is a memorial to victims of the 21 March 1960 massacre in which 69 protesters were shot dead and at least 180 wounded when police opened fire on anti-pass protesters.

Liliesleaf Farm

Liliesleaf Farm was, for many years, a meeting place and hideout for top ANC and South African Communist Party members. It is widely regarded as the birthplace of the ANC's military wing, Umkhonto weSizwe (MK), and was the site of the infamous police raid that resulted in the Rivonia Trials and eventual incarceration of many senior ANC leaders, including Nelson Mandela (who was not arrested in the raid), Govan Mbeki, Ahmed Kathrada, Raymond Mhlaba and Walter Sisulu.

Hector Peterson Museum

The Soweto Uprising of 16 June 1976 is remembered at the Hector Peterson Museum, the premier heritage site in Soweto. Situated in Orlando West on Khumalo Street, a short distance from where the shootings took place, it is a double-storey red-brick building with a memorial to Hector Peterson in the same grounds. From here it is a short walk along a tree-lined avenue to the fine restaurants and Mandela House in Vilakazi Street.

Constitution Hill

Constitution Hill, between Braamfontein and Hillbrow in Johannesburg, is a human rights precinct and world-class heritage tourist attraction incorporating cultural, historical, artistic, educational and recreational spaces that celebrate South Africa's ability to negotiate a peaceful transition to democracy. It is also the home of the South African Constitutional Court, which was opened on 21 March 2004. The complex includes a coffee shop, bookshop, tourist office and exhibition spaces.

Walter Sisulu Square of Dedication

By the advent of democracy in April 1994, much of Kliptown had become derelict. Due to the national significance of the signing of the Freedom Charter, an urban regeneration and business tourism project, known as The Greater Kliptown Regeneration Development, was initiated to transform the township and establish it as a major national and international heritage site. Its showpiece is the Walter Sisulu Square of Dedication, a site symbolising the right to freedom. As a place of the people, it incorporates informal traders, shops, art galleries and a luxury hotel. Holiday Inn Soweto Freedom Square, decorated with embroidery by local artists and photographs by Alf Kumalo, offers 46 rooms, 2 suites, boardrooms and a jazzy restaurant.

a buffer between Soweto and Johannesburg. Its cosmopolitan aspect allowed a certain degree of freedom and mobility, even after the advent of apartheid, and it was for this reason that it was chosen as the site for the convention. Described by ANC president Chief Albert Luthuli as 'a people's parliament', the Congress of the People adopted the Freedom Charter, which is now the cornerstone of the Bill of Rights and the South African Constitution. The Freedom Charter declared that 'South Africa belongs to all who live in it, black and white, and that no government can justly claim authority unless it is based on the will of all the people'.

But Soweto is best known for the children's revolt that changed the course of history. Soon after coming to power the National Party introduced Bantu Education, which was placed under Hendrik Verwoerd's Ministry of Native Affairs. This schooling was appallingly sub-standard – designed only to provide the most basic numeracy and literacy skills necessary for the increasingly technical demands of modern industry. For black children the school system provided an opportunity for solidarity and the sharing of ideas for liberation, fanned by the authorities' misguided attempts to make Afrikaans the compulsory teaching medium in black schools after Grade 3 – a decree that was to mobilise decisive resistance.

On the frosty morning of Wednesday, 16 June 1976, scholars assembled in school

TSWAING METEORITE CRATER

Situated 40 km northwest of Pretoria, the Tswaing Meteorite is one of the best-preserved meteorite craters in the world. Artefacts of the Later Stone Age have been found there.

grounds to sing *Nkosi Sikelel i'Afrika* before beginning their march to Orlando Stadium, where a protest against Afrikaans was to be held. On the way, at a rocky knoll not far from Phefeni Junior Secondary School, schoolboy Hector Peterson joined several thousand scholars led by Hastings Ndlovu. Facing them was a police patrol consisting of 48 policemen, 4 police cars, 3 anti-riot vehicles and 2 vans carrying dogs. The standoff ended with the police opening fire on the scholars, killing Ndlovu and Peterson.

It took a dumbfounded moment for the enormity of the brutal police action to sink in – then all hell broke loose, unleashing the Soweto Uprising. It was the single most important moment in South African history as it mortally wounded the apartheid beast. The uprising inspired black people countrywide, motivated workers, boosted liberation movements, forever changed the perception of white South Africa and sowed panic in National Party ranks.

HISTORY AND HERITAGE – PRETORIA

For over 150 years Pretoria was at the heart of South Africa's torment. As the executive capi-

GAUTENG NIGHTLIFE

Johannesburg and Pretoria offer a number of noteworthy nightlife spots. In Johannesburg, start out with cocktails at The Westcliff Hotel (overlooking the city's green belt), followed by dinner in Parkhurst, Parktown North or Norwood, where alfresco dining is the norm. If you are up for a big night out, Newtown has a range of jazz clubs, music lounges and bars worth discovering. An evening at one of the many taverns or restaurants in Soweto is also an option. In the north, Rivonia, Rosebank and Sandton have lots of late-night venues. Pretoria also has a number of notable nightspots and a thriving gay scene. For pubs, bars and restaurants in one spot, visit the suburb of Hatfield.

tal, between 1948 and 1994, it earned notoriety as the symbol of Grand Apartheid.

When the first white people arrived in 1829, the region where Pretoria now stands was occupied by Mzilikazi, a breakaway Zulu chief who founded the Matabele nation. Between then and 1854, Boers settled the area that was to become Irene. That year Commandant-General Marthinus Wessel Pretorius, the son of the Hero of Blood River, Andries Pretorius, purchased land at Elandspoort for a *kerkplaas* ('church farm') to serve the central Boer Zuid-Afrikaansche Republiek, or Transvaal Republic. Within a year a town had begun developing round the church square and it was christened Pretoria Philadelphia, later shortened to Pretoria.

Pretoria would have remained a small town had gold not been discovered 80 km to the south on the Witwatersrand in 1886, heralding the greatest gold rush ever. While the pious Boers in the capital looked on in horror as a veritable Gomorrah mushroomed on their doorstep, the wealth generated allowed them to transform Pretoria into the elegant city it is today.

But the new wealth brought with it turbulence and insecurity as imperial Britain cast its rapacious eye on the goldfields. Soon, the region was engulfed in the cataclysmic second Anglo-Boer War (also known as the South African War), the first phase culminating in Field Marshal Lord Roberts entering Pretoria at two o'clock in the afternoon of 5 June 1900. However, the fall of the city did not herald the end of the war, but the start of a guerrilla phase that would continue for another two years.

Pretoria would once again rise to prominence in 1910 when it was selected as the executive or administrative capital of the new union. In mark of this honour, the streets were planted with avenues of alien jacarandas, and Herbert Baker, the celebrated architect, was commissioned to find a suitable site and design and build a grand edifice.

He eventually settled on Meintjieskop, where he constructed the Union Buildings, a semicircular colonnaded acropolis that incorporates a natural amphitheatre.

ABOVE LEFT: A 6-m-high statue of Nelson Mandela greets visitors to Sandton's Nelson Mandela Square shopping centre. TOP: Sidewalk hawkers offer their wares in Newtown Precinct. ABOVE RIGHT: The Market Theatre in Newtown is at the heart of Jozi's cultural epicentre.

NOTEWORTHY PLACES
Johannesburg

Some love it, others hate it. The only thing on which everyone agrees is that the city has a spirited, swashbuckling character. Johannesburg is the wealthiest city in South Africa, and the hub of the country's commercial, financial, industrial and mining activities.

For the arty, the biggest gallery on the subcontinent, the Johannesburg Art Gallery, is worth a visit. The gallery is housed in a three-storey building and is a national monument. There are 15 exhibition halls with temporary displays and permanent exhibitions. The notable South African collection boasts names such as Gerard Sekoto, Sydney Kumalo, Ezrom Legae and Alexis Preller.

Zoo Lake, close to the Johannesburg Zoo, is a fun destination for families on weekends. The grounds are extensive and the popular Moyo restaurant is located here. Regular events are held at the lake, including cycling marathons, art-in-the-park exhibitions and live jazz concerts.

The Johannesburg Botanic Garden, adjacent to Emmarentia Dam, is a great place for picnics and walks. Canoeists and kayakers enjoy the dam and families visit on weekends to feed the ducks and relax in the sunshine. The Johannesburg Botanic Garden is renowned for its roses and also stages regular musical concerts.

Lion Park, where over 80 lions, including the white lions of Timbavati can be viewed, is situated close to Lanseria Airport and is within easy reach of both Pretoria and Johannesburg. There are also other predators such as brown, spotted and striped hyaena, as well as wild dog and cheetah. Travellers can take a self-drive through the park or go on a guided game drive. Cub World is a real highlight for the children, giving them the opportunity to interact with lion cubs.

Newtown and the Cultural Arc

Once a dilapidated corner of the Johannesburg inner city, Newtown is today a bustling centre of creativity. In the 1980s the renowned Market Theatre, the first nonracial theatre in Johannesburg, opened in the east wing of what used to be the old market building. It was followed by the Dance Factory and MuseuMAfricA in the same complex. Other developments in the dis-

BELOW LEFT: A progression of skulls illustrates human evolution. BELOW RIGHT: Little Foot, a relatively complete fossil hominid skeleton, is said to be 3,3 million years old, which makes it a candidate for the ancestor of humanity.

ARCHAEOLOGICAL TRIUMPHS

On 24 November 1924, two boxes were mailed by the Northern Lime Company at Taung in the present North West Province to Professor Raymond Dart, head of the University of the Witwatersrand's (WITS) Department of Anatomy. From the second box emerged 'a face which would look out onto the world after an age-long sleep of nearly a million years'. It was that of a child with a full set of milk teeth and its first molars just erupting. Its unique mixture of ape and human characteristics convinced Dart that this creature had to be somewhere between humans and the rest of the anthropoid apes on the evolutionary family tree. He named the fossil *Australopithecus africanus*, meaning southern ape of Africa; the skull is more commonly known as the Taung Child.

One of the few scientists who supported Dart, Dr Robert Broom, made some enquiries about the limestone mines and caves in the vicinity of Pretoria and Johannesburg, which had been mined for decades. Within a week he found fragmentary fossil evidence of *Australopithecus* at Sterkfontein. But it was not until 18 April 1947 that he would find an almost perfect adult ape-man skull – a discovery nicknamed Mrs Ples that would rank alongside the Taung Child.

Australopithecus was an immensely strong, dark-skinned creature with a skeleton shorter but remarkably similar to ours. It had an apelike face with jutting jaw, human-like teeth, heavy brow, flaring cheeks, and a brain a third the size of ours.

As the *Australopithecus* evolved so did the Sterkfontein Caves, which were slowly opening to the surface as the dolomite was dissolved by water. It is believed the caves first opened 3,5 million years ago, and rather than provide shelter they seem to have been death traps for creatures, including the *Australopithecus* dubbed Little Foot who fell into the Silberberg Grotto.

Over thousands of years Little Foot was buried under debris that fell or was washed into the grotto. Then came the find by Dr Ron Clarke of the WITS Palaeoanthropology Research Group. By chance, in 1994, he found foot bones among a box of sundry fossils at WITS. These were a revelation in that they represented the oldest hominid fossils found at Sterkfontein.

In June 1997, Clarke announced his discovery and stated his belief that the rest of the skeleton was encased in the breccia of Silberberg Grotto. At the end of that month he gave a cast of the foot to two fossil preparatories, Nkwane Molefe and Stephen Motsumi, and asked them to search the cave for the exact embedded match. What they found was a virtually complete skeleton of a 3,33-million-year-old *Australopithecus* hominid.

trict include the South African Breweries World of Beer and the Workers' Museum and Library, which features an exhibit of a compound in which black municipal workers were housed.

The rejuvenation of Newtown provided the spark for reviving the inner city. Part of the vision included building the Nelson Mandela Bridge, creating a cultural arc through Braamfontein to Constitution Hill on the border of Hillbrow. The idea was to make Newtown the hub of this link and began with making the area safe by installing closed-circuit cameras and cleaning up the public environment. Mary Fitzgerald Square, situated in the heart of the Cultural Quarter of the precinct, was upgraded. With lighting designed by renowned French designer, Patrick Rimoux, it has been transformed into a well-lit space where public performances, gatherings and concerts are often held. The square is now the key venue for large events, including the Joy of

BELOW: A model of *Homo heidelbergensis*, an extinct Homo species as discovered in Germany, links the human race across continents. BOTTOM LEFT: South African and international casts of fossil discoveries are displayed.

EXPERIENCE STERKFONTEIN

Sterkfontein Caves

A complex near the entrance to the Sterkfontein Caves includes a virtual reality auditorium, exhibition spaces, lecture theatre, restaurant and shop. From here tours are conducted through the iconic caves – revealing the unfolding journey of humankind in a mesmerising setting.

Maropeng Visitor Centre

The Maropeng Visitor Centre exhibition facility at Mohale's Gate is a world-class flagship initiative within the Cradle of Humankind. Maropeng, a Setswana word meaning 'return to the place of origin', is 10 minutes from the Sterkfontein Caves. At its heart is a circular tumulus, a grassed-over, state-of-the-art visitor's centre designed to resemble an ancient burial ground and symbolising the voyage of humankind from its beginnings into an uncertain future. One of its features is the Diversity Ramp, which leads to a human-made lake and a boat ride from the dawn of time to a look at what is to come. Amid the extraordinary exhibits are an education resource centre, conference facilities and a restaurant. In the grounds are a shopping area, amphitheatre, scientific activities and a luxury boutique hotel.

The magnificently appointed five-star Forum Homini boutique hotel offers dramatic views across the Cradle of Humankind. The decor incorporates images related to the cultural evolution of humans, including rock art, ancient totems and sculptures. For the ultimate culinary experience, book a table at the award-winning Roots restaurant.

In 2005, Maropeng won the British Guild of Travel Writers award for the best new tourism project worldwide. It has subsequently won the Sustainable Tourism Investment of the Year Award at the Africa Investor Tourism Awards.

Highlights of the Sterkfontein Valley

• Kromdraai, the second site discovered in the area, contains specimens of *Paranthropus robustus*, a hominid that existed one to two million years ago.

• Coopers Cave has yielded a molar tooth and the skull of a *P. robustus*.

• Godolin also has *P. robustus* remains and an astonishing array of a further 90 000 fossil specimens.

• At Swartkrans scientists have collected more than 200 hominid specimens, mostly *P. robustus*. It was the first site in Africa to produce remains

of *Homo ergaster*, and burnt bones point to the earliest controlled use of fire at least one million years ago.

• Drimolen, discovered in 1992, has yielded 74 specimens of *P. robustus*, including a near complete female cranium with articulated mandible, and five of *Homo ergaster*.

• The visually spectacular Wonder Cave is renowned for its drip stone formations and enormous chamber.

• Bolt's Farm has yielded the oldest deposits in the Sterkfontein Valley, with some fossil rodents dating back 4,5 million years.

• Gladysvale preserves some of the most extensive time sequences, with sediments dating from 250 000 to 3 million years ago.

• Significant fauna remains as well as animal deposits have been found at Plover's Lake and Haasgat. The former may have been the site of a leopard lair, while deposits of early forest-dwelling monkeys dating back 1,3 million years have been found at the latter.

• Pienaar's Cave has not yet been excavated, while diggings at Motsetse began in 2001.

Jazz festival, Arts Alive, Africa Day, the New Year Carnival, Diwali Festival of Lights, concerts and corporate events. Around it are fantastic restaurants, music venues and crafts outlets.

Sandton

Fifty years ago Sandton was farmland, but since then the area has grown into a significant business, shopping and entertainment district. Sandton City Shopping Centre was built more than 30 years ago and became known as the biggest mall in the Southern Hemisphere. Other developments followed and the mall grew, as did the commercial district around it. It is now home to the expanded Sandton City Mall, Nelson Mandela Square precinct, Village Walk, Sandton Convention Centre, the JSE and hundreds of blue-chip company offices and numerous world-class hotels – not to mention fantastic shopping, dining and entertainment venues.

Rosebank

Once a small, mixed commercial/residential node of Johannesburg, Rosebank is known for its entertainment, shopping and markets. The Rosebank Rooftop Market, held on Sundays, has been running for years and is still extremely popular with those who enjoy flea markets and bargain hunting, while the Rosebank African Craft Market is a favourite place for African artefacts. Rosebank Mall and the adjacent shopping precinct, The Zone, are known for designer stores, chichi restaurants and relaxed coffee-shop culture.

Soweto

Soweto is a thriving, iconic part of the greater Johannesburg metropole, and countless tourist buses carry visitors to the many important heritage sites located here. A must-do is to visit the eateries on Vilakazi Street, the popular Wandie's Restaurant, or those in the Maponya Mall. There is a four-star hotel at the Walter Sisulu Square of Dedication and numerous B & Bs offer comfortable accommodation.

Pretoria

Pretoria, in the Municipality of Tshwane, is an elegant city and home to most of the local contingent of international embassies. This has led to a profusion of fine restaurants and a cosmopolitan culture. One of the highlights of the city is the National Zoological Gardens, which is ranked in the world's top five. The Union Buildings are impressive, as is the Voortrekker Monument.

Pretoria's ambitious Freedom Park, which pays tribute to those who have fallen during South Africa's turbulent history, is already showing signs that it will become one of the country's premier heritage sites. The park features an interactive museum, open-air amphitheatre, conference centre, commercial precinct, and the Pan-African library and audio-visual library. Through interactive exhibitions, the museum serves to present and preserve South Africa's pre-colonial, colonial, apartheid and post-apartheid history.

Hatfield

Known for its lively student population, the suburb of Hatfield is something of a party zone in Pretoria. There are a number of pubs, bars, restaurants and live music venues frequented by revellers in search of a good time. Hatfield Plaza has more than 50 shops, stores and restaurants and keeps the commercial hub of the area turning.

Dinokeng

Dinokeng, Setswana for 'place of many waters', covers 281 000 ha of bushveld and grassland terrain in the northeastern quadrant of Gauteng. This area was once home to a rich variety of wild animals, including the legendary Big Five. However, the mass influx of people to the region following the discovery of gold and diamonds depleted the wildlife, and this corner of Gauteng lagged economically behind other parts of the province. A study on the future of the area, conducted in the late 1990s, recommended that it be developed into a premier tourist destination, showcasing its natural, cultural and historical attractions. This involved establishing traditional African villages where tourists could get to know the cultures of the area (Pedi, Tsonga, Ndebele and Tswana); upgrading sites to highlight the great sweep of the region's history, from the Stone Age to the present; improving visitor facilities and promoting activities and experiences, including

ABOVE RIGHT: Freedom Park, situated on Salvokop in Pretoria, is dedicated to heroes of the Struggle as well as those who died in the Anglo–Boer wars, World War I and World War II. OPPOSITE TOP: In Cullinan, be sure to visit the barnyard-cum-theatre at Jan Harmsgat se Agterplaas. OPPOSITE RIGHT: The Sterkfontein Caves have revealed many secrets about the history of humanity.

DID YOU KNOW?
Soweto's Vilakazi Street is the only place in the world where two Nobel Peace laureates (former president Nelson Mandela and Archbishop Emeritus Desmond Tutu) lived on the same street.

- Bungee jumping, abseiling, swinging or rapp jumping off the Orlando Cooling Towers in Soweto
- Water sports along the Vaal Meander and at Rietvlei Dam in Pretoria
- Spelunking (caving) in the Magaliesberg
- Abseiling into a dark cave in the Cradle of Humankind World Heritage Site, near Krugersdorp
- Skydiving in Edenvale
- Sandboarding down an old mine dump known as Mount Mayhem in Boksburg
- Golfing in and around Gauteng

ROUTES AND TRAILS

- Crocodile River Ramble (60 km), an arts and crafts route beginning in Krugersdorp and ending at Brits, including the Cradle of Humankind
- Three walks (1–7 hours) at Suikerbosrand Nature Reserve near Heidelberg
- Tswaing Crater Trail (3 hours) around the Tswaing Meteorite Crater, 40 km northwest of Pretoria

adventures such as hiking and mountain biking and sangoma consultations; and creating a 90 000-ha game reserve, the Dinokeng Big 5 Game Reserve.

Cullinan

The historic Victorian diamond-mining village of Cullinan developed around the Premier Diamond Mine. The mine opened in 1902 and is still operational. The world's largest rough diamond ever found, the 3 106-carat Cullinan, was recovered here and presented to King Edward VII of England. Two of its biggest polished pieces, known as Cullinan I and Cullinan II (or the Great and the Lesser Star of Africa), form part of the British Crown Jewels. The mine also produced the Golden Jubilee Diamond, which at 545,67 carats is the largest polished diamond in the world.

The Cradle of Humankind

The Cradle of Humankind in the Sterkfontein Valley was listed by UNESCO as a World Heritage Site on 2 December 1999. Ranked alongside such marvels as the Great Wall of China and the Victoria Falls, it comprises a unique band of palaeoanthropological sites across 47 000 ha in the northwestern corner of Gauteng and parts of the North West Province. It has yielded some of the most extensive fossil and artefact finds on earth, particularly for the period between four and one million years ago. The valley provides important information on the early development of humans and the environment in which prehumans and early humans lived. There are 13 explored sites within the World Heritage Site, and probably many more yet to be discovered.

CHAPTER 19

THE MPUMALANGA HIGHLANDS AND GREAT ESCARPMENT

ABOVE: Winding Long Tom Pass makes up part of Mpumalanga's scenic Panorama Route, one of the country's finest drives.

The Mpumalanga Highlands and Great Escarpment is a stretch of the eastern section of the interior plateau on the edge of the Drakensberg. It is here that the land plunges down to meet the Lowveld, a low-lying region that stretches along South Africa's border with Mozambique. It is cradled by the provinces of Limpopo to the north, Gauteng to the west and KwaZulu-Natal to the southeast. The scenery that accompanies so dramatic a change of territory is equally theatrical, with a full geographical cast that includes rivers,

gorges, cliffs, waterfalls and sweeping views. Steep and winding mountain passes show off the scenery to dazzling effect.

A wealth of information on earth's evolution is contained in the Barberton Greenstone Belt, also known as the 'Genesis of Life', located in the Makhonjwa Mountains around Barberton. Here, rocks dating back 3,5 billion years contain fossils that yield not only the secrets of the planet but also gold, a precious metal that has shaped the history of the province.

NDEBELE CULTURE

The distinct beadwork and geometric mural art of the South Ndebele were born of a need by one of the smallest groups in South Africa to express their cultural identity, and a desire by its womenfolk to assert their individuality in a patriarchal society.

The beautiful dress and accessories of South Ndebele women are rich with symbolism: the adornments most often reflect the age and social and marital status of their wearers, and a love of colour is evident in the garments and beadwork, from the front aprons of little girls to the colourful blankets and spectacular costumes worn by married women. Married women wear stacked rings around the neck, arms and legs, and those whose husbands are yet to build them a home wear a broad studded necklace known as a *rholwani*. When her house is ready, the woman replaces her necklace with copper, brass or plastic bands called *idzilo*, the quantity of which denotes her husband's wealth.

LONG TOM PASS

The 55,6-km Long Tom Pass linking Mashishing with Sabie is one of South Africa's highest tarred roads, with its summit at 2 150 m. The modern version, built in the 1950s, replaced one built in the 1870s by pick and shovel, as the Voortrekkers literally had to carve a road over the mountains to the Mozambican port of Delagoa Bay, now Maputo. The pass was also the scene of an Anglo–Boer War engagement, when the retreating Boers, pursued by British troops, turned back to fire from the Mauchsberg sentinel at the south end of the pass, using field guns dubbed Long Toms. Under fire cover the Boers were able to escape. The scenic pass came to be known as the Long Tom Pass and the battle is commemorated at a memorial 31 km from Mashishing, where a replica of the gun is located.

CLIMATE

Mpumalanga is said to have two climates, one for its high-lying escarpment and another for its subtropical Lowveld. Temperatures on the escarpment are more extreme with colder, frosty winters and hotter, drier summers. Low-lying areas experience a greater amount of summer rain.

FLORA AND FAUNA

Where the Drakensberg exceeds heights of 2 000 m, alpine grasslands and patches of Afromontane forest can be found. The wetlands that characterise the Highlands, with their high bird and botanical diversity, are a natural treasure.

Many species of antelope can be seen, along with predators such as caracal and leopard. Twitchers will find plenty of birds, and three endangered crane species – the blue, wattled and grey-crowned cranes – can all be spotted at the Verloren Vallei Nature Reserve near Dullstroom.

HISTORY AND HERITAGE

The groups who inhabit this area today – the Shangaan, Swazi and Ndebele – appear to have moved into this region in the 1800s.

The first Voortrekkers, led by Andries Hendrik Potgieter, arrived here in June 1845, founded a village called Andries-Ohrigstad. At about the same time the British annexed Natal, causing the Boers there to trek into the interior, with one group arriving at Andries-Ohrigstad. Clashes between Potgieter and the new arrivals resulted in their moving south to found Lydenburg, while Potgieter took a small commando to the Orange Free State. The Boers that stayed established farming communities and small towns along the Eastern Escarpment.

NOTEWORTHY PLACES
eMakhazeni (Belfast)

Located high up in the Drakensberg, eMakhazeni is a popular trout-fishing spot; the

ABOVE: Colourful Ndebele homesteads, with their distinctive geometric patterns, can be seen in the rural areas of the province.

town features six well-stocked dams under the supervision of the Belfast Fly Fishing Association. Tulips farmed in the area are another local attraction: an annual festival takes place in September. There is a second Anglo–Boer War (1899–1902) heritage site at Bergendal, a war cemetery and a knife-making studio. Small as eMakhazeni is, it has no less than 12 churches.

Wakkerstroom

One of the earliest white settlements of the old Transvaal, Wakkerstroom is an important birdwatching centre, offering easy sightings of some 40 species endemic to South Africa. Grassland birds are a particular attraction. Off-road and mountain biking as well as horse riding and hikes are some of the less sedentary activities on offer in this quaint village.

The local Opikoppi Private Museum is worth a visit for a general history of the village. The nearby Balele Mountain Lodge has 12 dams for fly fishing. A recommended scenic drive is that between Wakkerstroom and Luneberg. There is a varied choice of accommodation in the area.

SEE:
Limpopo &
Mpumalanga, p. 246
Mpumalanga, Swaziland
& Mozambique p. 247

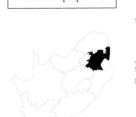

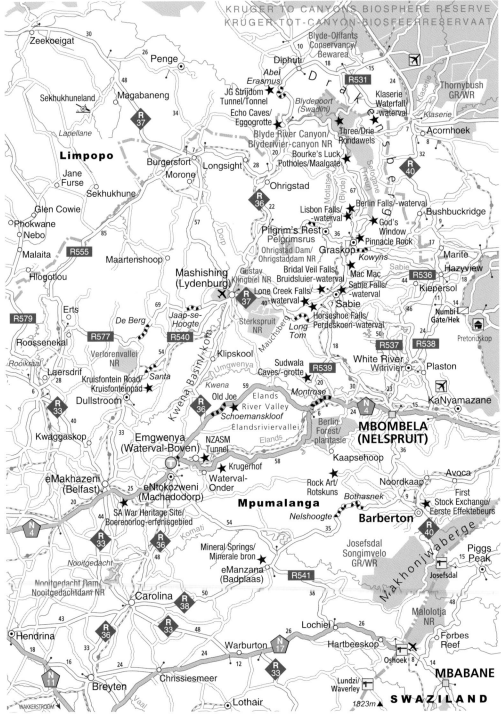

Amsterdam

This sheep-farming town may not have much to draw the attention of tourists, but its history is worth a mention for the lofty but unrealised ambition behind its establishment. A Glaswegian, Alexander McCorkindale, dreamt of a New Scotland republic here, in which he planned to settle 300 of his countrymen. He had plans for towns and farms and even went as far as naming a capital city – Roburnia, after Scottish poet Robert Burns. He succeeded in attracting 50 Scots to his new 'republic', but died before he could complete his plans. Roburnia became Amsterdam instead, reflecting the old Transvaal's link with the Netherlands. Farms in the area bear distinctively Scottish names.

Dullstroom

Dullstroom, founded in the 1880s by a group of Dutch immigrants headed by a merchant named Wolterus Dull, is renowned as a destination for trout fishing. Local tourism sings the virtues of its five F's – fly fishing, fireplaces (its high altitude means bracing winters), fauna and flora, fine food and fresh air. There are opportunities for both still-water and river fishing in the vicinity of the town, with brown and rainbow trout the sought-after catches. There are some pretty drives, such as along the Kruisfontein Road, which loops around the town. The Verloren Vallei Nature Reserve, comprising over 30 wetlands, offers some unusual avian and botanical sightings. It is a Ramsar-listed site, and must be visited by arrangement.

eNtokozweni (Machadodorp)

eNtokozweni, on the Elands River, originated as a staging post for transport riders on the way to the port at Delagoa Bay (Maputo) in Mozambique, and evolved into a railway town

TOP: The Gables shopping centre in the heart of Dullstroom is a one-stop location for accommodation, retail shopping and dining. ABOVE LEFT: From wooden sculptures to scrap-wire models, intricate beadwork and clay pots, Mpumalanga's artists fashion all sorts of artistic souvenirs. ABOVE RIGHT: The Kruger to Canyons Biosphere Reserve protects two of the country's main attractions – Blyde River Canyon and the Kruger National Park, where lucky visitors may spot the shy leopard.

BLYDE RIVER CANYON

The 20-km long Blyde River Canyon is one of South Africa's most prized scenic riches. It begins at the confluence of the Motlatse (Blyde) and Sefogane (Treur) rivers and is surrounded by the Blyde River Canyon Nature Reserve, which is rich in fauna and flora. The views are breathtaking: a circular drive beginning at Graskop leads visitors to some of the best viewpoints in the vicinity of the canyon. Must-sees include geological phenomena like the Bourke's Luck Potholes (cylindrical holes eroded in rocks by whirlpools), the hut-shaped promontories known as the Three Rondavels and the towering Pinnacle Rock. God's Window, an aptly named viewing point, provides unsurpassed vistas of the Mpumalanga Lowveld. A holiday resort is situated at the impressive Blydepoort (Swadini) Dam.

GOLD PANNERS LIVE ON

A taste of the wild old gold-rush days can be experienced at the annual South African Open Gold Panning Championships held in Pilgrim's Rest in September/October. The event is organised by the South African Gold Panning Association, the Pilgrim's Rest Museum and Mpumalanga's Department of Culture, Sport and Recreation. Competitors are given a gold pan and a bucket of sand in which gold nuggets are hidden. The winner is the contestant who pans out the most nuggets in the shortest time. Other amusements include a wheelbarrow race, pub crawl and dance.

TOP: Mpumalanga's lush Blyde River Canyon is the world's largest green canyon. ABOVE RIGHT: The historic town of Pilgrim's Rest is a living museum, reminiscent of the gold-rush days of the 1870s.

on the completion of a railway line in 1894. This spot is also good fly-fishing and hiking terrain, and a local health resort is known for its thermal sulphur springs.

Emgwenya (Waterval-Boven) and Waterval-Onder

The 75-m-high Elands River Falls separate these two villages, with Emgwenya (Waterval-Boven) situated above the falls and Waterval-Onder below. Located on the railway track that linked the old Transvaal Republic with Mozambique, the station at Emgwenya commemorates the thousands of labourers who died in the construction of the line, mostly of fever. Attractions include the NZASM Tunnel and a five-arch railway bridge nearby. The Kwena Basin on the outskirts of the village boasts good scenery, nature reserves and fishing lodges, while rock climbing in Emgwenya is reputed to be among the country's best.

Mashishing (Lydenburg)

Lydenburg was established in 1849 by a party of Voortrekkers. Nearly 25 years later, in 1873, it experienced an influx of prospectors when alluvial gold was found in the Spekboom (or Dorps) River. Today, mining and agriculture are the lifeblood of the town. Mashishing has one of the oldest Dutch Reformed churches, as well as Anglo–Boer War sites, two nature reserves – Sterkspruit and Gustav Klingbiel – and the spectacular twin Lydenburg Falls.

Barberton

For a few short years, Barberton, founded in the wake of a gold rush in 1884, boomed as fortune-seekers flocked to the small settlement. It was all beer and barmaids, until prospectors left for the promise of greater riches on the Witwatersrand. There are still some active gold mines in Barberton, as well as many old buildings that testify to

LYDENBURG HEADS

In 1957, a 10-year old boy first spotted six human and one animal clay masks on a farm outside Mashishing (Lydenburg). These were to become known as the Lydenburg Heads. Much later, he would bring them to the attention of the University of Cape Town. Subsequent excavations revealed that his finds dated to around 490 CE, making these heads one of the earliest records of southern African civilisation. The heads are, believed to have been crafted by Iron Age Bantu-speaking people, for use in initiation ceremonies. The Lydenburg Museum contains replicas; the originals can be seen at the Iziko South African Museum in Cape Town.

ACTIVITIES

- Fly fishing and hiking throughout the province
- Rock climbing and mountain biking at eNtokozweni
- Abseiling, river rafting and other water-based adventure sports at Sabie and Blyde River Canyon
- Stargazing and birdwatching at eMakhazeni

ROUTES AND TRAILS

- Cottonwood Tours offer tailor-made tours of the battlefields, a popular itinerary including a circular route covering eMakhazeni, eNtokozweni, Mashishing and Dullstroom (1 day)

the frenetic early times, such as De Kaap Stock Exchange, Stopforth House and the Lewis and Marks building. Keep an eye out for the statue of the bull terrier Jock, the canine hero of a well-loved South African tale, Sir Percy FitzPatrick's *Jock of the Bushveld*. Worth seeing are the cheerful indigenous *Barberton Daisy*, a disused steam locomotive, and the 20-km aerial cableway that once ferried goods between the town and neighbouring Swaziland. There are also several nature reserves in the area.

Sabie

With its extensive pine and blue-gum plantations, Sabie is set in one of the world's largest man-made forests. A forestry museum tells the story of the timber industry in the region. Set on the Sabie River, which once teemed with crocodiles, the town is famed for the waterfalls in its vicinity, such as the Bridal Veil, Lone Creek, Horseshoe and Sabie falls and the Mac Mac Falls and Pools, where swimming is possible. Hiking is a popular activity in and around the town, with routes ranging in difficulty from easy to gruelling, and there are several adventure activities available, such as abseiling.

Graskop

Perched on a spur of the Mauchsberg, Graskop, like other towns in the region, is a one-time gold-mining camp. Drivers making their way from Sabie to the forestry town must stay alert as they climb the steep 11-km incline of the Abel Erasmus Pass, which offers some amazing views. Graskop's attraction is its convenient location to the scenic wonders of the Blyde River Canyon as well as some awe-inspiring cascades such as the Lisbon and Berlin falls. It is also a good destination for twitchers, with three Important Bird Areas – sites that have been marked for conservation – in the vicinity. Here, some rare bird species, such as Taita and Peregrine falcon, blue swallow and blackwinged plover, can be seen.

Pilgrim's Rest

Pilgrim's Rest, too, had its beginnings in the feverish gold rush of the 1870s, an all-too-short moment of glory, when 'Wheelbarrow' Alex Patterson came upon the first payload of gold in the region. Nowadays, Pilgrim's Rest is a national heritage site, a well-preserved tribute to this exciting era in South Africa's history. Its old buildings have been converted into museums, art galleries and arts-and-crafts outlets and the old diggings site has been reconstructed.

LEFT: The exquisite Horseshoe Falls, so named because of their shape, are located along the Sabie River. BOTTOM LEFT: Although Mashishing had a brief alluvial gold rush, it now thrives on agriculture as well as platinum and chrome mining.

DID YOU KNOW?
Harrie's Pancakes in Graskop is lauded for making the best pancakes in the country. Savoury or sweet, no visit to Mpumalanga is complete without a bite at Harrie's.

CHAPTER 20

THE MPUMALANGA LOWVELD

ABOVE: The southern section of the Kruger National Park, located in the Mpumalanga Lowveld, has a healthy population of lion.

The Mpumalanga Lowveld is rich in resources, both below and above ground. Mining yields copper, iron, phosphates and vermiculite, while the land boasts some of the planet's greatest wildlife reserves. The Lowveld is also South Africa's fruit basket and vegetable garden, supplying citrus, nuts and avocados.

The Lowveld lies in the eastern half of the province, nudging up against the Great Escarpment in the west and the Mozambique border in the east, where it includes parts of the Kruger National Park. To the south is KwaZulu-Natal and to the north the Limpopo prov-ince. The town of Mbombela (Nelspruit) is the largest urban centre in the region. Displaying a largely savannah-type habitat, the terrain of the Lowveld is generally flat.

CLIMATE

Situated close to the warm Indian Ocean, the Mpumalanga Lowveld has a subtropical climate with humid summers and mild winters. Mbombela, the largest town in the area, experiences average temperatures of 19 °C–29 °C during summer and 6 °C–23 °C during winter. Rainfall occurs in the summer months.

FLORA AND FAUNA

The Lowveld is blessed with one of South Africa's star attractions, the Kruger National Park. The southern section holds the greatest concentration of game and some of the most popular rest camps. It also includes the Sabi Sand Game Reserve, incorporating a clutch of upmarket private game lodges. Here you will find an animal kingdom second to none, from the Big Five (buffalo, rhinoceros, lion, leopard and elephant) down to the smallest insect. The park features a variety of ecosystems and includes 336 tree, 49 fish, 34 amphibian, 114 reptile, 507 bird and 147 mammal species.

HISTORY AND HERITAGE

The Kruger National Park is a window to a long-gone past: its sometimes romantic, often turbulent history reflects that of southern Africa.

Humankind has come and gone in the Lowveld for aeons. Handaxes, cleavers and other artefacts found in the region are evidence that our earliest ancestors lived here long before the arrival of the Bantu-speaking farmers from the north and white explorers and settlers from the east and south. The first African farmers migrated from the central and eastern parts of the continent, settling in southern Africa around 1 700 years ago. But it was the arrival of another group of migrants, many centuries later, that ushered in a different era.

White explorers and settlers arrived in what is today known as Mpumalanga in the early 1800s. Solitary ivory hunters, slavers and adventurers preceded the flood of Boers escaping British hegemony in the Cape Colony. Around 1838, Boer leaders Hans van Rensburg and Louis Trichardt, in search of a route to Delagoa Bay and the sea, organised expeditions to cross the Lowveld and set up outposts there.

While the Boers did not settle on the Lowveld proper, they did establish themselves in the foot-hills of the Drakensberg. The picture changed dramatically in the 1870s with the discovery of gold near Lydenburg, now Mashishing, on the Highveld Plateau. As a result, shack communities mushroomed in the valleys and forests of the Great Escarpment, with disastrous effects on the region's wildlife.

By the time the Transvaal regained its independence in 1881 it had become clear that the wildlife resources of the region were in danger

WILDERNESS TRAILS

Did you ever imagine striding briskly through the bush à la Percy FitzPatrick, author of *Jock of the Bushveld*? A series of guided wilderness trails in the Kruger National Park will help bring such fantasies to life. Much in demand, the trails are generally restricted to groups of eight and operate over three nights with two full days in which you cover approximately 20 km a day. Be prepared to rough it as you overnight in rustic huts, although meals are included.

LEFT: Impala lilies brighten up the rugged bushveld landscape of the Lowveld. BELOW: The famous Kruger National Park has over 507 bird species, including the petite red-headed weaver.

SABI SAND GAME RESERVE

Sabi Sand Game Reserve, taking its name from the Sabi and Sand rivers, is situated to the north of Paul Kruger Gate and shares an unfenced 50 km boundary with the reserve. It boasts close on 20 privately owned reserves, each featuring a number of luxury lodges. For no small fee, they offer an upmarket, close-up encounter with the bush, utilising open game-viewing vehicles, keeping guest volumes small and pampering them with top-notch cuisine, spa treatments and personalised service. They attract Hollywood celebrities, global business moguls and world-famous politicians.

of disappearing. Legislation was put in place to preserve these resources, but it was ineffectual.

In 1895 the parliament of the Transvaal adopted a resolution to proclaim a government game reserve in the Lowveld. Eventually, in 1898, President Paul Kruger allowed for the establishment of the Sabie Game Reserve. The British soon arrived, and after they defeated the Boers Major (later Colonel) James Stevenson-Hamilton took up the position of game warden.

In 1926 the park was expanded and re-named the Kruger National Park. To protect his domain from human predators Stevenson-Hamilton opened the park to visitors. Soon, guests were arriving in their hundreds and the park began to provide accommodation in the form of traditional thatched huts. In 1998, its centenary year, a million visitors attested to the fact that the Kruger National Park, is one of the world's greatest tourist attractions.

NOTEWORTHY PLACES
Mbombela (Nelspruit)

Mbombela, a growing city in the fertile valley of the Umgwenya River (previously the Crocodile River), is the gateway to the Kruger National Park and Mozambique. This provincial capital lies in a lush agricultural area, particularly known for its citrus farming.

Just on the edge of town is one of the main reasons to stop awhile in Mbombela – the Lowveld National Botanical Garden with its 600 local plants, including shrubs and cycads. It is also the spot where the Umgwenya and Nels rivers meet, one gushing through a pot-holed gorge and the other tumbling down as a waterfall. Other attractions in and around Mbombela include the Croc River Enviro Park, where a variety of local and exotic species can be seen, and the Jane Goodall Insitutute Chimpanzee Eden, a sanctuary dedicated to the rescue and care of displaced chimpanzees.

If you have some time on your hands, join a tour of the KaNyamazane township, east of Mbombela. The day-long tour includes visits to a local school, a shebeen, an arts and crafts centre, as well as a traditional healer.

SUDWALA CAVES

Some 35 km northwest of Mbombela (take the R539 from Montrose) are the Sudwala Caves, a system of ancient caverns 30 km in length, formed around 3 000 million years ago. They come with well-preserved stalactites and stalagmites (the largest is 11 m high) and draw a large number of visitors on their way to or from the Kruger National Park. In the section that is open to the public, the main feature is a circular chamber 70 m in diameter and 37 m at its highest point, known as the amphitheatre because of its natural acoustics.

SEE:
Mbombela (Nelspruit) p. 217
Limpopo & Mpumalanga p. 246
Mpumalanga, Swaziland & Mozambique p. 247

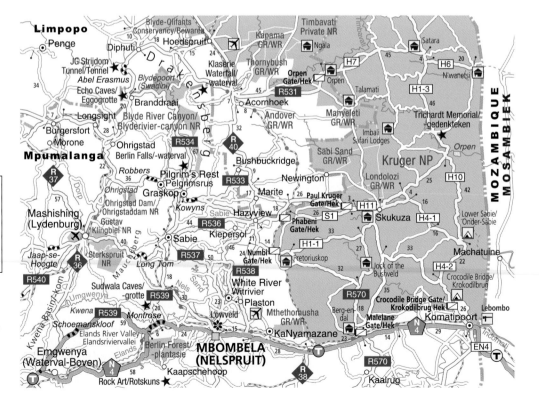

KRUGER NATIONAL PARK'S SOUTHERN REGION

The southern section of the famed Kruger National Park has the highest concentrations of wildlife and the easiest access. The gates into this region are the Paul Kruger, Numbi and Phabeni gates on the western boundary, and the Malelane and Crocodile Bridge gates on the southern border. They lead to the Pretoriuskop, Berg-en-Dal, Malelane, Crocodile Bridge, Lower Sabie and Skukuza rest camps, as well as the Biyamiti Bushveld Camp.

ACTIVITIES

- Horse riding in Mbombela and Kaapschehoop
- River rafting and balloon safaris at White River
- Hot-air ballooning at Hazyview

ROUTES AND TRAILS

- Kaapschehoop Trail (3–6 days) through forested plantations, historical sites and spectacular scenery, in Kaapschehoop

FESTIVALS

There are two major festivals in the Lowveld. The Uplands Festival, an arts festival and country market, is held in White River in May, and the InniBos Lowveld National Arts Festival is held in Mbombela in June or July.

In town, the beehive-shaped Mpumalanga Provincial Government Complex has a good collection of South African art, but call ahead to make arrangements if you want to view the art works.

White River

Peaceful White River is an agricultural centre on the doorstep of the Kruger National Park. It has somewhat of a reputation as an arts and crafts locale: just outside the town, Casterbridge Farm Shopping Centre offers craft shops, coffee bars, a cinema, a theatre, a vintage car museum and a farmyard petting zoo. There are a number of excellent restaurants, although these do tend to change names, themes and owners at quite a rapid rate. Follow the unofficial 'artist's route' and visit the showrooms and studios of Mpumalanga's finest potters, weavers, sculptors and glassblowers.

Hazyview

The town of Hazyview, so-named for the haze that settles over it on hot days, offers convenient access to the Numbi, Paul Kruger and Phabeni gates of the Kruger National Park. Many tourists visiting the park base themselves in this town and take day trips to the game reserve and surrounding attractions. An agricultural centre, it is surrounded by banana plantations. Perry's Bridge is a good place to stop over if you're looking for safari gear, arts and crafts, art galleries and curio shops all in one space.

Kaapschehoop

The village of Kaapschehoop, 27 km southwest of Mbombela and located next to the Berlin Forest, is said to be one of the few destinations in South Africa where wild horses are still found. Their origin is subject to much speculation, but it seems they are the offspring of horses that were abandoned in the area after the gold-mining boom of the late 1800s. There are currently three herds in Kaapschehoop, with many more in the surrounding forests.

LEFT: At about 5,5 m, gentle giraffe are the tallest land animals on earth, and their average lifespan is 20–25 years. BELOW: A juvenile bateleur (left) and a young female adult tawny eagle (right) fight over a monitor lizard in the Kruger National Park.

CHAPTER 21

THE LIMPOPO LOWVELD

ABOVE: Beautifully crafted Venda pots can be bought in scenic Hoedspruit and along various roadsides in Limpopo province.

The Limpopo Lowveld extends from the town of Tzaneen in the west to the Mozambique border in the east and Hoedspruit in the south, with the Limpopo River forming a natural boundary to the north. Into this region fall the northern reaches of the Kruger National Park and a group of exclusive game lodges in neighbouring protected areas. It is a land of myth and legend, with queens, half-human spirits and reptilian gods to tease the imagination.

CLIMATE

In general, Limpopo is hot and dry with high temperatures in the summer – as high as 40 °C in Lowveld towns such as Phalaborwa. In the Kruger National Park summer temperatures

VENDA CULTURE

Far from being a homogenous grouping, the Venda have their origins in a mixture of various groups that migrated across the Limpopo and eventually settled in the northern reaches of present-day South Africa.

In Venda tradition there are many sacred sites, including Lake Fundudzi in a valley in the Soutspansberg Mountains. Even today, it is believed that this is where the White Python – the god of fertility – lives. In reverence of the python, young female initiates perform the Domba dance. The girls form a chain of bodies and move to the rhythm of beating drums, replicating the movement of a snake and of a baby in the womb.

The Thathe-Vondo Forest, where the royal, ancestral burial ground is located, is another sacred site. It is protected, the Venda believe, by a half-man, half-lion creature called Nethane.

hover around the 30 °C mark. Tumultuous thunderstorms accompany the hot weather, while winters are mild. The higher regions of the Soutpansberg are cool, damp and misty.

FLORA AND FAUNA

In the northern part of the Kruger National Park are some species not found in the southern section, including antelope such as Sharpe's grysbok, Lichtenstein's hartebeest, roan antelope and the shy suni. This is also the realm of the samango monkey and the yellow-spotted rock dassie. Wild dog are more common here than in the southern region. Rare bird species include Arnot's chat, the yellow-billed oxpecker, variable sunbird and racket-tailed roller. The Lepelle River, formerly the Olifants River, marks the start of mopane vegetation, a favourite food of elephants.

The baobab tree, so iconic of Africa, becomes a more common sight in the northern parts of the province. The town of Modjadjiskloof is home to the world's third biggest baobab, which measures over 40 m in circumference.

HISTORY AND HERITAGE

The first herders started arriving in southern Africa about 2 000 years ago, bringing with them sheep and cattle. They were followed – between 300 and 400 years later – by Bantu-speaking farmers, skilled in the cultivation of sorghum and millet, the manufacture of pottery and the smelting of iron and copper. Some of these newcomers settled in the hills and valleys south of the Limpopo River, where they lived in small communities, relying on their herds, crop farming and hunting for their survival. Pottery fragments found near places such as

BELOW: A reconstruction of the Masorini Iron Age site, once inhabited by the baPhalaborwa people, can be seen close to Phalaborwa gate in the Kruger National Park. BOTTOM LEFT: The colourful mopane pomegranate tree is found in the bushveld areas of the Limpopo Lowveld.

MODJADJI, THE RAIN QUEEN

Since the publication of Rider Haggard's novel *She*, the Rain Queen of the Lobedu, on whom the tale was based, has captured imaginations. The story hinges on a princess who bore a child of an incestuous relationship and was banished from her kingdom, but she left equipped with the secret of how to make rain. So impressive were her powers that she was left untouched by armies during the Difaqane, a series of wars that occurred in the 1820s and 30s, causing chaotic migrations in southeastern Africa.

The Lobedu Kingdom comprises over 150 villages. Each has a headman who represents the Modjadji, or Rain Queen. The seat of the reclusive Rain Queen is Modjadjiskloof, a small town previously known as Duiwelskloof. Renamed in post-apartheid South Africa, the choice of name reveals the deep regard for the Balobedu dynasty. There is currently no reigning queen, the last one having died prematurely in 2005.

TIMBAVATI PRIVATE GAME RESERVE

This 53 000-ha tract of land, wedged between the Klaserie Private Nature Reserve and Kruger National Park, has been painstakingly brought back from a state of degradation. Now restored and healthy, it shares an unfenced border and diverse wildlife with the northern Kruger. There are family-style accommodation facilities in the reserve such as Gomo Gomo Game Lodge and Kambaku Safari Lodge, plus some luxury lodges.

The discovery in the 1970s of white lions in the Timbavati area brought much media attention. The colour of the animals is popularly attributed to albinism, but their colouring is in fact the result of a condition known as leucism, in which the coat is white but the eyes and skin retain pigmentation. It occurs when both parents carry a recessive 'white' gene that is inherited by cubs from both parents. The lions are believed by some to hold spiritual powers.

SEE:
Limpopo &
Mpumalanga p. 246
Mpumalanga, Swaziland
& Mozambique p. 247
Zimbabwe & Limpopo
p. 250
Zimbabwe &
Mozambique p. 251

Tzaneen and Mashishing, and in the Soutpansberg, have been carbon-dated to between 250 and 450 CE, and the discovery of slag remains suggests that iron was being smelted during this period.

From around 900 CE significant economic and political changes, perhaps driven by environmental and climatic conditions, began to take place. Trade became more common as settlements began exchanging goods with people on the Indian Ocean coast. Evidence of early commercial activity along the east coast of Africa includes the remains of glass beads, Chinese porcelain and textiles as well as gold, copper and iron objects found at archaeological sites including Mapungubwe, Schroda and K2 – all Iron Age sites south of the Limpopo River. Notable Later Iron Age sites include Thulamela and Masorini, both located within the Kruger National Park.

NOTEWORTHY PLACES
Hoedspruit

Hoedspruit's advantage lies in its proximity to the Kruger National Park and the privately owned lodges of Timbavati Private Nature Reserve and Klaserie Private Nature Reserve. It has the convenience of an airport too. For those who wish to tarry a while, the secluded Klaserie waterfall is nearby, the Hoedspruit

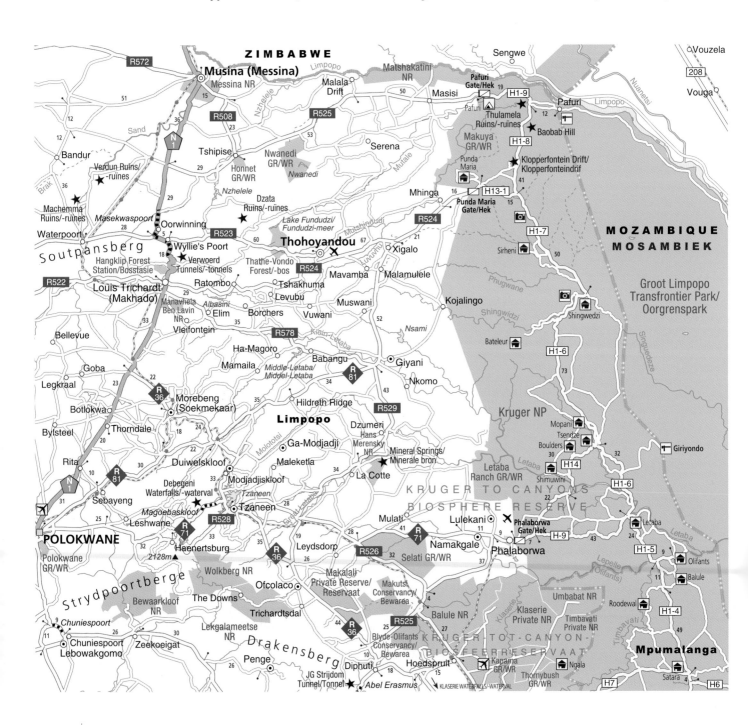

ACTIVITIES

- The Magoebaskloof Canopy Tour over Letaba Gorge (2.5 hours) between Tzaneen and Haenertsburg
- Hot-air ballooning at Klaserie Private Nature Reserve in the Greater Kruger National Park
- Golf at the Hans Merensky Country Club in Phalaborwa
- Quad biking, kloofing and tubing in the Magoebaskloof area between Tzaneen and Haenertsburg

ROUTES AND TRAILS

- A circular drive (40 km) from Tzaneen along the Great Letaba River, through George's Valley, across Magoebas-kloof Pass and past the mist-covered Wolksberg
- The much-lauded Magoebaskloof Pass road, which drops steeply down from the Great Escarpment to Tzaneen in the Lowveld, bypassing lush cultivated and forested lands
- The 4x4 African Ivory Route (more than 2 000 km) is a superb but rugged self-drive trail through Limpopo, which extends along the western, eastern and northern boundaries of Limpopo and is said to follow the original trail of ivory traders and elephant hunters
- A range of hiking trails from just 4 km to over 60 km (1–6 days), offered by Komatiland Eco-Tourism
- The Louis Changuion hiking trail (up to 1 day) near Haenertsburg, located in a 240-ha stretch of grassland and indigenous forest
- Walking trails (3–4 days), including the Sweni and Olifants trails, in the northern section of the Kruger National Park

Endangered Species Centre hosts day visitors, and the Khamai Reptile Park, a pioneer in the rehabilitation of snakes, lizards, crocodiles, tortoises, frogs, spiders and scorpions, is open for tours and lectures. The Nyani Tribal Village, which reflects an authentic Shangaan village, is worth a visit. The Blydepoort or Swadini Dam with a range of water-based adventure activities is 35 km away.

Phalaborwa

It is likely that the baPhalaborwa, also known as the baMalatshi, arrived in the district more than 300 years ago from present-day Zimbabwe. They were metal workers and engaged in the mining of copper and iron ore in the area. The discovery of extensive mine workings in the Phalaborwa region indicates that mining activity started here as long ago as 770 CE. Today the town mines substantial amounts of phosphate and copper. The Foskor Mine Museum offers a history on phosphate mining, while an opencast mine (Phalaborwa's 'Big Hole') can also be toured.

Tzaneen

The subtropical climate of the Lowveld is a natural hothouse for crops such as tropical fruit, citrus and nuts, which flourish in Tzaneen. There is also a cheese farm, the Wegraakbosch Organic Cheese Dairy, where visitors can see how cheese is made. On the northeastern boundary of the town the Great Letaba River flows into the Tzaneen Dam, which offers a number of recreational opportunities. The Debegeni Falls are a well-frequented site, the Cheerio Gardens bring you flowering cherry trees in September and October, and the Hans Merensky and Legalameetse nature reserves encourage you to commune with the natural world.

GAME VIEWING

Central and northern Kruger National Park

Of the Kruger National Park's 14 entrances, the Orpen, Phalaborwa, Punda Maria and Pafuri gates offer the easiest access to the central and northern sections. Rest camps here include Satara, Olifants, Letaba, Mopani, Shingwedzi, Tsendze and Punda Maria. There are also four bushveld camps, namely Talamati, Sirheni, Shimuwini and Bateleur, and luxury lodges operating in private concessions include the Imbali Safari Lodges and Pafuri Camp.

LEFT: Striking views can be enjoyed from parking lots on either side of the JG Strijdom tunnel, where local hawkers sell their wares. BELOW: One of the joys of travelling through the Limpopo Lowveld is buying fresh produce along the side of the road. Depending on the season, mangoes, litchis or avocadoes may be found.

CHAPTER 22

THE LIMPOPO BUSHVELD

ABOVE: The iconic baobab tree is found all over the rugged Limpopo Bushveld region.

The Limpopo Bushveld is situated in the western part of Limpopo province. To the south is North West Province, to the north and west is Botswana, while the N1 highway makes up the eastern border. The terrain becomes more interesting further west, away from the N1, around the hills and valleys of the Waterberg, and in the rainforest of the Soutpansberg, in the far northern reaches of the province that push up against the Zimbabwe border.

CLIMATE

This is hot and dry country with daytime temperatures spiralling upwards in the summer and remaining pleasant in the winter. Rain falls in summer and amounts to around 350 mm in the west and 600 mm in the northeast.

BAOBABS

The baobab defines the northern Limpopo landscape. It is often referred to as the 'upside-down tree' because its crown looks more like a root system than branches. There are some spectacular examples to view in the Musina area, which is ringed by a baobab tree reserve. On the road to Malala Drift a specimen known as Elephant's Trunk can be seen, so named for the shape of one of its branches. There is another, planted at the Musina railway station in 1915 which is still going strong. On the farm Nonsiang, outside of town, there is one said to be 4 500 years old; it is 26 m tall with a circumference of 19 m. There are more noteworthy baobabs in the Musina Nature Reserve, which also has antelope to view and rock formations, many millions of years old.

FLORA AND FAUNA

Shrub and tree species found in the Limpopo Bushveld include karee, boekenhout, acacia and combretum in the south, and mopane, knob thorn, tamboti and leadwood in the north. In the far north the baobab is common. Iron-wood, stinkwood and yellowwood are found in the well-watered Soutpansberg.

Animal life in the Waterberg can be experienced at a number of game lodges; a high point is a sighting of the endangered black rhino. Bird life is plentiful too, and aquatic birdwatching is recommended at the Nylsvley Nature Reserve, an official Ramsar site.

THE WATERBERG

The Waterberg Biosphere is some 15 000 km² stretching in an arc from Thabazimbi in the west to Modimolle in the centre and Mokopane in the east, with a basin of dissecting rivers in the centre. It was named a Biosphere Reserve in 2001, an international conservation designation conferred by UNESCO. Such reserves include a 'mosaic' of ecological systems that demonstrate a balanced relationship between humans and nature. The biodiversity of the Waterberg includes dry deciduous forest, high plateau savannah, shaded cliff vegetation and marsh habitats.

The Waterberg is Big Five territory and includes the privately owned Welgevonden Game Reserve, which has undergone an intensive game-restocking programme. Game farms and lodges in the Waterberg offer a range of accommodation facilities from five-star, full-service luxury lodges to more modest self-catering and guest-farm facilities.

HISTORY AND HERITAGE

As in other parts of South Africa, the more recent history of Limpopo is closely associated with the turbulence and conflict that characterised the Difaqane and the arrival of Voortrekkers who had left the Cape in defiance of British rule. However, the area's historical legacy extends much further back than that.

At the confluence of the Shashe and Limpopo rivers – where modern-day South Africa, Botswana and Zimbabwe meet – are the remains of an Iron Age settlement that thrived there for more than 300 years between 900 and 1300 CE.

The cultural heritage of Mapungubwe came to light in 1933, when a small party, led by one Ernst van Graan, discovered gold fragments on a hill on the farm Greefswald in the then northern Transvaal. Archaeological excavations

LEFT: The tranquil Waterberg, just three hours from Johannesburg, is a perfect weekend getaway.

SEE:
Limpopo, North West &
Gauteng p. 245
Limpopo &
Mpumalanga p. 246
Botswana, Zimbabwe &
Limpopo p. 249
Zimbabwe & Limpopo
p. 250

at and near the site revealed gold, copper, iron, ceramic and ivory objects, shells, animal bone tools, and indigenous and glass trade beads. The glass beads originated from India, North Africa, Arabia and Asia and their discovery provides evidence that Iron Age communities were actively involved in Indian Ocean trade networks as early as the 10th century. In exchange for items such as glass beads and cloth, Mapungubwe exported gold, ivory and other goods.

Mapungubwe Hill has also been referred to as 'The Lost City of Gold' due to further discoveries that included a golden rhinoceros figurine, a golden sceptre and a golden bowl. These objects, along with more than 156 000 other artefacts found at the site, are now housed in the Mapungubwe Museum at the University of Pretoria.

The remains unearthed at Mapungubwe are proof of the existence and subsequent decline of an African state, which, at its height, was the largest kingdom in the subcontinent. In recognition of its historic and cultural importance the Mapungubwe Cultural Landscape

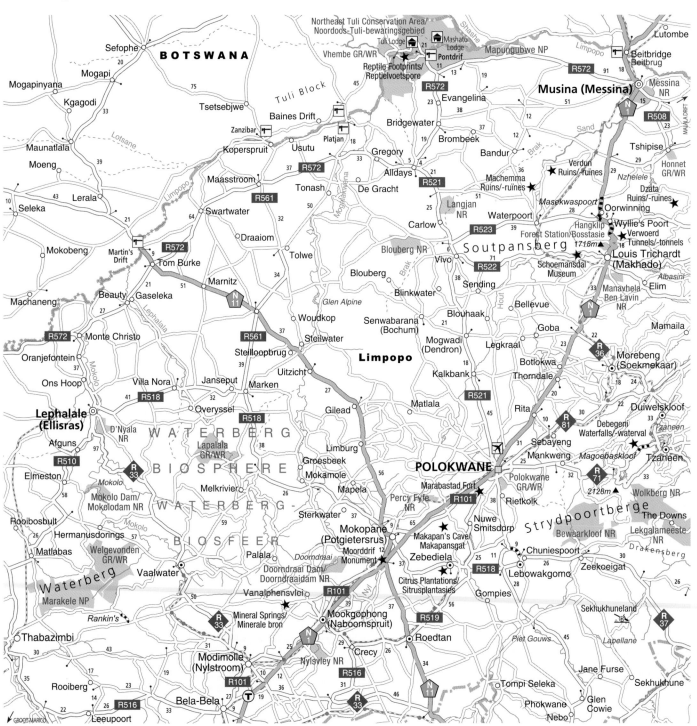

MAPUNGUBWE NATIONAL PARK

Proclaimed in 1995, the 20 216-ha Mapungubwe National Park is not only rich in cultural history, but boasts a wealth of flora and fauna as well as spectacular scenery. Elephant, white rhino, giraffe and a number of antelope species can be found here, and there are more than 300 bird species in the area. The location is wild and pristine, comprising riverine forest, baobab trees, mopane woodland and sandstone formations.

For accommodation, visitors can choose between various camps including Leokwe Camp, Limpopo Forest Tented Camp, Vhembe Wilderness Camp and the Mazhou Camping Site. Another option is the luxurious Tshugulu Lodge, which sleeps 12. There are heritage tours available, as well as morning walks, a tree-top walk and game drives.

was proclaimed a World Heritage Site in 2003. But the region's history goes even further back: there is ample evidence of San occupation near the Limpopo–Shashe confluence. More than 150 rock-art sites, dating back some 5 000 years, have been found in the area.

NOTEWORTHY PLACES
Polokwane

The provincial capital, Polokwane ('place of safety'), is a Voortrekker-founded town that took its former name, Pietersburg, from Petrus (Piet) Joubert. Today it is a centre of manufacturing and commerce, as well as the headquarters of the Limpopo Tourism & Parks Board. It offers a number of animal attractions, such as the Polokwane Game Reserve, Polokwane Bird and Reptile Park, Moletzie Bird Sanctuary and Chuene Crocodile Farm. Interesting museums include the Bakone Malapa Northern Sotho Open-Air Museum, the Polokwane Art Museum and the Hugh Exton Photographic Museum. There are also sites associated with Voortrekker history, the second Anglo-Boer War of 1899–1902 and the discovery of gold.

TOP: Mapungubwe National Park, in the remotest corner of Limpopo province, is one of the most pristine parks in the country. ABOVE: Several golden treasures, dating back centuries, have been found in the ancient graves at Mapungubwe Hill. LEFT: Rustic accommodation at Mapungubwe National Park is designed to let nature play a starring role.

RIGHT: The hot springs at Bela-Bela are a popular family holiday destination, and there are a number of resorts catering to families travelling with children.

Musina

Musina (previously Messina) is South Africa's northernmost town. The busy border at Beit-bridge, to the north, controls traffic in and out of Zimbabwe, while some 40 km to the south-east the sulphurous mineral springs of Tship-ise ('hot spring') beckon in the grounds of a holiday resort.

Thanks to the mineral-rich Messina Fault, modern Musina thrives as a copper and dia-mond mining town, but its prehistory is also closely associated with mining and metal work-ing in South Africa, for extensive Iron Age cop-per workings have been discovered in the area. Shafts or trenches, some reaching a depth of 25 m, were dug to follow the veins of ore, which, once excavated, were lifted to the sur-face in baskets. The ancient miners used ham-merstones and chisels made of iron to break the ore, before melting it in furnaces. Copper was valued by Iron Age societies for its orna-mental use and as a trade object.

Louis Trichardt (Makhado)

Louis Trichardt, named after the Voortrekker leader who set up camp here in 1836, has a tinge of the 'Wild West' as it once attracted ivory hunters and traders, as well as gunrun-ners. It is also known as Makhado, after Chief Makhado of the Venda who took a dim view of these shenanigans and overran the town. This story is retold in exhibits at the open-air Schoemansdal Museum, west of the town.

Other attractions in the area include San rock art, Voortrekker heritage sites, the Manavhela Ben Lavin Nature Reserve and the Albasini Dam, which offers water sports and other recreational activities. Some 35 km south of Makhado on the N1 is a sign indicating the Tropic of Capricorn.

Mokopane (Potgietersrus)

Mokopane is another town originally named for a Voortrekker leader (Piet Potgieter), later renamed after a local chief (Makapan) – in this instance the adversaries in a tragic tale. In 1854, a group of Voortrekkers resting in the area was set upon by Tlou warriors under chiefs Makapan and Mapela, and the entire party of 28 Boers lost their lives. Expecting a reprisal, Makapan led his 2 000-strong army into some limestone caves, now known as Makapansgat (Makapan's Cave), where they planned to hide. They took grain with them, expecting the caves to yield an adequate water supply.

A Voortrekker commando led by Potgie-ter then laid siege to the caves for a period of 30 days, during which periodic skirmishes were fought and Potgieter was killed. Finally, when no further shots came from the cave, the Voortrekkers stormed in and found the bodies of 1 500 warriors who had succumbed to thirst and hunger. The remainder are believed to have escaped.

The caves have also revealed significant fos-sil finds of early humans and animals, and are today a heritage site. The Arend Dieperink Museum in Mokopane and nature reserves in the vicinity are other sites worth visiting.

Mookgophong (Naboomspruit)

This town in the Waterberg owes its existence not to a gold rush, but to the discovery of tin that resulted in an influx of prospectors and the start of a boom town. In 1925 platinum was discovered here too. The naboom tree (euphorbia) is a common sight, and the Nylsvley Nature Reserve is a good spot for aquatic birding, with some 470 species recorded.

Modimolle (Nylstroom)

The tale behind the establishment of this Waterberg town is intriguing: a group of Voor-trekkers from Groot Marico decided that their best bet to escape British rule was to head as far north as possible … all the way to the Holy Land. When they happened upon a river and a hill that resembled a pyramid they believed they had arrived in Egypt. The river, they assumed, was the Nile (*Nyl*), and they named their settlement Nylstroom ('Nile stream').

The town's new name, Modimolle, means 'the spirits have eaten' and honours the local tribal tradition of offering food to the ancestors. Tourist highlights include churches and museums, and the entrance pillars of a second Anglo–Boer War concentration camp.

Bela-Bela (Warmbaths)

The therapeutic hot springs first discovered here by the Tswana 200 years ago, who named them Bela-Bela ('the water which boils on its own'), are modern Bela-Bela's biggest selling point. The Afrikaans name, Warmbad ('warm bath'), was dropped in 2002 in favour of the original Tswana appellation. A holiday resort has grown up around the 53 °C springs, and if you can tear yourself away from the soothing mineralised waters and spa treatments, there are restaurants and shopping facilities at the waterfront in this town.

Thabazimbi

Life in the town of Thabazimbi revolves around the mining of iron ore. Some 10 km west is the Marakele National Park that boasts not only elephant, rhino and feline predators, but also one of the world's largest remaining colonies of endangered Cape vulture.

Lephalale (Ellisras)

Ellisras, named for its founders Patrick Ellis and Piet Erasmus, changed its name to Lephalale, meaning 'heartbeat of the Bushveld'. This Waterberg town is the site of a large colliery. In its environs are a good number of game- and trophy-hunting farms. The Mokolo Dam is popular with anglers and the D'Nyala Nature Reserve is a choice picnic, hiking and birding spot.

ACTIVITIES

- Camping outside Mokopane
- Angling at Frikkie Geyser Dam and the Doorndraai Dam Nature Reserve near Mookgophong and the Mokolo Dam near Lephalale
- Birdwatching and picnicking at the Nylsvley Nature Reserve near Mookgophong
- Relaxing in the hot springs at Bela-Bela
- Game viewing at Marakele National Park near Thabazimbi

ROUTES AND TRAILS

- Hanglip Trail (2 days) at Makhado from the Hanglip forest station, which includes a climb up a 1 700-m peak
- Horse trails (2 hours–1 day) in the Waterberg
- Two Kransberg nature trails (6 and 9 hours) outside Thabazimbi
- Three Wag 'n Bietjie hiking trails (2–6 hours) near Bela-Bela
- Vasbyt Hiking Trail (2 days) near Mookgophong

FESTIVALS

Since 1986, the Bushveld Festival has become an annual event at Lephalale. It includes horse-jumping contests and dog shows, a three-day battle for the best 4x4, as well as bird- and tree-identification competitions.

LEFT: Mapungubwe National Park is not only of cultural importance, but also stocked with a great variety of wildlife.

CHAPTER 23

THE NORTH WEST

ABOVE: As a result of Operation Phoenix, a massive relocation programme, Madikwe Game Reserve has a diverse mammal population, including white rhino.

Northwest Province is bordered by Botswana, the Free State, the Northern Cape, Limpopo and Gauteng. The land is rich in platinum and the North West is sometimes referred to as the country's 'platinum province'.

The area is known for agriculture (maize, beef and sunflower seeds) and mining (platinum, gold and diamonds) as well as its tourism attractions, including Sun City, the Pilanesberg Game Reserve, Madikwe Game Reserve, the Magaliesberg and Hartbeespoort Dam.

PILANESBERG GAME RESERVE

Adjacent to the famous Sun City resort, Pilanesberg Game Reserve is home to a large variety of wildlife, including the Big Five and the rare wild dog. The reserve is set in the crater of an extinct volcano some 1 200 million years old, and is considered geologically unique due to the rare rocks and interesting rock formations scattered across its landscape. There are some significant Iron and Stone Age sites in the reserve.

CLIMATE

The North West is known for its excellent climate, long sunny days and wide blue skies. Summer temperatures range between 22 °C and 34 °C and afternoon thunderstorms are a regular event. Winters are dry and sunny although the evenings do get chilly. Average winter temperatures range from 2 °C (early mornings) to 20 °C (mid-day), and annual rainfall totals 360 mm.

THE TSWANA

The Tswana people emerged from the larger Sotho group and today number some two million, spread throughout the Northern Cape, Gauteng and North West provinces.

Tswana tradition measures wealth and status in cattle, the number of which also determines the size of households. Today, cattle, along with money, are usually paid as bride wealth (*bogadi*).

A typical Tswana family consists of a husband, his wife (or wives) and their unmarried children. The man is regarded as the head of the household and is shown immense respect. It is predominantly in the rural countryside where divisions between men and women are still upheld. This often means women are often excluded from political and religious meetings. Certain places in the village are reserved for the use of men, while at social gatherings women and men sit apart.

A Tswana woman's dress, which has evolved over the centuries, indicates her position. It is usually a voluminous outfit of plain colour with tucks at the bottom, over which she wears a specific multicoloured apron tied at the back. This is finished off with a headdress.

The Tswana way of life is celebrated at the Gaabo Motho Cultural Village at Hebron between Ga-Rankuwa and Mabopane. This cultural village gives insight into Venda, Zulu, Sotho, Tsonga and Ndebele cultures.

FLORA AND FAUNA

Most of the province falls within the Savannah biome (bushveld vegetation), the remainder being part of the Grassland biome. A range of different habitats and ecosystems contribute to the high level of biodiversity in the region.

The province has a number of national parks and provincial and private nature reserves, the most well known being the Pilanesberg and Madikwe game reserves, both home to the Big Five. The North West also shares the Magaliesberg Protected Natural Environment with Gauteng.

HISTORY AND HERITAGE

When the Sotho-Tswana moved into the region around the 14th century, they came as herders and farmers, arriving from across the Limpopo River. They settled in the northern part of South Africa, but by the early 1500s they had separated into different chiefdoms and spread out to the south and west, as far as present-day Botswana.

By the 1700s, the Sotho-Tswana had started to build dwellings and enclosures using stone, with stonewalled settlements becoming more widespread. Many of these were abandoned in the wake of the political and social upheaval associated with the Difaqane in the late 18th and early 19th centuries, and large, defensive village-like settlements such as Kaditshwene near Zeerust were established. Adding to the turmoil was the arrival of white settlers on the Highveld, looking for space uncontaminated by the English.

After the Battle of Vegkop, when the Ndebele attacked a Voortrekker laager, the Boers entered into an alliance with the Tswana in 1837 that would force Mzilikazi to flee north of the Limpopo River to present-day Zimbabwe. But the Boers did not stick to the pact for long and soon they and the Tswana became involved in a contest for land that lasted almost half a century and ended when Britain annexed British Bechuanaland in 1885.

In their relief over British protection, the Tswana did not realise that Mahikeng, the seat of the Tsidi-Barolong, was along the route at the heart of Cecil John Rhodes's vision to expand the empire from Cape Town to Cairo, and that it proved to be the perfect launching spot from which to unseat Transvaal president Paul Kruger. With the Transvaal border now pushed slightly eastwards, the way was clear for Rhodes, which spelt disaster for the Tswana and other indigenous groups to the north.

LEFT: The variety of reptiles in Pilanesberg Game Reserve includes geckos, skinks, chameleons and monitor lizards (shown). BELOW LEFT: Warthog roam the wild spaces of the North West province.

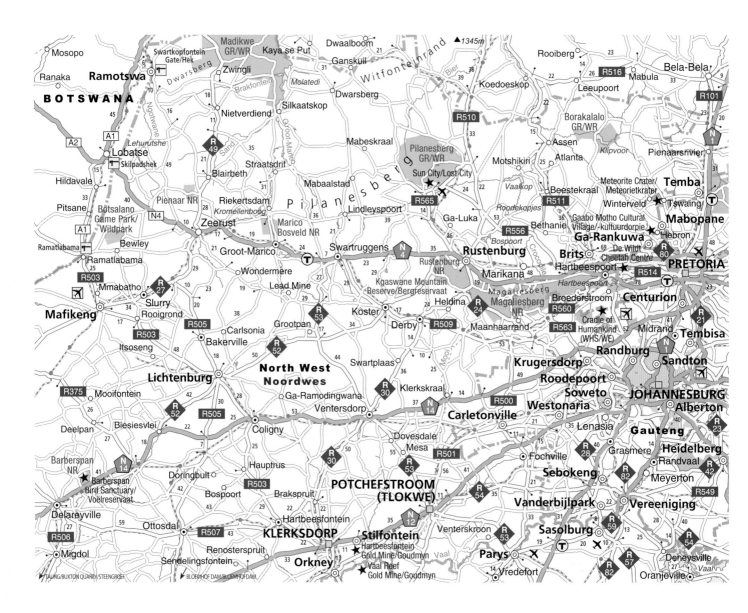

In the 1890s, Mahikeng, its name changed to Mafeking, became a 'Wild West' frontier town. It was from here that the fateful Jameson Raid was launched in 1896. While it was a disaster, it contributed directly to the second Anglo–Boer War of 1899.

Shortly before the second Anglo–Boer War, Colonel Robert Baden-Powell, against orders to keep mobile, invested his small force in Mafeking. On 12 October 1899 the first shots of the war were fired at nearby Kraaipan when Boers fired on a train bringing arms to the town. The following day the town was besieged, with the siege lifted only in May the following year.

The events at Mafeking had a direct influence on South African politics. The court interpreter during the siege was Sol Plaatje, who became so disillusioned with the conduct of the British that he would dedicate the rest of his life to reversing the worsening lot of black South Africans. His efforts were instrumental in the 1912 founding of the South African Native National Congress, forerunner of the ANC, which was the one of the first liberation movements in Africa.

After the lifting of the siege, the northwestern areas of the country became something of a backwater. In 1977 Mafeking became Mafikeng, the capital of the nominally independent Bophuthatswana homeland under Chief Lucas Mangope. He resisted reincorporation into South Africa until shortly before the first democratic elections in April 1994, even calling on right-wing Afrikaner elements to bolster his government. But that was a disaster and he was deposed, and Mafikeng and most of the North West Province returned to the fold.

NOTEWORTHY PLACES
Mafikeng

Known as 'the place of stones', Mafikeng was founded in the 1880s and offers an interesting mix of colonial and modern Africa. It is the provincial capital and contains a number of historic sites. The Mafikeng Cemetery and Mafikeng Museum are notable attractions as is Maratiwa House – the home of Sol Plaatje, the mission-educated intellectual, writer and campaigner against the infamous 1913 Natives Land Act.

Groot Marico

The town of Groot Marico takes its name from the Groot Marico River. A good place to start an exploration is at the local tourism information centre with Santa and Egbert van Bart – who not only do their bit for tourism but also run the local Herman Charles Bosman Literary Society, dedicated to the writer whose tales of the Groot Marico immortalised the best and the worst of the town and its people. The region is also famous for its mampoer – distilled liquor made from fruit.

Lichtenburg

The town of Lichtenburg is known for the discovery in 1926 of a valuable gemstone on the farm Elandsputte. As a result, hordes of fortune-seekers converged on the diggings and it became a boom town overnight. The rumpus soon died down – as it did in many other gold-rush towns in the region – leaving behind a settlement with a fascinating history. These days agriculture (sunflower seeds and maize) is at the core of this community. A few notable attractions in town include the De la Rey memorials, dedicated to this famous Afrikaner general, as well as the Lichtenburg Museum and the Lichtenburg Game Breeding Farm.

Taung

Taung ('place of the lion') was named after Tau, chief of the Bataung people. It achieved global renown in 1924 when a small hominid skull, now known to science as the 'Taung child', was discovered in the Buxton quarry. This discovery provided early evidence for the theory that humankind originated in Africa. Although still

THE LEGEND OF MAMPOER

The folklore of the bushveld (especially Groot Marico) is linked to mampoer, a pure, strong brandy distilled from peaches or other fruit. Many stories surround the origins of this tipple and the root of its name; some believe it to be the first cousin of the equally potent Cape witblits ('white lightning'). Although the history of the word mampoer is unknown, it has been suggested that the potent liquor was named after the Pedi chief Mampuru.

BELOW LEFT: The Valley of the Waves at The Lost City, with its man-made wave pool and numerous themed rides, is a popular haunt for families all year round. BELOW RIGHT: The Lost City, brainchild of hotelier Sol Kerzner, is world famous for its fantasy themed on an ancient African city.

SUN CITY

This giant entertainment complex is built on an ancient volcano and is a major tourist attraction. It offers a wealth of entertainment options including gambling, restaurants, theatres, live performances and children's activities.

The Palace of the Lost City at Sun City is a popular fantasy park and luxury hotel built to resemble the stronghold of an ancient African civilisation. One of the key attractions here is the Valley of the Waves theme park. Visitors can also enjoy excursions into the nearby Pilanesberg Game Reserve or play a round of golf at the Lost City Golf Course or the Gary Player Country Club.

a centre for archaeological research, the Taung Heritage Site is also open to the public and includes the picturesque Blue Pools, a tranquil picnic venue.

Klerksdorp
Settled in 1837, Klerksdorp is today a large mining and agricultural centre. Visitors can explore the history of mining in the area by visiting the Stock Exchange Building constructed in 1888 during the gold rush, and mining shafts dating back to the 18th century at Goudkoppie Hill. Tours of the local mine are available on request.

Potchefstroom (Tlokwe)
The town of 'Potch' started off as a farming settlement along the banks of the Mooi River. Andries Potgieter and his trekkers moved here in 1838 and it is known as the old Transvaal's oldest Voortrekker town. Today it is a student town, and the North-West University is a respected learning institution. There are a number of historic sites in town including the City Hall, Old Gunpowder House, Krugerskraal Opstal, Old Magistrate's Office and Andrew Carnegie Library.

Broederstroom
Broederstroom is in the foothills of the scenic Magaliesberg. It is an excellent base from which to explore the Hartbeespoort region and there are a number of guest houses and B & Bs in the area. The Margaret Roberts herbal farm, which is open to the public only on Wednesdays, is well worth a visit.

Hartbeespoort
Situated in the Magaliesberg, the village of Hartbeespoort on the shore of the dam after which it was named is a very popular weekend getaway spot for people living in Gauteng's urban hubs of Pretoria and Johannesburg. Water sports such as jet- and water-skiing are popular, as are boat cruises. Hartbeespoort Dam Cableway offers excellent views of the area. Land-based attractions include a reptile and snake park, an elephant sanctuary and several fun farm stalls, such as Tan' Malie se Winkel en Van Gaalen se Kaasmakerij.

Rustenburg
Rustenburg is the industrial and commercial centre of the Bojanala region, the section of the province closest to neighbouring Gauteng. Visit the Anglican church on Van Staden Street, view the Paul Kruger heritage site or go to the Rustenburg Museum, where there are a number of archaeological displays. The Kgaswane Mountain Reserve is situated on 5 200 ha and has numerous antelope and bird species. There are lovely hikes and trails here.

MADIKWE GAME RESERVE

Madikwe Game Reserve – close to the Botswana border – extends over 76 000 ha bordering the Dwarsberg Mountains. The area consists of distinct biomes that include the bushveld and Kalahari sandveld, supporting a wide range of habitats. The reserve is home to the Big Five and is also known for its cheetah and wild dog. There are a number of lodges in the reserve ranging from basic to five-star accommodation, as well as several community-owned lodges.

Madikwe's Operation Phoenix was one of the largest game translocations ever in southern Africa. The initiative saw 8 000 animals from 28 different species, including lion, black rhino, buffalo and elephant, being released into the reserve between 1992 and 1999.

ACTIVITIES

• Visiting mampoer stills on surrounding farms in the Groot Marico district

• Picnicking at Blue Pools at the Buxton quarry near Taung

• Mine tours at Hartbeesfontein Gold Mine

• Jet-skiing, water-skiing, picnicking, boat cruises and cable-car rides at Hartbeespoort Dam

• Hot-air ballooning over the Pilanesberg Game Reserve from Sun City

• Hang-gliding at Hartbeespoort, Magaliesburg and Pilanesberg

• Zip-lining near Sun City

• Gaming at Sun City

• Fishing at Vaalkop Dam near Sun City and Bloemhof Dam outside Bloemhof

• Game viewing at Pilanesberg and Madikwe game reserves

ROUTES AND TRAILS

• Uitkyk Hiking Trail (1 day) at Hartbeespoort Dam in the Magaliesberg

• Two Hennops hiking trails (3 and 5 hours) at Hartbeespoort Dam

• Guided walks (2–3 hours) in the Pilanesberg Game Reserve

DE WILDT CHEETAH AND WILDLIFE CENTRE

The De Wildt Cheetah Centre, near Brits and the Hartbeespoort Dam, is renowned for its successful cheetah breeding programme. Other animals that can be seen here include brown hyaena, African wild dog, antelope, blue duikers, vultures and owls. The centre also has a dedicated unit for vultures. Tours need to be booked in advance.

LEFT: Hot-air ballooning safaris over the scenic Magaliesberg are the perfect way to see the area's beautiful landscape.
ABOVE: Hartbeespoort Dam offers great water sports opportunities for the residents of nearby Johannesburg and Pretoria.

CHAPTER 24

THE KALAHARI AND DIAMOND FIELDS

ABOVE: Rain in the Kalahari is usually accompanied by violent thunderstorms and spectacular displays of lightning.

The landscape that makes up the vast north-western corner of South Africa, at the southern edge of the Kalahari, alternates between spectacular red sand dunes, woodlands, gently undulating plains, barren pans and expanses of scenic thornveld.

This harsh land is home to the iconic gemsbok (oryx) and other plains antelope, the black-maned lion of the Kalahari and the pygmy falcon. The bateleur is the undisputed master of the sky, while the huge communal nests of sociable weavers are a characteristic sight on telephone poles and in camel thorn trees.

Bounded by the Orange River Valley in the south, the region shares its western boundary with Namibia. To the north, its boundary is defined by Botswana and the North West Province, and in the east by the Free State. Agriculture centres on cattle, small stock and game

farming, but mining is the backbone of the region's economy. Diamonds played an important role in the development of the area, where immense iron ore, manganese and limestone deposits also occur.

CLIMATE

The Kalahari is known for its extremes – in mid-summer, temperatures can soar into the 40s, while winters in the southeast can be freezing cold at well below zero.

Heavy thunderstorms are common in summer, at other times spectacular displays of lightning, are accompanied by short bursts of rain. Precipitation is unpredictable, however, and years can pass without a single drop. When the rains do finally come, an entire year's quota can fall in a few hours. Average rainfall ranges from 175 mm in the northwest to 500 mm in the east.

FLORA AND FAUNA

The vegetation varies from open savannah, dominated by acacias and thornveld, to shrubveld. The camel thorn is the tree most closely associated with the Kalahari. Other characteristic plants include the umbrella thorn, black thorn, shepherd's tree, silver cluster-leaf, three-thorn rhigozum and raisin-bush.

Fields of bright-yellow flowering devil's thorn are conspicuous after good summer rains when a variety of other flowers and creepers come into bloom. Among them is the tsamma, the desert melon that is an important source of water and nutrition for animals.

With its rapier horns, the gemsbok has uniquely adapted to survive in this harsh landscape. The plains and dunes of the region were once also home to vast herds of migratory springbok, blue wildebeest, red hartebeest and eland. Lion and other predators were plentiful, but as farmers began settling in the area the wildlife was hunted relentlessly; only those that roamed the most remote parts escaped their guns.

THE KALAHARI – SEA OF SAND

The Kalahari, the largest continuous sand mantle in the world, covers most of Botswana and extends into western Zimbabwe, Zambia, eastern Namibia and Angola. Clay, sand and gravel gradually filled the basin which formed here some 65 million years ago. The most recent event took place 2 to 3 million years ago when strong winds blew vast quantities of sand into the basin.

Today, the Kgalagadi Transfrontier Park, which straddles South Africa and Botswana, is sanctuary to a vast array of animals and birds, while several game farms have been stocked with antelope and other game.

The Kalahari is renowned for its raptors and more than 50 species, including 35 residents, have been recorded to date. Summer is the best time for birding when the numbers of resident species are swelled by migrants. The *Kalahari Raptor Route* map is an excellent guide to raptor viewing along 15 drives in the Kalahari. It is available free from the Northern Cape Tourism Authority and outlines almost 2 000 km of roads in the area.

HISTORY AND HERITAGE

The Kalahari is the ancestral home of San hunter-gatherers who lived there for thousands of years; rock engravings at Wildebeest Kuil and elsewhere in the region are testimony to these early inhabitants.

They lived in harmony with nature until the arrival of new groups of people, namely Khoekhoen (black pastoralists), Bantu-speaking Tswanas (who migrated onto the Highveld about 1 000 years ago and practised a mixed economy of cattle-farming and agriculture), Basters (seminomadic pastoralists of mixed Khoekhoe and Dutch descent) and *trekboers* (white migratory stock farmers).

The Basters arrived in the area known as Transorangia (a territory beyond the Orange River, now known as Griqualand West) in the early 1800s from Little Namaqualand. They

BELOW LEFT: The bateleur takes its name from the French for tightrope walker – a reference to the way it balances its wings in flight. BELOW RIGHT: Blue wildebeest are one of the most commonly seen antelope in the Auob and Nossob valleys in the Kgalagadi Transfrontier Park.

SEE:
Kimberley p. 217
Northern Cape & North
West p. 235
Free State & North West
p. 236

settled at fountains around Klaarwater ('clear water'), renamed Griquatown in 1813, before later spreading out to more distant water sources at Campbell and Daniëlskuil. A new community thus began developing and they adopted the name Griqua in 1813 – after the ChariGuriQua, the Khoekhoe group from which they partly descend.

The lucky discovery of a diamond on the bank of the Orange River near Hopetown in 1866, followed by further, even more promising finds along the banks of the Vaal River in 1869, sparked a diamond rush to the region. While the Griquas and the two independent Boer republics (the South African Republic and the Orange Free State) laid claim to the area, the diggers simply went ahead and declared their own republic in 1870. However, the abundant lands of Griqualand West were annexed by Britain in 1871. That same year, a diamond was found at a hill called Colesberg Kopje, on a farm owned by the De Beers brothers, and so the diamond rush into what would become the town of Kimberley was triggered.

NOTEWORTHY PLACES
Griquatown

The first mission station north of the Orange River was established at the home base of the

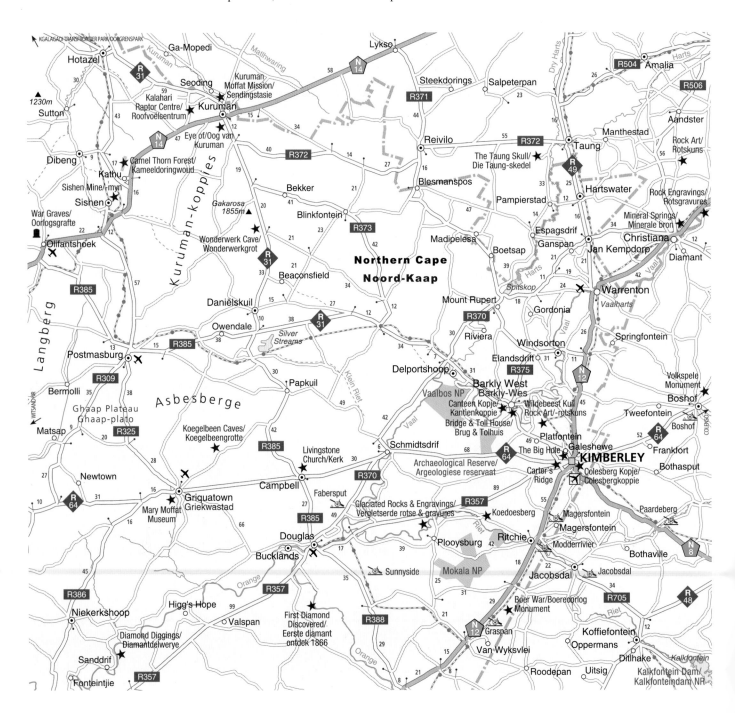

WITSAND NATURE RESERVE

The pure white dunes of Witsand Nature Reserve near Postmasburg are in stark contrast to the characteristic red dunes of the Kalahari. The 'island' of white sand, some 9 km long and about 2 km wide, formed when subsurface water leached off the iron oxide coating the sand grains.

Also of interest is the Brulsand, or Roaring Sand. When the air is dry, the uniform sand grains produce an ominous rumble when the dunes are disturbed.

Herds of springbok, gemsbok and red hartebeest roam the dunes and plains. Steenbok, common duiker, bat-eared fox and ground squirrel are among the smaller mammals to look out for.

Facilities consist of self-catering chalets, two swimming pools, a group camp and camping sites, as well as a conference centre.

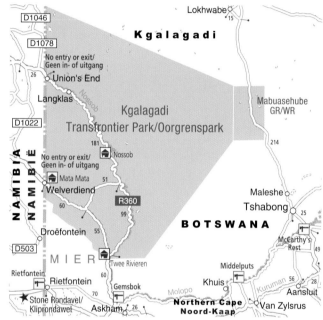

Griquas at Klaarwater by the London Missionary Society in 1804. The name was changed to Griquatown in 1813 and the town was laid out in 1879.

The Mary Moffat Museum in the main street was named after the eldest daughter of Dr Robert Moffat, who was born in Griquatown while her missionary father worked here in 1820 and 1821, before the family left for Kuruman. Mary later married the famed explorer Dr David Livingstone. A pulpit, said to have been made by Dr Moffat, and personal items of the Griqua chief Andries Waterboer are among the historic objects in the museum. One of the rooms has been furnished as a bedroom typical of the 1820s, while various documents and articles relating to the town's history are also displayed.

Other places of interest include the Griqua Monument near the hospital and the Execution Tree. Murderers and stock thieves were sent to hang from the seringa tree when Waterboer had his headquarters here.

Mokala National Park

The Mokala National Park, 80 km southwest of Kimberley, was officially proclaimed in June 2007 following a successful land claim on a section of the earlier Vaalbos National Park, which was established near Barkly West in 1986.

Within just three months, 860 animals were translocated from Vaalbos to Mokala (a Setswana name for the camel thorn tree), while nearly 390 animals were moved to other parks in the country. Mokala is home to black and white rhino, buffalo, tsessebe, roan, eland, red hartebeest, gemsbok, springbok and plains zebra, as well as various smaller mammals and a rich variety of birds.

Accommodation is available in two lodges, each with a restaurant and conference facilities.

SEE:
Northern Cape & Namibia p. 233
Northern Cape p. 234
Namibia p. 241
Botswana p. 242

ABOVE LEFT: A ground squirrel nibbles on a tsamma – an annual creeper with a melon-like fruit that has a moisture content of over 90%. ABOVE RIGHT: Gemsbok, icons of the Kalahari, are well adapted to survive in arid areas.

ABOVE: Synonymous with Kimberley is the Big Hole, the largest non-mechanically-dug hole in the world.
BELOW RIGHT: Kimberley's Old Town gives visitors an idea of what life was like here in the glory days of diamond mining.

There is also a small camp with hot-water ablutions and campsites overlooking a waterhole.

Kimberley

Kimberley – the 'Diamond City' and the 'City that Sparkles' – developed around a mining camp that sprang up after diamonds were found there in 1871.

Miners, fortune-seekers and swindlers rushed to the scene. With picks, shovels and their bare hands, they excavated the largest non-mechanically-dug hole in the world, and called it the Big Hole. When the mine closed in 1914, it covered an area of 17 ha and was 215 m deep. The 22,5 million tonnes of earth that were excavated had yielded 2 722 kg of diamonds.

The Diamonds & Destiny Visitor Centre at the Big Hole provides a fascinating insight into the story of diamonds. A viewing platform suspended over the sheer edge of the Big Hole provides awe-inspiring views of the mine, while a 19th-century mineshaft has been recreated in the Underground Mine. The locally found 616 Diamond and the Eureka, the first diamond found in South Africa (near Hopetown in 1866), are among the treasures on display in the centre's Diamond Vault.

Adjacent to the Big Hole is Old Town, where period buildings recreate the hectic mining days when fortunes were rapidly made and just as quickly lost. It features a replica of one of the more than 100 pubs that flourished in Kimberley's heyday, a digger's house built in 1878, the original Barney Barnato's Boxing Academy and a pawnbroker's shop. The oldest church, the German Lutheran Church of St Martini, the oldest house (a prefabricated structure im-

DID YOU KNOW?

The 616 Diamond is named after its weight in carats, and is the largest single diamond crystal in the world, remaining uncut.

MUSEUMS OF KIMBERLEY

Founded in 1907, the McGregor Museum in the 1897-built Kimberley Sanatorium has excellent displays on the town's history, including the Siege of Kimberley and the forced removals of the Malay Camp, as well as on natural history and the origins of humankind.

The museum has 8 satellite exhibitions, among them the Duggan-Cronin Gallery with its unique collection of 8 000 ethnographic photographs taken mainly between 1919 and 1939. Apart from these images taken by Alfred Duggan-Cronin, there are also the photographic collections of Jean Morris, Aubrey Elliot and Alice Mertins, as well as displays of beadwork, costumes and pottery.

An extensive collection of San rock art, traditional African art and a representative collection of South African art can be viewed at the William Humphreys Art Gallery, that also houses works by 16th- and 17th-century Dutch, Flemish, English and French masters.

ported from England in 1877), and a diamond buyer's office are among the many other interesting buildings in Old Town.

The early days of transport in Kimberley can be relived by boarding a tram that runs between the City Hall (built in Roman-Corinthian style in 1899) and the Big Hole. The restored tram, Car Number 3, was used between 1906 and 1914.

Situated at the highest point of Kimberley, where five roads converge, the imposing Honoured Dead Memorial commemorates those who died during the 124-day siege of Kimberley during the second Anglo–Boer War of 1899–1902.

Places of interest in Galeshewe, a township in Kimberley that is one of the oldest in the country, include the building where Pan Africanist Congress (PAC) leader Robert Sobukwe had a law office and the Mayibuye Memorial, which honours those who died during the 1952 Kimberley Uprising.

Wildebeest Kuil

More than 400 engravings have been etched into the rocks on a small hill at Wildebeest Kuil, about 16 km northwest of Kimberley. Eland, rhinoceros, red hartebeest and elephant are among the animals depicted, but unlike other such sites in the Northern Cape there are few engravings of geometric images. A 25-minute-long film introduces visitors to the rock-art site and the !Xun and Khwe San communities of Wildebeest Kuil. Information boards have been erected at engravings along the 800-m-long pathway and visitors can listen to an audio commentary. Facilities at the Wildebeest Kuil Rock Art Centre include displays, an auditorium, arts and crafts shop and a tearoom.

Barkly West

Miners began working the diamond-rich alluvial gravels on both banks of the Vaal River at a fording place call Klipdrift ('stone ford') in 1869, and at the height of the diamond-mining frenzy some 20 000 diggers lived in the area. The settlement was named after the governor at the Cape at the time, Sir Henry Barkly, who paid a visit to the diamond fields in 1870.

The first bridge over the Vaal River was opened at Barkly West on 24 June 1885. The old tollhouse on the northern bank of the river now serves as the Barkly West Museum, which focuses on the early diamond diggings. St Mary's Anglican church, built in 1871, the old jail and the house of Cecil John Rhodes are among the other attractions in the town.

Canteen Kopje, once the site of frantic diamond digging, is also of great archaeological importance. Large numbers of Stone Age

ABOVE: The fallen of the Scottish Highland Regiments are remembered by this Celtic cross.

artefacts have been uncovered at this hill, among them a 4,7-kg handaxe – one of the largest ever to have been discovered in South Africa.

Daniëlskuil

Daniëlskuil lies in the southern foothills of the Kuruman Hills. It was named after a 6-m-deep limestone sinkhole that somehow reminded the early inhabitants of the biblical story of Daniël and the lions' den.

Archaeological research at Wonderwerk Cave, a 139-m deep grotto in a dolomite hill 43 km north of Daniëlskuil, has provided evidence of human habitation for the past 800 000 years and early attempts to make fire. Ostrich, eland, elephant and abstract motifs are depicted by the 'finger paintings' near the mouth of the cave, where there is also a large stalagmite. Facilities include an information and exhibition centre at the cave entrance and three self-catering cottages.

Kuruman

Situated on the Ghaap Plateau on the edge of the Kalahari, Kuruman is also known as the 'Oasis of the Kalahari'. It was laid out on the banks of the Kuruman River in 1887 and is a centre for the surrounding farms and mines in the area.

The first mission station of the London Missionary Society for the Tswana people was founded about 90 km north of Kuruman in 1816. It was later moved to Maruping until the Scottish missionary, Dr Robert Moffat, arrived at Kuruman in 1824. Then it was moved once more – to its present site on the western outskirts of Kuruman – and became known as the Kuruman Moffat Mission. The Moffat homestead, wagon shed, the mission church and original water furrow dug by Dr Moffat to irrigate the mission gardens form part of the complex. The foundation stone of the church was laid in 1830 and the 800-seat church was consecrated 3 years later.

The Kalahari Raptor Centre is situated on a 600-ha private nature reserve, 31 km northwest of Kuruman. The centre has aviaries that house raptors that cannot be released back into the wild, as well as an enclosure for vultures. The reserve has been stocked with gemsbok, eland, springbok, red hartebeest, blue wildebeest and plains zebra. There is an education centre and a luxury two-bed self-catering chalet.

Not to be missed is the seemingly endless stream of crystal-clear water that pours out of the dolomite rocks at the Eye of Kuruman, known as Ga-Segonyana ('little water calabash') in Setswana.

Kathu

Kathu was established as a mining town for employees of the nearby Sishen Mine in the late 1950s and was laid out amid an exceptionally dense forest of tall camel thorn trees. Covering some 4 000 ha, the camel thorn forest was declared a natural heritage site in 1995.

The Sishen Mine, a few kilometres southwest of Kathu, ranks among the five largest opencast mines in the world and has one of the biggest iron-ore deposits globally. What is more, the iron ore is transported on some of the longest trains in the world along an 800-km-long railway line to the harbour at Saldanha on the West Coast.

Mier

Sandwiched between the Namibian border in the west and the Kgalagadi Transfrontier Park

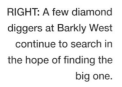

RIGHT: A few diamond diggers at Barkly West continue to search in the hope of finding the big one.

ACTIVITIES

• Camping and game viewing at Mokala National Park southwest of Kimberley
• Viewing rock art at Wonderwerk Cave, 43 km north of Daniëlskuil, and at Wildebeest Kuil, about 16 km northwest of Kimberley
• Viewing raptors and game at the Kalahari Raptor Centre, 31 km northwest of Kuruman
• Dune boarding and 4x4 driving on the dunes of Mier
• Birding and game viewing at the Kgalagadi Transfrontier Park
• Listening to the Roaring Sand, game viewing, swimming and camping at Witsand Nature Reserve near Postmasburg

ROUTES AND TRAILS

• Three 4x4 trails in the South African section of the Kgalagadi Transfrontier Park: Nossob 4x4 Eco Trail (214 km), guided over four days; Bitterpan Trail (120 km), only accessible to residents of Bitterpan Wilderness Camp; and Leeuwdril 4x4 Loop (13,2 km)
• Kalahari Raptor Route entails 15 different routes covering a total 2 000 km in the Northern Cape Kalahari
• Belgravia Walk (2 hours) and Great Kimberley North Walk (4 hours) in Kimberley

in the north, Mier occupies one of the remotest corners of South Africa.

This almost forgotten piece of land forms part of the ancestral home of the !Khomani San, who were dispossessed of their land in 1930 when the Mier area was declared a settlement for coloured people.

The !Khomani San and those Mier families living north of the settlement were forced to leave that area too, when shortly afterwards,

in 1931, the Kalahari Gemsbok National Park was proclaimed.

Rietfontein is the main centre of Mier. The rectangular mission church with its decorative end gables is a reminder of the Baster people who settled here under the leadership of *Kaptyn* (Captain) Dirk Philander, after migrating from the southwestern Cape in the 1860s.

Years later, in March 1999, Mier made headline news when 25 000 ha of land just outside the Kgalagadi Transfrontier Park were returned to the !Khomani San. The !Khomani San and the Mier community were subsequently also successful in their claims to ownership of land in the southern section of the transfrontier park. This area has been incorporated into the reserve as a contractual park, and the two communities operate a lodge in the area.

The dunes of Mier are ideal for dune boarding and are a challenge to the driving skills of 4x4 enthusiasts.

Kgalagadi Transfrontier Park

The Kgalagadi Transfrontier Park is a vast wilderness of red sand dunes, gently undulating sandveld and tree savannahs punctuated by pans and the dry courses of the Nossob and Auob rivers.

One of Africa's great game parks, it became the first transfrontier conservation area on the continent when South Africa's Kalahari Gemsbok National Park and Botswana's Gemsbok National Park were amalgamated in 1999.

It is a sanctuary to large herds of gemsbok, blue wildebeest, red hartebeest, eland, springbok and smaller creatures such as the honey badger, black-backed jackal, bat-eared fox, suricate and ground squirrel. Large predators are represented by the famous black-maned Kalahari lion, leopard, cheetah and brown and spotted hyaena.

Birding is especially rewarding in summer, and bateleur, pygmy falcon, secretarybird, martial eagle, red-necked falcon and six varieties of vulture count among the park's rich diversity of raptors. Kori bustard, ostrich, Burchell's sandgrouse, Kalahari scrub-robin, crimson-breasted shrike and sociable weaver are among the conspicuous birds to be ticked.

Accommodation ranges from three rest camps (Twee Rivieren, Mata Mata and Nossob) and tented and wilderness camps in the South African side of the park, to campsites with basic facilities in the Botswana section, which is accessible by four-wheel drive vehicles only.

LEFT: The southern pale chanting goshawk is among the more than 50 raptors occurring in the Kalahari.

CHAPTER 25

THE CENTRAL KAROO

ABOVE: Victorian cottages and flat-roofed Karoo houses line the streets of historic Colesberg.

Situated on the South African plateau in the vast expanse of the Great Karoo, the Central Karoo is a tract of land dominated by stony plains punctuated by windmills, the occasional dolerite hill and small mountains.

The Khoekhoen called this vast semi-desert region *Kuru*, a name meaning 'hard' or 'dry' – an apt description of this harsh land. The aromatic Karoo *bossies* (bushes) and grasslands are ideally suited to small-stock farming and the area is a major producer of wool, lamb and mutton.

The region is bounded by the Kalahari and diamond fields in the north, while the Koup and the Camdeboo lie along its southern boundaries. It extends from the Hantam Ka-

roo east to the Eastern Cape Interior and the Orange River.

CLIMATE

The climate of the Central Karoo is similar to that of other regions in this semidesert area – extremely hot summers with temperatures exceeding 40 °C, and cold winters. Snowfalls are rare, but frost is common between April and November and temperatures can plunge to -5 °C in midwinter.

The region lies in the summer rainfall area and the rains are accompanied by heavy thunderstorms. Precipitation averages between 200 and 250 mm over much of the region, but increases to more than 400 mm in the north.

FLORA AND FAUNA

A mixture of grassveld and typical Karoo shrubs dominate the vegetation of the region, which lies in an area where the Karoo and the Grassland biomes meet. Grassveld once dominated large areas of the region, but it has been invaded by Karoo plants as a result of overgrazing and poor veld management.

Large herds of springbok, gemsbok, buffalo, elephant, rhino and other game roamed the plains when the first explorers and *trekboers* (migratory stock farmers) arrived in the region. But it did not take long before the prolific herds disappeared from the *vlaktes* (plains) and the guns fell silent.

The region lies in the main breeding ground of the lesser kestrel, a Palaearctic migrant from Europe and Asia. The birds begin arriving in November and their numbers peak in January and February.

HISTORY AND HERITAGE

The region was once home to the !Xam, one of several groups of San hunter-gatherers who occurred throughout much of southern Africa. They lived in small nomadic bands and survived by collecting plants and hunting game with bows and poisoned arrows.

The smooth boulders of the dolerite ridges punctuating the Karoo landscape provided the canvas for San shamans to depict the visions they had under trance. There are numerous rock engraving sites in the region but permission to view them has to be obtained in advance as they are on private land.

The Korana inhabited the region's northern reaches, moving along the Orange River with their livestock in search of grazing.

Dutch *trekboers* were already settled widely in the Upper Karoo by the first decade of the 1800s. They needed water to sustain themselves and their livestock and occupied waterholes within the territories of the !Xam. The San struck back by raiding the isolated farms but were powerless against the guns of the *trekboers* and were soon driven out of the region.

The dominant positions of Dutch Reformed churches in the region suggest that most of the towns were established to serve the spiritual needs of farmers in the surrounding areas.

Hopetown saw a brief flurry of activity after the first diamond was found in the district in 1866. But the miners soon abandoned the town when diamonds were found at Colesberg Kopje and Barkly West.

NOTEWORTHY PLACES
Nelspoort

Nelspoort is usually bypassed by travellers as it is situated off the N1. But for those interested in rock art, a detour will be well rewarded. San hunter-gatherers and Khoekhoe pastoralists left a fascinating legacy of engravings on the dolerite boulders just outside the village.

Engravings of elephant (including one that is 1,2 m long), eland, rhino, ostrich, as well as human figures, animal spoor and geometric patterns abound. Several 'rock gongs' (dolerite boulders balanced on top of each other that resonate when struck) can also be seen. Prior

LEFT: The herds of springbok that once roamed across the Karoo are slowly returning to the plains, which are punctuated by typical Karoo *koppies* (hillocks).

SEE:
Northern Cape p. 227
Eastern Cape & Free
State p. 228

arrangements must be made with the custodian of the Restvale Primary School in Nelspoort for a guided tour. It is advisable to wear sturdy footwear and a hat and to take a water bottle along.

Three Sisters

This well-known refuelling stop at the junction of the main routes to Johannesburg via Kimberley and Bloemfontein owes its name to three typical Karoo *koppies* (hillocks) nearby. The

pointed tops of the *koppies* consist of dolerite. The shales and sandstones immediately below this were baked hard by the heat of the dolerite intrusions, making this layer more resistant to erosion and giving rise to the trademark cliffs of the *koppies*.

Victoria West

This town was originally called Victoria in honour of the British monarch at the time it was founded in 1844. It was later renamed Victoria

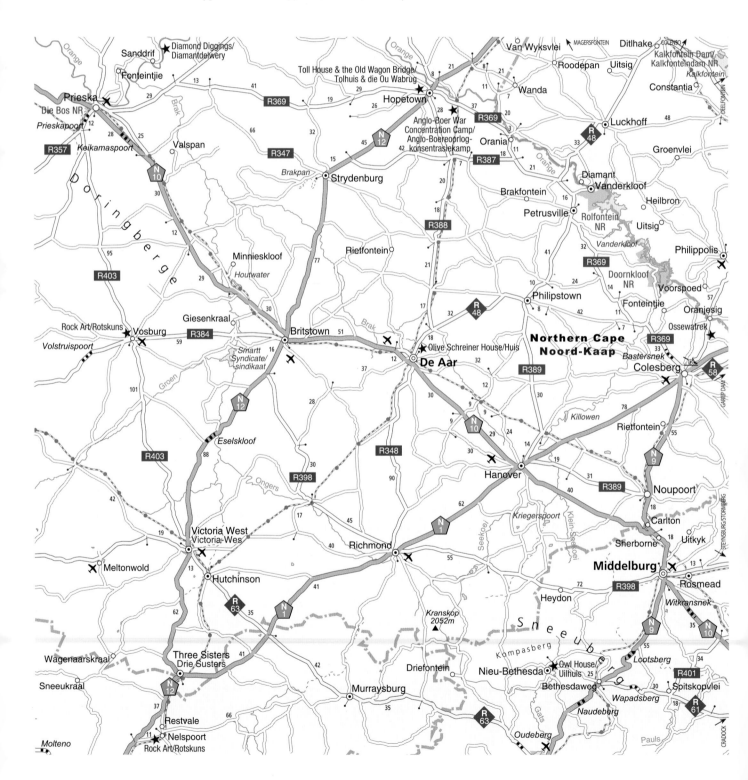

DEELFONTEIN

Following the setbacks suffered by the British forces during the second Anglo–Boer War in the battles at Stormberg (10 December 1899), Magersfontein (11 December 1899) and Colenso (15 December 1899), a campaign was launched in Britain to raise funds for a military hospital.

The hospital at Deelfontein Station opened in March 1900 and more than 6 000 wounded and sick soldiers were treated here within the first 9 months. The largest surgical and convalescent hospital in the Cape Colony at the time, it was even equipped with X-ray machines. Many of the patients died of dysentery and enteric fever, however. They lie buried in two nearby cemeteries – one with five graves and the other with 128.

West to distinguish it from the Victoria East district which was proclaimed in the Eastern Cape in 1847.

The Victoria West Regional Museum houses displays on the cultural and natural history of the Karoo. A fossil of a prehistoric fish dating back 250 million years is among its fossil collection.

Victoria West is the hometown of Francois du Toit 'Mannetjies' Roux, the legendary Springbok rugby player of the 1960s. Rugby fans can visit the Mannetjies Roux Museum at the Victoria Trading Post. Also of interest is the Apollo Theatre, the only remaining 1950s Art Deco cinema in South Africa.

The 1846 Oude Pastorie ('old parsonage'), the 1869 Anglican church, the 1847 Dutch Reformed church and the Print Shop, where the *Victoria West Messenger* has been published since 1876, are among the many other historic buildings in the town.

Britstown

Britstown developed around the settlement established between Victoria West and Kimberley in 1877 to provide accommodation to streams of travellers heading to the diamond fields. Following the discovery of gold on the Witwatersrand, the little settlement thrived, but its fortunes waned when the railway line between Cape Town and Johannesburg bypassed the town.

TOP: The Three Sisters, a trio of dolerite-capped Karoo *koppies* (hillocks), are a familiar landmark for motorists travelling between Cape Town and Johannesburg. ABOVE: The Victoria Trading Post in Victoria West is a typical general dealer's store of yesteryear. LEFT: Grassy plains and tabletop mountains dominate the landscape around Victoria West.

ORANIA

Situated on the banks of the Orange River, midway between Hopetown and Petrusville, Orania is, without doubt, the most peculiar cultural destination in South Africa. Built as a construction village for workers on the Orange River Development Project in 1963, the 430-ha village was bought by a group of 40 right-wing Afrikaner families in December 1990 to provide a refuge for Afrikaners wanting to preserve their cultural heritage. Only people who subscribe to the values of Orania are permitted to live and work here. Self-reliance is one of Orania's fundamental principles and all work is performed by whites.

An adjacent farm was bought in 1991 for irrigation farming, and pecan nuts, almonds, melons, watermelons, fruit and lucerne are produced on 50 smallholdings.

Attractions include the Orania Museum with its collection of firearms and displays on the Afrikaners' struggle for independence. Also of interest is the Verwoerd Commemorative Collection in the house where the widow of Dr HF Verwoerd, one of the architects of the National Party's apartheid policy, lived. A statue honouring Verwoerd and the Koeksister Monument, which pays tribute to this traditional Afrikaner confectionary, are among other interesting sites.

TOP: The Orange River flows lazily past Hopetown – once the scene of frantic searches for diamonds. ABOVE: Tiger's-eye stone was used to build the British military fort at Prieska during the Anglo–Boer War.

The Britstown Museum is housed in the Holy Trinity church, a beautiful dressed-sandstone building with small arched windows. Other attractions include the Dutch Reformed church, built 1877, and the Smartt Syndicate Dam to the west of town, built in 1964.

Prieska

Laid out against the backdrop of the Doringberge, Prieska was established at a drift (fording place) on the southern banks of the Orange River in 1882. It is a centre for the surrounding sheep farms and is well known for its semiprecious stones, especially tiger's-eye.

The Dutch Reformed church, with its unusual spire, was completed in 1878. Prieska Koppie, on the town's eastern edge, is an ideal vantage point and during the second Anglo–Boer War

the British built a stone fort on the hill.

Situated at the confluence of the Prieskapoort and Orange rivers on the northeastern outskirts of the town, Die Bos Nature Reserve is characterised by lush riverine forest and offers good birding possibilities. The Ria Huysamen Aloe Garden in the main street has a fine collection of aloes and other succulents, and is especially attractive when most species are in bloom in July and August.

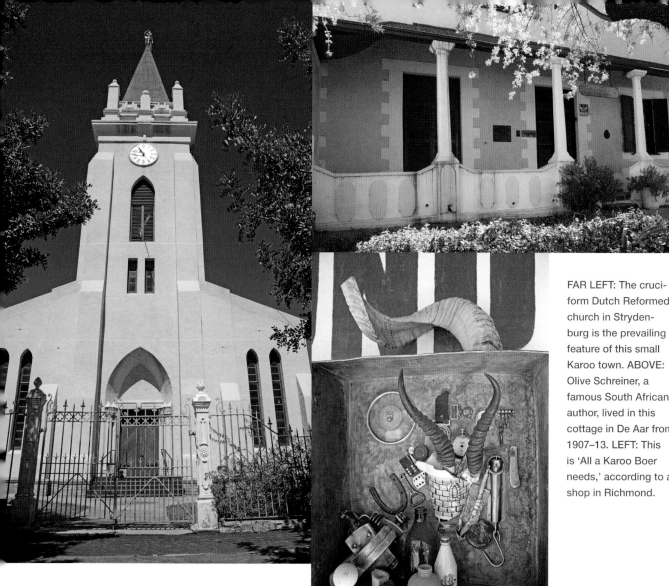

FAR LEFT: The cruciform Dutch Reformed church in Strydenburg is the prevailing feature of this small Karoo town. ABOVE: Olive Schreiner, a famous South African author, lived in this cottage in De Aar from 1907–13. LEFT: This is 'All a Karoo Boer needs,' according to a shop in Richmond.

Hopetown

Founded in 1854 on the southern bank of the Orange River, Hopetown became a hive of activity when a diamond, later named Eureka, was found on the farm De Kalk in 1866. Two letters cut into a windowpane of a building at 33 Church Street are reminders of a simple experiment carried out to establish whether a stone found on the farm Zandfontein in 1869 was a diamond. It was – all 83,5 carats of it. The stone was later named the 'Star of South Africa'.

The remains of the toll house and the old wagon bridge built across the Orange River in 1875 can be seen about 10 km west of the town.

Strydenburg

A disagreement over the location of a new settlement between Britstown and Hopetown caused so much discontent that when the choice fell on the farm Roodepan the town was named Strydenburg ('town of disagreement').

Large numbers of flamingos are attracted to Brakpan, a saltpan to the west of town, after good rains.

De Aar

Unlike most Karoo towns, which were established to serve the religious needs of farmers, De Aar ('the vein') developed around the railway junction established here in 1883. Situated almost midway between Cape Town and Johannesburg, its location was also perfect as a junction for the railroads to Port Elizabeth and Upington. The availability of large volumes of water from the strong *aar* (underground water source), on the farm after which the town was named, also counted in its favour.

The house in Grundling Street where Olive Schreiner lived from 1907–13 is now a restaurant. There is also a small display on the author who is best known for her classic novel, *The Story of an African Farm*.

Other attractions in the town include the 1894 St Paul's Anglican church and the Ammunition Museum (the largest ammunition depot in the Southern Hemisphere is at De Aar).

ABOVE: Colesberg's Dutch Reformed church was built in 1863, but the tower was added later.
OPPOSITE: Memorabilia of Springbok rugby legend 'Mannetjies' Roux are on display in Victoria West.

Richmond

Established in 1843 as a parish for the Dutch Reformed Church, Richmond occupies one of the highest and coldest places of the inland plateau. It was named after the father-in-law of the governor of the Cape at the time, the Duke of Richmond. The Dutch Reformed church was consecrated in 1847, but the tower was only added in 1909. Of special interest is the enormous pulpit, which dates back to 1854.

The area is famous for its horse studs and the Saddle Horse Museum, one of only two in the world, is dedicated to this breed. Housed in the old public school built in 1863, the museum has displays on the American saddle horse and the Anglo–Boer War, as well as rooms decorated in Cape Dutch and Victorian period styles.

Hanover

Flanked by two *koppies*, Hanover was laid out on the farm Petrusvallei in 1854. It was named after the German city where the ancestors of Gert Gouws, owner of the farm, were born.

The delightful country town with its water furrows and flat-roofed Karoo houses clustered around the old Market Square has changed little since Olive Schreiner described it as the prettiest village she had ever seen.

Schreiner, one of South Africa's most celebrated authors, and her husband, Samuel 'Cron' Cronwright-Schreiner, lived in Grace Street from 1900–7. Because of her forthright sympathy for the cause of the Boers she was placed under house arrest during the second Anglo–Boer War.

The 1895 Anglican church, magnificent 1895 dressed-sandstone Dutch Reformed church and old library are among the town's many architectural treasures. The original farmhouse on Petrusvallei has been put to use as the Hanover Museum with displays on the town's history and development.

A walk up Trappieskop ('staircase hill'), on the western side of the town, to watch the sunrise or sunset, is rewarded with an all-round view of the surrounding Karoo plains.

Middelburg

Middelburg lies more or less at equal distance from Cradock, Colesberg, Steynsburg and Richmond. It was established as a centre for the Dutch Reformed Church and as a seat of the district's magistracy in 1852.

The Middelburg Cultural History Museum is housed in a fine Victorian building that dates back to 1898 and was used by the Dutch Reformed Church as a school for underprivileged children. It has exhibits on the second Anglo–Boer War when 10 000 British troops were stationed near the town, San artefacts and traditional Xhosa beadwork. The PW Vorster Museum, on the town's northern outskirts, is housed in the old gabled homestead built in 1827 on the farm Grootfontein. It focuses on the history and development of the town and has an interesting collection of farming implements.

Noupoort

Noupoort, founded in 1881, owes its name to a narrow valley northwest of the town. The

ROLFONTEIN NATURE RESERVE

The terrain of the Rolfontein Nature Reserve, which lies on the southern shores of the Vanderkloof Dam, ranges from rugged ridges and grassy plains to densely wooded valleys. White rhino and herds of eland, gemsbok, black wildebeest, red hartebeest, plains zebra and springbok have been reintroduced. The Douglas Hey Limnological Research Station was established in 1979 to conduct research on the fish of the dam. The reserve has a network of roads for game viewing and there are picnic sites for day visitors.

ACTIVITIES

- Hang-gliding and paragliding in Middelburg, one of the prime sites in the country
- Canoeing and angling on the Orange River
- Game viewing, birdwatching and picnicking at Rolfontein Nature Reserve near Vanderkloof
- Game viewing, birdwatching, camping and picnicking at Doornkloof Nature Reserve near Colesburg
- Water-skiing, windsurfing and other water sports on the Vanderkloof Dam
- Visiting rock engravings on farms in the region
- Viewing 'rock gongs' at Nelspoort
- Mountain biking, hiking and 4x4 trails on farms in the region
- Hunting on farms in the region

ROUTES AND TRAILS

- Two trails with Trans-Karoo Adventures (5 hours or 2–3 days) on the farm Rietpoort, 26 km from Noupoort
- Pied Barbet Trail (2 hours) in the Rolfontein Nature Reserve near Vanderkloof
- Bokmakierie Trail (3 days) in the Doornkloof Nature Reserve near Colesberg

settlement developed around a railway station. The All Souls Anglican church and the British blockhouse on Hospital Hill are interesting historic buildings to visit.

Colesberg

Set among Karoo *koppies* and dolerite boulders, Colesberg lies almost midway between Cape Town and Johannesburg and was once a major staging post on the Great North Road. The town was established in 1830 and owes its name to the British Governor at the Cape at the time, Sir Lowry Cole. The town is a major centre for the surrounding sheep and game farms, but the district is also renowned for its racehorse stud farms.

Colesberg has retained much of its 19th-century charm and typical flat-roofed Karoo houses flank Bell and Stockenstroom streets in the historical heart of the town.

The Colesberg-Kemper Museum is housed in the old Colesberg Bank building that dates back to 1862. It has an interesting collection of fossils, a 19th-century toy collection and photos of the second Anglo–Boer War. Also of interest is the UNISA photographic display on the Karoo *donkie-karretjie* people – nomads who travel from one place to the next by donkey cart.

Other attractions include the 1840 Trinity Methodist church, the 1854 Anglican church, the 1863 Dutch Reformed church (the clock tower was added in 1926), and the mill in Bell Street – one of the country's last working horse mills.

Philipstown

Philipstown was established in 1863 and named in honour of the British Governor at the Cape at the time, Sir Philip Wodehouse.

The town's streets are lined by many fine 19th-century Karoo houses; the magistrate's court building, the old jail (housing a small museum) and the dressed-sandstone Dutch Reformed church are also of architectural interest.

Vanderkloof

Situated northeast of Petrusville, the village of Vanderkloof was established in the 1960s to accommodate workers of the Vanderkloof Dam, before being turned into a holiday resort.

The dam forms part of the Orange River Development Project and is the largest man-made lake in South Africa, after the Gariep Dam. The water backs up for 100 km behind the 108-m-high wall, which is the highest in the country and houses a hydroelectric power station.

CHAPTER 26

THE ORANGE RIVER VALLEY

ABOVE: Below the Augrabies Falls the Orange River wends its way through rugged, spectacular scenery.

The course the mighty Orange River carved through the landscape in its middle and lower reaches brings life to an inhospitable area where only the hardiest can survive. Away from the lush banks with their verdant vineyards the terrain alternates between red sand dunes and gently undulating sand and gravel plains dissected by ancient dry river courses and vast pans.

The Orange River Valley occupies one of the most remote corners of the Northern Cape. It stretches along either side of the middle and lower reaches of the Orange River, from Groblershoop in the east to Goodhouse in the west. With its abundance of water, alluvial soil and warm climate, the Orange River Valley is a fertile agricultural area. Crops include sultanas, table and wine grapes, lucerne, wheat, maize, beans, peas, lentils and groundnuts.

CLIMATE

The Orange River Valley is blessed with an abundance of sunshine. Summer stretches from October to March and temperatures of between 35 °C and 40 °C in midsummer are the rule rather than the exception. A record high of 47,8 °C was recorded at Goodhouse on the Orange River in 1939. Daytime temperatures in winter (April to September) are mild and enjoyable, but the nights can be chilly.

Rain occurs during the summer months when heavy afternoon thundershowers bring temporary relief from the oppressive heat. Rainfall ranges between 50 mm and 400 mm per annum, but is unpredictable. Prolonged droughts are a common occurrence.

FLORA AND FAUNA

The vegetation ranges from thickets along the Orange River to Karoo plains dotted with dwarf shrubs, small trees, annuals and short grasses. Fields of bright yellow devil's thorns are conspicuous after good summer rains when a variety of other creepers and flowers also come into bloom.

The large herds of springbok and other game encountered by early travellers and explorers have long since disappeared, but the Augrabies Falls National Park and private game farms offer opportunities to view typical plains antelope such as gemsbok and springbok, as well as blue wildebeest, red hartebeest and eland.

The enormous communal weaver nests clinging sociably, but precariously, to telephone poles are a familiar site along roads in the region. Keep an eye out for pygmy falcon, which can often be spotted in the vicinity of the nests. A variety of larks, typical Karoo species such as Burchell's courser and Ludwig's bustard, and a rich diversity of raptors can also be seen.

HISTORY AND HERITAGE

San hunter-gatherers roamed the plains and dunes for thousands of years before Koranna pastoralists moved in. The islands in the middle reaches of the Orange River provided a safe haven for rival Koranna groups, while freebooters and renegades fleeing the authorities at the Cape also sought refuge there, as did people of mixed descent, Dutch hunters and *trekboers* (migratory stock farmers).

By the mid-1800s, the northern frontier had become notorious for its illegal trade in firearms and alcohol, skirmishes and commando-style stock raids. To bring order to the lawless region, British forces fought two wars against the Koranna: the first from 1868–69 and the second from 1878–79. A peace agreement was reached in January 1880, and the agricultural industry along the Orange River was established in 1883, when the first irrigation canals were built at Upington.

NOTEWORTHY PLACES
Groblershoop

Groblershoop, a centre of the surrounding grape- and livestock-farming district, developed around a camp built to house workers during the construction of the Boegoeberg Dam in 1929.

THE GREAT RIVER

Rising in the highlands of Lesotho, the Orange River, South Africa's largest waterway, enters the Atlantic Ocean at Alexander Bay after a journey of 2 300 km. British explorer Colonel Robert Jacob Gordon, who reached the course in 1777, named it in honour of Prince William V of the House of Orange in the Netherlands. Its Khoekhoe name, !Gariep, simply means 'great river'.

ABOVE: The pygmy falcon, southern Africa's smallest diurnal raptor, is closely associated with sociable weaver nests, which they use for roosting and nesting. LEFT: Blue wildebeest, close relatives of black wildebeest, race across sparsely vegetated plains.

WINE OF A THIRSTLAND

A patchwork of vineyards lines the meandering Orange River over a distance of 300 km as it moves westwards from Groblershoop to Blouputs. Over 900 producers deliver their grape harvests to the Orange River Wine Cellars, which produced its first wine at Upington in 1968. It also has cellars in Kakamas, Keimoes, Grootdrink and Groblershoop and is the second-largest cooperative in the world. The area is especially known for its fortified and dry white wines, but also produces red cultivars.

ABOVE: Verdant vineyards grow along the Orange River, in sharp contrast to their arid surroundings.

SEE:
Northern Cape & Namibia pp. 232–233
Northern Cape p. 234

The 10-m-high weir and irrigation canals were built by white labourers left destitute by the Great Depression and a devastating drought.

Attractions in the area include the historic (1911) water turbines built on the farm Winstead, 25 km from Groblershoop on the road to Griquatown. Also to be seen on this farm is a military cemetery where seven South African soldiers were buried in November 1914 after a battle with rebels loyal to Boer General Manie Maritz. The rebels were on their way to join Maritz, who was sympathetic to the German administration in South West Africa (now Namibia), when the two sides clashed.

Upington

Upington, the commercial centre of the region, was founded in 1871 as a mission station named Olyvenhoutsdrift ('ford of the olive trees') by a Rhenish missionary, Reverend Christiaan Schröder. When the town was proclaimed in 1884 it was named after Sir Thomas Upington, Prime Minister of the Cape Colony from 1884–86.

Two rather unusual statues can be seen in the town. The life-size bronze donkey in the grounds of the Kalahari Oranje Museum is a tribute to the contribution this animal made to the region's early development; the camel-and-rider in front of the police station recalls the days when the police patrolled their vast territory on camels, which were ideally suited to the desert terrain.

Domestic implements and photographs documenting the history of Upington and the Lower Orange River area are displayed in the Kalahari Oranje Museum. Originally, the building housed the historic Rhenish Mission church, consecrated in 1875. The adjacent parsonage was added eight years later.

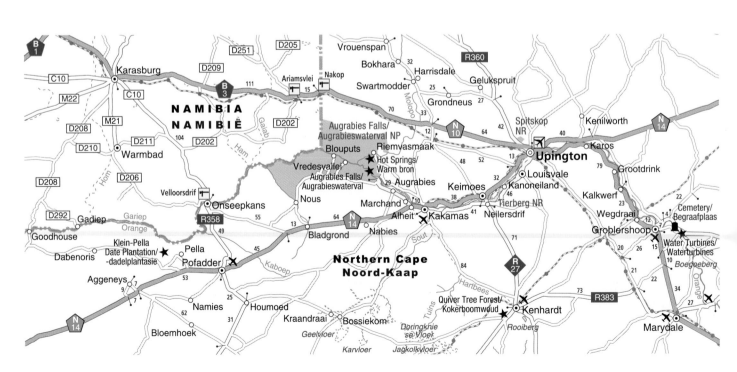

THE INGENIOUS *BAKKIESPOMP*

Waterwheels similar to those used in ancient Egypt provided a solution to the challenge of how to lead water from the Orange River canals to higher ground. Small buckets (*bakkies*) are fitted to paddle wheels powered by the flow of the water. As each wheel turns the water in the buckets is dropped into a furrow. The wooden water wheels of the 1800s were later replaced by wrought-iron models.

More than 200 date palms line the 1 041-m-long Palm Tree Avenue leading to The Eiland Holiday Resort on Olyvenhout Island. Planted in 1935, it is one of the longest and densest palm avenues in the Southern Hemisphere.

Upington is a major centre of the dried fruit industry and each year many tonnes of sultanas and raisins are processed at the South African Dried Fruit Co-operative – the second largest factory of this kind in the world. Visitors can purchase dried fruit on site.

The Spitskop Nature Reserve, 13 km north of the town, has been stocked with herds of gemsbok, springbok, red hartebeest and eland.

Kanoneiland

The name Kanoneiland ('cannon island') recalls the region's turbulent pioneering days when Koranna river pirates, based on the island, were bombarded with a cannon for six days in 1878, during the Second Koranna War. Half a century later, 52 farmers defied gov-ernment orders prohibiting the occupation of Orange River islands and began cultivating crops there. Over the years the 50-odd islands were linked by landfills, and today Kanoneiland, about 14 km long and 3 km wide, is the largest inhabited inland island in South Africa.

Keimoes

At Keimoes the Orange River splits into a labyrinth of channels to create a mosaic of islands linked by roads and footbridges. Keimoes is famous for its *bakkiespomp* (waterwheel) mounted on the water furrow along the main street.

Diagonally across from the waterwheel is the historic Dutch Reformed Mission church, which was built in 1889 and used as a school until 1916. The neo-Gothic windows were added in 1920.

Nature lovers can explore the Tierberg Nature Reserve and enjoy spectacular views from its lookout point. In August and September the drab rocks are adorned in red as thousands of Gariep aloes burst into bloom.

Kenhardt

The pleasant country town of Kenhardt played an important role in bringing order to the northern frontier in the second half of the 19th century. A camel thorn tree marks the spot where Magistrate Maximillian Jackson and his police

TOP LEFT: Kanon-eiland in the Orange River has been turned into highly productive agricultural land. TOP RIGHT: Kenhardt's old buildings lend the town an atmos-phere reminiscent of the days when it was one of the most remote settlements in the Northern Cape. ABOVE LEFT: The historic bakkiespomp (waterwheel) along the main street in Keimoes is a heritage site, as is the Dutch Reformed Mission church diag-onally across. ABOVE: Upington's Donkey Statue is one of only two statues in South Africa that pays tribute to the role this draught animal played in the development of the region.

force spent the night of 27 December 1868, en route to the volatile Lower Orange River.

Founded in 1876, Kenhardt was once the most remote administrative, police and military outpost in the northwestern Cape. The old library (1897) with its corrugated iron roof and plain veranda is an excellent example of a typical pioneer house.

About 8 km south of town the plains give way to dolerite outcrops where an unusually dense concentration of 4 000–5 000 quiver trees has created a 'forest' of tree aloes.

Kakamas

Kakamas was established in 1897 by the Dutch Reformed Church as a settlement for farmers impoverished by drought. The extensive system of irrigation canals and furrows they built laid the foundations for today's vineyards and fields of lucerne and cotton. On the farm Baviaans Kranz, a few kilometres east of Keimoes, Cornish miners dug two tunnels through solid rock. Work on the 97-m and 172-m-long tunnels was completed in 1911.

Kakamas is famous for its waterwheels on the outskirts of the town many of which are still in working order. Also of interest is the old Transformer Building, which housed one of South Africa's first hydroelectric power stations. The double-storey building resembles an Egyptian temple and was completed in 1914.

The first sultana vine was planted in Kakamas in 1928, and the Orange River Valley is now the major producer of sultanas in South Africa. The town is also famous for the Kakamas peach, a yellow clingstone variety ideally suited to canning.

A rocky *koppie* (hillock), 4 km east of Kakamas on the road to Keimoes, marks the spot where seven German and two South African soldiers were killed when a German force attempted to open a corridor from South West Africa (now Namibia) into South Africa in February 1915.

Riemvasmaak

Riemvasmaak, a little-known tract of semi-desert land defined by the Namibian border in the west and the Orange River in the south, made headlines when the first land restoration claim was awarded to the former inhabitants of the area in February 1994.

The Riemvasmakers, as they are generally known, trace their origins to a group of pastoralists under the leadership of *Koning* (King) Dawid, who settled here in the 1870s after fleeing conflict in southern Namibia. People of mixed descent and Xhosa-speaking migrants also settled here and a Roman Catholic mission station was established in 1947 to serve the spiritual needs of the community.

Riemvasmaak's 1 500 residents were forcefully removed to Namibia and the Eastern Cape in 1973 and 1974 when the area was declared a military training ground by the then South African Defence Force.

Following their successful land claim in 1994, the first Riemvasmakers returned from Namibia in March 2005. Currently, agriculture centres on goat, sheep and cattle farming, as well as table-grape production at Vredesvallei ('valley of peace') along the Orange River.

Millions of years of erosion have fashioned a landscape of dolerite outcrops, flat-topped mountains, plains and sand dunes. The usually dry Molopo River has carved a spectacular 80-m-deep gorge through the rugged landscape and the hot spring that rises from its rocky bed is a lifeline to the people of Riemvasmaak. It is also a popular campsite for outdoor enthusiasts.

Augrabies Falls National Park

At Augrabies, the Orange River has carved a deep passage through the granite rocks to create one of the world's great cataract-type waterfalls. Viewing platforms afford awe-inspiring vistas of the main fall, which plunges 56 m into an 18-km-long gorge with sheer, smooth walls. When the Orange River is in full flood a cur-

tain of water thunders into the gorge, which has an average depth of 240 m. The Khoekhoen appropriately named this spectacle *Akoerabis* – 'the place of the great noise'. Self-drive routes lead to vantage points such as Ararat and Oranjekom from where there are good views of the gorge and the swirling river far below.

A scramble up Moon Rock, which can either be reached on foot or by car, provides a 360-degree view of the surrounding landscape. The granite-gneiss outcrop, or whaleback, is an excellent example of onion-skin weathering, which is the flaking off of slabs of rock.

Giraffe, kudu and herds of gemsbok, springbok, red hartebeest and eland roam the game-viewing area, while the rocky terrain is an ideal habitat for klipspringer as well as family groups of baboon and rock dassie. Cape clawless otter, ground squirrel, bat-eared fox and vervet monkey are among the smaller mammals to be seen. Guided night drives may provide glimpses of nocturnal animals such as leopard, caracal, small-spotted genet and aardvark.

Accommodation is available in stone chalets and there are shaded campsites. Facilities include picnic sites for day visitors, two swimming pools, a restaurant, shop and filling station.

Pella

Nestling in a valley between rugged hills, Pella's palm trees and lush green gardens appear like an oasis. The settlement was founded in 1814 by the London Missionary Society for Khoekhoen who had fled conflict in southern Namibia.

Pella was abandoned in 1872, but the mission station was reopened when the Roman Catholic Church established its presence in the Northern Cape in 1878. Construction of a cathedral started in 1888, and it took seven years of hard labour before it was inaugurated in 1895. Wounded German soldiers were treated in the church hall that served as a hospital during World War I, when South African troops invaded South West Africa, then under German administration.

Other reminders of Pella's origins include the marble tombstones of the founding Catholic missionaries and the historic millstone, which dates back to the end of the 1800s.

With some 14 000 palms under cultivation, the date plantation at Klein Pella, about 25 km west of Pella, is the largest in the Southern Hemisphere. The picking season extends from mid-February to April.

ACTIVITIES

- Mountain and quad biking at Riemvasmaak
- Gariep 3-in-1 Adventure, a combination of canoeing (3 km), hiking (4 km) and mountain biking (11 km) in the Augrabies Falls National Park
- Game viewing at Spitskop Nature Reserve and Augrabies Falls National Park
- Waterfall viewing, picnicking, swimming and camping at Augrabies Falls National Park
- Date picking at Klein Pella from mid-February to April

ROUTES AND TRAILS

- Three 4x4 trails (41–71 km) at Riemvasmaak
- Rockery Route (44 km) along a scenic gravel road between Kakamas and Neilersdrif near Keimoes; suitable for sedan cars
- Hiking trails of varying length and moderate difficulty at Riemvasmaak
- Dassie Nature Trail (2 hours), a self-guided interpretative walk in Augrabies Falls National Park
- Self-guided circular Klipspringer Hiking Trail (3 days) in Augrabies Falls National Park

CHAPTER 27

THE HANTAM KAROO

ABOVE: Striking tabletop mountains are seen in the vicinity of Fraserburg, north of the Nuweveldberge.

The Hantam Karoo is a land of wide-open spaces and seemingly never-ending plains where slowly turning windmills represent the only movement during the heat of the day. Dinosaur tracks and scour marks left by ancient glaciers reveal the fascinating prehistory of the region, while gigantic high-tech telescopes survey the crystal-clear night sky to help reveal the evolution of the universe.

The region is named after the landmark Hantamsberg, which owes its name to a Nama word, *hyentama*, for the edible roots of a pelargonium species. Autumn sees a variety of geophytes (plants with bulbs, corms and tubers) burst into bloom, and in spring the plains are transformed into a brilliant array of colours when the annuals have their turn.

Gently undulating plains punctuated by hills, dolerite outcrops and pans dominate the landscape in this southwestern corner of South Africa's inland plateau. The Hantam Karoo is bounded by the Bokkeveldberge in the west and the Central Karoo in the east. The Roggeveld- and Nuweveldberge form the southern boundary, while Bushmanland, which stretches towards the Orange River, occupies the northern section of the region.

Sheep farming, with dorpers for mutton and merinos for wool, is the main agricultural activity, while wheat is also grown. The natural pans in the region are major producers of salt.

CLIMATE

The climate is one of extremes, and temperatures of above 40 °C are not uncommon in midsummer. In winter the mountains are often blanketed in snow and minimum temperatures can drop to well below freezing. Most of the rain in the west of the region falls during the winter months and spring, while the east lies in the summer rainfall area where heavy afternoon thunderstorms are the rule.

Rainfall decreases from 650 mm a year at the edge of the escarpment to less than 300 mm further inland.

FLORA AND FAUNA

The fynbos, succulent Karoo and Nama Karoo biomes converge in the Hantam Karoo, and the region has an exceptionally high diversity of species with many endemics.

Some 1 350 plant species, including 80 endemics, are known to occur on the Bokkeveld Plateau. The region is especially rich in geophytes, among them eight of southern Africa's 17 bulbinella species.

Nieuwoudtville lies at the northern limit of the mountain fynbos vegetation, which is char-acterised by proteas, ericas, reeds and rushes, while a variety of typical Karoo *bossies* (bushes), shrubs and succulents dominate the Karoo vegetation further inland.

The large herds of game that once roamed the plains have long been replaced by flocks of sheep, but the area still offers exciting birding possibilities – especially Bushmanland, which boasts one of the highest diversity of larks in the world.

HISTORY AND HERITAGE

Rock paintings in the Bokkeveldberge and engravings on clusters of boulders on the plains of the interior are testimony to the !Xam San, hunter-gatherers who lived in harmony with nature for thousands of years before the arrival of Khoekhoe, Dutch and Xhosa stock farmers.

The extermination of the large migrant game herds brought the San into conflict with Dutch stock farmers, and competition over water and grazing sparked fierce battles between the stock farmers.

As a result of the harsh winter conditions, many Hantam farmers have two farms – one on the plateau and one in the lowlands. In the cold months they herd their sheep to the Onder-Karoo ('lower Karoo'), where they remain until October when they move their stock back to the high plateau.

THE CORBELLED HOUSES OF THE HANTAM

The Hantam's architecture reflects the ingenuity of the early *trekboers* who built the unique corbelled houses. In the absence of timber, flat stones were used to erect square or round houses with an internal diameter of up to 5,5 m. The walls were built upright for about 2 m, followed by successive courses of inward-overlapping flat stones until the roof was completely closed. The beehive-shaped dwellings were usually roughly plastered and then whitewashed.

BELOW LEFT: These beehive-shaped houses built from flat stones are unique to Fraserburg, Williston and Carnarvon.
BELOW: Nieu-woudtville, in the southwest of the Hantam Karoo, is renowned for its diversity of geophytes and annual flowers that burst into bloom each spring.

BULB CAPITAL OF THE WORLD

Nearly half of the 600 plant species known to occur in the vicinity of Nieuwoudtville are geophytes and the town has aptly been dubbed the 'bulb capital of the world'. About 22 geophytes are restricted to the Nieuwoudtville area, while another 28 species are endemic to the Bokkeveldberge.

The Hantam Karoo's flower season stretches from late March to October, but peaks in August and September. A variety of bulbs burst into bloom after late summer rains and showers of pink March lilies are especially conspicuous in early autumn, while fields of cat's tails transform the veld into carpets of yellow in winter. The mass displays of succulents and annuals usually start in midautumn.

NOTEWORTHY PLACES

Nieuwoudtville

The first *trekboers* (migratory stock farmers) settled in the area in 1730, but it was not until 1897 that a settlement was established on land bought from HC Nieuwoudt, the farmer after whom the town was named.

Prominent among the many beautiful dressed sandstone buildings, which are a special feature of the village, are the Dutch Reformed church with its clock tower above the entrance, the parsonage, the post office and the adjacent shop.

Despite its small size, the Nieuwoudtville Wildflower Reserve, just east of the town, supports over 300 plant species. Geophytes account for nearly 40% of the reserve's checklist – the highest number reported for any area in South Africa. The 6 200-ha Hantam National Botanical Garden located just outside the town also protects an incredibly rich variety of geophytes and was declared South Africa's ninth national botanical garden in 2007.

SEE:
Northern Cape p. 225
Northern Cape p. 226

The Oorlogskloof Nature Reserve, 16 km southwest of Nieuwoudtville, is a wilderness of fascinating sandstone formations, breathtaking scenery and rock paintings that are only accessible on foot. Rock paintings can also be seen on the farm Papkuilsfontein, adjacent to the reserve.

Between 6 000 and 8 000 quiver trees grow among the dolerite outcrops at Gannabos – the largest concentration tree aloes in South Africa. A visit is especially rewarding in May or June when the yellow flowers are in full bloom.

The Nieuwoudtville Falls 4 km north of town are a spectacular sight in winter, when a swelled Doring River plunges 90 m into the gorge.

Loeriesfontein

The quiet settlement of Loeriesfontein, in the southeastern corner of Bushmanland, developed around a spring where the first *trekboers* settled. The museum in the old Baptist church has a small but interesting collection of farming

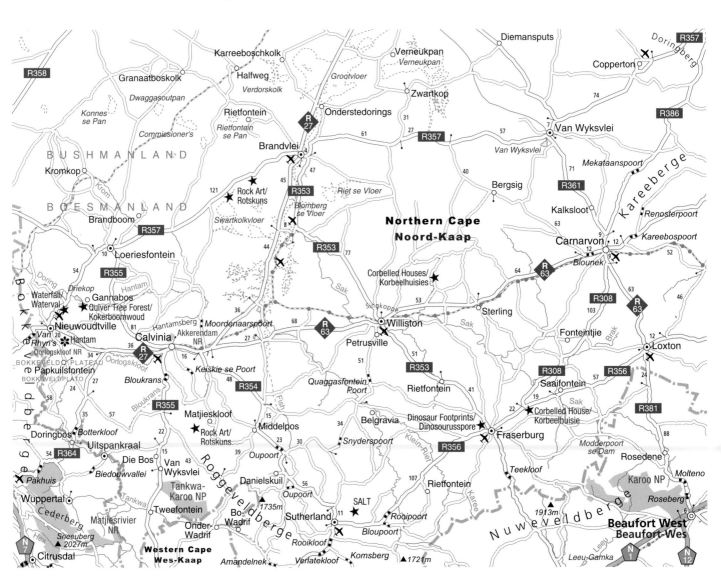

OORLOGSKLOOF GLACIAL PAVEMENTS

The glacial pavement on the farm Oorlogskloof, 7 km south of Nieuwoudtville, is testimony to the movement of vast ice sheets across the southern African landscape some 300 million years ago. Sediments were later deposited on the glacially sculpted landscape when the ice began melting. Later still, the ice sheets readvanced and rock fragments embedded in the ice carved grooves and striations into the soft sediments.

VERNEUKPAN

Verneukpan northeast of Brandvlei owes its name to the mirages which create the illusion that the salt pan is filled with water. The pan first made headlines in 1929 when British racing driver, Sir Malcolm Campbell, attempted to break the world land speed record of 372 km/h here in his Bluebird. Campbell's attempt was unsuccessful, but he later roared to success at Daytona Beach, Florida, USA.

Verneukpan was in the news again when it hosted a major international rave, the Desert Storm Trance-Karoo Tribal Festival, in 1996. The event was repeated the following year and then, not so surprisingly, disappeared from the annual calendar of events.

and domestic implements, while a collection of windpumps of all sizes is displayed in the adjacent Fred Turner Windpump Museum – one of only two such museums in the world.

Brandvlei

Brandvlei, a typical Karoo town on the plains in the heart of Bushmanland, is an important centre for the surrounding sheep farms and salt works. It developed near a vlei close to the Sak River, where a farmer named Brand first settled. The handsome, cruciform Dutch Reformed church, built in neo-Gothic style in the town's main street, was completed in 1905.

Attractions in the vicinity of Brandvlei include the rock engravings on the farms Lekkerlê and Kans. The area also offers excellent birding: red and Sclater's lark, Karoo eremomela, Burchell's courser and Ludwig's bustard are among the species to be seen.

Calvinia

Calvinia, named in honour of the religious reformer Johannes Calvin, is the main hub in the Hantam Karoo. It was established against the backdrop of the flat-topped Hantamsberg on the banks of the Oorlogskloof River in 1851, and is today the centre of one of the largest wool-producing districts in South Africa.

Pride among the many historic houses are Hantam House, a Cape Dutch country homestead built around 1853, and the Dorpshuis, a Victorian home dating from the 1860s. The *nagmaalkamer*s ('Holy Communion rooms') at the rear of the Dorpshuis date back to the days when farmers travelled long distances to cel-

TOP LEFT: After good winter rains the main fall in the Doring River, just north of Nieuwoudtville, plunges over a 90-m-high cliff. TOP RIGHT: A large collection of windmills, synonymous with the Karoo, can be seen at the Fred Turner Windpump Museum in Loeriesfontein. ABOVE LEFT: Farm workers living in the Hantam Karoo eke out a modest existence in the villages and towns. ABOVE RIGHT: The Cape Dutch-style Hantamhuis in Calvinia has a fascinating collection of period furniture, and houses a coffee shop, restaurant and gift shop.

SOUTHERN AFRICAN LARGE TELESCOPE

With its brilliant night skies unaffected by light and air pollution, Sutherland is one of the best stargazing locations in the world. High on a plateau, 14 km from the town, are the 11 telescopes that comprise the Sutherland station of the South African Astronomical Observatory. One of these is the Southern African Large Telescope (SALT). With a mirror diameter of 11 m, it is the largest telescope in the Southern Hemisphere. The mirror consists of 91 identical hexagonal segments, each about 1 m wide and weighing 100 kg.

Also known as Africa's Giant Eye, the telescope is used to study distant galaxies and the evolution of the universe. SALT is 25 times more powerful than any other telescope in Africa and a billion times more powerful than the naked eye. To put this into perspective: SALT can detect something as faint as candlelight on the moon. Africa's Giant Eye is a collaborative partnership of 11 institutions from 6 countries on 4 continents.

HANTAM MEAT FESTIVAL

Calvinia is renowned for its annual Hantam Meat Festival, held during the last weekend in August. A variety of meat dishes, mainly lamb, are prepared in the traditional way. Some unusual fare such as curry tripe, lamb's tails, baked sheep's head, *peertjies* (sheep's testicles), *skilpadjies* (minced sheep's liver mixed with onion, cloves and bread wrapped in a layer of caul fat) may also be sampled.

TOP: With its clear skies, Sutherland is the perfect location for the Southern African Large Telescope (SALT). ABOVE: Modest Karoo-style cottages and grand sandstone buildings line the streets of Sutherland.

ebrate the Eucharist and needed accommodation. The displays on sheep and wool farming, and life in the Hantam during the pioneering days, make the Calvinia Museum an interesting stop.

Postal items dropped into Calvinia's gigantic red postbox are stamped with a special postal mark. The structure, originally a water tower, is a strong contender for the title of largest postbox in the world.

Energetic visitors can explore the Akkerendam Nature Reserve on the slopes of the Hantamsberg.

Sutherland

Sutherland enjoys the double distinction of having the largest telescope in the Southern Hemisphere and being one of the coldest towns in the country – its lowest recorded temperature being -16,4 °C.

It is a pleasant town with beautiful old sandstone buildings and clay-roof houses. Attrac-

tions include the Dutch Reformed church, used as barracks by British forces during the second Anglo–Boer War of 1899–1902 (also known as the South African War), and the Louw Museum, once the home of the Afrikaans poet brothers NP van Wyk Louw and WEG Louw.

Williston

Williston lies at the foot of Singkoppe, two dolerite outcrops that were first used in 1846 as an open-air stage for religious choirs. The Dutch Reformed church, built from local sandstone, was consecrated in 1913, and its crucifix design, porches on three sides, and Gothic windows and doorways make it unique among churches in South Africa. The Rhenish Mission church was consecrated in 1857, and the Dutch Reformed Mission church, that now serves as a museum, dates back to 1884.

A unique art form developed in the Williston district when stonemasons began carving magnificent tombstones from sandstone in the 1840s. An excellent example can be seen in the Amandelboom section of the town's old cemetery and on farms along the Tombstone Route.

Several well-preserved corbelled houses can also be seen on farms in the Williston district.

Fraserburg

Fraserburg lies on a plateau to the north of the Nuweveldberge. Typical Karoo houses, Victorian cottages and dressed sandstone buildings line the streets and lend the town an old-world

ACTIVITIES

- Paragliding from the summit of Van Rhyns Pass, near Nieuwoudtville, especially in January when the thermals are at their best
- Flower viewing throughout the region in August and September
- Stargazing in Sutherland
- Viewing evidence of dinosaurs at Gansfontein, just outside Fraserburg
- Viewing rock engravings at Lekkerlê and Kans farms near Brandvlei
- Viewing rock paintings on Papkuilsfontein farm, south of Nieuwoudtville
- Birdwatching at Brandvlei and in Bushmanland

ROUTES AND TRAILS

- Banksgate 4x4 Trails (10–66 km), from Banksgate farm in the Sutherland district
- De Postjes 4x4 Trails of various distances in the Fraserburg district
- Ouberg Pass, 45 km from Sutherland
- Tombstone Route (60 km one way) starting in Williston
- Kambrokind Walking Trail (1.5–4 hours) just outside Sutherland
- Two day walks (8 and 9 hours respectively) in Oorlogskloof Nature Reserve outside Nieuwoudtville
- 52,2 km hiking trail (4–7 days) in Oorlogskloof Nature Reserve, Nieuwoudtville
- Kareeboom (1 hour) and Sterboom (6–7 hours) walks in the Akkerendam Nature Reserve near Calvinia

FOSSILISED DINOSAUR FOOTPRINTS

Dinosaurs reigned supreme when the Karoo was a vast alluvial plain some 250 million years ago. The tracks of large, five-toed mammal-like reptiles, known as dino-cephalians, tracks of a bradysaurus reptile and scrape marks made by fish fins can be seen at the Gansfontein palaeo-surface, 6 km north of town. Visits must be arranged through the Hoogland Municipality in Fraserburg.

charm. The iconic Peperbus ('pepper pot') is an architectural curiosity and the only one of its kind in South Africa. The hexagonal building with a dome-shaped roof was completed in 1861 and served as the office of the municipal market master at one time.

An interesting collection of costumes and household utensils, as well as a small but fascinating fossil exhibition, can be seen in the Fraserburg Museum which is housed in the old parsonage that was built in 1856. A replica of a corbelled house can be viewed in the town square opposite the museum.

Carnarvon

Laid out in a basin to the southeast of the Kareeberge, Carnarvon is a centre for the surrounding farms and the eastern gateway to the spring flowers of the Hantam. The first mission station was established in 1847 at Schietfontein ('shoot fountain'), a few kilometres west of Carnarvon, for a Xhosa-speaking community that had settled at the spring in the early 1800s.

Carnarvon has an impressive heritage of typical Karoo architecture, especially in the De Bult ('the hill') area, the town's historic heart. The Dutch Reformed Mission complex on the town square is one among many heritage sites. It comprises the old parsonage, dating back to the 1850s, the 1850 Rhenish Mission church, the 1873 mission school and the 1912 Edwardian parsonage.

The celebrated Afrikaans poet, AG Visser, lived and worked in Carnarvon as a teacher, headmaster and doctor.

The Blik Bar ('can bar') with its unique collection of 4 000 beer tins, the Carnarvon Museum and the adjacent replica of a corbelled house are other attractions.

LEFT: Although evident at other times of the year, flowers in the Hantam Karoo are especially prevalent in August and September. BELOW: One of its kind, Carnarvon's Blik Bar has a collection of over 4 000 beer cans.

CHAPTER 28

NAMAQUALAND

ABOVE: Fields of the glansooggousblom, an indigenous daisy, transform the landscape of the Namaqua National Park into an orange blaze in spring.

Namaqualand, a vast arid region in the northwestern corner of South Africa, is renowned for its spectacular seasonal displays of spring flowers. Nature has blessed this area, aptly named the 'Garden of the Gods' by photographer Freeman Patterson, with a wealth of succulents.

The rolling hills strewn with small quartz pebbles, and red sandy plains in the south of Namaqualand, are known as the Knersvlakte – a name alluding to early travellers, who gnashed their teeth when travelling through this harsh and waterless terrain. North of Nuwerus, the Knersvlakte gives way to the smooth round granite hills and domes of the Namaqualand Klipkoppe ('rocky hills'). To the west lies the sandveld, a 30-km-wide strip of white and red sandy soil extending from the Olifants River northwards along the coast. The Orange River forms the northern boundary, while the Bokkeveldberge and the escarpment, and the Atlantic Ocean make up the eastern and western boundaries respectively.

Small-stock farming and wheat production are the main agricultural activities. The region is also rich in copper ore and diamond deposits, while gypsum is mined on the plains just north of Vanrhynsdorp. There are also marble and granite mines in the region.

CLIMATE

Situated in a semidesert area, the climate of Namaqualand is one of extremes. Midsummer temperatures are swelteringly hot, but it can be freezing cold in winter. Namaqualand lies in a winter rainfall area and precipitation varies from less than 50 mm at the coast to 200 mm a year further inland. Fog is common along the coast.

FLORA AND FAUNA

Namaqualand is synonymous with mass displays of annuals – among them the Namaqua daisy and species with descriptive names like botterblom ('butter flower'), beetle daisy and gansogie ('goose eye').

The secret of Namaqualand's floral displays lies in the way the plants have adapted to survive the harsh conditions. After the first good winter rains the seeds of the annuals germinate and for a few weeks the drab landscape is transformed into a blaze of colour – provided there have been good follow-up rains to ensure that the plants reach maturity.

The peak flowering season is usually from early August to mid-September. By the end of September the flowers wilt and disperse their seeds, which then lie in wait for the next year's rains. In order to survive, the seeds have ingenious built-in safety mechanisms. Each species has its own temperature and moisture requirements for germination and not all the seeds germinate after one good shower. This ensures that the natural seed bank is not depleted if there are no follow-up rains to sustain the new growth.

The flowers are usually at their best between 10h00 and 16h00 on sunny, windless days. They should be viewed from the north (with the sun behind the viewer), as the flowers orientate themselves towards the sun.

Succulents account for a third of the region's more than 3 000 plant species and include miniature 'stone plants' (lithops) and a rich variety of mesembs, commonly referred to as *vygies*.

More than 480 species of geophytes occur in the region. They escape the relentless summer heat because their bulbs, corms and tubers are protected underground. Water is retained in their underground storage organs to sustain them during droughts.

The harsh environment does not support many large mammal species, but the region is rich in reptiles, including many endemic species such as the Namaqualand dwarf leaf-toed gecko, the Rooiberg girdled lizard and the Namaqua dwarf adder.

Birding is best in winter and spring and Karoo eremomela, cinnamon-breasted warbler, Verreaux's eagle, ground woodpecker and mountain wheatear are among the species likely to be seen.

HISTORY AND HERITAGE

The region is home to the Nama people, a Khoekhoe group that migrated from northern Botswana westwards along the Orange River some 2 000 years ago and then split into two groups. The Little Namaqua settled south of the Orange River, while the Great Namaqua occupied southern Namibia.

Copper bangles worn by the Khoekhoen aroused the interest of officials of the Dutch settlement established at the Cape by Jan van Riebeeck in 1652. The first expeditions to find the source of the copper set out north, and by 1660 the Olifants River was reached.

Following the return of Ensign Isaq Schrijver from the Khamiesberg with samples of copper in 1684, Governor Simon van der Stel led an expedition to Namaqualand the following

BELOW: Namaqualand is renowned for its extraordinary diversity of spring annuals, perennials, succulents and geophytes such as this beautiful pink bobbejaantjie. BOTTOM: The branches of quiver trees are covered in a thin layer of whitish powder that helps to deflect the sun's hot rays.

QUIVER TREE

Quiver trees are a characteristic feature in the arid landscape of the Northern Cape, occurring widely in rocky areas in Namaqualand and the northern reaches of the Hantam Karoo. The San once used their branches as quivers for their arrows, hence the unusual name.

One of South Africa's five tree aloe species, they can grow to a height of up to 7 m and bear clusters of bright yellow flowers from June to August.

SEE:
Western & Northern
Cape p. 224
Northern Cape p. 225
Northern Cape &
Namibia pp. 232–233

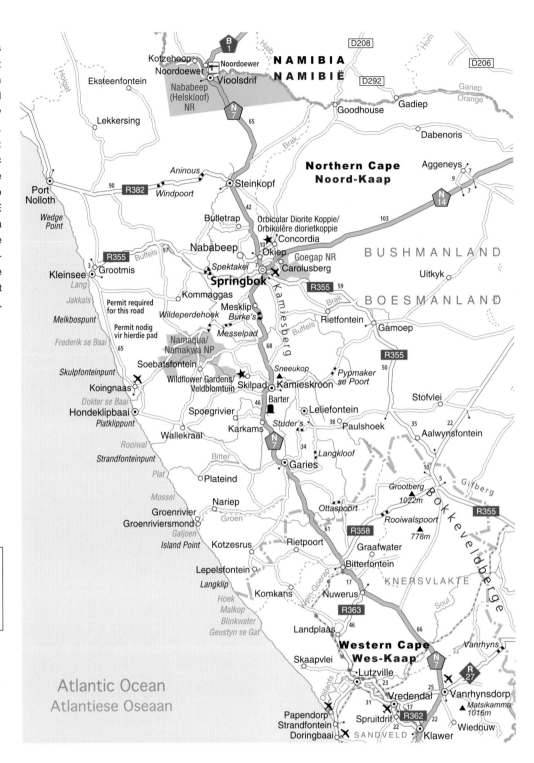

OPPOSITE TOP: Fields of annuals carpet the usually barren Namaqualand plains for a few weeks each spring. OPPOSITE MIDDLE: Vanrhynsdorp's historic old gaol was built more than 100 years ago in 1895. OPPOSITE BOTTOM: Some Nama women may still be seen wearing the traditional Nama *kappie* – a large white bonnet made from linen.

year. After a two-month journey, the expedition reached the 'copper mountain'. One of the mineshafts dug by the expedition in 1685 can still be seen at the Koperberg, near the disused Carolusberg mine, a few kilometres east of Springbok.

However, commercial exploitation of copper in Namaqualand only began in 1859. Over the next 140 years, vast quantities of ore were extracted from 23 mines in the area, but by the beginning of the 21st century the last mine was closed.

NOTEWORTHY PLACES

Vanrhynsdorp

Set against the backdrop of the Matsikamma Mountain, Vanrhynsdorp, the southernmost town in Namaqualand, was established on farm land in 1751. Originally named Troe-Troe, the settlement was renamed Vanrhynsdorp in 1881 after the owner of the farm.

The town has a distinctly Victorian atmosphere with many well-preserved houses dating back to the early 1900s. The old gaol, built in 1895, now houses the Vanrhynsdorp Museum and the tourism bureau. The town is a popular refilling stop on the N7.

A unique collection of valve radios and wireless equipment dating back to 1920 is displayed in the Latsky Radio Museum – a private collection that is open only during the flower season or by appointment.

Many rare succulents are among the 500 plant species on sale at the Kokerboom Nursery in the town, which is the largest indigenous succulent nursery in South Africa.

Rock paintings, including red and 'decorated' hand prints, human figures and images resembling nets, can be seen south of Vanrhynsdorp at Wiedouw and further along in the Gifberg ('poison mountain'), so named for the endemic hyaena poison-bush.

Garies

Heading north from Vanrhynsdorp, the N7 passes the towns of Nuwerus and Bitterfontein before reaching Garies. Situated midway between Vanrhynsdorp and Springbok, Garies was laid out against the backdrop of granite hills after land was made available for a Dutch Reformed church in 1845.

British forces occupied a cluster of granite outcrops overlooking the town from 1901 to 1902 during the second Anglo–Boer War. The lookout was fortified with stone walls and during their free time the soldiers engraved their names and regimental badges into the rock.

The outcrop, which has since become known as Letterklip ('alphabet rock'), is about 1 km from the town on the Studer's Pass.

Kamieskroon

The tranquil town of Kamieskroon was named after the crown-shaped rock on the crest of the Khamiesberg. Dominating the landscape to the northeast of the town, the 1 591-m-high Sneeukop is the second-highest point in Namaqualand.

The first Dutch Reformed church in Namaqualand was built in 1864 in a valley on a farm 6 km north of Kamieskroon. When it became obvious that the valley was too small for the Bowesdorp settlement, which had grown around the church, Kamieskroon became the new centre of the surrounding farming community in 1924.

The town is an ideal base for a day drive to Leliefontein Mission Station, which lies to the east of the Khamiesberg, an area that is home to some 1 000 plant species.

Namaqua National Park

The Namaqua National Park northwest of Kamieskroon is renowned for its springtime carpets of orange daisies. The park's foundations were laid in 1998 with the establishment of the Skilpad Wildflower Reserve by the World Wide Fund for Nature (WWF). The Namaqua National Park was officially opened in August 1999 and has since been enlarged to include the low-lying sandveld to the west. Plans are afoot to extend the park eastwards to incorporate the Khamiesberg where many endemic succulents occur.

The most spectacular wildflower displays can be found on former wheat fields in the Skilpad section of the park that are dominated by two showy daisy species – one with orange ray florets and the other with black disc-like florets. A variety of other annuals, geophytes and perennial species also thrive in the surrounding unploughed areas. Succulents and perennial bushes grow among the granite outcrops and in the adjacent mountains. Typical sandveld vegetation occurs on the low-lying coastal plains.

Picnic facilities are provided for day visitors and self-catering accommodation is available. The reserve is reached 22 km northwest of Kamieskroon along a gravel road.

Leliefontein

Situated in the eastern foothills of the Khamiesberg, the settlement of Leliefontein lies along what has aptly been named the Garden Route of Namaqualand.

The oldest Methodist mission station in the country was founded here by the Reverend Barnabas Shaw in 1816. The historic church dates back to 1855, while the adjoining parsonage was built a few years earlier.

A plaque in the church serves as a memorial to the 35 inhabitants massacred by a Boer war force under the command of General Manie Maritz in January 1902. An altercation broke out when they were accused of being sympathetic to the British, after which Maritz ordered their annihilation.

Hondeklip Bay

The choice of a port from which to export copper originally fell on Hondeklip Bay. The town owes its name to a 5-m-high rock (*klip*) that resembled a seated dog (*hond*) – until its 'head' was struck off by lightning.

The settlement was declared a magisterial district in 1862 and the rough track along which the copper was transported from Springbok to the coast was improved when the Messelpad Pass (named after dressed-stone embankments) was built between 1867 and 1869.

However, the completion of the railway line to Port Nolloth brought about the rapid decline of the settlement, and these days it functions predominantly as a summer-holiday destination for Namaqualand farmers.

Springbok

Springbok, the commercial centre of Namaqualand, owes its existence to the rich cop-

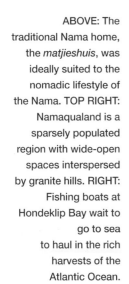

ABOVE: The traditional Nama home, the *matjieshuis*, was ideally suited to the nomadic lifestyle of the Nama. TOP RIGHT: Namaqualand is a sparsely populated region with wide-open spaces interspersed by granite hills. RIGHT: Fishing boats at Hondeklip Bay wait to go to sea to haul in the rich harvests of the Atlantic Ocean.

THE TRADITIONAL *MATJIESHUIS*

The dome-shaped traditional Nama *matjieshuis* ('mat house') consists of a framework of 40 to 50 bent branches that are covered with reed mats. Not only do the mats regulate the temperature inside the dwelling, they also allow for ventilation.

These semipermanent structures were ideally suited to the nomadic lifestyle of the Nama, as they could swiftly be taken down and reassembled when the time came to find new pastures for their livestock.

Although no longer as common as they once were, such traditional homes can still be seen in villages in the Richtersveld and at small settlements in the Leliefontein area. Nowadays, black plastic and sacking is used to cover the frame.

ORBICULE KOPPIE

An extremely rare type of rock, orbicular diorite, can be seen at Orbicule Koppie, a rocky hillock south of a village called Concordia situated 10 km east of Okiep. Known to occur outside of Namaqualand only in Scandinavia, orbicular diorite consists of egg-shaped 'orbs' surrounded by a matrix of pegmatites.

ACTIVITIES

- Canoeing on the Orange River; several operators conduct trips from base camps downstream of Vioolsdrif or Noordoewer in Namibia
- Mountain biking in the Goegap Nature Reserve and in the Khamiesberg, along the road to Leliefontein
- Experiencing Nama culture at Paulshoek in the Khamiesberg
- Birdwatching all over the region

ROUTES AND TRAILS

- Messelpad and Wildeperdehoek passes from Springbok to Hondeklip Bay; suitable for sedan cars
- Circular drive (17 km) in the Goegap Nature Reserve near Springbok; suitable for sedan cars
- 4x4 route (40 km) in the Goegap Nature Reserve near Springbok
- Travelling from Vioolsdrif to Eksteenfontein (40 km) through the Nababeep (Helskloof) Nature Reserve and on to the Richtersveld
- Caracal 4x4 Ecoroute (153 km) in Namaqua National Park, from Skilpad to Groen River
- Shipwreck 4x4 Trail (3–4 hours) from Kleinsee to Koingnaas; travellers need to carry a passport or identity document as part of the route is in a restricted diamond-mining area
- Two day walks (2 and 5 hours) in the Goegap Nature Reserve near Springbok
- Two day walks (2 and 3 hours) in the Namaqua National Park

per deposits occurring in the area, known to geologists as the Okiep Copper District. The open-cast Blue Mine, on the northwestern outskirts of the town, came into operation in 1852 and was the first commercial mine in the country. The stone smokestack built at the Springbokfontein reduction works in 1863 is a reminder of the town's early mining days.

Services of the first Dutch Reformed church congregation were held in an oblong stone building, built in 1877, until the new dressed-stone church was taken into use in 1921. Springbok's synagogue was built in 1929 when the town had a sizeable Jewish community, but now serves as the town's history museum.

The Goegap Nature Reserve, 15 km south-east of Springbok, is a sanctuary for Hartmann's mountain zebra, gemsbok, springbok, klipspringer and a host of small mammals and birds, including flocks of ostrich. For most of the year the reserve attracts few visitors, but in the spring flower season large numbers of people pass through the gates to enjoy the spectacular natural floral show. A succulent display and a rock garden have been developed in the Hester Malan Wild Flower Garden that forms part of the reserve.

Okiep

More than a decade after the first shaft was sunk at Okiep in 1856, the mine was ranked as the richest copper mine in the world. It eventually closed in 1971, and in 1997 the houses in the town were given to the people who occupied them at that time. Relics of Okiep's mining history include the old smelter stack, which was in use from 1880 to 1929, and the adjoining steam-driven Cornish beam pump erected in 1882 to pump water from the mine.

Nababeep

Exploitation of copper ore at Nababeep began in 1857. Closed in 1919, the mine reopened in 1939, but mining activities finally ceased in the early 1980s. The smelter, however, was kept going with concentrates until December 2003, when it, too, was shut down.

The history built on the region's copper riches is the theme of the Nababeep Mine Museum. *Clara*, the quaint steam engine in front of the museum, was the last steam locomotive used on the Okiep–Port Nolloth narrow-gauge railway line, which was closed in 1941 after the track proved to be uneconomical.

ABOVE: The historic smelter stack at Okiep was built by Cornish miners in 1880 for the boilers that supplied steam for the nearby Cornish beam pump. LEFT: *Clara*, a narrow-gauge locomotive used on the Okiep–Port Nolloth line, is the centrepiece of the displays at the Nababeep Mine Museum.

CHAPTER 29

THE RICHTERSVELD

ABOVE: The Richters-
veld, South Africa's
only mountainous
desert, is renowned for
its spectacular scenery.

Occupying the northwestern corner of Namaqualand, the greater Richtersveld area extends from the Orange River in the north and the cold Atlantic Ocean in the west to the R382 in the south and the N7 in the east. The coastal strip seems bleak and lifeless, but further inland towering mountain peaks and deep valleys create the spectacular scenery of South Africa's only mountainous desert.

Despite the rugged terrain and the harsh climate, the Richtersveld is renowned for its unique flora. It is also one of the few places in the country where traditional semi-nomadic stock farming is still practised. In recognition of its exceptional botanical and cultural value, a 160 000-ha tract of the Richtersveld, coinciding with the Richtersveld National Park, was declared a UNESCO World Heritage Site in June 2007.

CLIMATE

The climate of the Richtersveld is as harsh as its terrain. The rainfall is sparse and erratic, ranging from a mere 15 mm along the coast to 300 mm in the interior. The coast enjoys mild temperatures (10–22 °C), but further inland they can soar above 45 °C in midsummer and drop to zero in winter.

FLORA AND FAUNA

One of the most outstanding features of the Richtersveld is the floral diversity, especially of its succulents – which account for more than a third of the region's 1 615 plant species. Contributing to this natural heritage are some 255 species of mesembs, or *vygies*. About 140 of the Richtersveld's plant species are endemic and occur nowhere else in the world.

Best known among the region's botanical treasures is the halfmens, a succulent also known as elephant's trunk. Colonies of this strange-looking plant grow on rocky slopes, while diminutive 'stone plants' or 'flowering stones' are inconspicuous among the quartz pebbles.

The giant quiver tree, which can reach a height of 10 m, the quiver tree (also called *kokerboom*), Pearson's aloe and the multi-stemmed maiden's quiver tree are among the 17 aloe species that occur in the Richtersveld. The botterboom ('butter tree') with its yellowish, papery bark, the candelabra-like noorsdoring and the bushman's candle are other common plants.

Hartmann's mountain zebra, gemsbok, klipspringer and steenbok are among the antelope that live in this harsh land. The desert is also a haven for reptiles, and some 52 species can be found here.

With a bird checklist of over 200 species, birding in the Richtersveld is especially rewarding.

HISTORY AND HERITAGE

Nama Khoekhoe pastoralists settled in the Richtersveld some 2 000 years ago after migrating with their herds of small stock from present-day northern Botswana. They lived in nomadic family clans headed by a chief; a number of clans were united as a tribe led by a captain. It was not until 1840 that the first permanent settlement was established at Kuboes by the Rhenish Missionary Society. The Richtersveld is named after Dr E Richter, an inspector of the Rhenish Missionary Society who visited the area in 1830.

In the ongoing search for copper and other minerals in the northwestern parts of the country, prospectors and geologists turned their attention to the Richtersveld. In the second half of the 1830s, Captain (later Sir) James Alexander began mining copper at Kodas, about 5 km southwest of the 979-m-high Kodas Peak, and shipped the ore on barges to the mouth of the Orange River, where it was then transferred onto coasters.

Many other prospectors followed in his footsteps, among them Fred Cornell who prospected in the Richtersveld between 1910 and 1920 and gave a wonderful description of the region in his book *The Glamour of Prospecting*.

The discovery of alluvial diamonds along the Namaqualand coast in the mid-1920s caused a diamond rush and the coastal strip north of Port Nolloth was declared State Alluvial Diggings in 1928, a move that denied the people of the Richtersveld access to their ancestral land. In an historic ruling, the ancestral rights of the Richtersveld people over the strip of land were restored by the Constitutional Court in October 2003.

THE STRIKING *HALFMENS*

The halfmens, an unusual stem succulent, is one of the most striking plants of the Richtersveld. Folklore has it that a group of Nama who were driven out of southern Namibia looked back longingly to the fertile lands north of the Orange River. The gods felt pity for the grief-stricken people and transformed them into *halfmense* ('half people').

NOTEWORTHY PLACES

Steinkopf

The first mission station of the London Missionary Society in the Richtersveld was established in 1818, about 5 km south of Kookfontein ('boiling spring'), as Steinkopf was originally known. The mission station was moved to Kookfontein in 1820 and renamed after a benefactor of the Society, Dr Karl Steinkopf. In 1840, the mission station was transferred to the Rhenish Missionary Society. A collection of paintings donated by the family of the Reverend Ferdinand Brecher, who was a missionary at Steinkopf in the late 1800s, can be viewed in the town's stone church, built in the 1840s. Also worth visiting is the succulent nursery run by the Immanuel Centre for the Disabled.

Port Nolloth

Port Nolloth was established in 1855 as a small-vessel harbour for the export of copper. The port was linked to Okiep by a narrow-gauge railway line which was taken into use on 1 January 1876, but the difficult entrance to the

LEFT: Halfmens, a stem succulent, is endemic to the Richtersveld and the southernmost reaches of Namibia. It is also known as 'elephant's trunk'.

SEE:
Western & Northern
Cape p. 224
Northern Cape &
Namibia p. 232

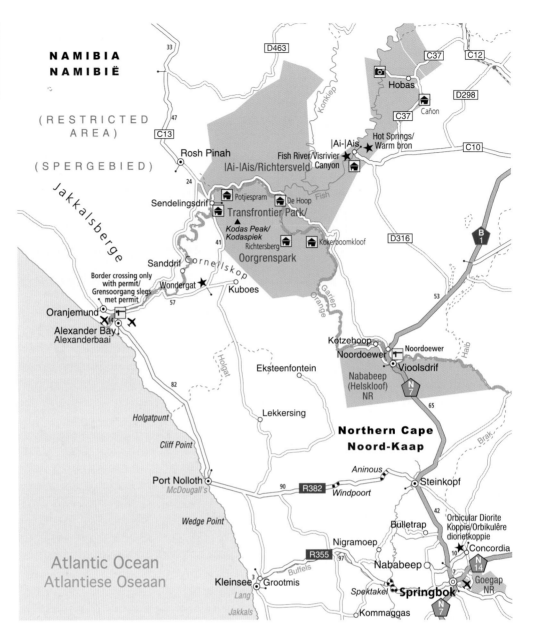

harbour prevented large vessels from docking and the railway was eventually closed in 1944.

The town's fortunes improved in 1925 when local storekeeper, Jack Carstens, discovered a diamond a few kilometres south of the small settlement. Today, Port Nolloth is a centre of the marine diamond industry.

The Port Nolloth Museum, located in the historic clubhouse built for officers of the Cape Copper Company in the 1880s, portrays the history of the town and the diamond and copper industries. Some of the wooden houses that were imported from Denmark in 1895 can still be seen in the town.

In summer, large numbers of Namaqualanders flock to the unspoilt beach resort of McDougall's Bay, 3 km south of Port Nolloth, to escape the heat of the interior.

Alexander Bay

The town of Alexander Bay, on the southern bank of the Orange River, was named after the British explorer, Sir James Alexander, who began mining copper in the Richtersveld in the 1830s.

Diamonds were discovered here in the late 1920s, and the mine and town that developed subsequently were transferred to a state-owned enterprise, Alexkor, in 1989. A tour of the mine includes viewing mining operations and visiting the museum, harbour, oyster farm and seal colony. Tours must be booked at least 24 hours in advance to obtain security clearance, and children under the age of 18 are not permitted.

The Orange River mouth, proclaimed a Ramsar site in 1991, is the sixth most important coastal wetland in South Africa. The wetland

RICHTERSVELD VILLAGES

About 6 000 people live in the Richtersveld settlements of Kuboes, Sanddrif, Eksteenfontein and Lekkersing, outside the Richtersveld National Park.

The Nama settlement of Kuboes was founded as a substation of Steinkopf by the Rhenish missionary, Johan Hein, in 1840. The whitewashed mission church dates back to 1893.

Also known as the 'Rainbow Town' of the Richtersveld, Sanddrif was established in the 1970s to accommodate mainly Xhosa and Basotho employees working at the nearby diamond mine of TransHex. Nama people have also settled there and today Sanddrif has a curious multicultural feel about it.

In 1949 a group of marginalised Basters (people of mixed Khoekhoe and Dutch descent) from Kenhardt in Bushmanland was resettled at Eksteenfontein. The settlement was named after the Reverend Pieter Eksteen who assisted them in their plight.

Baster people also settled at Lekkersing, an Afrikaans name meaning 'joyful singing'.

ACTIVITIES

- Viewing the diverse flora of the region, especially succulents, in the Richtersveld National Park and surrounds
- Spotting antelope and reptiles in the Richtersveld National Park and surrounds
- Birdwatching at the Orange River mouth
- Swimming at McDougall's Bay
- Touring the diamond mine at Alexander Bay
- Experiencing Nama culture in the Richtersveld villages of Kuboes, Lekkersing and Eksteenfontein

ROUTES AND TRAILS

- Three guided hiking trails in the Richtersveld National Park from 1 April to 30 September only – Vensterval Trail (4 days), Lelieshoek–Oemsberg Trail (3 days) and Kodaspiek Trail (2 days)

supports up to 26 000 birds of 26 species, including significant numbers of Cape cormorant, Hartlaub's gull, lesser flamingo, chestnut-banded plover and black-necked grebe.

Cornellskop

A large colony of bastard quiver trees grows on Cornellskop, a limestone hill named after prospector, Fred Cornell. The Wondergat ('mystery hole') at the foot of Cornellskop is believed to be the home of a snake that features prominently in Nama folklore. According to one such legend, the snake can transform itself into a maiden who lures men into the hole and then drowns them in an underground river.

Richtersveld National Park

The 162 000-ha Richtersveld National Park was proclaimed on 20 July 1991, nearly two decades after the establishment of a conservation area in the area was first proposed. In terms of an agreement with the Richtersveld communities, the park is being leased from the local people for a 30-year period, allowing them to preserve their culture and continue their traditional lifestyle and semi-nomadic stock farming practices. The park is jointly managed by the local communities and South African National Parks (SANParks), with the four Richtersveld villages of Kuboes, Sanddrif, Lekkersing and Eksteenfontein represented on the management committee.

A 4x4 is recommended for the park's rough tracks, although some roads are accessible to vehicles with a high ground clearance. Sedans are not permitted.

Accommodation ranges from self-catering chalets at Sendelingsdrif, where the park headquarters is situated, to camping sites with basic facilities at Potjiespram, De Hoop, Richtersberg and Kokerboomkloof. Two wilderness camps with self-catering units and a hiking trail base camp are other accommodation options.

LEFT: De Hoop, on the banks of the Orange River, is a popular campsite in the Richtersveld National Park, which protects an incredible diversity of succulents.

IAI–IAIS/RICHTERSVELD TRANSFRONTIER PARK

The 508 600-ha IAi–IAis/Richtersveld Transfrontier Park was established following the signing of an agreement between the governments of South Africa and Namibia in August 2003. The vast conservation area comprises the Richtersveld National Park in South Africa and the IAi–IAis Game Park in southern Namibia, where the Fish River Canyon is the main attraction. Travellers can cross the Orange River by means of a pontoon which operates daily at Sendelingsdrif – provided they have the necessary travel documents.

FURTHER READING

Brett, M. 2010. *Touring South Africa's national parks*. Cape Town: Struik Travel & Heritage.

Cape Town Routes Unlimited. 2008. *Cape Town & Western Cape Official Travel Guide 2008–09*. Cape Town.

Carruthers, V. 2005. *The wildlife of southern Africa – A field guide to the animals and plants of the region*. Cape Town: Struik Nature.

Eastwood, E. and C. 2006. *Capturing the spoor – An exploration of southern African rock art*. Cape Town: David Philip.

Fraser, S. 2008. *Seven days in Cape Town*. Cape Town: Struik Travel & Heritage.

Giliomee, H. and Mbenga, B. 2007. *New history of South Africa*. Cape Town: Tafelberg.

Hayward, J., Loubser, J. and Velásquez Rojas, C. (Consultant eds). 2010. *Shoreline – Discovering South Africa's coast*. Based on the acclaimed SABC2 documentary series *Shoreline*. Cape Town: Struik Travel & Heritage.

Hopkins, P., Slabbert, D. and Ngwenya, B. 2009. *The South African fact book*. Johannesburg: Penguin Books.

Knight, I. and Castle, I. 2004. *The Zulu War – Then and now*. Oxford: Osprey Publishing.

Mandela, N. 1995. *Long walk to freedom*. London: Abacus.

Manning, J. 2007. *Field guide to fynbos*. Cape Town: Struik Nature.

McCarthy, T. and Rubidge, B. 2005. *The story of earth and life – A southern African perspective on a 4.6 billion-year journey*. Cape Town: Struik Nature.

Michler, I. and Van Schaik, T. 2009. *South Africa – The insider's guide*. Cape Town: Struik Travel & Heritage.

Nell, L. 2003. *The Garden Route and Little Karoo – Between the desert and the deep blue sea*. Cape Town: Struik Nature.

Norman, N. and Whitfield, G. 2006. *Geological journeys – A traveller's guide to South Africa's rocks and landforms*. Cape Town: Struik Nature.

Olivier, W. 2010. *Hiking trails of South Africa*. Cape Town: Struik Travel & Heritage.

Palmer, E. 1974. *The plains of Camdeboo*. London: Fontana.

Pienaar, A. 2009. *The Griqua's apprentice*. Cape Town: Umuzi.

Sinclair, I. and Ryan, P. 2009. *Complete photographic field guide – Birds of southern Africa*. Cape Town: Struik Nature.

Slabbert, D. 2009. *South Africa through the seasons*. Cape Town: Struik Travel & Heritage.

Taylor, W., Hinde, G. and Holt-Biddle, D. 2003. *The Waterberg – The natural splendours and the people*. Cape Town: Struik Nature.

The Tourism Blueprint CC. 2009. *Tourism Blueprint guide to the nine provinces of South Africa including Swaziland & Lesotho*. Cape Town.

Theron, E. and Radcliff, J. 2009. *Dirty Boots adventure guide – The definitive guide to the best adventures in southern Africa*. Cape Town: Dirty Boots™ Publishing.

Wilson, F. 2009. *Dinosaurs, diamonds and democracy – A short, short history of South Africa*. Cape Town: Umuzi.

INDEX

Legend to Road Guide

Tarred — Untarred
Under Construction

Freeway / National Road

Main Road

Secondary Road

N1 R21 R110 Route Numbers

T T Toll Route and Toll Plaza

Mountain Pass

15 Distance in Kilometres

Railway with Station

International Boundary

Provincial Boundary

Water Feature

Pan

Marsh

National Park and Nature Reserve

▲ Place of Interest

Waterfall

☐ Capital or City

◎ Major Town

○ Secondary Town

⊙ Other Town

○ Settlement

🏠 Accommodation

⍳ Historical Site

◁ Border Control

✈ Major Airport

⊢ Airfield

▲ Major Spot Height

16°00'E   Okahandja   18°00'E   20°00'E   22°00'E   24°00'E

Dipros Krater

Kutse Game Reserve

Black Cliff

Bay

Namib Naukluft Park

Kalkrand

Aranos

Kgalagadi

Kalahari Game Reserve
(y Permit Required)

A2

BOTSW...

Stampriet

Union's End

Gemsbok National Park

Mabuasehube Game Reserve

Sou...

243

K...

Hardap

Mariental

Gochas

241

242

Mattahöhe

Hardap Dam
Hardap Recreation Resort

Gibeon

240

NAMIBIA

Namib Rand Nature Res.

Helmeringhausen

Koës

Kgalagadi Transfrontier Park

Kalahari Gemsbok National Park

Tshabong

Molopo Nature Reserve

North West

Tiras Mountain Conservancy

Koichabpan

Easter Point
Knoll Point

Black Rock

Black Cliffs

North Point
Spencer Bay

Mercury Island

Hottentotsbaai

Bethanie

Aus

Keetmanshoop

Aroab

Molopo

Kuruman

Moshaweng

Hotazel

Matthwaring

Kokgole

Vrybur...

Sch...

Lüderitz
Diaz Point

Naute Recreation Area

DIAMOND AREA 1

Karas

Molopo

Dibeng

Kuruman

Tau
Reivilo

Jan Kemp...

Elizabeth Bay

Possession Island

(RESTRICTED AREA)

Fish River Canyon National Park

Grünau

Karasburg

233

B3

234

N14

Sishen

Postmasburg

235

Danielskuil

Rosh Pinah

232

Warmbad

N10

Upington

Keimoes

Groblershoop

Delportshoop

Barkly West

Oranjemund

Richtersveld National Park

Noordoewer

ViooIsdrif

Orange

Augrabies Falls National Park

Onseepkans

N14

Kakamas

Campbell

Griquatown

Mokala National Park

Douglas

Ritchie

Alexander Bay

Port Nolloth

Steinkopf

Pofadder

Kenhardt

N10

10

Niekerkshoop

Prieska

Hopetown

McDougall's Bay

Nababeep Okiep

Goegab Nature Reserve

Geelvloer

Karvloer

Marydale

Copperton

Strydenburg

Luc...

Wedge Point

Springbok

Namaqua National Park

Grootvloer

Verneuk Pan

N10

Petrusvill...

Melkbospunt

Konnes se Pan

Dwaggassoutpan

Northern Cape

Van Wyksvlei

Britstown

P

Skulpfonteinpunt

Hondeklipbaai

Kamieskroon

Commissioner's Salt Pan

Brandvlei

Riet se Vloer

226

De Aar

Strandfonteinpunt

Garies

224

225

Carnarvon

227

Hanover

Island Point

Klein Doring

Swartkolkvloer

Loeriesfontein

Williston

Victoria West

Richmond

Mid...

Nieuwoudtville

Victoria West

Hutchinson

Atlantic Ocean

Vredendal

Vanrhynsdorp

Calvinia

Loxton

Nieu Bet

Rooiduinpunt

Klawer

Fish

Fraserburg

Murraysburg

Graaff-Reinet

Lambert's Bay

Uitspankraal

Tankwa-Karoo National Park

Aberdeen

Adendorp

Baboon Point

Clanwilliam

Wuppertal

Sutherland

Karoo National Park

Rietbron

9

St Helena Bay

Citrusdal

Beaufort West

Stompneuspunt
Paternoster

Velddrif

Piketberg

Porterville

Laingsburg

Prince Albert

De Rust

Willowmore

Ste...

Vredenburg
Saldanha

Hopefield

Moorreesburg

Swartberg N.R.

Dysselsdorp

Baviaanskloof Wildernes...

Langebaan

West Coast National Park

Dassen Island

Malmesbury

Ceres

Western Cape

Touws River

Ladismith

Buffels

Uniondale

22...

Joubertina

Kareed...

218

Melkbosstrand

Wellington

Worcester

Montagu

Marloth Nature Reserve

220

Oudtshoorn

George

Paarl

219

Robertson

Albertina

Mossel Bay

221

CAPE TOWN

Milnerton

Bellville

Stellenbosch

Swellendam

Riversdale

Wilderness Section (GRNP)

Knysna

Plettenberg Bay

Hout Bay

Strand

Caledon

Riversonderend National Park

Heidelberg

Albertinia

Cape Barracouta

Knysna Section (GRNP)

Simon's Town

Table Mountain National Park

Hermanus

Walker Bay

Napier

De Hoop N.R.

Cape Infanta

Cape Vacca (Kanonpunt)

Cape of Good Hope

False Bay

Bredasdorp

Gansbaai

Struis Bay

Quoin Point

Cape Agulhas

16°00'E   18°00'E   20°00'E   22°00'E   24°00'E

Copyright © Map Studio 20...

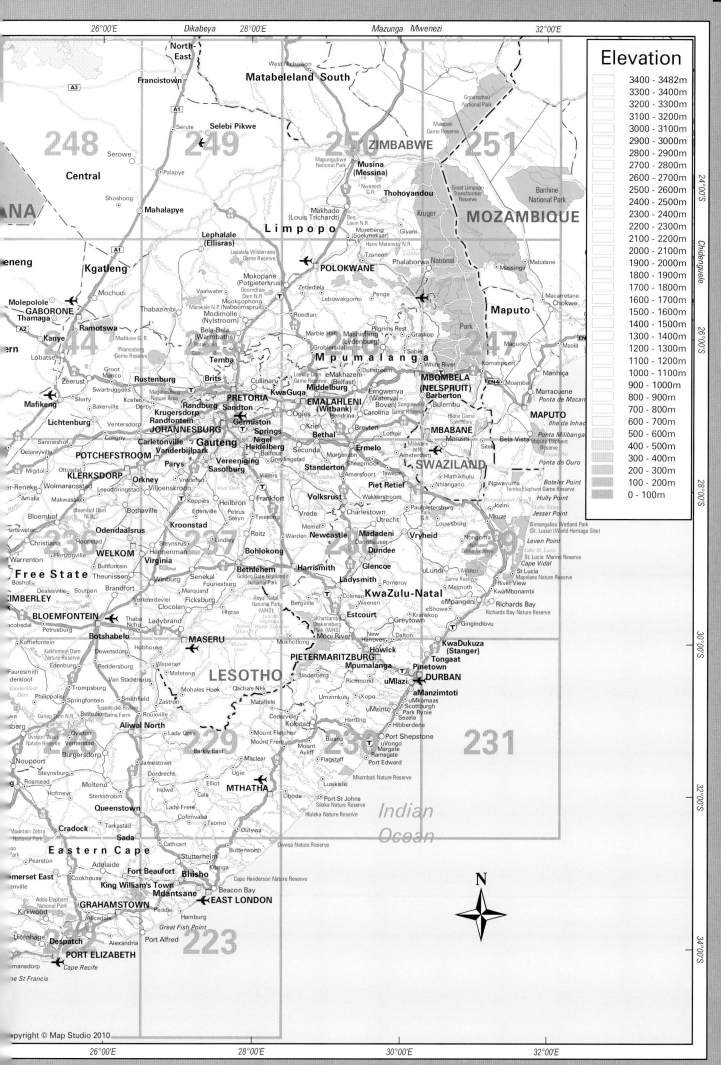

Elevation

	3400 - 3482m
	3300 - 3400m
	3200 - 3300m
	3100 - 3200m
	3000 - 3100m
	2900 - 3000m
	2800 - 2900m
	2700 - 2800m
	2600 - 2700m
	2500 - 2600m
	2400 - 2500m
	2300 - 2400m
	2200 - 2300m
	2100 - 2200m
	2000 - 2100m
	1900 - 2000m
	1800 - 1900m
	1700 - 1800m
	1600 - 1700m
	1500 - 1600m
	1400 - 1500m
	1300 - 1400m
	1200 - 1300m
	1100 - 1200m
	1000 - 1100m
	900 - 1000m
	800 - 900m
	700 - 800m
	600 - 700m
	500 - 600m
	400 - 500m
	300 - 400m
	200 - 300m
	100 - 200m
	0 - 100m

Copyright © Map Studio 2010

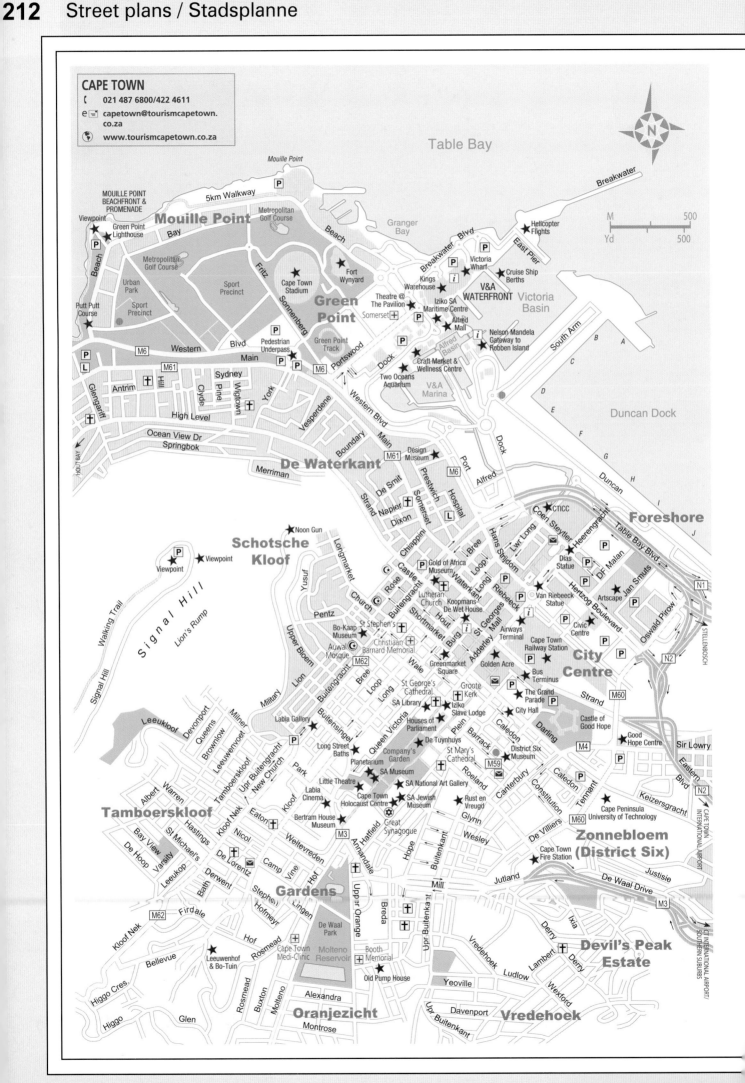

Table Bay

CAPE TOWN
021 487 6800/422 4611
e capetown@tourismcapetown.co.za
www.tourismcapetown.co.za

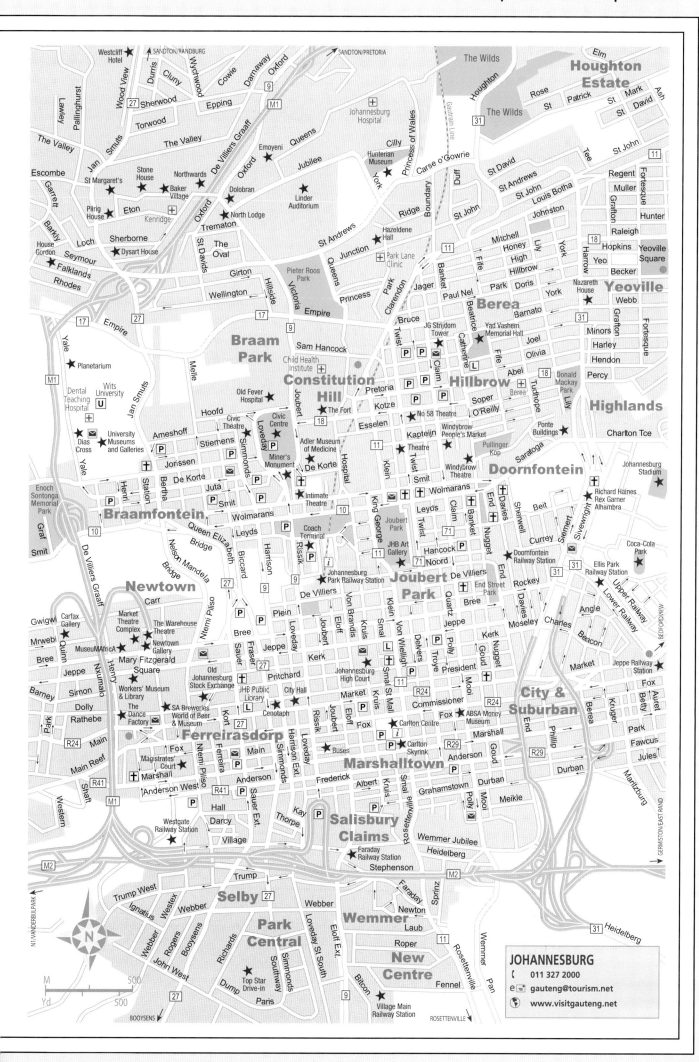

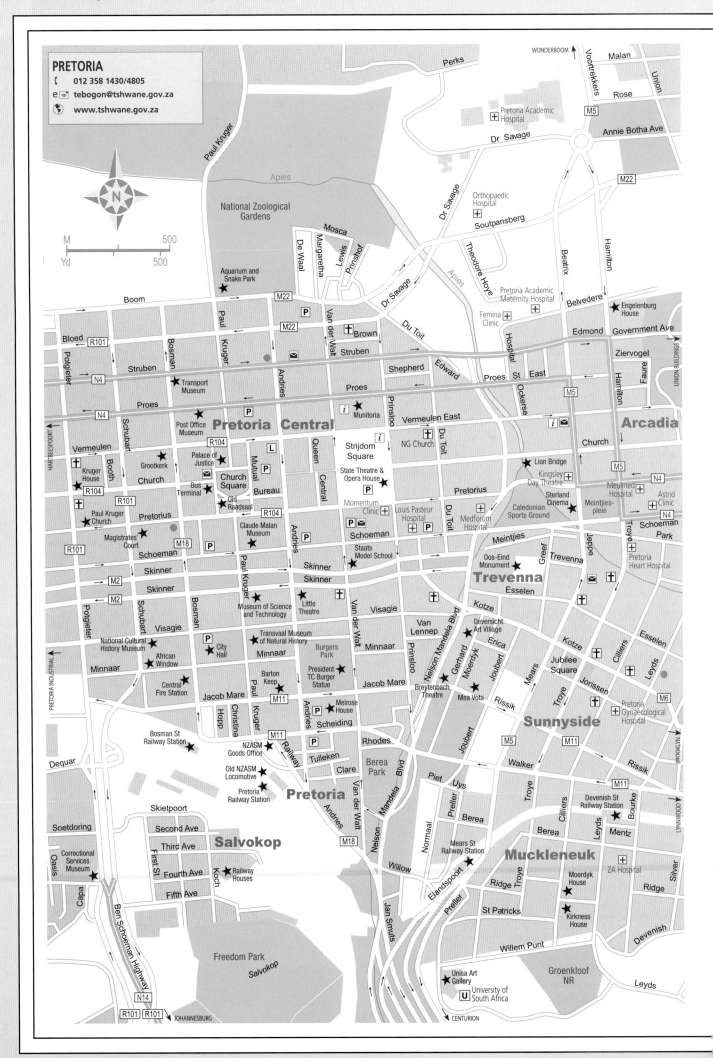

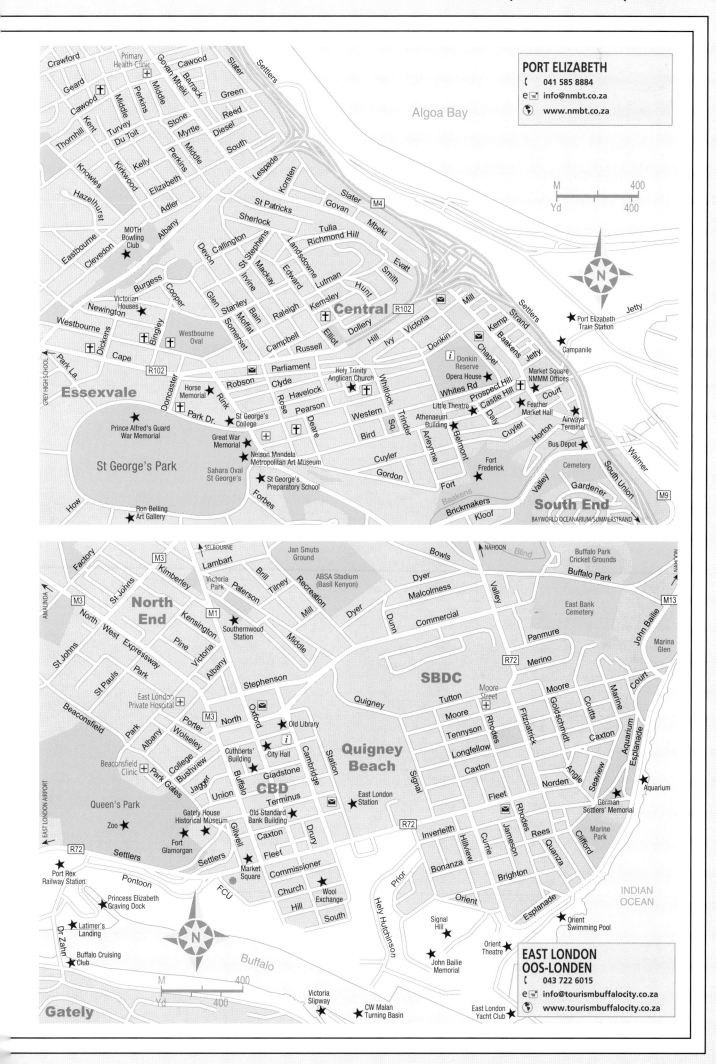

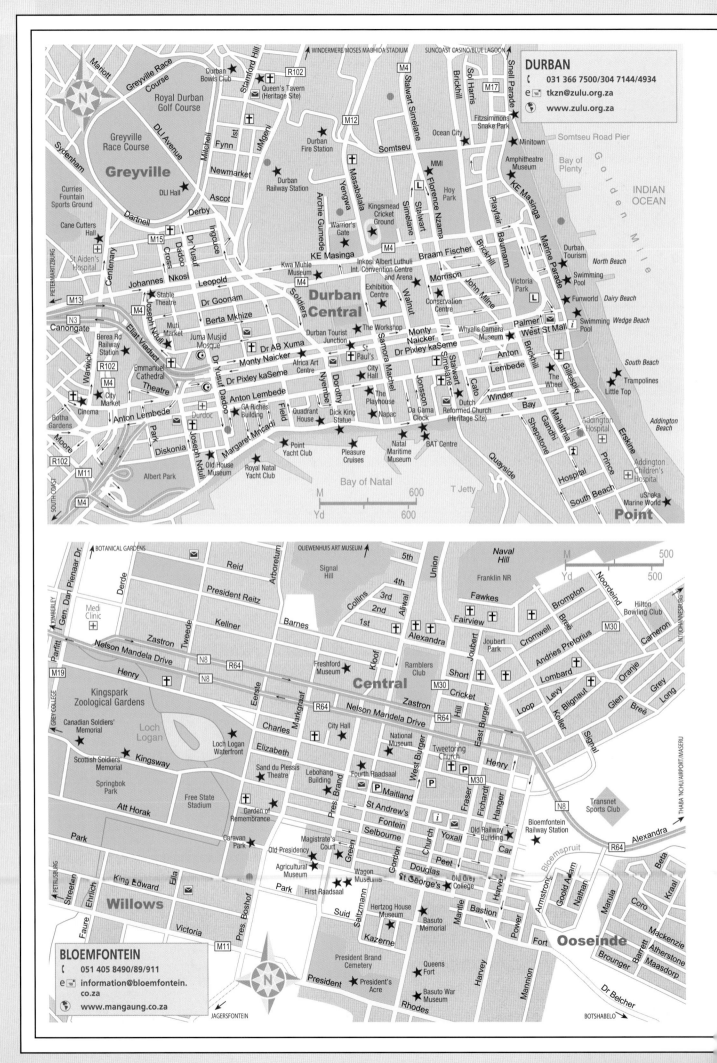

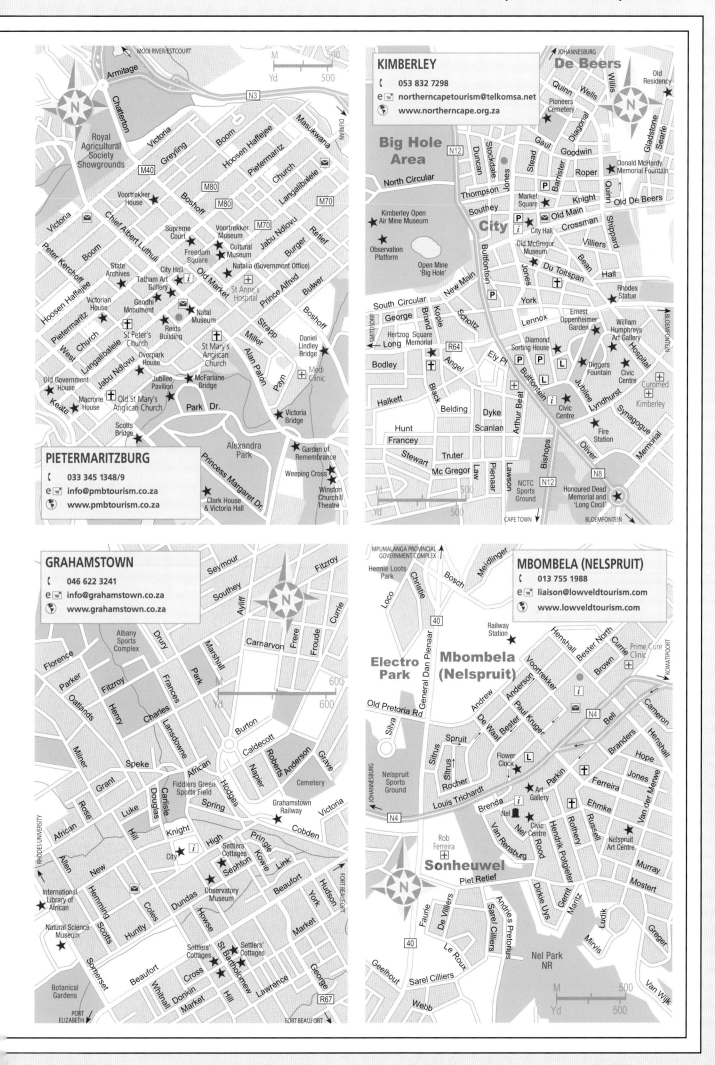

KIMBERLEY
- 053 832 7298
- northerncapetourism@telkomsa.net
- www.northerncape.org.za

PIETERMARITZBURG
- 033 345 1348/9
- info@pmbtourism.co.za
- www.pmbtourism.co.za

GRAHAMSTOWN
- 046 622 3241
- info@grahamstown.co.za
- www.grahamstown.co.za

MBOMBELA (NELSPRUIT)
- 013 755 1988
- liaison@lowveldtourism.com
- www.lowveldtourism.com

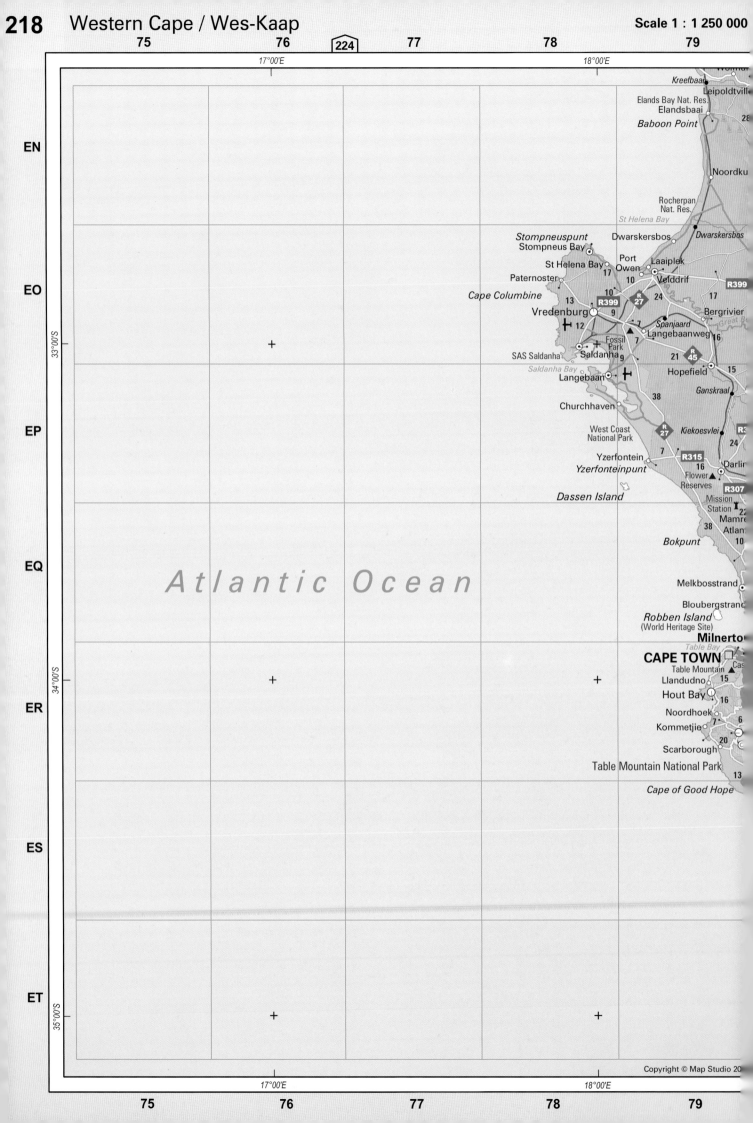

Atlantic Ocean

Kreefbaai

Elands Bay Nat. Res.
Elandsbaai
Baboon Point

Noordku

Rocherpan
Nat. Res.

St Helena Bay

Leipoldtville

28

Woltar

Stompneuspunt
Stompneus Bay
St Helena Bay
Paternoster
Cape Columbine
Vredenburg
13
12
SAS Saldanha
Saldanha
Saldanha Bay
Langebaan
Churchhaven
Dwarskersbos
Port
Owen
17
10
10
9
R399
Fossil
Park
9
7
38
*West Coast
National Park*
R27
Yzerfontein
16
Yzerfonteinpunt
7
Dassen Island

Dwarskersbos
Laaiplek
Velddrif
24
R399
R27
24
Spanjaard
Langebaanweg
7
7
21
Hopefield
R45
Ganskraal
Kiekoesvlei
R315
Darlin
Flower ▲
Reserves
R307
Mission
Station
Mamre
Atlan
Bokpunt
Bergrivier
Great
17
16
15
R3
24
22
38
10

Melkbosstrand
Bloubergstrand
Robben Island
(World Heritage Site)
Milnerto
Table Bay
CAPE TOWN
Table Mountain
Llandudno
Hout Bay
Noordhoek
Kommetjie
Scarborough
Cas
15
16
7
6
20
Table Mountain National Park
13
Cape of Good Hope

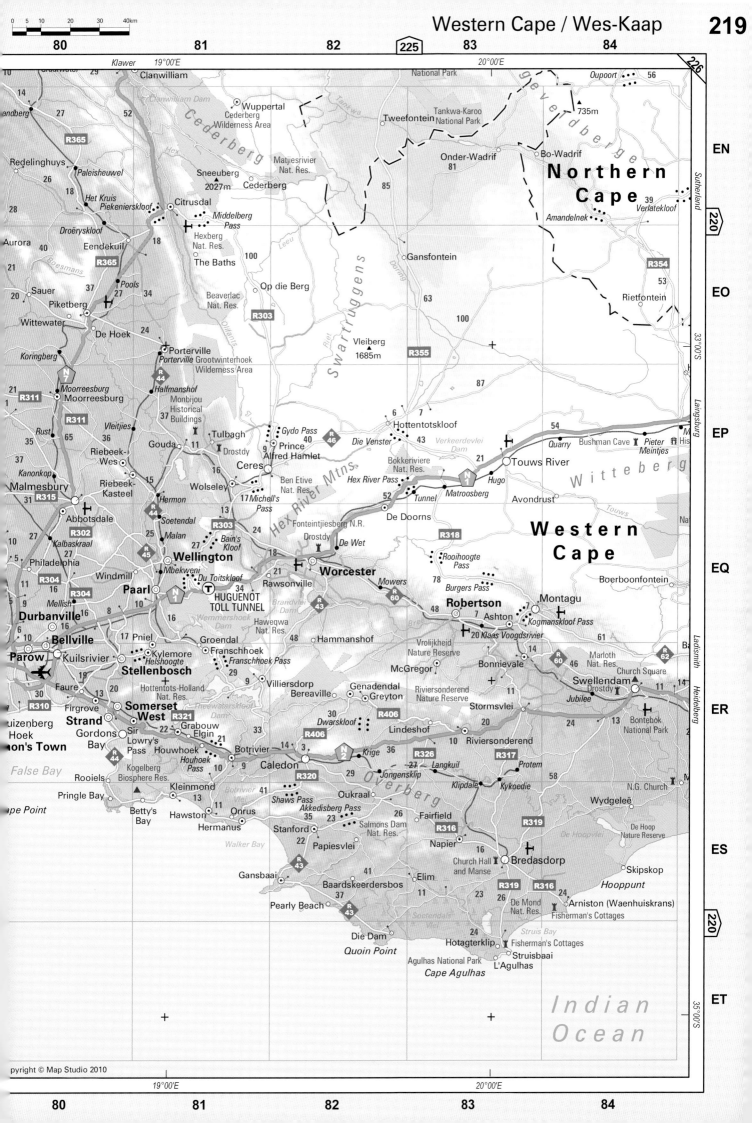

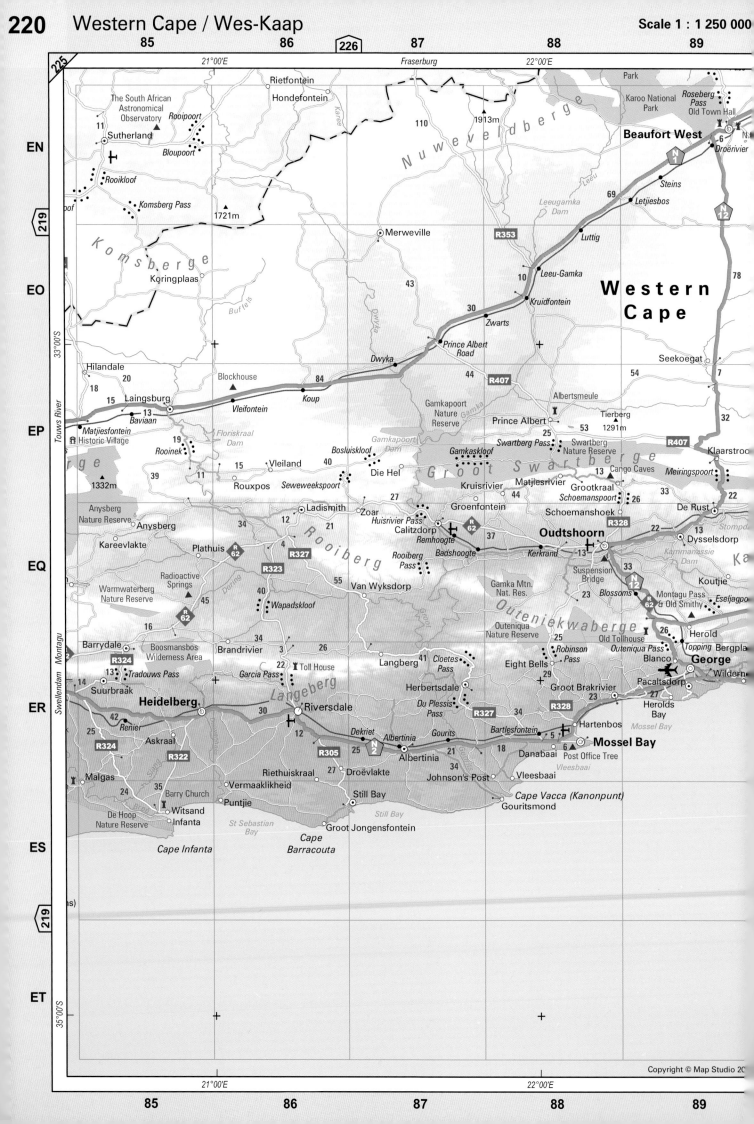

85   86   226   87   88   89

21°00'E   Fraserburg   22°00'E

Park

Rietfontein

Hondefontein

The South African
Astronomical
Observatory   Rooipoort

11   1913m   Karoo National Park   Roseberg Pass
Old Town Hall

Sutherland   110   Beaufort West

Bloupoort   Droërivier

EN   N1   6

Rooikloof   Steins

Komsberg Pass   69   Letjiesbos   N12

1721m   Merweville   Leeugamka Dam   Luttig   78

Koringplaas   R353

43   10   Leeu-Gamka   W e s t e r n
C a p e

EO   30   Kruidfontein

Buffels   Zwarts   32

33°00'S   Dwyka   Prince Albert Road   Seekoegat   7

Hilandale   20   84   Gamkapoort Nature Reserve   44   R407   Albertsmeule   54

18   Blockhouse   Koup   Prince Albert   Tierberg   R407
1291m

15   Laingsburg   Vleifontein   25   53   Swartberg Nature Reserve   Klaarstroo

EP   13   Baviaan   Swartberg Pass   22

Matjiesfontein   19   Gamkaskloof   13   Cango Caves   Meiringspoort

Historic Village   Rooinek   Bosluiskloof   G r o o t   S w a r t b e r g e

39   11   Vleiland   40   Die Hel   Kruisrivier   44   Grootkraal   33

1332m   Rouxpos   Seweweekspoort   27   Groenfontein   Schoemanspoort   26   De Rust   22

Anysberg Nature Reserve   Ladismith   Zoar   Matjiesrivier   Schoemanshoek   R328

EQ   Anysberg   12   21   Huisrivier Pass   Calitzdorp   62   37   Oudtshoorn   22   Dysselsdorp   13

Kareevlakte   34   Remhoogte   Kerkrand   -13   Kammanassie Dam

Plathuis   R62   4   Badshoogte   Suspension Bridge   33   N12   Koutjie

Radioactive Springs   R327   Rooiberg Pass   23   Blossoms   62   Montagu Pass   Eseljagpo

Warmwaterberg Nature Reserve   R323   55   Van Wyksdorp   Gamka Mtn. Nat. Res.   & Old Smithy

45   40   Doring   Outeniqua Nature Reserve   25   Old Tollhouse   26   Herold

16   R62   Wapadskloof   O u t e n i e k w a b e r g e   Robinson Pass   Outeniqua Pass   Topping   Bergpla

Barrydale   Boosmansbos Wilderness Area   34   26   Langberg   41   Cloetes Pass   Eight Bells   29   Blanco   George

ER   R324   Brandrivier   3   Herbertsdale   Groot Brakrivier   23   Wildern

13   Tradouws Pass   22   Toll House   Langeberg   Du Plessis Pass   R327   34   R328   Hartenbos   Pacaltsdorp   27

14   Garcia Pass   Gourits   Bartlesfontein   5   Herolds Bay   Mossel Bay

Suurbraak   **Heidelberg**   30   Riversdale   Dekriet   Albertinia   6   Post Office Tree   **Mossel Bay**   Mossel Bay

42   Renier   12   N2   25   Albertinia   21   18   Danabaai

25   Askraal   Gourits   34   Vleesbaai

R324   R322   R305   Droëvlakte   Johnson's Post   Cape Vacca (Kanonpunt)

Malgas   35   Riethuiskraal   27   Still Bay   Vleesbaai   Gouritsmond

24   Barry Church   Vermaaklikheid   Puntjie   Still Bay

De Hoop Nature Reserve   Witsand   Groot Jongensfontein

ES   Infanta   St Sebastian Bay   Cape Barracouta

Cape Infanta   Cape Barracouta

ET   35°00'S

21°00'E   22°00'E

85   86   87   88   89

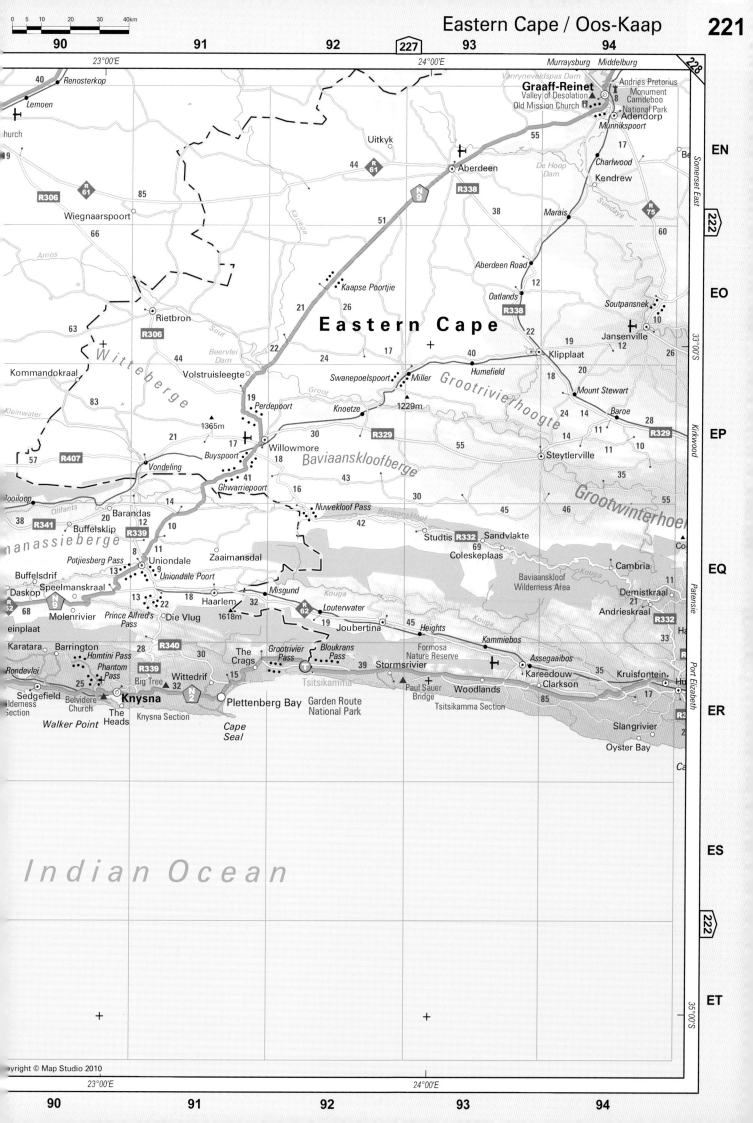

0 5 10 20 30 40km

90 91 92 227 93 94 228

23°00'E 24°00'E Murraysburg Middelburg

EN

40 Renosterkop
Lemoen
church
19

Vanryneveldspas Dam
Graaff-Reinet Andries Pretorius
Valley of Desolation Monument
Old Mission Church Camdeboo
National Park
Adendorp
Munnikspoort

55
17

Charlwood
Kendrew

Be

EO

Uitkyk

44 R61
Aberdeen
R338
N9

51

38
Marais

De Hoop
Dam

222

Soutpansnek
10

R75

60

Somerset East

33°00'S

Wiegnaarspoort
66

85
R306

R61

63
Rietbron
R306

Amos

Kaapse Poortjie

21 26

Eastern Cape

17

Aberdeen Road

Oatlands
R338

Klipplaat

1229m

12

22

19

Jansenville
12

26

Kirkwood

EP

Kommandokraal
Witteberge

Beervlei
Dam
44

Volstruisleegte

22

19
Perdepoort

1365m
17

Buyspoort
18

Vondeling

Sout

Groot

Swanepoelspoort Miller

Knoetze

30

R329

Baviaanskloofberge

Humefield
40

55

18

Grootrivierhoogte

24

14

11

Steytlerville
11

20

Mount Stewart
Baroe
28

R329

10

35

EQ

Kleinwater
83

57
R407

21

Ghwarriepoort

41

16

43

Nuwekloof Pass

Baviaanskloof

30

45

46

Grootwinterhoek

55

Co

Rooiloop
Olifants

14

Barandas
12
R339
10

8

Uniondale

Zaaimansdal

42

Studtis
R332
Coleskeplaas

69

Sandvlakte

Kouga

Baviaanskloof
Wilderness Area

Cambria
11

Demistkraal
21
Andrieskraal
R332

Patensie

38
R341
Buffelsklip

hanassieberge

Potjiesberg Pass
13

11
9

Uniondale Poort

13

22

18

Haarlem

32

Misgund

Kouga

Louterwater

45

Heights

Kammiebos

33

Ha

ER

Buffelsdrif
Daskop
R32
68
N9
Molenrivier

Speelmanskraal

einplaat

Prince Alfred's
Pass
Die Vlug

1618m

R62

19

Joubertina

Formosa
Nature Reserve

Assegaaibos

R

Karatara
Barrington
Homtini Pass

R340

30

The
Crags

Grootrivier
Pass

Bloukrans
Pass

39

Stormsrivier

Kareedouw
Clarkson

35

Kruisfontein

R32

Rondevlei
Phantom
Pass

25

R339

Big Tree

Wittedrif
32
N2

15

T

Tsitsikamma

Paul Sauer
Bridge

Woodlands

85

17

Hu

Port Elizabeth

Sedgefield
Belvidere
Church

Knysna

Walker Point

The
Heads

Knysna Section

Plettenberg Bay

Cape
Seal

Garden Route
National Park

Tsitsikamma Section

Slangrivier

Oyster Bay

Ca

ilderness
Section

I n d i a n   O c e a n

ES

222

ET

23°00'E 24°00'E

90 91 92 93 94

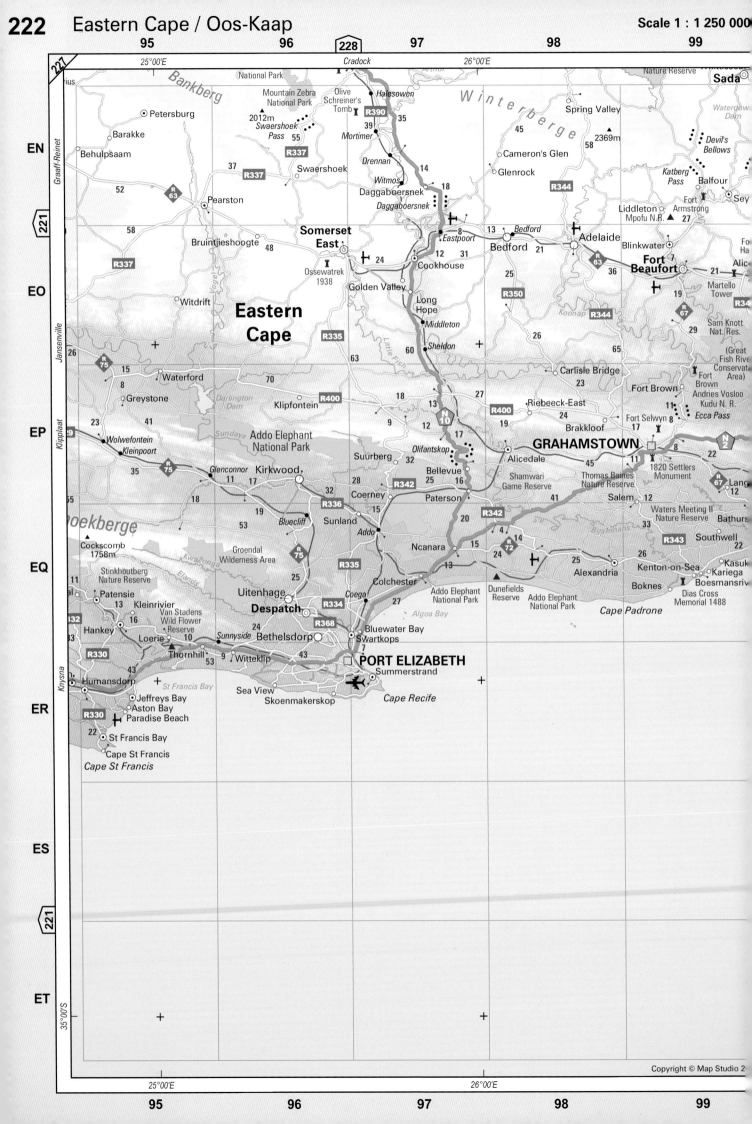

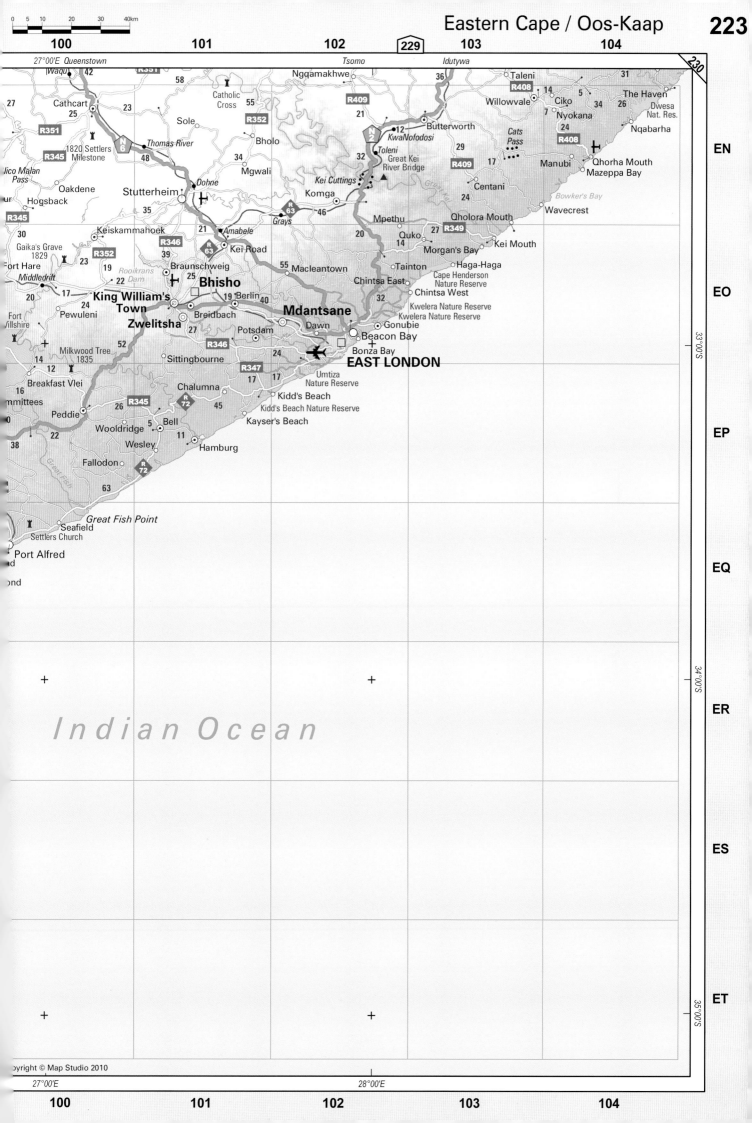

0 5 10   20   30   40km

EN

EO

EP

EQ

ER

ES

ET

27°00'E Queenstown
|Waqu| 42
Cathcart
27
25
R351
1820 Settlers
Milestone
R345
Jico Malan
Pass
Oakdene
Hogsback
58
23
Thomas River
48
Dohne
35
Catholic
Cross
Sole
Bholo
34
Mgwali
Stutterheim
Dohne
R352
55
Tsomo   Idutywa
Ngqamakhwe
R409
21
Butterworth
KwaNofodosi
Toleni
Great Kei
River Bridge
32
Kei Cuttings
Komga
46
Grays
R63
36
Taleni
Willowvale
R408
14
Ciko
7
Nyokana
29
17
Centani
24
Bowker's Bay
5
34
26
31
The Haven
Dwesa
Nat. Res.
Nqabarha
R408
Manubi
Qhorha Mouth
Mazeppa Bay
Cats
Pass

R345
30
Gaika's Grave
1829
R352
23
19
Fort Hare
Middledrift
22
Rooikrans
Dam
17
20
King William's
Town
Zwelitsha
Keiskammahoek
21
Amabele
R346
R63
Kei Road
39
Braunschweig
25
Bhisho
19
Berlin
40
Breidbach
Pewuleni
27
Fort
Willshire
Milkwood Tree
1835
52
Sittingbourne
R346
Potsdam
24
Dawn
Macleantown
55
Mpethu
20
Quko
14
Tainton
Chintsa East
32
Chintsa West
Kwelera Nature Reserve
Kwelera Nature Reserve
Gonubie
Beacon Bay
Bonza Bay
27
R349
Morgan's Bay
Kei Mouth
Haga-Haga
Cape Henderson
Nature Reserve
Qholora Mouth
Wavecrest

+
14
12
Breakfast Vlei
16
mmittees
Peddie
22
38
Wooldridge
Wesley
Fallodon
R345
26
5
Bell
11
Hamburg
R72
63
Chalumna
R72
45
R347
17
17
EAST LONDON
Umtiza
Nature Reserve
Kidd's Beach
Kidd's Beach Nature Reserve
Kayser's Beach
Mdantsane

Great Fish Point
Seafield
Settlers Church
Port Alfred
ond

Indian Ocean

+   +

+   +

27°00'E   28°00'E

33°00'S

34°00'S

35°00'S

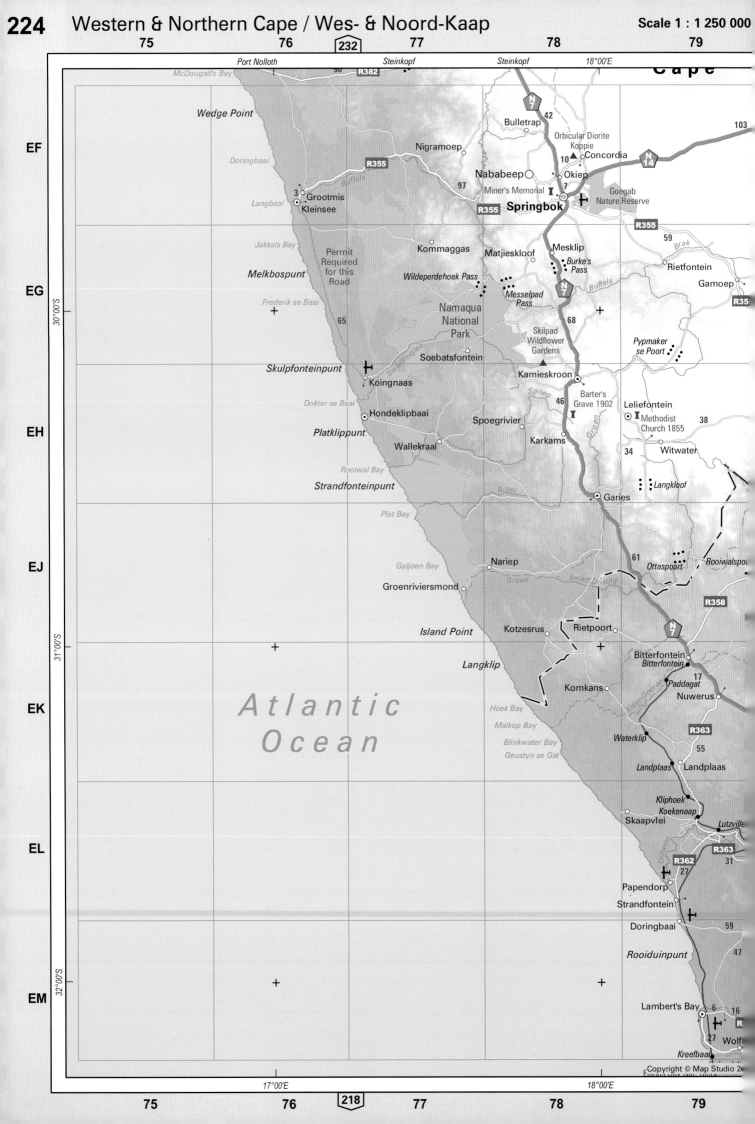

40km

Pofadder   19°00'E
Bloemhoek   Namies   25   Houmoed

62   31

EF

Uitkyk   48

Northern Cape

Dagab   226   EG

R358

50

Karreeboschkolk

Granaatboskolk   Halfweg   Kenhardt   30°00'S

Katkop   Verdorskolk

Stofvlei   Rietfontein

latbakkies   Konnes se Pan   Rietfontein se Pan   EH

35   22

Aalwynsfontein   Dwaggasoutpan   Commissioner's Salt Pan   Brandvlei   4

15   Kromkop   121   Rock Paintings   47   R353   EJ

Grootberg
1022m   R355   R27   47

778m   R357   8   Sakrivier

R355   75   44   Tontelbos
Bodam

Windmill
Museum   Oumuur

10   Loeriesfontein

Western
Cape   R357   Swartkolkvloer   Blomberg se Vloer   EK

54   Kootjieskolk
Koosdrif   Hoedjies

66   Brandkop   81   36   Swawel   R63   68   Williston

Nieuwoudtville   Vlakhoeksberg
1530m   Moordenaarspoort   Stuurman   27

Vanrhyns Pass   20   R27   34   36   Calvinia   16   Downes   7   31°00'S

Grootdrif   49   Oorlogskloof
N.R.   29   Oorlogskloof

R27   R364   Bloukrans Pass   Keiskie se Poort   48   EL

sand   25   24   42   R354
Vredendal   Urionskraal   R355

17   R362   22   35   57   15
Spruitdrif   58

22   Klawer   Middelpos   R354

Olifants River
Irrigation Scheme   Botterkloof   22   Rock
Paintings   23   30
15   Doringbos   43
eipan   Trawal   39   Oupoort
Heerenlogement
Cave   38   Uitspankraal   Die Bos
Heerenlogement   R364   56
9   Ratelfontein   Pakhuis Pass   54   Biedouwvallei   85   Tankwa-Karoo
National Park   Oupoort
Graafwater   29   Cederberg
Wilderness Area   Clanwilliam

Citrusdal   19°00'E   20°00'E   220

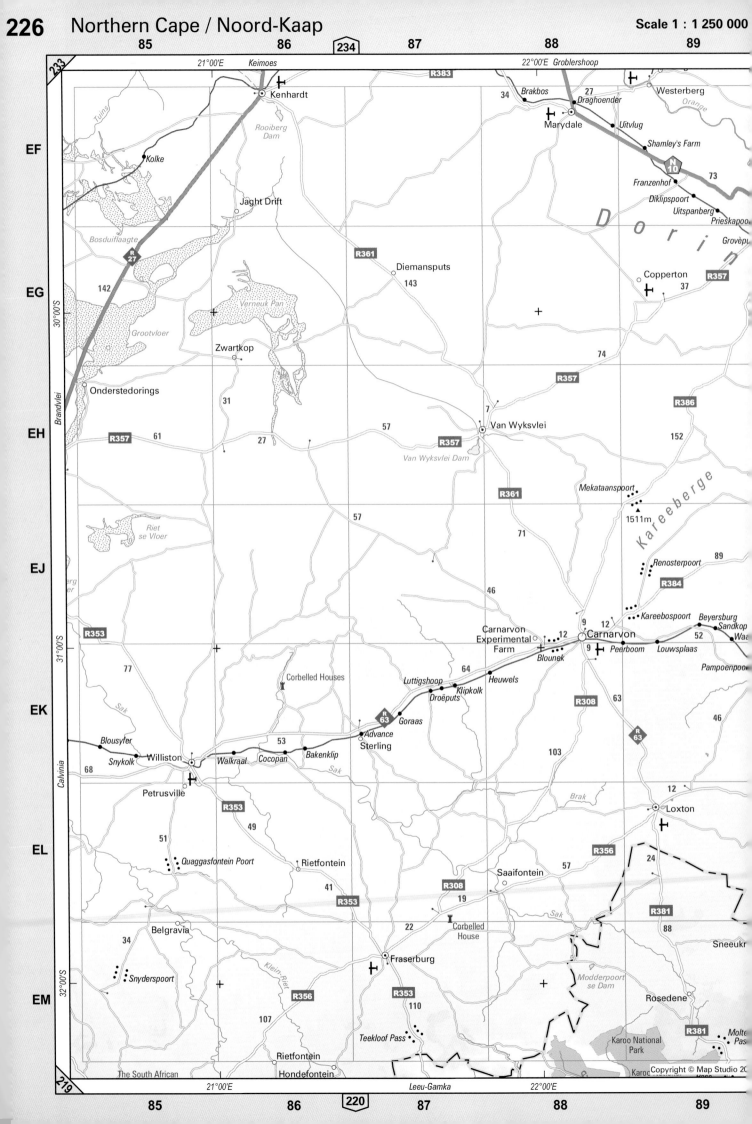

Free State

Northern Cape

Eastern Cape

Western Cape

Niekerkshoop
Higg's Hope
Valspan
Douglas
First Diamond Discovered 1866
Hayfield
Ritchie
Graspan
1899-1902
Graspan 1899
Oppermans
R388
Sheephouse
Van Wyksvlei
Belmont 15
Roodepan
Diamond Diggings
R357
Witput
Wanda
Prieska
R369
R369
Old Wagon Bridge
Hopetown
Oranjerivier
Orania
Diamant
Vanderkloof
Karabee
Keikamaspoort
Anglo-Boer War Concentration Camp
Kraankuil
R387
Brakfontein
Petrusville
Redlands
Strydenburg
R387
Poupan
Rolfontein Nature Reserve
Grootdoring
Omdraaisvlei
Sodium
Potfontein
Ongers
Minnieskloof
Houtwater Dam
Voëlgeraas
Houtkraal
Philipstown
Broken Dam
Bushman Paintings
Giesenkraal
Vosburg
R384
Britstown
Sweetfontein
Brand
Olive Schreiner House
De Aar
Volstruispoort
Smartt Syndicate Dam
Die Put
Bletterman
Riet
Burgerville
R389
Eselskloof
Mynfontein
Frans
Killowen Dam
Hanover Road
Marthasput
Deelfontein
Dwaal
Kweekwa
Sterkaar
Hanover
Welvanpas
De Klerk
Merriman
R398
R348
Kriegerspoort Dam
Van Amstel
Wildebeeste
Brakpoort
Richmond
Victoria West
Barnard
Meltonwold
Hutchinson
R398
Heydon
Verster
R63
Biesiespoort
Kranskop 2052m
Sneeuberg
Nieu-Bethesda
Wagenaarskraal
R63
Bethesdaweg
Naudeberg Pass
Three Sisters
Kromrivier
Murraysburg
R63
Restvale
Nelspoort
Oudeberg Pass
Andries Pretorius Monument
Renosterkop
Vanryneveldspas Dam
Graaff-Reinet
Valley of Desolation
Camdeboo

Copyright © Map Studio 2010

Free State

Northern Cape

Eastern Cape

Copyright © Map Studio 20

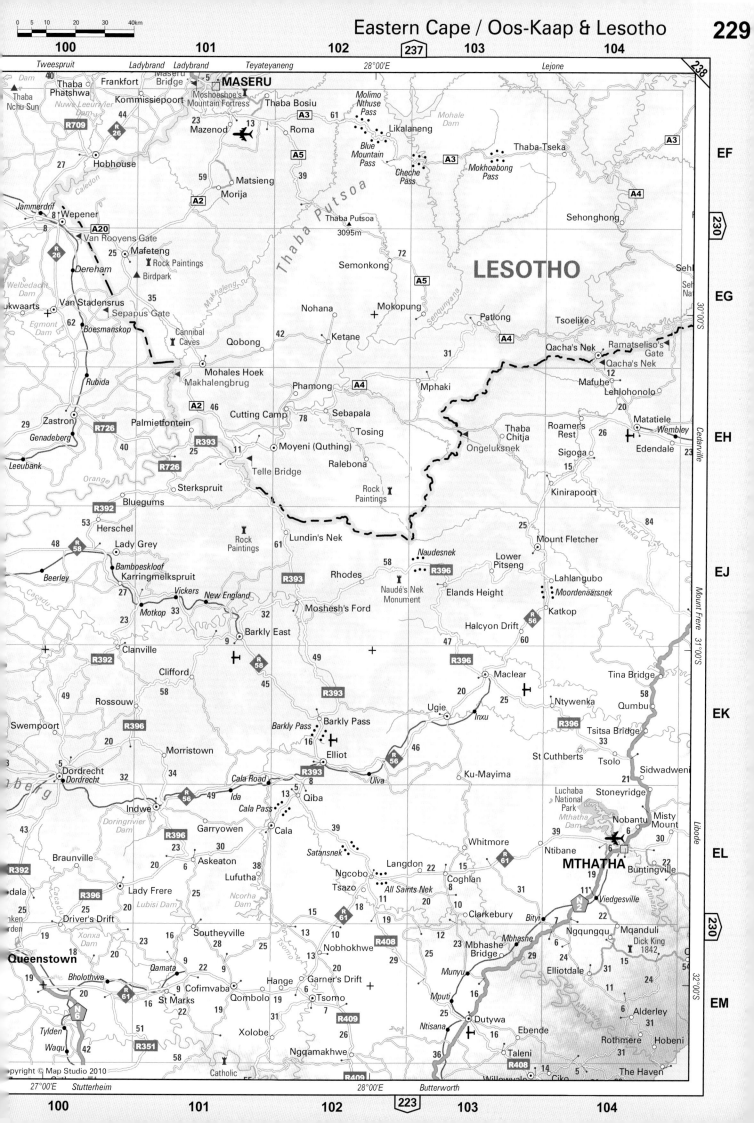

Map: Eastern Cape / Oos-Kaap & Lesotho

0 5 10 20 30 40km

100 101 102 237 103 104

LESOTHO

MASERU

Tweespruit Ladybrand Ladybrand Teyateyaneng 28°00'E Lejone

Thaba Phatswa Frankfort Maseru Bridge Moshoeshoe's Mountain Fortress Thaba Bosiu Molimo Nthuse Pass Likalaneng Mohale Dam Thaba-Tseka

Thaba Nchu Sun Hobhouse Mazenod Roma Blue Mountain Pass Cheche Pass Mokhoabong Pass

R709 Matsieng Morija Thaba Putsoa 3095m Semonkong

Jammerdrif Wepener Van Rooyens Gate Mafeteng Rock Paintings Birdpark Nohana Mokopung Patlong Tsoelike Sehonghong

Welbedacht Dam Dereham Van Stadensrus Sepapus Gate Cannibal Caves Qobong Ketane Semonkong Qacha's Nek Ramatseliso's Gate

Egmont Dam Boesmanskop Mohales Hoek Makhalengbrug Phamong Sebapala Mphaki Qacha's Nek Mafube Lehlohonolo

Zastron Genadeberg Palmietfontein Cutting Camp Tosing Thaba Chitja Roamer's Rest Matatiele Wembley Edendale

Leeubank Sterkspruit Moyeni (Quthing) Ralebona Ongeluksnek Sigoga Kinirapoort

Bluegums Telle Bridge Rock Paintings Mount Fletcher

Herschel Rock Paintings Lundin's Nek Naudesnek Lower Pitseng Lahlangubo Moordenaarsnek

Lady Grey Bamboeskloof Karringmelkspruit Rhodes Naudé's Nek Monument Elands Height Katkop Halcyon Drift

Beerley Vickers New England Moshesh's Ford Maclear

Motkop Barkly East Ntywenka Qumbu Tina Bridge

Clanville Clifford Ugie Inxu Tsitsa Bridge Tsolo Sidwadweni

Rossouw Morristown Barkly Pass Elliot Ulva Ku-Mayima St Cuthberts

Swempoort Dordrecht Cala Road Qiba Luchaba National Park Stoneyridge Misty Mount

Indwe Ida Cala Pass Whitmore Mthatha Dam Nobantu

Braunville Garryowen Cala Satansnek Langdon Coghlan Ntibane MTHATHA Buntingville

Lady Frere Askeaton Lufutha Ngcobo Tsazo All Saints Nek Clarkebury Viedgesville

Driver's Drift Southeyville Nobhokwe Bityi Ngqungqu Mqanduli Dick King 1842

Queenstown Bholothwa Qamata Hange Garner's Drift Munyu Mbhashe Bridge Elliotdale Alderley

Tylden Cofimvaba Qombolo Tsomo Mputi Dutywa Ebende Rothmere Hobeni

Waqu St Marks Xolobe Ngqamakhwe Ntisana Taleni Ciko The Haven

27°00'E Stutterheim 28°00'E Butterworth

100 101 102 223 103 104

Eastern Cape

KwaZulu-Natal

Indian Ocean

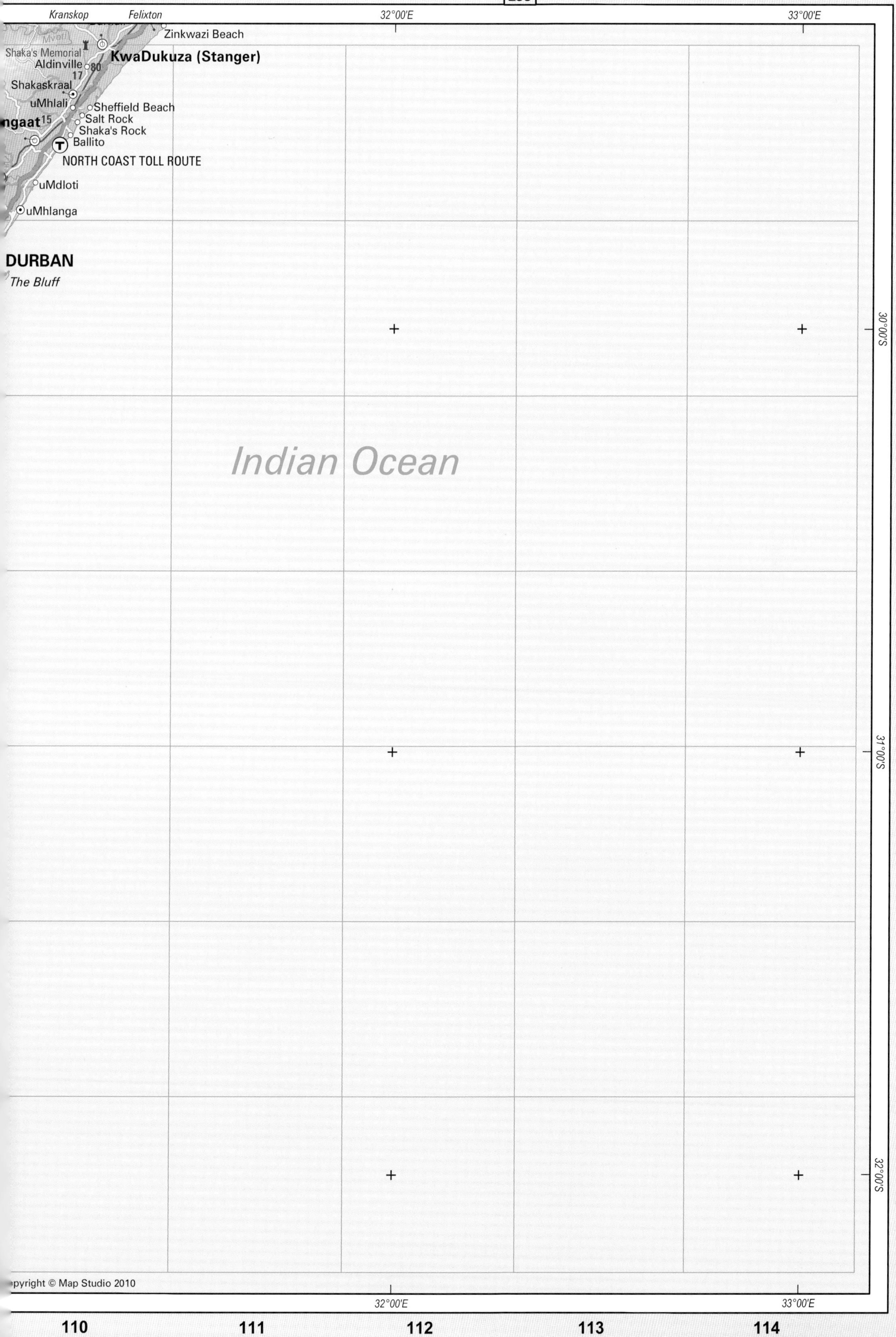

0 5 10   20   30   40km

Kranskop   Felixton   32°00'E   33°00'E

Zinkwazi Beach

Shaka's Memorial   **KwaDukuza (Stanger)**
Aldinville   80
17
Shakaskraal

uMhlali   Sheffield Beach
Salt Rock
ngaat 15   Shaka's Rock

T Ballito

NORTH COAST TOLL ROUTE   EF

uMdloti

uMhlanga

DURBAN

The Bluff   EG   30°00'S

+   +

Indian Ocean   EH

EJ

+   +   31°00'S

EK

EL

+   +   32°00'S

Zinkwazi Beach   EM

KwaDukuza (Stanger)

Copyright © Map Studio 2010

32°00'E   33°00'E

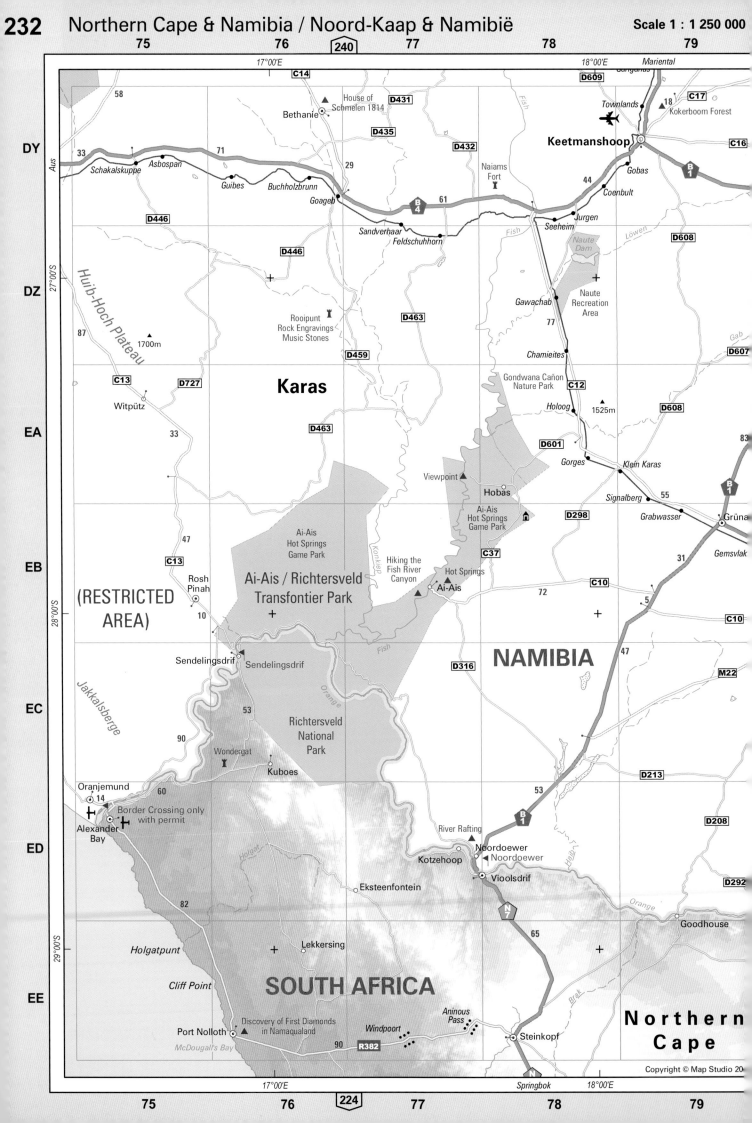

This is a topographic map showing the Northern Cape & Namibia region.

Grid references (top): 75, 76, 240, 77, 78, 79

Grid references (side): DY, DZ, EA, EB, EC, ED, EE

Coordinates: 17°00'E, 18°00'E, 27°00'S, 28°00'S, 29°00'S

Labels and place names:

58, C14, Mariental, D609, C17, 18, Kokerboom Forest, Townlands, House of Schmelen 1814, D431, Bethanie, D435, D432, Keetmanshoop, C16, 33, 71, 29, Schakalskuppe, Asbospan, Guibes, Buchholzbrunn, Goageb, 61, B4, Naiams Fort, 44, Gobas, Coenbult, Jurgen, Seeheim, D608, Fish, Löwen, D446, Sandverhaar, Feldschuhhorn, D446, Naute Dam, Gab, Gawachab, Naute Recreation Area, 77, Rooipunt Rock Engravings Music Stones, D463, Chamieites, D607, 87, 1700m, D459, Karas, Gondwana Cañon Nature Park, C12, Holoog, 1525m, D608, C13, D727, Witpütz, D463, D601, 33, Gorges, Klein Karas, 83, Viewpoint, Hobas, 55, Signalberg, Grabwasser, B1, Ai-Ais Hot Springs Game Park, D298, Grüna, 47, Ai-Ais Hot Springs Game Park, Gemsvlak, C13, Rosh Pinah, Hiking the Fish River Canyon, Hot Springs, Ai-Ais, 72, C10, 31, (RESTRICTED AREA), Ai-Ais / Richtersveld Transfontier Park, Konkiep, C37, 5, C10, 10, Fish, D316, NAMIBIA, M22, Sendelingsdrif, Sendelingsdrif, 47, 53, Orange, Jakkalsberge, 90, Richtersveld National Park, D213, Wondergat, Kuboes, 53, Oranjemund, 60, B1, D208, 14, Border Crossing only with permit, River Rafting, Noordoewer, D292, Alexander Bay, Holgat, Kotzehoop, Noordoewer, Eksteenfontein, Vioolsdrif, Orange, Goodhouse, 82, N7, 65, Holgatpunt, Lekkersing, Brak, Cliff Point, SOUTH AFRICA, Port Nolloth, Discovery of First Diamonds in Namaqualand, Windpoort, Aninous Pass, Northern Cape, McDougall's Bay, 90, R382, Steinkopf, N, Springbok

Copyright © Map Studio 20

Grid references (bottom): 75, 76, 224, 77, 78, 79

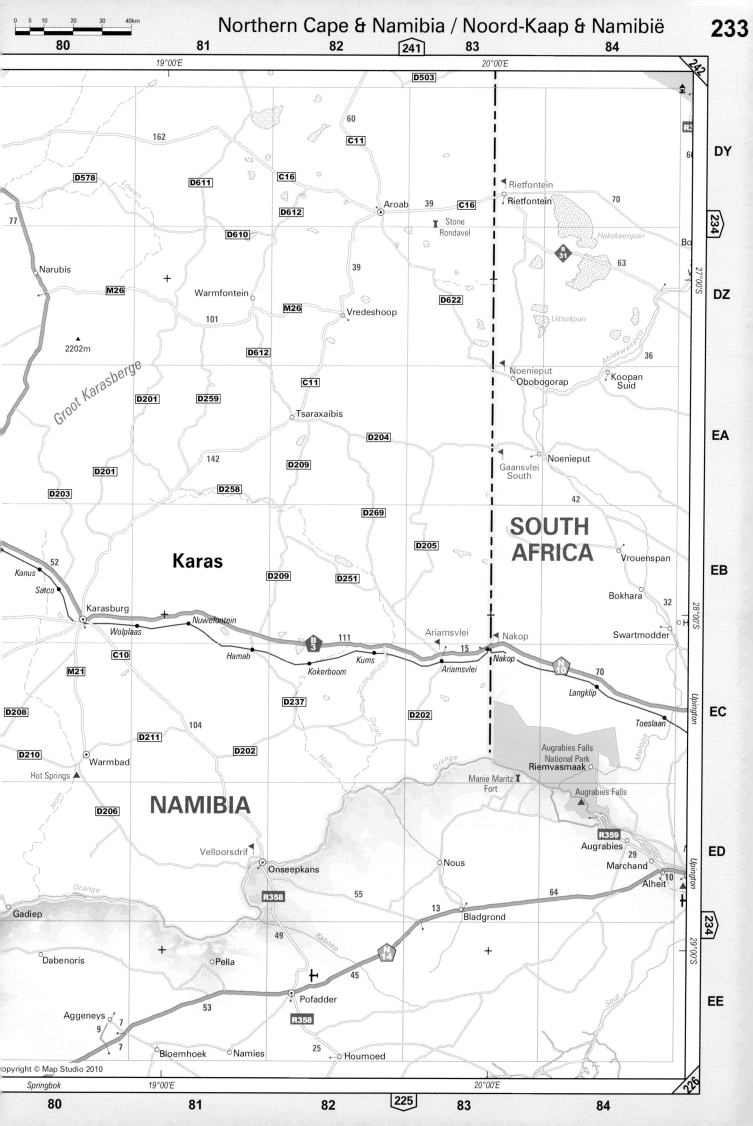

0 5 10   20   30   40km

80   81   82   [241]   83   84

19°00'E   20°00'E   [242]

DY

[D503]

60

[C11]   70   [R3]

162

[D578]   [D611]   [C16]   Rietfontein   DZ

[D612]   Aroab 39 [C16] Rietfontein   *Hakskeenpan*

77   [D610]   Stone   [R 31] 63

Rondavel

Narubis   [M26]   [D622]   *Uitsakpan*   DZ

Warmfontein   39   *Abiekwasputs* 36

101   [M26] Vredeshoop   Noenieput Koopan

▲   Obobogorap Suid

2202m   [D612]

[D201] [D259]   [C11]   EA

Tsaraxaibis   Noenieput

Groot Karasberge   142 [D204]   Gaansvlei

[D209]   South   42

[D201]   [D258]

[D203]   [D269]   **SOUTH**

[D205]   **AFRICA**   Vrouenspan   EB

Karas   [D209] [D251]   Bokhara 32

52   Swartmodder

Kanus   Nuwefontein 111   Ariamsvlei Nakop

Satco   [B 3]   15 Nakop [N 10] 70

Karasburg   Hamab Kums   Ariamsvlei   Langklip   EC

[C10]   Wolplaas Kokerboom   [D202]   Toeslaan

[M21]   [D237]   *Orange*   Augrabies Falls

[D208]   104 *Gaiab*   National Park

[D211]   [D202]   *Molopo* Riemvasmaak

[D210] Warmbad   Manie Maritz   Augrabies Falls ▲

Hot Springs ▲   Fort

[D206] **NAMIBIA**   [R359]

Velloorsdrif   Nous   Augrabies   ED

Orange Onseepkans   29 Marchand

[R358] 55   Bladgrond 64 Alheit 10

Gadiep   13

49   [N 14]   234

Dabenoris Pella   45   29°00'S EE

[R358]   Pofadder

Aggeneys 7 53   EE

9   [R358]

7 Bloemhoek Namies 25 Houmoed

Copyright © Map Studio 2010

Springbok 19°00'E   [225] 20°00'E   [226]

80   81   82   [225] 83   84

27°00'S

28°00'S

Upington

234

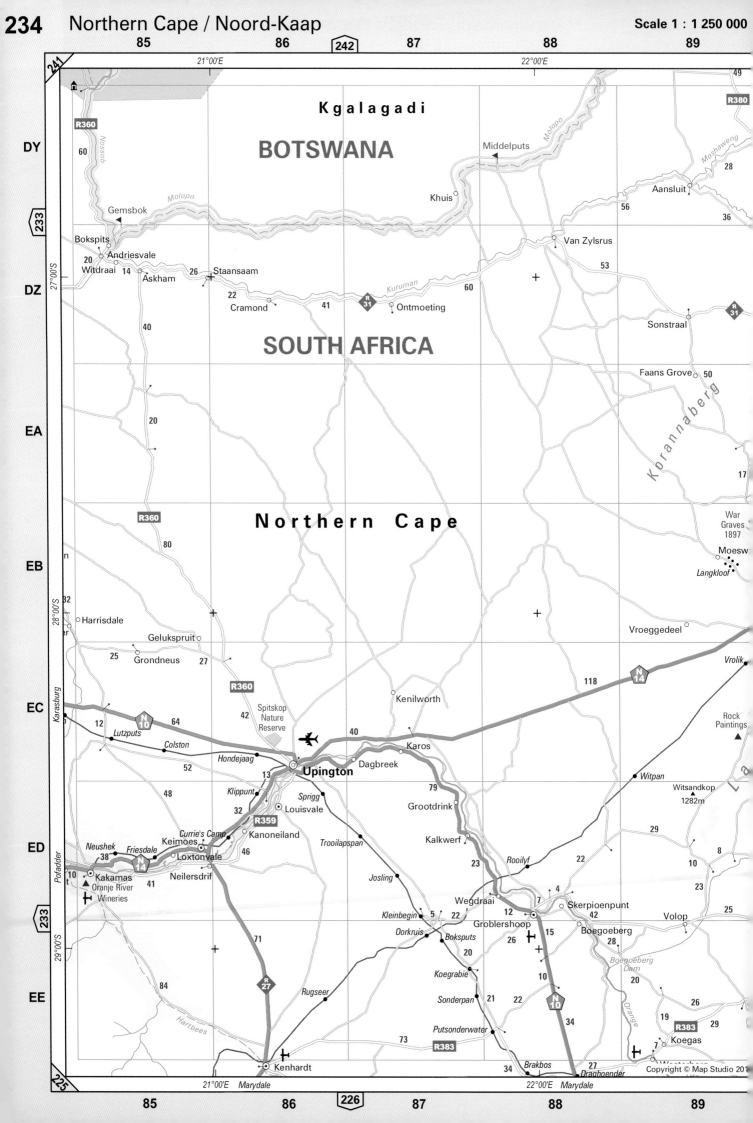

Kgalagadi

BOTSWANA

SOUTH AFRICA

Northern Cape

Middelputs

Khuis

Van Zylsrus

Gemsbok

Bokspits
Andriesvale
Witdraai
Askham
Staansaam
Cramond
Ontmoeting
Sonstraal

Faans Grove

Harrisdale
Gelukspruit
Grondneus

Vroeggedeel

Vrolik

Kenilworth

Karos

Spitskop
Nature
Reserve

Upington
Dagbreek

Lutzputs
Colston
Hondejaag
Klippunt
Sprigg
Grootdrink
Louisvale
Currie's Camp
Kanoneiland
Kalkwerf
Neushek
Friesdale
Keimoes
Trooilapspan
Rooilyf
Loxtonvale
Neilersdrif
Josling
Kakamas
Oranje River
Wineries
Wegdraai
Kleinbegin
Skerpioenpunt
Oorkruis
Boksputs
Volop
Groblershoop
Boegoeberg
Koegrabie
Boegoeberg
Dam
Sonderpan
Rugseer
Putsonderwater
Koegas
Kenhardt
Brakbos
Draghoender

War
Graves
1897
Moesw
Langkloof

Rock
Paintings

Witpan
Witsandkop
1282m

Copyright © Map Studio 20

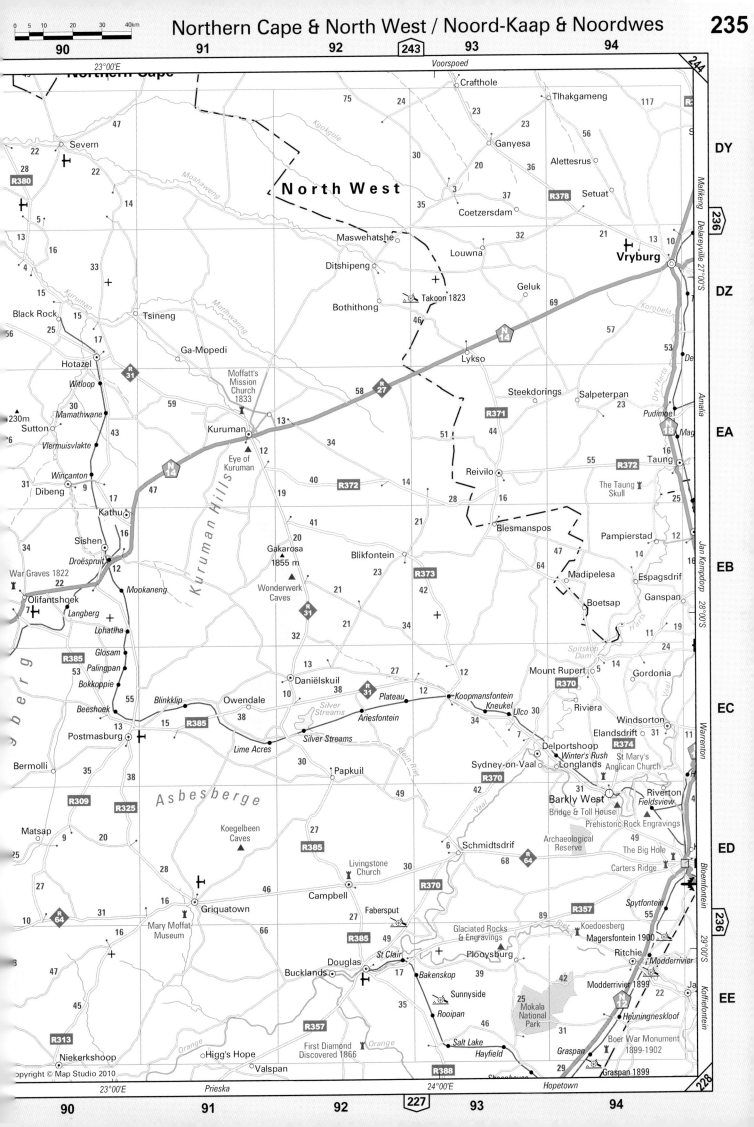

Scale 1 : 1 250 000

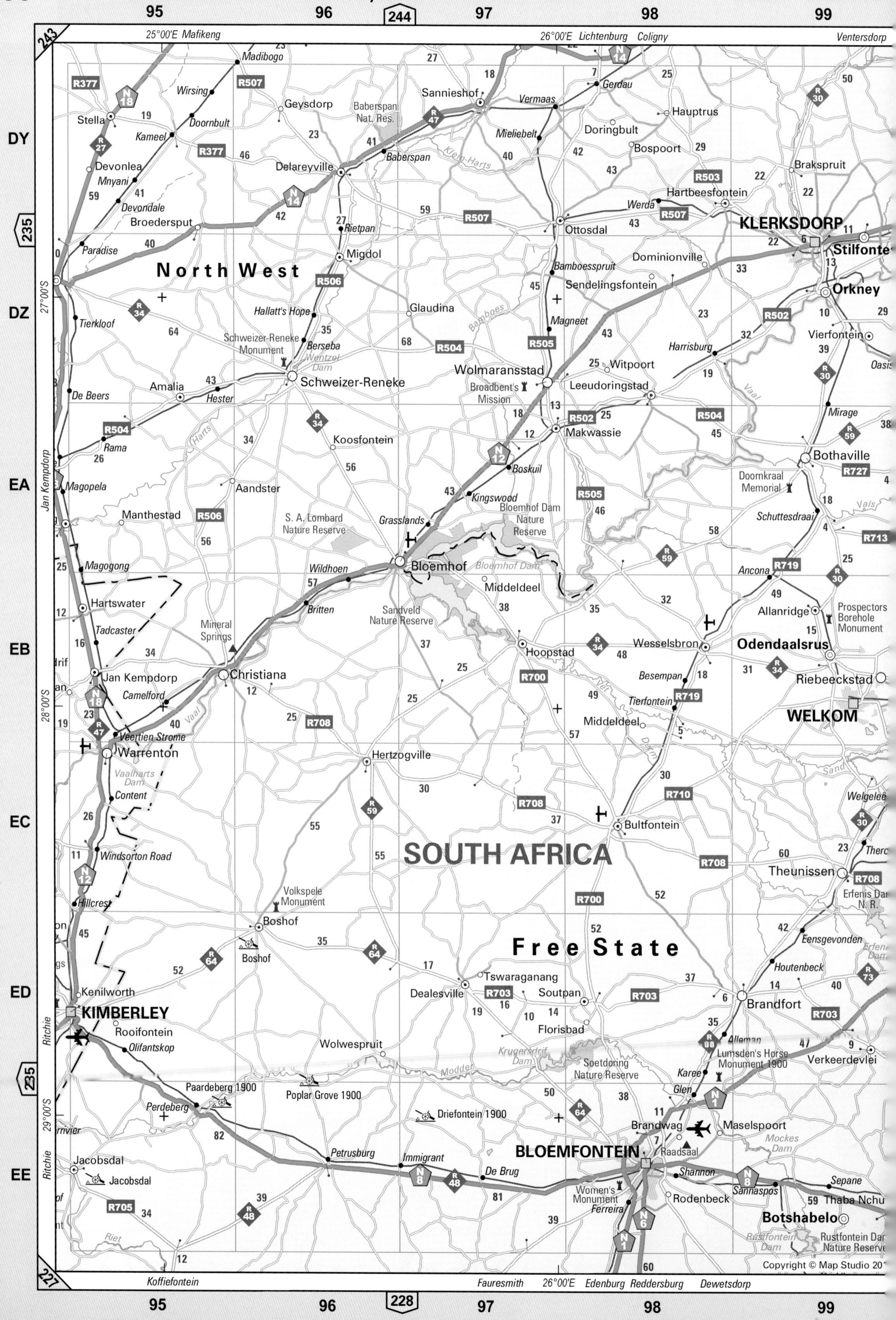

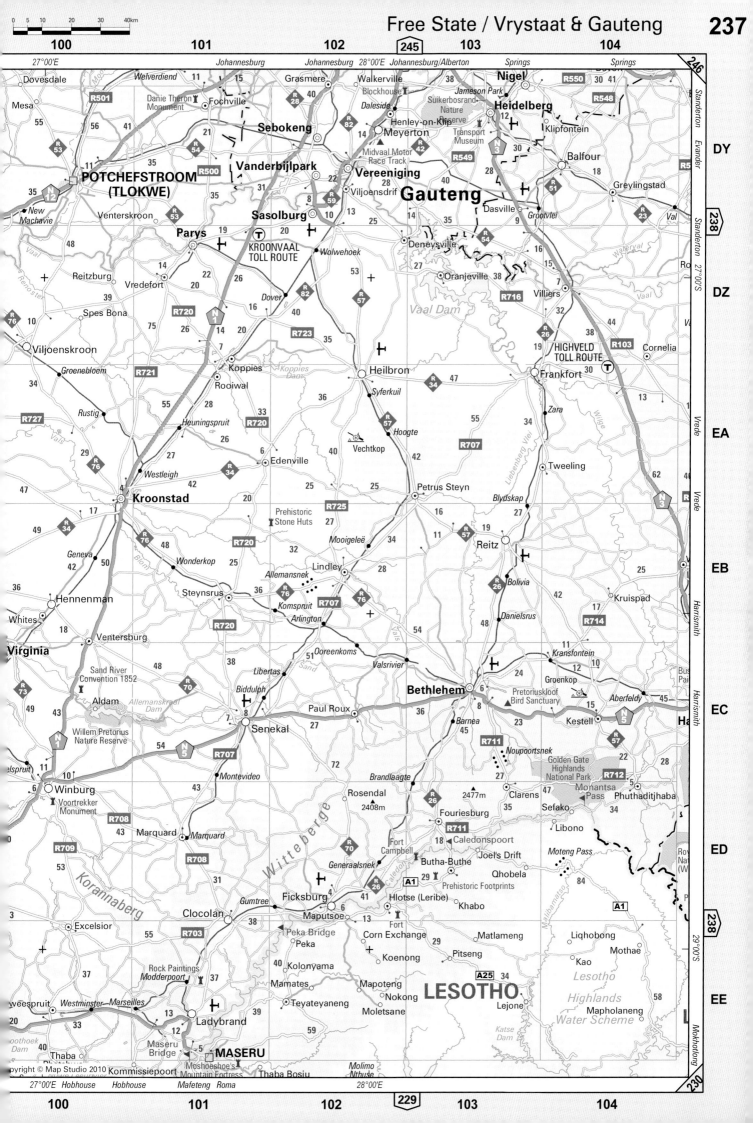

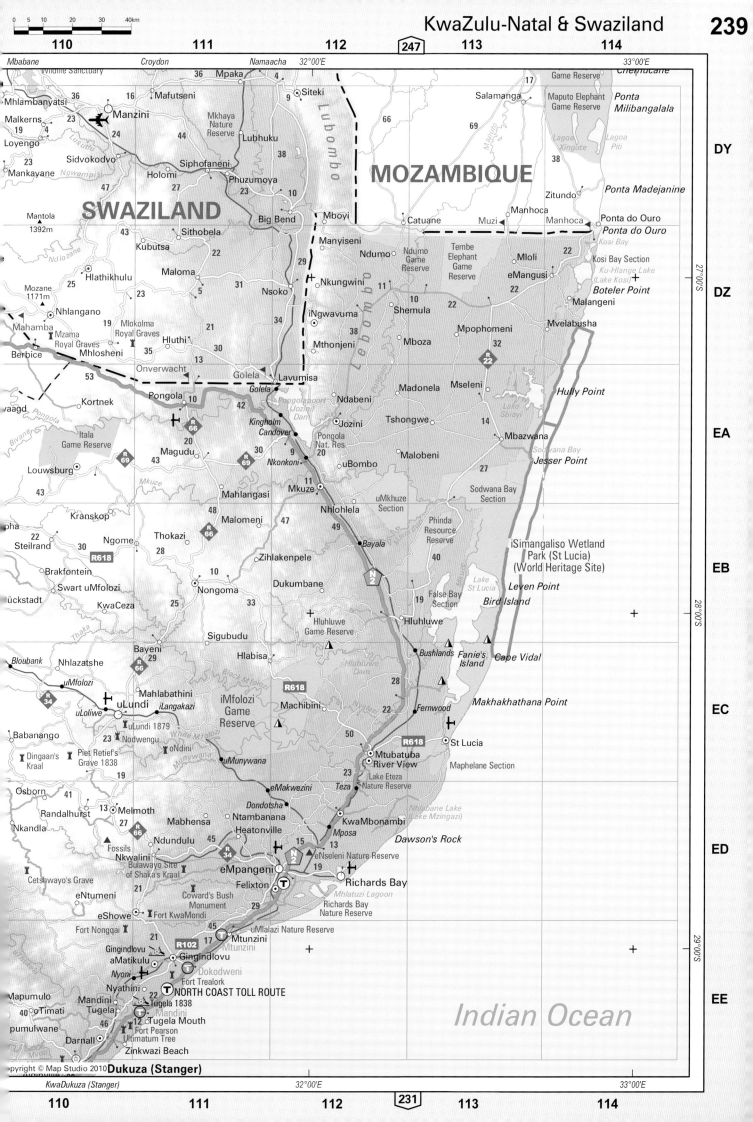

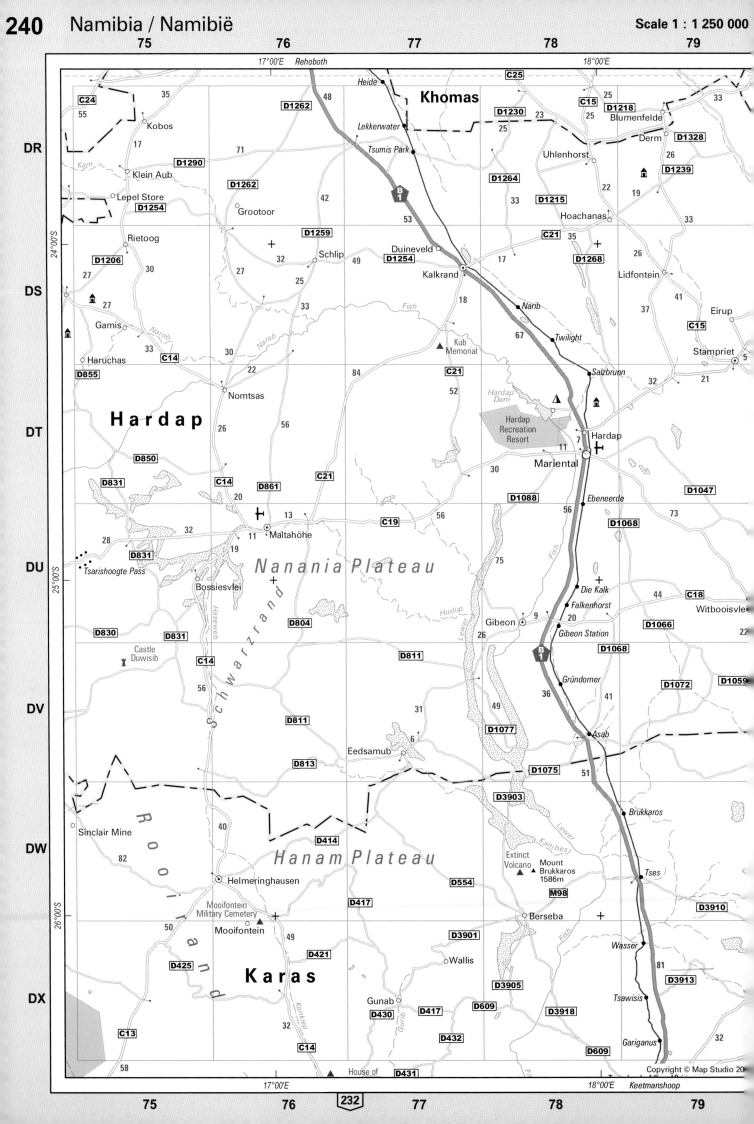

Khomas

Hardap

Nanania Plateau

Hanam Plateau

Karas

Kobos
Klein Aub
Lepel Store
Rietoog
Gamis
Haruchas
Nomtsas
Grootoor
Schlip
Duineveld
Kalkrand
Heide
Lekkerwater
Tsumis Park
Narib
Twilight
Salzbrunn
Hoachanas
Uhlenhorst
Blumenfelde
Derm
Lidfontein
Eirup
Stampriet
Kub Memorial
Hardap Dam
Hardap Recreation Resort
Hardap
Mariental
Maltahöhe
Bossiesvlei
Tsarishoogte Pass
Castle Duwisib
Ebeneerde
Die Kalk
Falkenhorst
Gibeon
Gibeon Station
Witbooisvlei
Gründorner
Asab
Eedsamub
Sinclair Mine
Helmeringhausen
Mooifontein Military Cemetery
Mooifontein
Brukkaros
Extinct Volcano
Mount Brukkaros 1586m
Berseba
Tses
Wallis
Wasser
Gunab
Tsawisis
Gariganus
House of

Schwarzrand
Rooiland
Haseweb
Lewer
Hudup
Fish
Narob
Kam
Konkiep
Gurib
Kanibes

Rehoboth
Keetmanshoop

17°00'E
18°00'E
24°00'S
25°00'S
26°00'S

75   76   77   78   79

C24   C25   C15   D1218   D1262   D1230   D1290   D1262   D1259   D1254   D1264   D1215   D1268   D1328   D1239   D1206   C21   C15   D855   C14   C21   C14   D850   D831   D861   C21   D1088   D1047   D1068   C19   D831   C18   D830   D831   D804   D1066   C14   D811   D1068   D811   D1077   D1072   D1059   D813   D1075   D3903   D414   D554   M98   D417   D3901   D425   D421   D430   D417   D609   D3918   D3905   D609   D432   D431   C13   C14   D3910   D3913

B1

232

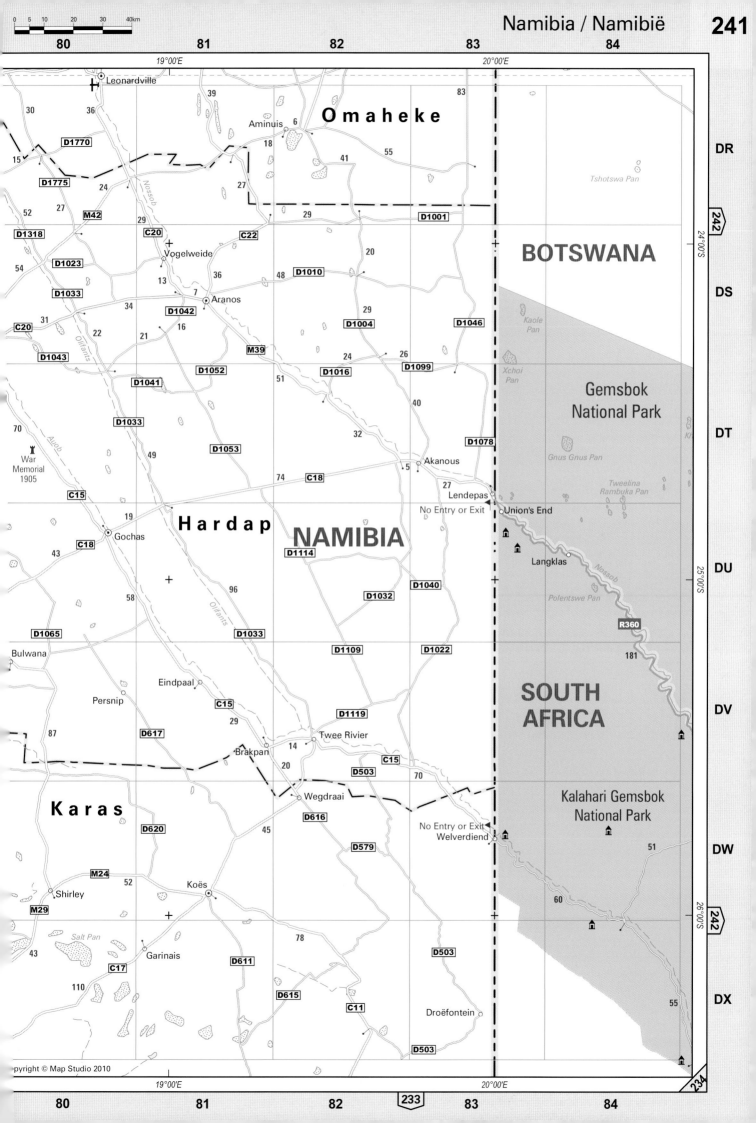

0 5 10 20 30 40km

80 · **81** · **82** · **83** · **84**

19°00'E · 20°00'E

Leonardville

O m a h e k e

30 · 36

D1770

Aminuis · 6

39

18

83

Tshotswa Pan

15

D1775

24

52 · 27

M42

29

C20

Vogelweide

C22

27

41 · 55

D1001

29

20

DR

242

24°00'S

BOTSWANA

DS

D1318

54

D1023

D1033

C20 · 31

D1043

13

D1042

7 · Aranos

34

22 · 21

16

M39

D1052

48 · D1010

D1004

29

24 · D1016

26

D1099

51

40

Kaole Pan

Xchoi Pan

Gemsbok National Park

DT

70

Auob

War Memorial 1905

D1041

D1033

D1053

49

74 · C18

32

5 · Akanous

D1078

27

Lendepas

No Entry or Exit

Union's End

Gnus Gnus Pan

Tweelina Rambuka Pan

C15

19

H a r d a p

NAMIBIA

D1114

Gochas

C18

43

58

96

D1040

D1032

Langklas

Nossob

Polentswe Pan

R360

181

DU

25°00'S

D1065

Bulwana

D1033

D1109

D1022

SOUTH AFRICA

DV

Eindpaal

Persnip

C15

29

D1119

Twee Rivier

D617

87

14

Brakpan

20

D503

70

C15

Wegdraai

K a r a s

D620

D616

45

D579

No Entry or Exit
Welverdiend

Kalahari Gemsbok National Park

51

DW

242

26°00'S

M24

52

Koës

Shirley

M29

60

43

Garinais

D611

78

D503

C17

110

D615

C11

Droëfontein

55

DX

Copyright © Map Studio 2010

D503

80 · **81** · **82** · **83** · **84**

19°00'E · 233 · 20°00'E · 234

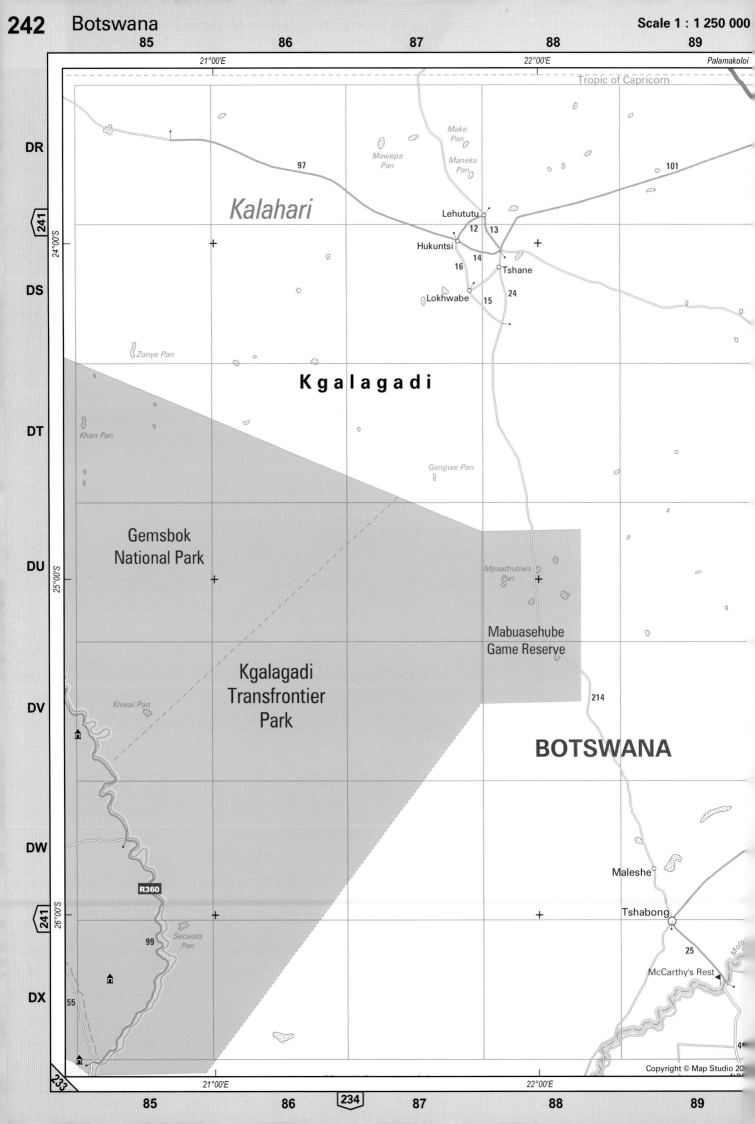

DR
DS
DT
DU
DV
DW
DX

21°00'E 22°00'E *Palamakoloi*

Tropic of Capricorn

Kalahari

97

Mawepa Pan

Make Pan

Maneka Pan

101

Lehututu

12 13

Hukuntsi

14

16 Tshane

Lokhwabe 15 24

Zonye Pan

K g a l a g a d i

Khan Pan

Gangwe Pan

Gemsbok
National Park

Mpaathutiwa Pan

Mabuasehube
Game Reserve

214

Khwai Pan

Kgalagadi
Transfrontier
Park

BOTSWANA

R360

Maleshe

99

Secwats Pan

Tshabong

25

55

McCarthy's Rest

Molo

24°00'S

25°00'S

26°00'S

241

241

233

234

85 86 87 88 89

Copyright © Map Studio 20

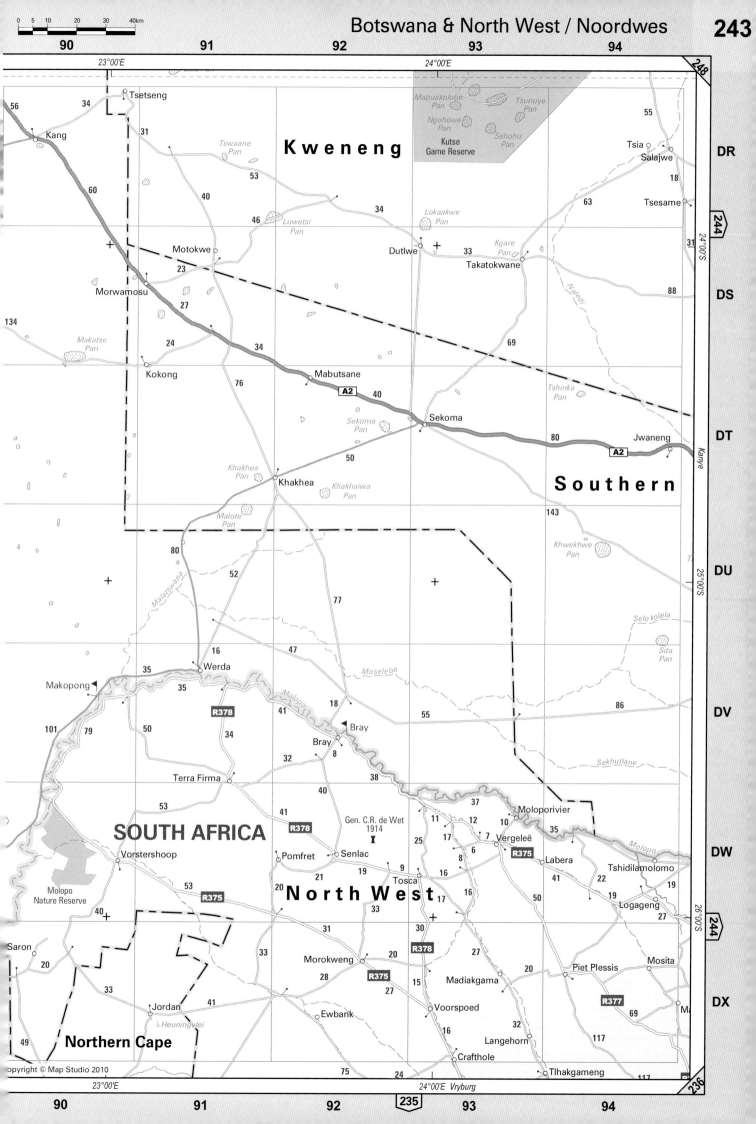

0 5 10   20   30   40km

90   91   92   93   94

23°00'E   24°00'E

Kweneng

Tsetseng
56   34
Kang   31
60   Tswaane Pan   53
40   34
46   Luwetsi Pan
Motokwe   Dutlwe   33   Kgare Pan   Takatokwane
23
Morwamosu   27
134
24   34   69
Kokong   76   Mabutsane   A2   40
50   Sekoma Pan   Sekoma   80   Jwaneng   A2
Khakhea Pan   Khakhaiwa Pan
Khakhea
143
Malote Pan
80
52   77
47   Moselebe
16   Werda
35   35   18   Bray
Makopong   41   Bray
101   79   50   34   8
32   38
Terra Firma   40
53   41   37   Moloporivier
SOUTH AFRICA   R378   Gen. C.R. de Wet 1914   11   12   10   35
Vorstershoop   25   17   7   Vergeleë   R375
Pomfret   Senlac   9   8   6   Labera   Tshidilamolomo
21   19   Tosca   16   41   22   19
20   North West   17   16   50   Logageng
33   30   27
31   R378   27   Mosita
Molopo Nature Reserve   40   33   20   Morokweng   20   R375   15   Madiakgama   20   Piet Plessis   R377
Saron   28   R375   Voorspoed   16   Langehorn   117   69
20   27
33   Jordan   41   Ewbank   32   Crafthole
49   Northern Cape   Heuningvlei   75   24   Tlhakgameng

23°00'E   24°00'E Vryburg

90   91   92   235   93   94

DR
244
DS
DT
DU
DV
244
DW
DX

Kutse Game Reserve
Mabuakolobe Pan   Tsunuye Pan
Ngohowe Pan   Sehohu Pan
55
Tsia
Salajwe
18
Tsesame
63   88
31
Naledi
Tshinka Pan
80
Southern
Khwekhwe Pan
Selokolela
Sita Pan
86
Sekhutlane
Molopo

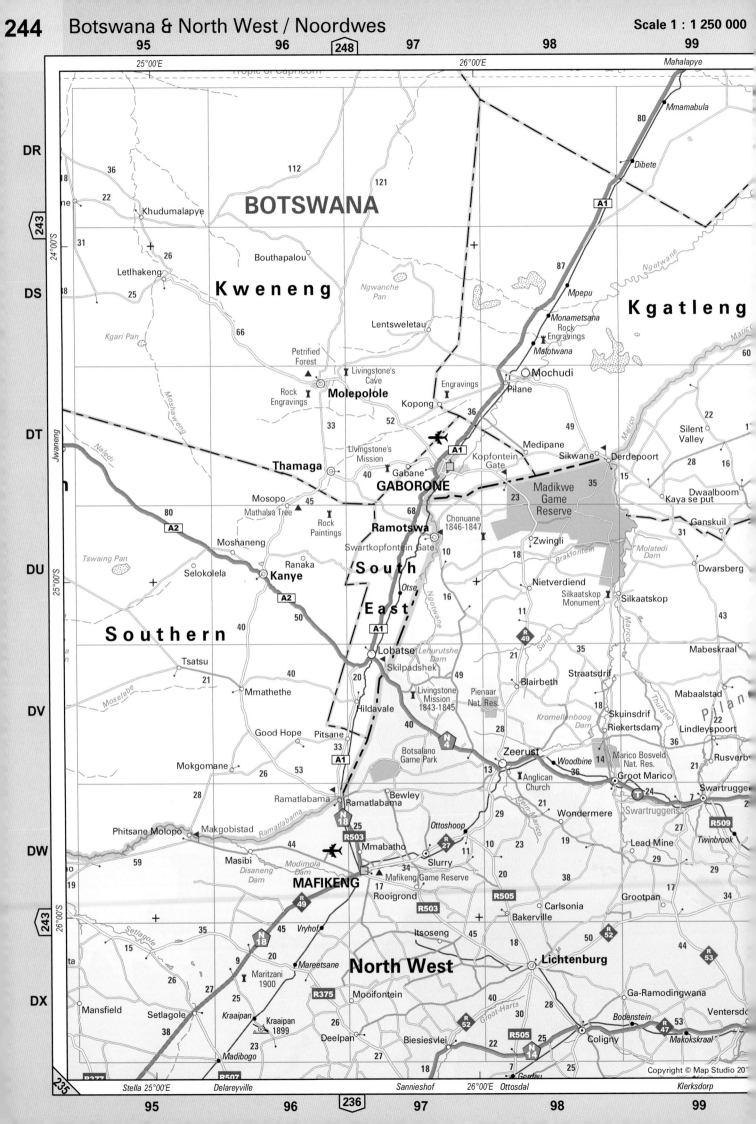

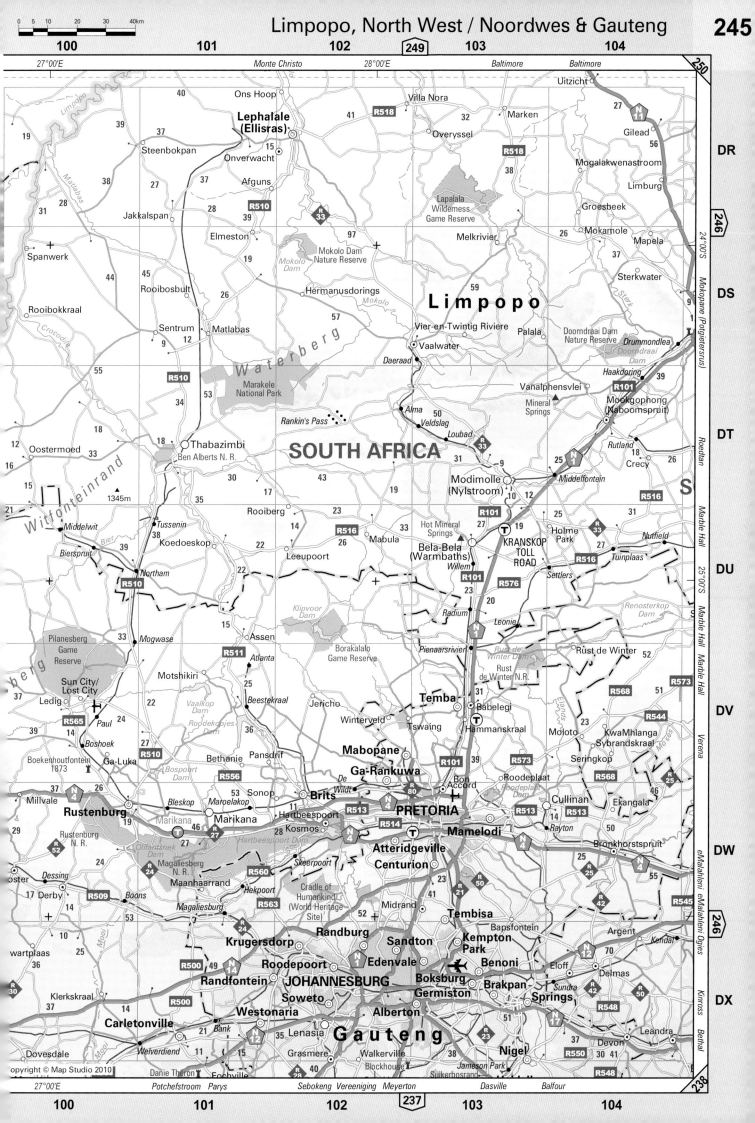

0 5 10 20 30 40km

100 | 101 | 249 | 103 | 104

27°00'E — Monte Christo — 28°00'E — Baltimore — Baltimore

DR
DS
DT
DU
DV
DW
DX

250
246
N11
Mokopane (Potgietersrus)
Roedtan
Marble Hall
Marble Hall
Verena
eMalahleni Ogies
246
Kinross
Bethal
238

24°00'S
25°00'S

Uitzicht
Villa Nora
Marken
Gilead
27
56
Overyssel
32
Mogalakwenastroom
Limburg
R518
38
Groesbeek
R518
Mokamole
26
Mapela
37
Sterkwater

Ons Hoop
40
41
Lephalale (Ellisras)
15
Onverwacht
Afguns
Steenbokpan
37
27
37
R510
33
39
28
39
Melkrivier

Limpopo
59
Lapalala Wilderness Game Reserve
Doorndraai Dam Nature Reserve
Drummondlea
Doorndraai Dam
9
1

19
38
31
28
Jakkalspan
Elmeston
97
Mokolo Dam Nature Reserve
Mokolo Dam
Hermanusdorings
Mokolo
57
Vier-en-Twintig Riviere
Palala
Vaalwater
Daeraad
Haakdoring
39
Vanalphensvlei
Mineral Springs
R101
Mookgophong (Naboomspruit)

Spanwerk
Rooibosbult
44
45
Sentrum
9
12
Matlabas
26
55
Waterberg
Marakele National Park
34
53
18
Thabazimbi
Ben Alberts N.R.
SOUTH AFRICA
Alma
50
Veldslag
Loubad
31
9
Rutland
18
Crecy
26
Modimolle (Nylstroom)
Middelfontein
10
12
R516
S

Oostermoed
33
16
Rankin's Pass
30
43
19
R101
25
N
Holme Park
27
R33
Nutfield
1345m
35
Rooiberg
23
Mabula
33
Hot Mineral Springs
27
19
KRANSKOP TOLL ROAD
R516
Tuinplaas

15
Witfonteinrand
Middelwit
Tussenin
38
Koedoeskop
14
R516
26
Leeupoort
Bela-Bela (Warmbaths)
Willem
R101
Settlers
21
Bier
39
22
22
23
20
Radium
Leonie
Renosterkop Dam
Rust de Winter Dam
R568
51
R573
52

Bierspruit
Northam
R510
15
Assen
Klipvoor Dam
Borakalalo Game Reserve
Pienaarsrivier
Rust de Winter
Rust de Winter N.R.
Rust de Winter
Rust de Winter
Moloto
23
KwaMhlanga
Sybrandskraal
R544

Pilanesberg Game Reserve
33
Mogwase
R511
Atlanta
25
Jericho
Winterveld
31
Temba
Babelegi
Seringkop
R568
R25
46
berg
37
Motshikiri
Beestekraal
Tswaing
Hammanskraal
Moloto
Ekangala

Ledig
Sun City / Lost City
22
Vaalkop Dam
Roodekopjes Dam
36
Mabopane
Ga-Rankuwa
Roodeplaat
Cullinan
50
R565
24
Paul
Bethanie
Pansdrif
De Wildt
Bon Accord
R101
39
R573
R513
R513
14
Rayton
Ekangala
39
14
Boshoek
R510
R556
Brits
R80
Roodeplaat Dam
R513
R25

Boekenhoutfontein 1873
Ga-Luka
Bospoort Dam
53
Sonop
Hartbeespoort
PRETORIA
R101
Bronkhorstspruit
26
N4
37
Millvale
Bleskop
Maroelakop
11
R513
N4
Mamelodi
N4
55
Rustenburg
19
Marikana
Marikana
28
Kosmos
R514
Babelegi
25
29
Rustenburg N.R.
R52
R27
27
Hartbeespoort Dam
N1
Atteridgeville
R25
R21
R50
N4
Olifantsnek Dam
46
Skeerpoort
Centurion
23

oster
Dessing
Magaliesberg N.R.
24
R560
Cradle of Humankind (World Heritage Site)
41
R545
17 Derby
Boons
R24
Maanhaarrand
Hekpoort
Midrand
52
R42
14
R509
Magaliesburg
R563
Tembisa
Bapsfontein
Argent
Kendal
53
R24
Randburg
Sandton
Kempton Park
Eloff
N12
70
wartplaas
10
25
Krugersdorp
Edenvale
Benoni
Delmas
36
R500
49
N14
Roodepoort
Boksburg
Sundra
R42
R50
R30
Randfontein
JOHANNESBURG
Germiston
Springs
R548
Klerkskraal
37
R500
Soweto
Brakpan
51
N17
Carletonville
14
21
Bank
Westonaria
Alberton
Leandra
Dovesdale
Welverdiend
11
Lenasia
Gauteng
R23
37
Devon
Danie Theron
15
Grasmere
Walkerville
38
R550
30 41
Blockhouse
Jameson Park
Nigel
Suikerbosrand
R548

Copyright © Map Studio 2010

27°00'E — Potchefstroom Parys — Sebokeng Vereeniging Meyerton — Dasville — Balfour

100 | 101 | 102 | 237 | 103 | 104

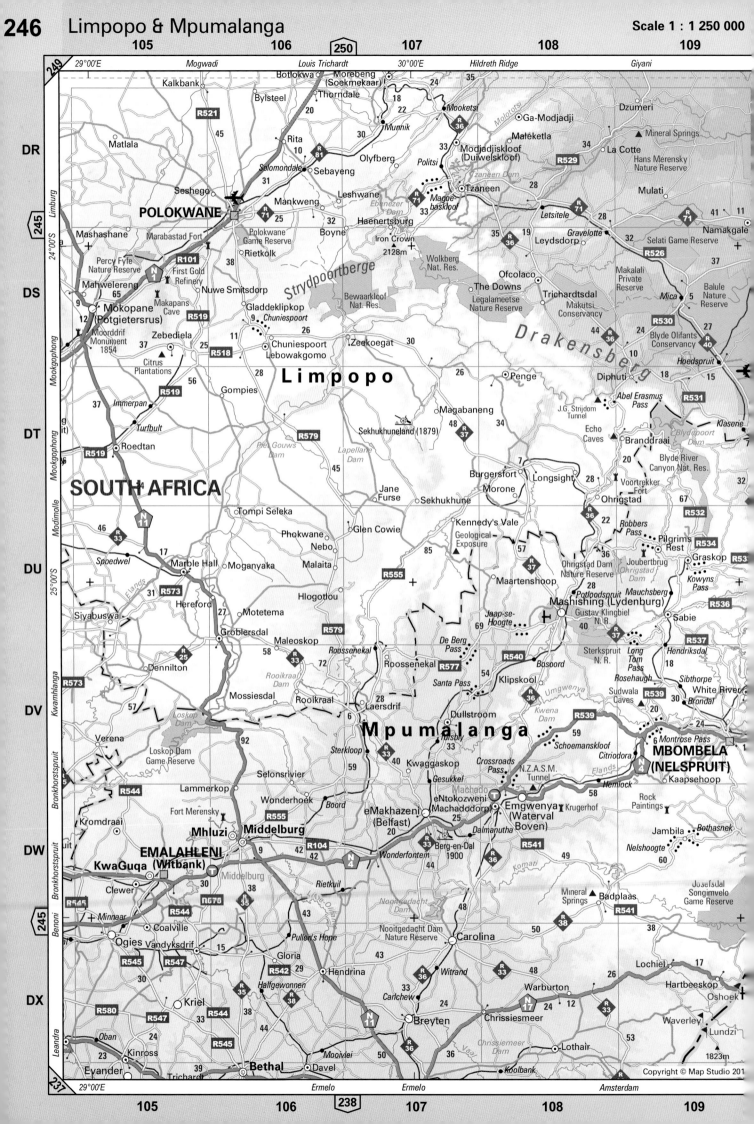

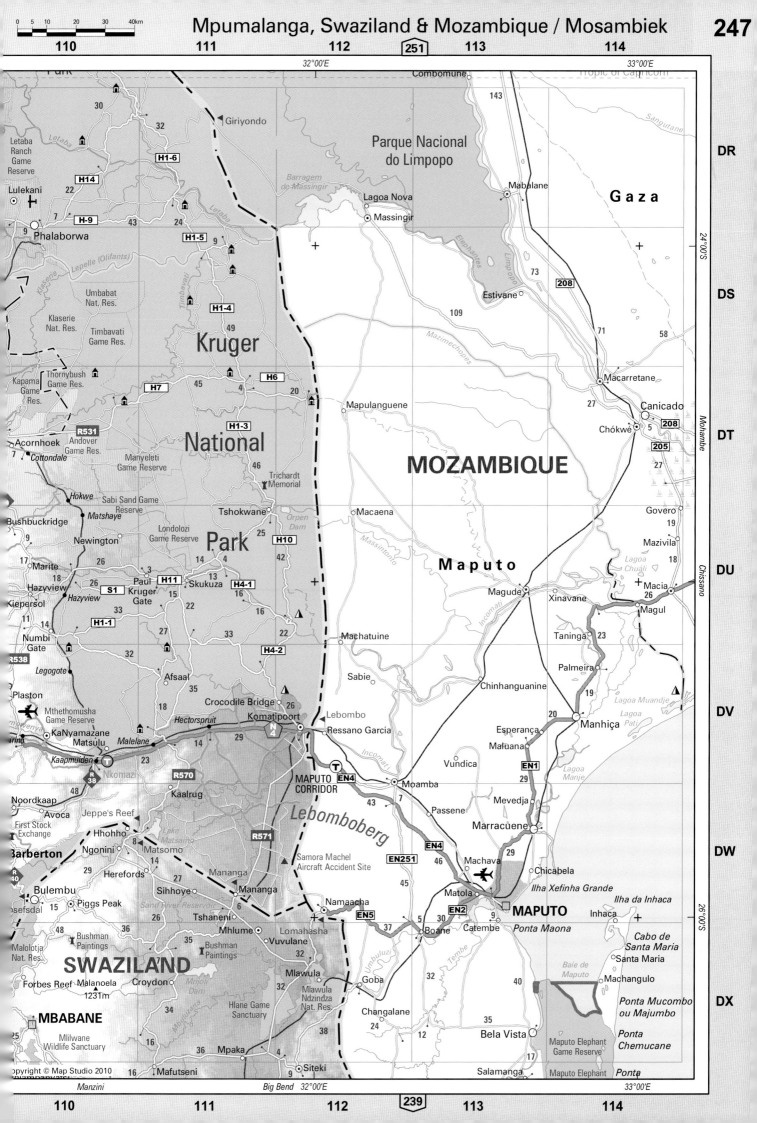

0 5 10   20   30   40km

32°00'E   Tropic of Capricorn   33°00'E

Combomune

DR

143

Giriyondo

Parque Nacional do Limpopo

Mabalane

Gaza

30

32

H1-6

H14

Letaba Ranch Game Reserve

Lagoa Nova

22

Lulekani

Massingir

Barragem de Massingir

73

208

DS

7

H-9

43

24

9

Phalaborwa

109

Estivane

71

58

H1-5

9

Umbabat Nat. Res.

H1-4

49

Kruger

Macarretane

Klaserie Nat. Res.

Timbavati Game Res.

27

Canicado

208

45

4

H6

20

Mapulanguene

Chókwé

5

205

DT

Kapama Game Res.

H7

H1-3

Thornybush Game Res.

National

27

7

Acornhoek

Andover Game Res.

MOZAMBIQUE

Cottondale

46

Manyeleti Game Reserve

Trichardt Memorial

Macaena

Govero

19

Hokwe

Sabi Sand Game Reserve

Park

Mazivila

18

Bushbuckridge

Matshaye

Londolozi Game Reserve

25

H10

42

Maputo

Lagoa Chuáli

Macia

DU

9

14

4

Marite

18

26

Paul

H11

13

Skukuza

H4-1

Magude

Xinavane

26

Magul

Newington

3

15

22

16

16

Taninga

23

Hazyview

Kiepersol

H1-1

33

27

33

22

Palmeira

Numbi Gate

32

H4-2

Machatuine

19

Lagoa Muandje

R538

Legogote

Afsaal

Sabie

Chinhanguanine

20

Manhiça

Lagoa Pati

DV

Plaston

35

Crocodile Bridge

26

Lebombo

Esperança

Mthethomusha Game Reserve

18

Hectorspruit

Komatipoort

Ressano Garcia

Maluana

EN1

KaNyamazane Matsulu

Malelane

14

29

Vundica

29

Kaapmuiden

23

MAPUTO CORRIDOR

T

EN4

Moamba

7

Mevedja

Nkomazi

R570

Kaalrug

43

Passene

Marracuene

Noordkaap

48

Lebomboberg

EN4

Machava

29

Avoca

First Stock Exchange

Jeppe's Reef

R571

EN251

46

Chicabela

DW

Hhohho

Lake Matsama

Samora Machel Aircraft Accident Site

45

Ilha Xefinha Grande

Barberton

Ngonini

8

Matsomo

Matola

Ilha de Inhaca

R40

14

Mananga

EN2

9

MAPUTO

Bulembu

29

Herefords

27

Mananga

Namaacha

30

Catembe

Inhaca

osefsdal

15

Piggs Peak

Sihhoye

6

5

Boane

Ponta Maona

Cabo de Santa Maria

48

36

35

EN5

37

Santa Maria

26

Tshaneni

Mhlume

Lomahasha

Machangulo

Bushman Paintings

Vuvulane

Goba

32

DX

Malolotja Nat. Res.

SWAZILAND

Bushman Paintings

32

Mlawula Ndzindza Nat. Res.

32

40

Ponta Mucombo ou Majumbo

Forbes Reef

Malanoela

Croydon

Changalane

24

12

Ponta Chemucane

1231m

Mpaka

38

36

35

Bela Vista

Ponta

MBABANE

16

Mpaka

4

Maputo Elephant Game Reserve

Baie de Maputo

Mlilwane Wildlife Sanctuary

16

Mafutseni

9

Siteki

Salamanga

Maputo Elephant

25

Copyright © Map Studio 2010

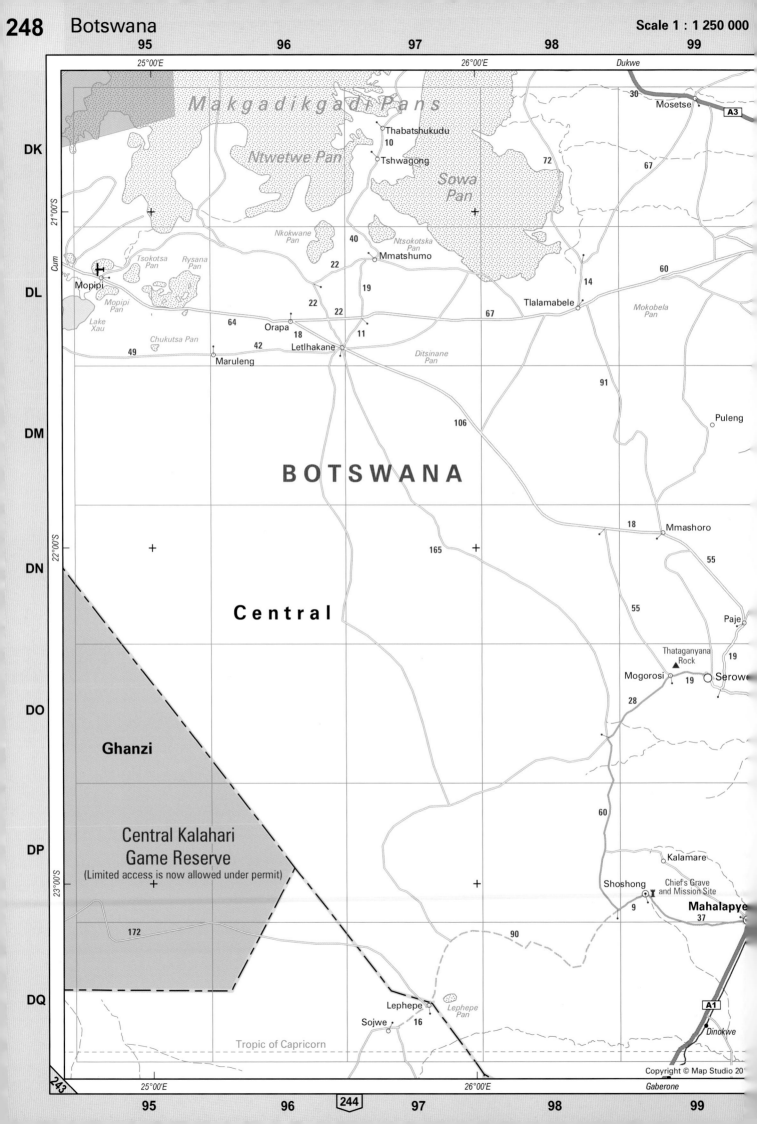

Makgadikgadi Pans

Ntwetwe Pan

Sowa Pan

Thabatshukudu

Tshwagong

Mosetse

A3

Dukwe

Nkokwane Pan

Ntsokotska Pan

Mmatshumo

Tsokotsa Pan

Rysana Pan

Mopipi

Mopipi Pan

Lake Xau

Chukutsa Pan

Tlalamabele

Mokobela Pan

Orapa

Letlhakane

Maruleng

Ditsinane Pan

Puleng

BOTSWANA

Central

Mmashoro

Paje

Thataganyana Rock

Mogorosi

Serowe

Ghanzi

Central Kalahari
Game Reserve
(Limited access is now allowed under permit)

Kalamare

Shoshong

Chief's Grave
and Mission Site

Mahalapye

A1

Lephepe

Lephepe Pan

Sojwe

Dinokwe

Tropic of Capricorn

Gaberone

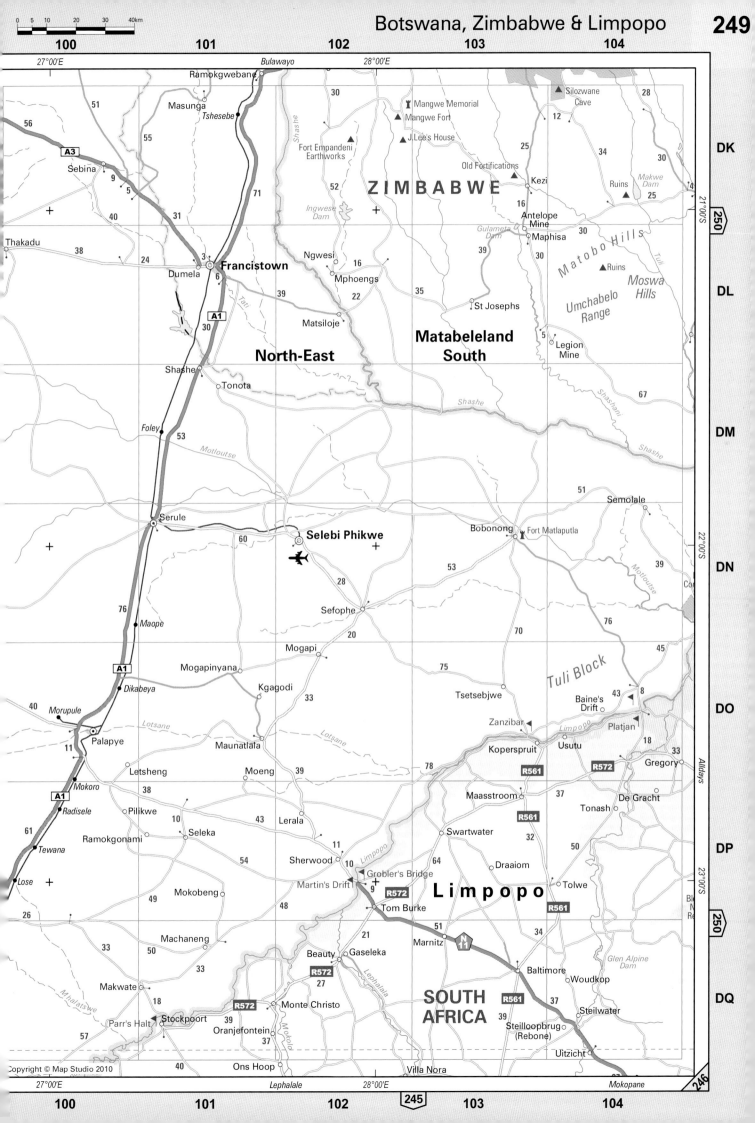

0 5 10 20 30 40km

27°00'E · Bulawayo · 28°00'E

Ramokgwebane
Masunga
Tshesebe

51
56

A3
Sebina

9
5

40

31

DK

30

Mangwe Memorial
Mangwe Fort
J.Lee's House

Silozwane
Cave

12

28

25

34

30

Fort Empandeni
Earthworks

52

Z I M B A B W E

Old Fortifications

Kezi

16

Ruins

Makwe
Dam

25

71

Ingwese
Dam

21°00'S

250

Thakadu

38

24

3

Dumela
6

Francistown

A1

30

Ngwesi

Mphoengs

16

22

39

35

Matsiloje

Antelope
Mine
Maphisa

30

30

Gulameta
Dam

39

M a t o b o   H i l l s

Ruins

Tuli

30

**Matabeleland
South**

St Josephs

5

Legion
Mine

Moswa
Hills

Umchabelo
Range

DL

North-East

Shashe

Tonota

Foley
53

Motloutse

Shashe

67

Shashani

DM

Serule

60

Selebi Phikwe

28

Sefophe

51

Semolale

Bobonong
Fort Matlaputla

53

Motloutse

39

Co

DN

22°00'S

76

Maope

20

Mogapi

70

76

45

Mogapinyana

Kgagodi

33

75

Tsetsebjwe

Tuli Block

43

8

Baine's
Drift

Dikabeya

Lotsane

Lotsane

Zanzibar

Koperspruit

Limpopo

Usutu

Platjan

18

Gregory

33

DO

40
Morupule

11

Palapye

Letsheng

Moeng

39

R561

R572

Maunatlala

78

Maasstroom

37

De Gracht

Tonash

DP

23°00'S

250

A1
Mokoro

Radisele

Pilikwe

38

10

Seleka

43

Lerala

11

Sherwood
10

Limpopo

Swartwater

R561

32

50

61
Tewana

Ramokgonami

54

64

Draaiom

Lose

26

Mokobeng

49

48

Grobler's Bridge
Martin's Drift
9

R572

Tom Burke

Tolwe

R561

Machaneng

50

33

21

Marnitz

51

34

Baltimore

Woudkop

DQ

33

Beauty
Gaseleka

R572

27

**SOUTH
AFRICA**

R561

37

Steilwater

18

R572
Monte Christo

Glen Alpine
Dam

Makwate

Parr's Halt
Stockpoort

39

Oranjefontein

37

Steiloopbrug
(Rebone)

39

Uitzicht

57

40

Ons Hoop

Villa Nora

Mokopane

27°00'E · Lephalale · 28°00'E

245

246

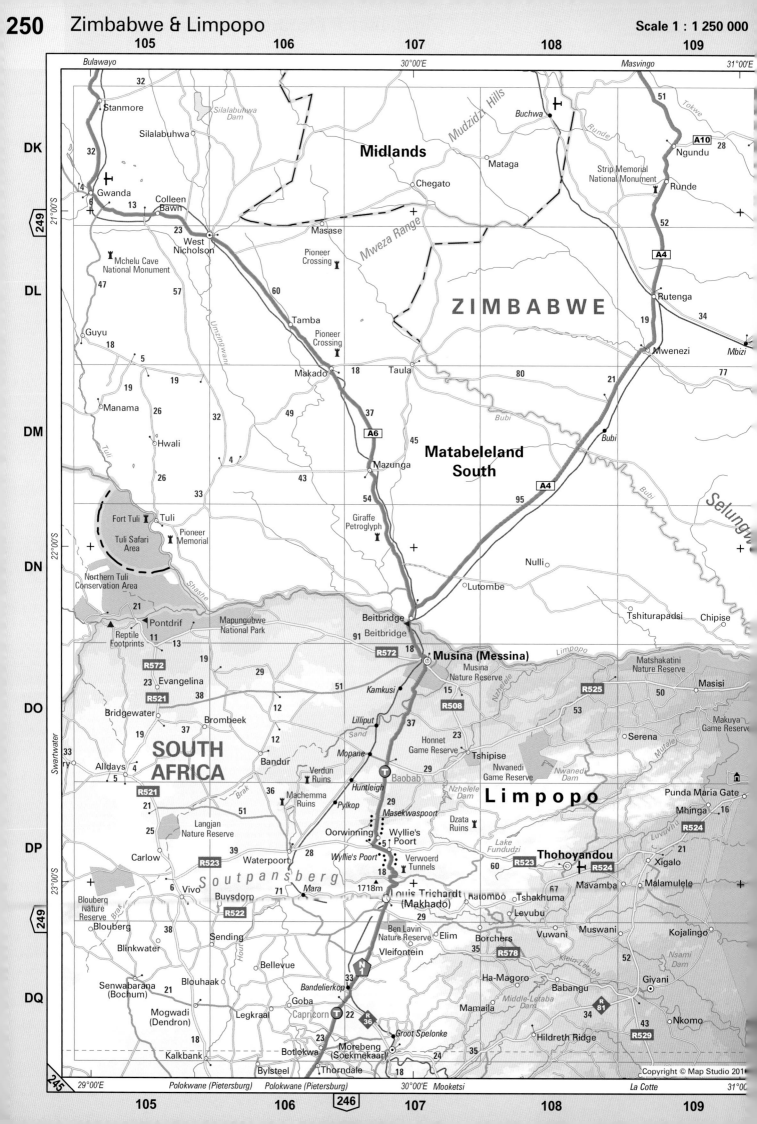

Bulawayo

105   **106**   **107**   **108**   **109**

30°00'E   Masvingo

Stanmore
Silalabuhwa
Silalabuhwa Dam
32
32

DK

249
21°00'S

Gwanda
13
Colleen Bawn
23
West Nicholson

Mchelu Cave
National Monument

47   57

DL

Guyu
18
5
19   19
Manama   26
32
Hwali
26
4
33
Tuli
Fort Tuli
Tuli Safari Area

Northern Tuli
Conservation Area

21

Reptile Footprints
Pontdrif
11   13

60
Tamba
Pioneer Crossing
Makado
49
37
A6
45
Mazunga
43
54
Giraffe Petroglyph

Pioneer Crossing

Masase
Chegato

Midlands

Mataga

Buchwa

ZIMBABWE

Ngundu
28
A10

Strip Memorial
National Monument

Runde

Rutenga
19   34
52
A4

Mwenezi
Mbizi
21
77
80

Bubi
A4
95
Bubi

**Matabeleland
South**

Nulli

22°00'S

Lutombe

Tshiturapadsi
Chipise

Selungw

Mapungubwe
National Park
Beitbridge
91   Beitbridge

R572   18

Musina (Messina)
Musina
Nature Reserve

Matshakatini
Nature Reserve
Masisi

DN

DO

R572
19
Evangelina
23
R521
38
Bridgewater
37
19
Brombeek
12
12
Bandur

Swartwater
33

Alldays
4
5

**SOUTH
AFRICA**

36

29
51

Kamkusi
15
R508
Lilliput
37
Sand
Mopane
Verdun Ruins
Huntleigh
Masekwaspoort
Pylkop
29

23
Honnet
Game Reserve
Tshipise
29

Nwanedi
Game Reserve
Nwanedi
Dam

R525
50
53
Serena
Makuya
Game Reserve

Punda Maria Gate
Mhinga
16
R524

Oorwinning
Wyllie's Poort
5
Dzata
Ruins
Lake
Fundudzi
Limpopo

Langjan
Nature Reserve
25

Carlow
R523
39
Waterpoort
28
Wyllie's Poort
18
1718m
Louis Trichardt
(Makhado)

R523
60
Thohoyandou
R524

Xigalo
21

Malamulele

Mavamba

DP

21

6
Vivo
Buysdorp
71
Mara
R522

Blouberg
Nature
Reserve

Blouberg
38
Sending
Blinkwater
Bellevue

Ben Lavin
Nature Reserve
Vleifontein
N1
Bandelierkop
33

Senwabarana
(Bochum)
21
Mogwadi
(Dendron)
Legkraal
18
Goba
Capricorn **T** 22
R36
Groot Spelonke
Botlokwa
Bylsteel
Thorndale
18

Verwoerd
Tunnels

Katombo
Tshakhuma
Levubu
Elim
Borchers
35
R578
Ha-Magoro
Mamaila
Middle-Letaba
Dam
24
35

Vuwani
Muswani
Kojalingo
52
Nsami
Dam
Babangu
Giyani
34
R81
43
Nkomo
R529
Hildreth Ridge

Luvubu
R524

Klein-Letaba

249
23°00'S

DQ

29°00'E
Polokwane (Pietersburg)

105   Polokwane (Pietersburg)
106   **246**   30°00'E   Mooketsi
107
108   La Cotte   31°00'
109

Morebeng
(Soekmekaar)

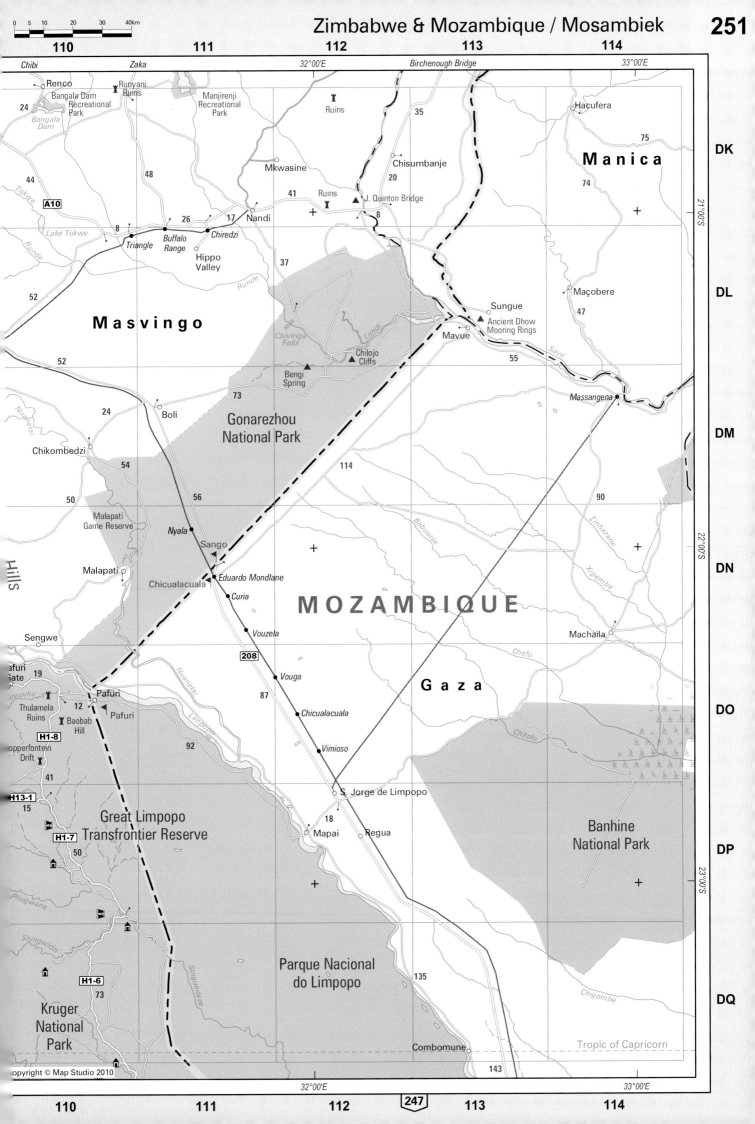

110 · **111** · **112** · **113** · **114**

DK
DL
DM
DN
DO
DP
DQ

0 5 10 20 30 40km

Chibi   Zaka   32°00'E   Birchenough Bridge   33°00'E

Renco
Bangala Dam
Recreational Park
Runyani Ruins
Manjirenji Recreational Park
Ruins
Hacufera

24
Bangala Dam
44   48
Mkwasine
Chisumbanje
20
35
74   75

M a n i c a

A10
41   Ruins   J. Quinton Bridge
Nandi
8
Maçobere
8   26   17
Triangle   Buffalo Range   Chiredzi
Hippo Valley
Lake Tokwe
Runde
37
Sungue
Ancient Dhow Mooring Rings
Mavue
47

M a s v i n g o

52
Chiviriga Falls
Chilojo Cliffs
55
Save
52
73
Bengi Spring
Massangena

24   Boli
Chikombedzi
Gonarezhou National Park
114
90
54
56
Malapati Game Reserve
Nyala
Babuatse
50   Sango
Malapati   Eduardo Mondlane
Zinhazane
Xipembe
Curia

M O Z A M B I Q U E

Sengwe
Vouzela
Machaila
Chefu
Hills
Pafuri Gate   19
208
Pafuri
Vouga
G a z a
Thulamela Ruins   12
Pafuri
87
Chicualacuala
Chitolo
Baobab Hill
H1-8
92
Vimioso
opperfontein Drift
Limpopo
41
H13-1
15
S. Jorge de Limpopo
Banhine National Park

Great Limpopo Transfrontier Reserve
18
Mapai   Regua
H1-7
50
Phugwane
Shingwidze

Parque Nacional do Limpopo
135
Chigombe
H1-6
73
Singuedeze
Kruger National Park
Combomune   Tropic of Capricorn
143

Copyright © Map Studio 2010   32°00'E   33°00'E

Index to Place Names

Abbreviations: Bot. – Botswana E.C. – Eastern Cape F.S. – Free State Gau. – Gauteng KZN – KwaZulu-Natal
Les. – Lesotho Lim. – Limpopo Moz. – Mozambique Mpum. – Mpumalanga Nam. – Namibia N.C. – Northern Cape
N.W. – North West Swa. – Swaziland W.C. – Western Cape Zim. – Zimbabwe

NAME	PG	GRID
FORT MTOMBENI	238	EE 109
FOURIESBURG	237	ED 103
FRANCISTOWN	249	DL 101
FRANKFORT	237	EA 104
FRANKLIN	230	EH 106
FRANS	227	EJ 94
FRANSCHHOEK	219	ER 81
FRANZENHOF	226	EF 89
FRASERBURG	226	EM 87
FRERE	238	ED 106
FRIESDALE	234	ED 85
FRISCHGEWAAGD	238	EA 109
G		
GABANE	244	DT 97
GABORONE	244	DT 97
GADIEP	233	ED 80
GA-LUKA	245	DV 100
GAMIS	240	DS 75
GA-MODJADJI	246	DR 108
GAMOEP	224	EG 79
GA-MOPEDI	235	DZ 91
GANSBAAI	219	ES 81
GANSFONTEIN	219	EO 83
GANSKRAAL	218	EP 79
GANSKUIL	244	DU 99
GANSPAN	235	EB 94
GANYESA	235	DY 93
GA-RAMODINGWANA	244	DX 99
GA-RANKUWA	245	DV 102
GARIEP DAM	228	EJ 96
GARIES	224	EH 78
GARIGANUS	240	DX 79
GARINAIS	241	DX 81
GARNER'S DRIFT	229	EM 102
GARRYOWEN	229	EL 101
GASELEKA	249	DQ 102
GAWACHAB	232	DZ 78
GEGE	238	DZ 109
GELUK	235	DZ 93
GELUKSBURG	238	ED 105
GELUKSPRUIT	234	EB 85
GELUKWAARTS	229	EG 100
GEMSVLAKTE	224	EB 79
GEMVALE	230	EL 106
GENADEBERG	229	EH 100
GENADENDAL	219	ER 82
GENERAALSNEK	237	ED 102
GENEVA	237	EB 100
GEORGE	220	ER 89
GERDAU	236	DY 98
GERMISTON	245	DX 103
GESUKKEL	246	DV 107
GEYSDORP	236	DY 96
GIBEON	240	DU 78
GIBEON STN.	240	DU 78
GIESENKRAAL	227	EH 91
GILEAD	245	DR 104
GINGINDLOVU	239	EE 111
GIYANI	250	DQ 109
GLADDEKLIPKOP	246	DS 106
GLAUDINA	236	DZ 97
GLEN	236	EE 98
GLEN BEULAH	230	EH 107
GLEN COWIE	246	DU 107
GLENCOE	238	EC 107
GLENCONNOR	222	EP 95
GLENMORE BEACH	230	EK 108
GLENROCK	222	EN 98
GLORIA	246	DX 106
GLOSAM	235	EC 90
GLÜCKSTADT	239	EB 110
GOAGEB	232	DY 76
GOBA (KZN)	230	EH 107
GOBA (LIMP.)	250	DQ 106
GOBA (MOZ.)	247	DX 112
GOBAS	232	DY 79
GOCHAS	241	DU 80
GOEDEMOED	228	EH 98
GOLDEN VALLEY	222	EO 97
GOLELA	239	EA 111
GOMPIES	246	DT 106
GOMVLEI	228	EG 98
GONUBIE	223	EO 102
GOOD HOPE	244	DV 96
GOODHOUSE	232	EE 79
GORAAS	226	EK 87
GORDONIA	235	EC 94
GORDONS BAY	219	ER 80
GORGES	232	EA 78
GOUDA	219	EP 81
GOURITS	220	ER 87
GOURITZMOND	220	ES 88
GOVERO	247	DU 114
GRAAFF-REINET	221	EN 94
GRAAFWATER	225	EM 80
GRABOUW	219	ER 81
GRABWASSER	232	EB 79
GRAHAMSTOWN	222	EP 98
GRANAATBOSKOLK	225	EG 83
GRASKOP	246	DU 109
GRASMERE	245	DX 102
GRASPAN	235	EE 94
GRASSLANDS	236	EA 97
GRAVELOTTE	246	DS 108
GRAYS	223	EN 102
GREGORY	249	DO 104
GREYLINGSTAD	237	DY 104
GREYSTONE	222	EP 95
GREYTON	219	ER 82
GREYTOWN	238	EE 108
GRIQUATOWN	235	ED 91
GROBLERSDAL	246	DU 106
GROBLERSHOOP	234	EE 88
GROENDAL	219	EQ 81
GROENEBLOEM	237	EA 100
GROENFONTEIN	220	EP 87
GROENRIVIERS-MOND	224	EJ 77
GROENVLEI	238	EA 108
GROESBEEK	245	DR 104
GRONDNEUS	234	EC 85
GROOT BRAKRIVIER	220	ER 88
GROOT JONGENS-FONTEIN	220	ES 86
GROOT MARICO	244	DV 99
GROOT SPELONKE	250	DQ 107
GROOTDORING	227	EG 90
GROOTDRIF	225	EL 81
GROOTDRINK	234	ED 87
GROOTKRAAL	220	EP 88
GROOTMIS	224	EF 76
GROOTPAN	244	DW 99
GROOTSPRUIT	238	EA 108
GROOTVLEI	237	DY 103
GROVÈPUT	226	EG 89
GRÜNAU	232	EB 79
GRÜNDORNER	240	DV 78
GUIBES	232	DY 76
GUMTREE	237	ED 101
GUNAB	240	DX 77
GUYU	250	DL 105
GWANDA	250	DK 105
H		
HAAKDORING	245	DT 104
HAARLEM	221	EQ 91
HACUFERA	251	DK 114
HAENERTSBURG	246	DR 107
HAGA-HAGA	223	EO 103
HALCYON DRIFT	229	EJ 103
HALESOWEN	222	EN 97
HALFGEWONNEN	246	DX 106
HALFMANSHOF	219	EP 81
HALFWEG	225	EG 83
HALLATT'S HOPE	236	DZ 96
HALSETON	228	EL 99
HAMAB	233	EC 81
HA-MAGORO	250	DQ 108
HAMBURG	223	EP 101
HAMILTON	238	EC 106
HAMMANSHOF	219	EQ 82
HAMMANSKRAAL	245	DV 103
HAMMERSDALE	230	EG 108
HANGE	229	EM 102
HANKEY	222	EQ 95
HANOVER	227	EK 94
HANOVER ROAD	227	EJ 94
HARDAP	240	DT 78
HARDAP REST CAMP	240	DT 78
HARDING	230	EH 107
HARRISBURG	236	DZ 98
HARRISDALE	234	EB 85
HARRISMITH	238	EC 105
HARTBEESFONTEIN	236	DY 98
HARTBEESPOORT	245	DW 102
HARTEBEESKOP	246	DX 109
HARTENBOS	220	ER 88
HARTSWATER	236	EB 95
HARUCHAS	240	DS 75
HARVARD	238	DZ 105
HATTINGSPRUIT	238	EB 107
HAUPTRUS	236	DY 98
HAWSTON	219	ES 81
HAYFIELD	235	EE 93
HAZYVIEW	247	DU 110
HEATONVILLE	239	ED 111
HECTORSPRUIT	247	DV 111
HEERENLOGEMENT	225	EM 80
HEIDELBERG (GAU.)	237	DY 103
HEIDELBERG (W.C.)	220	ER 85
HEIGHTS	221	EQ 93
HEILBRON	237	EA 102
HEKPOORT	245	DW 101
HELMERINGHAUSEN	240	DW 76
HELPMEKAAR	238	EC 108
HELVETIA	228	EG 99
HEMLOCK	246	DV 108
HENDRINA	246	DX 106
HENLEY-ON-KLIP	237	DY 102
HENNENMAN	237	EB 100
HENNING	228	EK 98
HERBERTSDALE	220	ER 87
HEREFORD	246	DU 105
HEREFORDS	247	DW 110
HERMANUS	219	ES 81
HERMANUSDORINGS	245	DS 102
HERMON	219	EP 81
HEROLD	220	EQ 89
HEROLDS BAY	220	ER 89
HERSCHEL	229	EJ 100
HERTZOGVILLE	236	EC 96
HESTER	236	DZ 95
HET KRUIS	219	EN 80
HEUNINGNESKLOOF	235	EE 94
HEUNINGSPRUIT	237	EA 101
HEUWELS	226	EK 88
HEYDON	227	EL 94
HHOHHO	247	DW 110
HIBBERDENE	230	EH 108
HIGG'S HOPE	235	EE 91
HIGHFLATS	230	EH 107
HILANDALE	220	EP 85
HILDAVALE	244	DV 97
HILDRETH RIDGE	250	DQ 108
HILLCREST	236	EC 95
HILTON	230	EF 108
HIMEVILLE	230	EF 106
HIPPO VALLEY	251	DL 111
HLABISA	239	EC 111
HLATHIKHULU	239	DZ 110
HLOBANE	238	EB 109
HLOGOTLOU	246	DU 106
HLOTSE (LERIBE)	237	ED 102
HLUHLUWE	239	EB 113
HLUTHI	239	DZ 111
HOACHANAS	240	DR 78
HOBAS	232	EA 78
HOBENI	229	EM 104
HOBHOUSE	229	EF 100
HOEDJIES	225	EK 84
HOEDSPRUIT	246	DS 109
HOFMEYR	228	EL 97
HOGSBACK	223	EN 100
HOKWE	247	DT 110
HOLBANK	238	DY 108
HOLMDENE	238	DY 105
HOLME PARK	245	DU 104
HOLOMI	239	DY 111
HOLOOG	232	EA 78
HOLY CROSS	230	EK 106
HONDEFONTEIN	220	EN 86
HONDEJAAG	234	EC 86
HONDEKLIPBAAI	224	EH 77
HOOGTE	237	EA 102
HOOPSTAD	236	EB 97
HOPEFIELD	218	EP 79
HOPETOWN	227	EF 93
HORSE SHOE	238	EB 106
HOTAGTERKLIP	219	ET 83
HOTAZEL	235	DZ 90
HOTTENTOTSKLOOF	219	EP 82
HOUMOED	233	EE 82
HOUT BAY	218	ER 79
HOUTENBECK	236	ED 99
HOUTKRAAL	227	EH 93
HOUWHOEK	219	ER 81
HOWICK	230	EF 107
HUGO	219	EP 83
HUHUDI	235	DZ 94
HUKUNTSI	242	DS 87
HUMANSDORP	222	ER 95
HUMEFIELD	221	EO 93
HUNTLEIGH	250	DP 107
HUTCHINSON	227	EL 91
HWALI	250	DM 105
I		
IDA	229	EL 101
IFAFA BEACH	230	EH 109
IKAGELENG	244	DV 98
IKAGENG	237	DY 100
IKHUTSENG	236	EC 95
ILANGAKAZI	239	EC 111
IMMERPAN	246	DT 105
IMMIGRANT	236	EE 97
IMPENDLE	230	EF 107
INANDA FARM	230	EF 109
INDWE	229	EL 101
INFANTA	220	ES 85
INGOGO	238	EA 107
INGWAVUMA	239	DZ 112
INHACA	247	DW 114
INVERUGIE	230	EH 108
INXU	229	EK 103
IPELEGENG	236	DZ 96
ISWEPE	238	DZ 108
ITSOSENG	244	DX 97
IXOPO	230	EG 107
IZINGOLWENI	230	EJ 107
J		
JACOBSDAL	236	EE 95
JAGERSFONTEIN	228	EG 96
JAGHT DRIFT	226	EF 86
JAKKALSPAN	245	DR 100
JAMBILA	246	DW 109
JAMESON PARK	237	DY 103
JAMESTOWN	228	EK 99
JAMMERDRIF	229	ED 100
JAN KEMPDORP	236	EB 95
JANE FURSE	246	DT 107
JANSENVILLE	221	EO 94
JEFFREYS BAY	222	ER 95
JERICHO	245	DV 102
JOEL'S DRIFT	237	ED 103
JOHANNESBURG	245	DX 102
JOHNSON'S POST	220	ER 87
JOJWENI	230	EM 105
JOLIVET	230	EH 108
JONGENSKLIP	219	ER 82
JORDAN	243	DX 91
JOSLING	234	ED 87
JOUBERTINA	221	EQ 92
JOZINI	239	EA 112
JOZUA	238	DZ 107
JUBILEE	219	ER 84
JURGEN	232	DY 78
JWANENG	243	DT 94
K		
KAALRUG	247	DW 111
KAAPMUIDEN	247	DV 110
KAAPSEHOOP	246	DV 109
KAKAMAS	234	ED 85
KALAMARE	248	DP 99
KALBASKRAAL	219	EQ 80
KALKBANK	250	DQ 105
KALKRAND	240	DS 77
KALKWERF	234	ED 87
KAMEEL	236	DY 95
KAMIESKROON	224	EH 78
KAMKUSI	250	DO 107
KAMMIEBOS	221	ER 93
KANANA	236	DZ 99
KANG	243	DR 90
KANONEILAND	234	ED 86
KANONKOP	219	EP 80
KANUS	233	EB 80
KANYAMAZANE	247	DV 110
KANYE	244	DU 96
KAO	237	EE 104
KARABEE	227	EG 90
KARASBURG	233	EB 80
KARATARA	221	ER 90
KAREE	236	ED 98
KAREEDOUW	221	ER 93
KAREEVLAKTE	220	EQ 85
KARG'S POST	230	EH 106
KARIEGA	222	EQ 99
KARINO	247	DV 110
KARKAMS	224	EH 78
KAROS	234	EC 87
KARREEBOSCH-KOLK	225	EG 84
KARRINGMELK-SPRUIT	229	EJ 100
KASUKA ROAD	222	EQ 99
KATHU	235	EB 90
KATKOP	229	EJ 104
KATKOP	225	EH 83
KAYA SE PUT	244	DT 99
KAYSER'S BEACH	223	EP 101
KEATE'S DRIFT	238	ED 108
KEETMANSHOOP	232	DY 79
KEI MOUTH	223	EO 103
KEI ROAD	223	EO 101
KEIMOES	234	ED 85
KEISKAMMAHOEK	223	EO 100
KELSO	230	EH 109
KEMPTON PARK	245	DX 103
KENDAL	245	DX 104
KENDREW	221	EN 94
KENHARDT	226	EF 86
KENILWORTH (N.C.)	234	EC 87
KENILWORTH (N.C.)	236	ED 95
KENNEDY'S VALE	246	DU 107
KENTON-ON-SEA	222	EQ 99
KERKRAND	220	EQ 88
KESTELL	237	EC 104
KETANE	229	EG 102
KEZI	249	DK 103
KGAGODI	249	DO 101
KGAKALA	236	DZ 98
KHABO	237	ED 103
KHAKHEA	243	DT 92
KHUDUMALAPYE	244	DR 95
KHUIS	234	DY 87
KIDD'S BEACH	223	EP 102
KIEKOESVLEI	218	EP 79
KIEPERSOL	247	DU 110
KIMBERLEY	236	ED 95
KING WILLIAM'S TOWN	223	EO 101
KINGHOLM	239	EA 111
KINGSBURGH	230	EG 109
KINGSCOTE	230	EG 105
KINGSLEY	238	EB 108
KINGSWOOD	236	EA 97
KINIRAPOORT	229	EH 104
KINROSS	246	DX 105
KIRKWOOD	222	EP 96
KLAARSTROOM	220	EP 89
KLAAS VOOGDS-RIVIER	219	EQ 83
KLASERIE	246	DT 109
KLAWER	225	EL 80
KLEIN AUB	240	DR 75
KLEIN KARAS	232	EA 79
KLEINBEGIN	234	ED 87
KLEINMOND	219	ES 81
KLEINPLAAT	221	EQ 90
KLEINPOORT	222	EP 95
KLEINRIVIER	222	EQ 95
KLEINSEE	224	EF 76
KLEIPAN	225	EM 80
KLERKSDORP	236	DZ 99
KLERKSKRAAL	245	DX 100
KLIPDALE	219	ES 83
KLIPFONTEIN (E.C.)	222	EP 96
KLIPFONTEIN (MPUM.)	237	DY 104
KLIPHOEK	224	EL 79
KLIPKOLK	226	EK 87
KLIPPLAAT	221	EO 94
KLIPPOORT	238	EC 107
KLIPPUNT	234	ED 86
KLIPRIVER	238	ED 108
KLIPSKOOL	246	DV 108
KLIPSPRUIT (E.C.)	230	EH 106
KLIPSPRUIT (KZN)	238	EA 107
KNAPDAAR	228	EJ 98
KNEUKEL	235	EC 93
KNOCKAGH	230	EH 108
KNOETZE	221	EP 92
KNYSNA	221	ER 90
KOBOS	240	DR 75
KOEDOESKOP	245	DU 101
KOEGAS	234	EE 89
KOEGRABIE	234	EE 87
KOEKENAAP	224	EL 79
KOENONG	237	EE 102
KOËS	241	DW 81
KOFFIEFONTEIN	228	EF 95
KOIINGNAAS	224	EH 77
KOJALINGO	250	DQ 109
KOKERBOOM	233	EC 82
KOKONG	243	DT 91
KOKSTAD	230	EH 106
KOLKE	226	EF 85
KOLONIESPLAAS	228	EM 95
KOLONYAMA	237	EE 102
KOMATIPOORT	247	DV 111
KOMGA	223	EN 102
KOMKANS	224	EK 78
KOMMAGGAS	224	EG 77
KOMMANDOKRAAL	221	EP 90
KOMMETJIE	218	ER 79
KOMMISSIEPOORT	229	EF 101
KOMSPRUIT	237	EB 102
KOOLBANK	238	DY 108
KOOPAN SUID	233	EA 84
KOOPMANSFONTEIN	235	EC 93
KOOSDRIF	225	EK 84
KOOSFONTEIN	236	EA 96
KOOTJIESKOLK	225	EK 84
KOPERSPRUIT	249	DO 103
KOPONG	244	DT 97
KOPPIES	237	EA 101
KORINGBERG	219	EO 80
KORINGPLAAS	220	EO 85
KORTNEK	239	EA 110
KOSMOS	245	DW 102
KOSTER	245	DW 100
KOTZEHOOP	232	ED 77
KOTZESRUS	224	EJ 78
KOUKRAAL	228	EH 99
KOUP	220	EP 86
KOUTJIE	220	EQ 89
KRAAIPAN	244	DX 96
KRAANKUIL	227	EG 93
KRANSFONTEIN	237	EC 104
KRANSKOP (KZN)	238	EE 109
KRANSKOP (KZN)	239	EB 110
KREEFBAAI	224	EM 79
KRIEL	246	DX 105
KRIGE	219	ER 82
KROMDRAAI	246	DW 105
KROMKOP	225	EH 82
KROMRIVIER	227	EM 90
KROONSTAD	237	EA 100
KRUGERS	228	EG 97
KRUGERSDORP	245	DX 102
KRUIDFONTEIN	220	EO 88
KRUISFONTEIN	221	ER 94
KRUISPAD	237	EB 104
KRUISRIVIER	220	EP 88
KUBOES	232	EC 76
KUBUSI	223	EN 101
KUBUTSA	239	DZ 111
KUILSRIVIER	219	ER 80
KU-MAYIMA	229	EK 103
KUMS	233	EC 82
KURUMAN	235	EA 91
KUTLWANONG	236	EB 99
KWACEZA	239	EB 110
KWADUKUZA (STANGER)	231	EF 110
KWADWESHULA	230	EH 108
KWAGGASKOP	246	DV 107
KWAGUQA	246	DW 105
KWAMASHU	230	EF 109
KWAMBONAMBI	239	ED 112
KWAMHLANGA	245	DV 104
KWAMSANE	239	EC 112
KWANOBUHLE	222	EQ 96
KWANOFODOSI	223	EN 102
KWANOJOLI	222	EO 97
KWANONQABA	220	ER 88
KWANONZAME	228	EL 95
KWASIZABANTU MISSION	238	EE 109
KWAZANELE	246	DX 107
KWEEKWA	227	EK 90
KYKOEDIE	219	ES 83
KYLEMORE	219	ER 81
L		
LA COTTE	246	DR 108
LAAIPLEK	218	EO 79
LABERA	243	DW 94
LADISMITH	220	EQ 86
LADY FRERE	229	EL 100
LADY GREY	229	EJ 100
LADYBRAND	237	EE 101
LADYSMITH	238	ED 107
LAERSDRIF	246	DV 107
LAGOA NOVA	247	DR 112
L'AGULHAS	219	ET 83
LAHLANGUBO	229	EJ 104
LAINGSBURG	220	EP 85
LAMBERT'S BAY	224	EM 79
LAMMERKOP	246	DW 105
LANGBERG (N.C.)	235	EB 90
LANGBERG (W.C.)	220	ER 87
LANGDON	229	EL 103
LANGEBAAN	218	EP 78
LANGEBAANWEG	218	EO 79
LANGEHORN	243	DX 93
LANGHOLM	222	EP 99
LANGKLAS	241	DU 84
LANGKLIP	233	EC 84
LANGKUIL	219	ER 83
LATEMANEK	238	DZ 107
LAVUMISA	239	EA 112
LEAD MINE	244	DW 99
LEANDRA	245	DX 104
LEBOWAKGOMO	246	DS 106
LEDIG	245	DV 100
LEEU GAMKA	220	EO 88
LEEUBANK	229	EH 100
LEEUDORINGSTAD	236	DZ 98
LEEUPOORT	245	DU 102
LEGION MINE	249	DL 104
LEGKRAAL	250	DQ 106
LEGOGOTE	247	DV 110
LEHLOHONOLO	229	EH 104
LEHUTUTU	242	DR 87
LEIPOLDTVILLE	218	EN 79
LEJONE	237	EE 103
LEKKERDRAAI	228	EJ 98
LEKKERSING	232	EE 76
LEKKERWATER	240	DR 77
LELIEFONTEIN	224	EH 79
LEMOEN	221	EN 90
LENASIA	245	DX 102
LENDEPAS	241	DT 83
LENTSWELETAU	244	DS 97
LEONIE	245	DU 103
LEPEL STORE	240	DR 75
LEPHALALE (ELLISRAS)	245	DR 101
LEPHEPE	248	DQ 97
LERALA	249	DP 102
LESHWANE	246	DR 106
LETJIESBOS	220	EN 89
LETLHAKANE	248	DL 96
LETLHAKENG	244	DS 95
LETSHENG	249	DO 100
LETSITELE	246	DR 108
LEVUBU	250	DP 108
LEYDSDORP	246	DS 108
LIBERTAS	237	EC 102
LIBODE	230	EL 105
LIBONO	237	ED 104
LICHTENBURG	244	DX 98
LIDDLETON	222	EN 99
LIDFONTEIN	240	DS 79
LIDGETTON	230	EF 107
LIKALANENG	229	EF 102
LILLIPUT	250	DO 107
LIMBURG	245	DR 104
LIME ACRES	235	EC 91
LINDESHOF	219	ER 83
LINDLEY	237	EB 102
LINDLEYSPOORT	244	DV 99
LINGELIHLE	228	EM 97
LIQHOBONG	237	EE 104
LLANDUDNO	218	ER 79
LOBATSE	244	DV 97
LOCH BUIDHE	230	EG 107
LOCHIEL	246	DX 109
LOERIE	222	EQ 95
LOERIESFONTEIN	225	EJ 82
LOFTER	228	EG 97
LOGAGENG	243	DW 94
LOHATLHA	235	EB 90
LOKHWABE	242	DS 87
LONG HOPE	222	EO 97
LONGLANDS	235	EC 94
LONGSIGHT	246	DT 108
LOSE	249	DP 100
LOSKOP	238	EE 106
LOSSAND	225	EL 80
LOTHAIR	246	DX 108
LOUBAD	245	DT 103
LOUIS TRICHARDT (MAKHADO)	250	DP 107
LOUISVALE	234	ED 86
LOUTERWATER	221	EQ 92
LOUWNA	235	DZ 93
LOUWSBURG	239	EA 110
LOUWSPLAAS	226	EK 89
LOVANE	228	EK 97
LOWER ADAMSON	228	EK 98
LOWER LOTENI	230	EF 106
LOWER PITSENG	229	EJ 103
LOXTON	226	EL 89
LOXTONVALE	234	ED 85
LOYENGO	239	DY 110
LUBHUKU	239	DY 111
LUCKHOFF	228	EG 95
LUFAFA ROAD	230	EG 107
LUFUTHA	229	EL 101
LULEKANI	247	DR 110
LUNDIN'S NEK	229	EJ 102
LUNEBERG	238	EA 109
LUSIKISIKI	230	EK 106
LUTOMBE	250	DN 107
LUTTIG	220	EO 88
LUTTIGSHOOP	226	EK 87
LUTZPUTS	234	EC 85
LUTZVILLE	224	EL 79
LYDENBURG (MASHISHING)	246	DU 108
LYKSO	235	DZ 93
M		
MAANHAARRAND	245	DW 101
MAARTENSHOOP	246	DU 108
MAASSTROOM	249	DP 103
MABAALSTAD	244	DV 99
MABALANE	247	DR 113
MABESKRAAL	244	DV 99
MABHENSA	239	ED 111
MABOPANE	245	DV 102
MABULA	245	DU 102
MABUTSANE	243	DT 92
MACAENA	247	DU 112
MACARRETANE	247	DT 114
MACHADODORP (ENTOKOZWENI)	246	DW 107
MACHAILA	251	DN 114
MACHANENG	249	DQ 101
MACHANGULO	247	DX 114
MACHATUINE	247	DU 112
MACHAVA	247	DW 113
MACHIBINI	239	EC 112
MACIA	247	DU 114
MACLEANTOWN	223	EO 102
MACLEAR	229	EK 103
MAÇOBERE	251	DL 114
MADADENI	238	EB 107
MADIAKGAMA	243	DX 93
MADIBOGO	244	DX 96
MADIPELESA	235	EB 94
MADISENG	246	DT 107
MADONELA	239	EA 112
MAFETENG	229	EG 100
MAFIKENG	244	DW 96
MAFUBE	229	EH 104
MAFUTSENI	239	DY 111
MAGABANENG	246	DT 107
MAGALIESBURG	245	DW 101
MAGNEET	236	DZ 97
MAGOGONG	236	EA 95
MAGOPELA	236	EA 95
MAGUDE	247	DU 113
MAGUDU	239	EA 111
MAGUL	247	DU 114
MAGUSHENI	230	EJ 106
MAHALAPYE	248	DP 99
MAHLABA	238	ED 108
MAHLABATHINI	239	EC 111
MAHLANGASI	239	EA 111
MAHWELERENG	246	DS 105
MAIZEFIELD	238	DY 106
MAKADO	250	DM 106
MAKANAS KOP	222	EP 99
MAKELEKETLA	237	ED 100
MAKHADO (LOUIS TRICHARDT)	250	DP 107
MAKOKSKRAAL	244	DX 96
MAKWASSIE	236	EA 98

Index to Place Names